Public Discourses of Gay Men

Paul Baker

 Routledge

Taylor & Francis Group

LONDON AND NEW YORK

First published 2005
by Routledge
2 Park Square, Milton Park, Abingdon, Oxon OX14 4RN

Simultaneously published in the USA and Canada
by Routledge
711 Third Ave, New York, NY 10017

Routledge is an imprint of the Taylor & Francis Group

First issued in paperback 2013
© 2005 Paul Baker

Typeset in Garamond by Wearset Ltd, Boldon, Tyne and Wear

British Library Cataloguing in Publication Data
A catalogue record for this book is available from the British Library

Library of Congress Cataloging in Publication Data
A catalog record for this book has been requested

ISBN 978-0-415-34973-4 (hbk)
ISBN 978-0-415-85022-3 (pbk)

Contents

Figures

Tables

Acknowledgements

Thanks go to Michael Hoey who gave many useful comments on the entire manuscript, and to the following people who all gave their feedback on one or more chapters: Bethan Benwell, Sally Johnson, Bill Leap, Tony McEnery, Jane Sunderland. I would also like to thank the members of the Lancaster Gender and Language research group and participants at the 2004 Lavender Linguistics Conference (American University, Washington).

1 What can I do with a naked corpus?

Introduction

The corridors in the linguistics department where I work tend to become crowded with students at certain periods – sometimes you have to navigate past groups gathered around noticeboards, particularly during exams. Recently, during one such busy period, I overheard a group of young women discussing an exam timetable which had just been posted on one of the noticeboards. 'I can't believe we have an exam at nine o'clock in the morning,' one student complained. 'That's so gay!'

How can an exam time be gay? Obviously this was the relatively new negative use of the word *gay*, a word whose meaning seems to undergo a semantic makeover every few decades. Once *gay* meant carefree and happy. However, this changed in the 1970s when people who had previously been labelled as sexual deviants started using it to refer to themselves. But now for many young people, *gay* also means lame or unfashionable.

It is difficult to ascertain whether the new use of *gay* will enter mainstream language or whether it will burn brightly and die fast as a temporary teenage fad. If it gains wider usage, then people who currently call themselves gay may decide to redefine themselves. Perhaps a more compelling issue is why one of my students would use *gay* in such a potentially insensitive way in a public space. I'm sure she would have been shocked had she been accused of homophobia (indeed, at the same time I heard this utterance, the university was decorated with posters declaring somewhat paradoxically that 'homophobia is gay'). However, at the same time, it could be argued that in appropriating one of the few words which positively represents a stigmatised minority group and recasting it as something negative, my student is not particularly helping to further the equal rights movement. Her utterance demonstrates a peculiar ambivalence towards a concept (homosexuality) which, for the past few decades, has been subject to multiple and conflicting representations. It is the intention of this book to examine and address such representations – to tease them apart from each other, and then show how ultimately each one is inter-related.

Homosexuality and discourse

Although sexual and romantic same-sex relationships between humans have existed for millennia, the ways that such relationships and the people who engage in them have been celebrated, normalised, accepted, ignored, problematised or persecuted has been subject to considerable variation over time and across different societies. For example, collections of poems written during the Zhou Dynasty (1122–256 BC) make it clear that court life incorporated open expressions of affection between men, and such relationships were often used as a means of social advancement or for political intrigue. In Ancient Greece, acceptance of male–male relationships as part of a 'balanced bisexuality' was viewed as normal (as long as one partner was an adult and the other was aged between twelve and fifteen), although effeminate adult males tended to incur social opprobrium. Attitudes to male–male sex in Hebrew cultures were based around the high value placed on male sexuality in marriage. For example, a man was forbidden to hold his penis even while urinating and the story of God's punishment of the 'sodomites' in the story of Sodom and Gomorrah is one of the most notorious passages in the Bible (although some religious scholars argue that the story has been selectively interpreted and that male prostitutes, rapists or even poor hosts were the real targets of God's wrath). By the thirteenth century, bisexuality in Europe had either been erased or redefined by the Church and state as sodomy or pederasty (Spencer 1995: 156).

In seventeenth- and early eighteenth-century Britain, a distinction was made between *fops* who were viewed as effeminate but promiscuously heterosexual and *rakes* who took the penetrative role in sex with younger males. However, rakes were viewed as bisexual and were not considered to be effeminate (Trumbach 1991: 105). By 1710, however, a new identity, the Molly, had emerged – one who was effeminate *and* engaged in anal sex. Such men existed within a subculture based around what were known as Molly Houses; clubs and taverns where working- and middle-class men (sometimes dressed as women) would meet, for the purposes of socialisation and to make sexual contacts (Norton 1992). In eighteenth- and nineteenth-century Western Europe, women formed 'romantic friendships' which contained all the elements of ardent love affairs and were accepted by society, although any sexual aspect of these relationships was unacknowledged. Contemporary western understanding of homosexuality is tempered by a medical/legal model of sexual deviance which gained ground during the late nineteenth century. According to Katz (1983: 147–50) the word 'homosexual' was first used in 1869, preceding 'heterosexual' by several years. Of this, Foucault (1976: 43) writes: 'We must not forget that the psychological, psychiatric, medical category of homosexuality was constituted from the moment it was characterised.'[1]

For Foucault this was an act of reification – the naming of homosexuality brought about its existence. Sedgwick (1991: 2) points out that with this naming, from that point on, every person could be assigned a homo- or hetero-sexuality as well as a gender. By the 1950s, oppression of homosexual men was de rigueur in the UK, resulting in violent attacks, blackmail, imprisonment, public scandals, suicides and medical treatments involving electric shocks, nausea-inducing drugs (David 1997: 181–4) and female hormones (Jivani 1997: 123). In 1967, homosexuality was partially decriminalised in the UK, which helped pave the way for the rise of a new conceptualisation of homosexuality based around the identity of *gay*, associated with concepts such as 'coming out' and 'gay pride'. By the 1990s, partly in response to inadequate government responses to AIDS, the concept of *queer* offered a political, inclusive label, focused on uniting oppressed identities and challenging the concept of 'normal'. So *queer* didn't just mean gay but encompassed a range of minority or stigmatised sexual or gender identities – bisexual, transsexual or transvestite. It could also refer to identities based around specific sexual behaviours: people who used prostitutes or engaged in S/M or a range of other sexual activities deigned to be against the heterosexual, married, missionary-position 'norm'. In addition, the notion of *queer* could be expanded even further beyond gender/sexuality in order to refer to and unite other non-sexual yet oppressed identities such as black, working-class, wheelchair-user or single parent.

Sexual identity has often been closely associated with a person's gender (whether they behave in a masculine or feminine manner) or distinctions within particular sexual activities (to penetrate versus to be penetrated rather than anal sex per se). It is the intention of this book to examine the ways that sexual identity is currently perceived – and in particular to focus on how the sexual category of gay men is constructed via discourse in western society. The 'problem' of male homosexuality has dogged governments, churches, armies, opinion formers, medical and teaching establishments, newspaper editorial writers and 'ordinary' people since the sexual category was created in the 1860s and, judging by the frequency of mentions of homosexuality in the media, continues to do so.[2]

Debates concerning the rights and representations of gay people are therefore far from over and I believe that a crucial factor in the outcome of such debates is the way that public discourse regarding homosexuality is shaped. Legal rights are inextricably connected to discourse, or a 'system of statements which constructs an object' (Parker 1992: 5). Discourse is further categorised by Burr (1995: 48) as

> a set of meanings, metaphors, representations, images, stories, statements and so on that in some way together produce a particular version of events... Surrounding any one object, event, person etc., there may be a variety of different discourses, each with a different story to tell about the world, a different way of representing it to the world.

Discourses are not merely descriptions of people's 'beliefs' or 'opinions' and they cannot be taken as representing an inner, essential aspect of identity such as personality or attitude. Instead they are connected to practices and structures that are lived out in society from day-to-day. Discourses are difficult to pin down – they are constantly changing, interacting with each other, breaking off and merging. As Sunderland (2004) points out, there is no 'dictionary of discourses'. In addition, any act of naming or defining a discourse is going to be an interpretative one. Where I see a discourse, you may see a different discourse, or no discourse. It is difficult, if not impossible, to step outside discourse. Therefore our labelling of something as a discourse is going to be based upon the discourses that we already (often unconsciously) live with.

To give a couple of examples, Holloway's (1981, 1984) 'male sexual drive' discourse constructs male sexuality as a biological drive – men are seen as having a basic need for sex which they cannot ignore and must be satisfied. Such a discourse could be used in law courts to ensure that male rapists receive lighter sentences. A discourse of 'compulsory heterosexuality' (Rich 1980) would involve practices which involve overlooking the existence of gay and lesbian people by assuming that everyone is heterosexual. The extent to which individuals agree with the existence of a discourse or whether such a discourse reflects an accurate representation of the world depends on how such a discourse impacts on their own identities, experiences and ideological positions.

While discourse is often conceptualised as an intangible, unstable concept which is difficult to quantify, it *is* tied to the way that society is organised and I believe that legal change can be a direct consequence of the way that a particular subject is discursively constructed. One aim in writing this book is therefore political. As a gay man, I am interested in making sense of how current discourses surrounding the way that a group I identify with are constructed. I also wish to make such discourses more transparent by carrying out an analysis of how language is used to create, maintain and contest them. My own position is that homosexual and heterosexual people should enjoy equal social and legal status. And while discourses affect laws, I also believe that the relationship is two-way: changes in the law can help to shape the course of future discourses around a subject – if something which was previously criminalised is then recategorised as legal, it will eventually come to be conceptualised in a very different way. I therefore approach the subject of analysis from a subjective position, although I am unsure what an 'objective' position regarding the subject of homosexuality would be in any case, and even if one *were* to claim this standpoint, it could be argued that such a person had, in effect, made a subjective choice to be objective, which would in itself have consequences for the way that analysis was carried out. As Parker and Burnman (1993: 159) note, 'we still do believe that a moral/political sensitivity to the way oppression is maintained in language is required of discourse analysis', although at the same time, researchers need to ensure that they do not attribute evidence for the existence of a discourse (particularly a prevailing discourse) that is based upon over-sensitivity, reliance on a small number of cases or intuition alone. For that reason, I address the second aim in writing this book: to carry out a number of related corpus-based studies of discourse.

Corpus analysis involves using computers to discover linguistic patterns within large bodies of text, which may then be subjected to more interpretative analyses. For reasons that I outline below, corpus linguistics is *not* a methodology which researchers who have looked at the relationship between language and sexuality/gender have ordinarily utilised. Similarly, corpus linguists have not tended to focus on sexuality/gender either. This book is therefore an attempt to build a bridge between these two, often incongruent, research areas, by showing that each has something to offer the other and that by working in tangent, they can produce illuminating research outcomes. One way that researchers can be more confident in their claims about the existence of discourses is to highlight the ways in which 'patterns of association – how lexical items tend to co-occur – are built up over large amounts of text and are often unavailable to intuition or conscious awareness. They can convey messages implicitly and even be at odds with an overt statement' (Hunston 2002: 109). A corpus linguistics approach may not allow us to step outside of discourse completely, but it should present the researcher with a perspective based on making sense of quantifiable patterns of language – at least ensuring that we are starting from a less-biased position with a reasonably large road map.

Quality research?

To expand upon the brief definition given above, corpus linguistics is 'the study of language based on examples of real life language use' (McEnery and Wilson 1996: 1). However, unlike qualitative approaches, corpus linguistics utilises bodies of electronically encoded text, implementing a more quantitative methodology, for example by using frequency information about occurrences of particular linguistic phenomena. Corpora are generally large (consisting of thousands or millions of words) and representative samples of a particular type of naturally occurring language use, so they can be used as a standard reference by which claims about language can be measured. The fact that they are encoded electronically means that complex calculations can be carried out on large amounts of text, revealing linguistic patterns and frequency information that would otherwise take days or months to uncover by hand, and which may run counter to intuition.

In addition, electronic corpora are often annotated with additional linguistic information, the most common being part-of-speech information, which allows large-scale grammatical analyses to be carried out. Other types of information can be encoded within corpora – for example, in spoken corpora (containing transcripts of dialogue), attributes such as sex, age, socio-economic group and region can be encoded for each participant. This allows language comparisons to be made about different types of speakers.

For example, Rayson *et al.* (1997) have shown that speakers from economically advantaged groups use *actually* and *really* more than those from less-advantaged groups, who are more likely to use words like *say*, *said* and *says* as well as numbers and taboo words.

Corpus-based (or equivalent) methods have been used from as early as the nineteenth century. The diary studies of infant language acquisition (Taine 1877, Preyer 1889), or Käding's (1897) frequency distribution of sequences of letters in an 11-million word corpus of German focused on collections of large, naturally occurring language use. However, up until the 1970s, only a small number of studies utilised corpus-based approaches. Quirk's (1960) Survey of English Usage began in 1961, as did Brown and Kucera's work on the Brown corpus of American English. It was not until the advent of widely available personal computers in the 1980s that corpus linguistics as a methodology became popular. Johansson (1991) shows that the number of such studies doubled for every five-year period between 1976–91.

Corpus linguistics has since been employed in a number of areas of linguistic enquiry, including dictionary creation (Clear *et al.* 1996), as an aid to interpretation of literary texts (Louw 1997), forensic linguistics (Woolls and Coulthard 1998), language description (Sinclair 1999), language variation studies (Biber 1988) and language teaching materials (Johns 1997). However, the corpus linguistics approach has not been without its share of criticism. For example, Widdowson (2000) argues that both corpus linguistics and critical discourse analysis are problematic, constituting *linguistics applied* rather than *applied linguistics*. Corpus linguistics only offers 'a partial account of real language' (2000: 7) because it does not address the lack of correspondence between corpus findings and native speaker intuitions. Widdowson also questions the validity of analysts' interpretations of corpus data and raises questions about the methodological processes that they choose to use, suggesting that the ones which computers find easier to carry out will be chosen in preference to more complex forms of analysis. Borsley and Ingham (2002) criticise corpus-based approaches because it is difficult to draw conclusions about language based on a finite sample of language – what is not in a corpus may be just as important as what is there. They also argue that language is endowed with meaning by native speakers and therefore cannot be derived from a corpus. See Stubbs (2001a, 2002) for rejoinders to these articles.

Despite these qualms, some discourse analysts *have* used corpora in order to analyse texts such as political speeches (Flowerdew 1997, Fairclough 2000, Piper 2000), teaching materials (Stubbs and Gerbig 1993, Wickens 1998), scientific writing (Atkinson 1999) and newspaper articles (Caldas-Coulthard and Moon 1999, van Dijk 1991). Such studies have shown how corpus analysis can uncover ideologies and evidence for disadvantage (see Hunston 2002: 109–23 for a summary).

However, corpus linguistics does not appear to have had a great impact in the more sociolinguistic areas of gender and language and queer linguistics[3] referred to hereafter as language and identities.[4] Some of the exceptions to this include Shalom's study of men's and women's personal adverts (1997), McEnery *et al.*'s (2000) work on swearing and demographic categories in the British National Corpus, and Schmid and Fauth's (2003) exploration of gender differences in the ICE corpus. Stubbs' (1996) analysis of the ways that gender is constructed within two of Robert Baden-Powell's speeches to boys and girls highlights the fact that ideological issues can be present even around a fairly innocuous word like *happy*. Stubbs showed that Baden-Powell (the founder of the Boy Scouts Association) instructed girls to make other people happy, whereas boys were merely advised to live happy lives. Holmes (2001) carried out a corpus-based study of gender representations in New Zealand English while Rey (2001) performed a corpus-based study of dialogue spoken in the television series *Star Trek* looking for differences between male and female language use, and Biber and Burges (2001) looked at changing gender differences in dramatic dialogue using the ARCHER corpus of dramatic texts from the seventeenth to the twentieth century. However, such studies represent a minority of existing corpus-based work and tend to be based around finding evidence for *differences* between men and women's language use – a theoretical starting point that has largely been abandoned by researchers of language and identities, as is outlined in more detail below.

An examination of recent conferences on language and identities or a look at edited collections in the area (e.g. Johnson and Meinhoff (1997), Livia and Hall (1997), Harvey and Shalom (1997), Bucholtz *et al.* (1999), Campbell-Kibler *et al.* (2002) and Litosseliti and Sunderland (2002)) suggests that in recent years there has been a move away from quantitative-based research, which is all the more notable considering that this is an area which emphasises an eclectic approach where there is no single set methodology. Eckert and McConnell-Ginet's exhaustive textbook *Language and Gender* (2003) only has one entry for corpus studies, which describes Precht's (2002) conference paper on gender and use of expletives.

Swann (2002: 49) lists seven 'warrants' or decision procedures which allow analysts to interpret data (such as an utterance, a linguistic construction or a set of linguistic features) as being gendered (although the same warrants could largely be used for forms of identity connected to sexuality, race, age, class, and so on). These warrants appear to be listed in increasing order of their relationship to researcher interpretation/intuition. For example, the first is 'quantitative and/or general patterns (derived from correlational studies ... corpora or systematic comparisons)', the fourth is 'speakers'/participants' solicited interpretations' and the sixth is 'analyst's intuitions'. While Swann outlines the advantages and limitations of each warrant, she concludes that 'On the whole ... there does seem to have been a shift towards more localised studies' and 'far less reliance is placed on quantifiable and/or general patterns' (2002: 59).

I would suggest that there are a number of possible reasons for this unease with methodologies based around finding quantifiable patterns in language, and particularly with corpus linguistics. The corpus-based approach did not really gain acceptance until the 1980s when the availability of computers demonstrated that techniques which, in the past, had largely been hypothetical, could in fact be carried out. However, by the time that researchers were in a position to accept corpus linguists as a valid means of language enquiry, there had already occurred a shift in the social sciences in the accepted ways that knowledge was collected via research methodologies. For much of the nineteenth and twentieth centuries, knowledge had been gathered by taking approaches which have been variously called scientific, positivist, essentialist, empirical or structuralist. Such approaches viewed the universe as containing facts or truths that could be discovered by objective researchers working under experimental conditions. They emphasised measurement and categorisation – for example, the classification of different species of plants or animals into related groups, or the measurement of human characteristics such as height, weight or IQ in order to discover averages or norms. Researchers would form hypotheses and test them under strict experimental conditions. While this approach is often still associated with the natural, physical and biological sciences, it has also been used in the social sciences – particularly in sociology, psychology and linguistics where phenomena such as social class, personality and attitude have been examined. However, by the 1980s, an alternative means of producing knowledge had become available, roughly based around the concept of *post-modernism* and referred to as post-structuralism or social constructionism. As Denzin (1988: 432) writes:

> Gone are words like theory, hypothesis, concept, indicator, coding scheme, sampling, validity, and reliability. In their place comes a new language: readerly texts, modes of discourse, cultural poetics, deconstruction, interpretation, domination, feminism, genre, grammatology, hermeneutics, inscription, master narrative, narrative structures, otherness, postmodernism, redemptive ethnography, semiotics, subversion, textuality, tropes.

While Denzin optimistically suggested that now researchers had a *choice* (1988: 432), I would agree with Swann that, for the most part, researchers working in the area of language and identities have tended to focus on methodologies that have emphasised qualitative analyses rather than looking for quantifiable patterns. Corpus linguistics largely became viable as a methodology at a point where this shift had already occurred, and its grounding in quantification did not make it attractive to social scientists. However, in order to understand *why* such a shift happened, it is useful to consider the historical trajectory of research into language and identities as falling under the larger remit of social science research.

In gender studies, earlier, more quantitative-based research is now often characterised as falling under at least one of the dreaded three 'D's of *deficit*, *dominance* and *difference* (Bergvall 1999, Eckert and MacConnell-Ginet 1992).

All three approaches had one aspect in common – a focus on inscribed gender binaries between the categories of men and women which led researchers to make statements such as 'the use of the intensive "so" . . . is more frequent in women's than men's language' (Lakoff 1975: 54). One criticism of such a study was that it was an unsubstantiated claim – it wasn't even grounded within the limits of empirical analysis, making it similar to Jespersen's (1922) unfounded assertion that women's language was *deficient* to men's. The more critical *dominance* approach (characterised by Fishman (1983) and West and Zimmerman (1983)) did attempt to empirically investigate claims about the ways that men and women used language with frequency counts of linguistic features.

Such an approach wasn't limited to sex differences. Other researchers claimed that gay men used language differently from heterosexual men – for example, Hayes (1976) who outlined three types of *GaySpeak* (secret, social and radical-activist), while Farrell (1972) and Stanley (1970) uncovered evidence that gay people use a specialist lexicon or argot, containing words not normally used in mainstream society.

However, such studies were criticised as taking an overly simplistic approach to identity. They assume that identity categories are fixed and stable – and that they can be reduced to norms – so we implicitly contrast the language of an imagined average gay man with that of an imagined average heterosexual man. This approach obscures the fact that language variation is subject to considerable 'intragroup differences and intergroup overlap' (Eckert and McConnell-Ginet 1999: 193), that membership to such identity 'groups' isn't necessarily fixed or the same for everyone and that people's identities are based on numerous interacting and fluid characteristics such as age, social class, gender, sexuality and race. The concentration on difference in quantitative research also often results in a disregard for similarities between groups – resulting in a form of cultural determinism which conflates gender (masculinity/femininity) with sex (male/female). Such a claim assumes a uni-directional relationship between language and gender – people are viewed as speaking a certain way *because* they are female or male.

In addition, pointing out differences doesn't do much to explain why they exist. Swann (2002: 51) writes: 'On its own, the establishment of general patterns in the distribution of linguistic features is a limited and potentially reductive exercise which tells us nothing about how language is used by women and men in specific contexts, nor about what speakers are doing as they talk.' So what then, if women use the intensive 'so' more than men? We would also need to explore the contexts in which the intensive 'so' appears (and doesn't appear) for different types of women (and men for that matter), what the intensive 'so' is used to achieve and why it is used. We'd also need to be careful about extrapolating frequency counts of 'so' based on a finite number of subjects measured at the same time onto the general population.

With these sorts of research issues, we are therefore moving away from quantitative analyses which simply quote numbers that translate into differences, and are starting to focus on a more qualitative kind of analysis which asks *why* differences exist. Thus introspective claims led to quantitative testing of hypotheses, which in turn led to qualitative investigations. An (admittedly anecdotal) demonstration of the respective values placed on quantitative and qualitative research can be found in the sorts of research that university students typically engage in: questionnaires that require subjects to tick boxes of pre-assigned categories are generally more associated with first-year undergraduate coursework in the social sciences (at least within departments where I have worked), whereas postgraduates are more likely to be encouraged to employ focus group, interview or other qualitative methodologies.

Quantitative studies could therefore be viewed as a simplistic precursor or necessary evil which must be reluctantly acknowledged before qualitative work can be done. Some researchers have taken the argument further and side-stepped quantitative data altogether, arguing that its focus on counting to indicate differences isn't particularly useful. For example, Parker and Burnman (1993: 161) warn that the 'slide to empiricism' in discourse analysis is 'paradoxical and disturbing' and that 'discourse research produces more interesting analyses than traditional psychology' (1993: 163).

While structuralists believed that people's identities determine how they speak, post-structuralist accounts of language and identities argue that the reverse is the case – that language (among other things) helps to *shape* gender (or sexuality or race, etc.). Therefore gender becomes associated with ways of *doing* rather than ways of *being*. People are who they are because of the way that they talk, rather than the way that they talk being due to who they are. In this sense, gender is viewed as performative (Butler 1990). Judith Butler's example of drag queens who act out a female identity suggests that gender is in a sense a performance – and one which everyone is engaged in, all the time. According to Butler (1990: 33), becoming a woman is 'a term in process, a beginning, a *constructing* that cannot rightfully be said to originate or to end'. Post-structuralism also eschews the idea of the objective 'scientific' researcher (objectivity being simply another subjective position), pointing out that there is no such thing as objective truth, only discourses (Burr 1995: 160).

Research into language and identities has therefore moved away from the quantitative approaches favoured by the physical sciences, and has instead been influenced by post-structuralist accounts which have favoured qualitative research that aims to deconstruct or contest categories such as male/female and homo/hetero. Such a shift is not restricted to language and identities but has occurred across a variety of related academic fields. For example, in psychology, researchers had created the notion of different 'personality' traits or scales, such as Eysenk's introversion/extroversion scale (1953), which could be quantified by asking subjects a list of questions such as 'Do you enjoy going on roller-coasters?', and then calculating a score based on their answers. However, an extreme social constructionist viewpoint would argue that the concept of a fixed personality is unreal because people behave differently in a range of contexts (e.g. depending on whether they are at work or with their parents or different groups of friends). Ironically, psychologists have labelled people's ability to adjust their behaviour according to social context as being yet another quantifiable personality trait – *self-monitoring* (Snyder and Gangestad 1986). Personality inventories therefore assume that there must be an essential identity, an 'inner me' or true personality, which social constructionists would dispute. In a similar way, Potter and Wetherell (1987: 43–55) questioned the notion of quantitative questionnaire-based 'attitude' research (e.g. Marsh 1976) by carrying out a qualitative analysis of interviews that attempted to elicit attitudes about immigrants. They found that the analyst's categories did not match the participant's terms, elicited attitudes were often contradictory and that defining the status of the object under discussion was problematic.

Corpus research, then, with its emphasis on comparing differences through counting, and creating rather than deconstructing categories, could therefore be viewed as somewhat retrograde and incompatible with post-structuralist thinking. Indeed, one area that corpus linguistics has excelled in has been in generating *descriptive* grammars of languages (e.g. Biber *et al.* 1999) based on naturally occurring language use, but focusing on language as an abstract system.

Another possible reason for the lack of corpus-based (or other quantitative) research on language and identities is also linked to the identities and ideologies of those who are engaged in such research. The words *qualitative* and *quantitative* are derived respectively from their base forms *quality* and *quantity*. The apparently dichotomous relationship between the two concepts implies a binary choice – quality is not quantity and quantity is not quality. And for many people, quantity is seen as a poor substitute for quality. There is another danger lurking in the notion of quantity and quantification. Hacking (1990) has shown that the avalanche of statistics that occurred in the nineteenth century was in effect a form of social regulation, defining normal behaviour in terms of averages, while Cicourel (1964) argued that quantitative researchers tend to fix meanings in ways that suit their preconceptions. Similarly, social psychologists in the 1960s and early 1970s argued that the discipline was implicitly voicing the values of dominant groups (see Harré and Secord 1972, Brown 1973, Armistead 1974). Additionally, Gergen (1973) has argued that all knowledge is historically and culturally specific and that it isn't possible to look for definitive accounts of people and society, because social life is continually changing.

Foucault, in *The Archaeology of Knowledge* (1972), points out that if we can trace back the origins of our current ways of understanding ourselves, we can begin to question their legitimacy and resist them. Marginalised voices – those of the mad, the delinquent, the abnormal and the disempowered – are viewed as important sources of resistance in challenging prevailing (constructionist) knowledge. It could also be argued that in academia (and perhaps particularly in the social sciences) people sometimes engage in research where they have a vested interest or feel a personal connection to the research topic, myself included. For example, the study of language and gay men is likely (but not exclusively) to be of particular interest to gay men, while the subject of motherhood is likely to be of interest to mothers and so on. Arguably the identity of the researcher is likely to inform their approach – different researchers are liable to bring with them a set of existing assumptions, agendas and ideologies which may influence their analysis. I do not believe that it is possible for a researcher to take a completely objective viewpoint (as already stated, even the desire for objectivity suggests that a subjective 'position' has been taken). As research on labelling theory has indicated, stigmatised or 'deviant' identities are likely to subsume other aspects of identity – the behaviour of people with a stigmatised identity will therefore be seen by others as a product of the stigmatised identity (Epstein 1998: 145). Goffman (1963: 14) notes that it is not only outsiders who place a premium on stigmatised identities; those who are stigmatised must constantly 'manage' their identities on dichotomies such as excuse/confront and reveal/conceal. Therefore, research into language and identities could be particularly associated with people who are viewed as holding or are closely connected to problematic, contested or powerless identities (for example, gay men and lesbians, women, deaf people, people from non-white ethnic groups). Such people are likely to be more aware of the oppression of such groups and therefore hold with forms of analysis that are more likely to be associated with questioning the status quo – e.g. queer theory, feminist linguistics, critical discourse analysis – rather than simply stating the ways in which people speak, think or behave differently from each other (which may have the effect of reinforcing categories of difference). Burr (1995: 162) refers to these newer forms of analysis as *action research*, forms of research which have change and intervention rather than the discovery of 'facts' as their explicit aim. Unsurprisingly, post-structuralist thinkers have explored the relationship between language, ideology and hegemony, based on the work of writers like Gramsci (1985) and Bakhtin (1984).

However, post-structuralism theory can also be applied to the split between qualitative and quantitative methodologies. Derrida (1974, 1978, 1981) argues that for thousands of years, western thought has been founded upon the logic of binary oppositions – resulting in questions such as 'Does language determine thought or vice versa?', 'Are we individuals or the product of society?' and 'Is our behaviour the result of nature or nurture?' Derrida argues that such oppositions are typical of ideologies, in that they create an inherent need to judge one side of the dichotomy as primary and the other as secondary, rather than thinking that neither can exist without the other. Instead, Derrida recommends that we reject the logic of *either/or* of binary oppositions, in favour of a logic of *both/and*. So, for example, we should view language and thought as inseparable components of a system, neither of which can make sense without the other. Language/thought should therefore be a unit of study within itself, rather than two separate processes.

We could apply exactly the same argument to allow us to question the validity of the categories *quantitative/qualitative* or *structuralism/post-structuralism*. Post-structuralism theory should therefore allow us to problematise the categories of *quantitative* and *qualitative*, asking why research methodology should have been conceptualised as a split in this way, whether these categories could complement each other and what the consequences of these oppositional *either/or* categories and the discourses that have grown up around them have had for the wider research community. I would argue that both forms of thinking are dependent on each other. A post-structuralist analysis requires a pre-existing structuralist counterpart, whereas a structure that is not subjected to deconstructionist principles is in danger of reification. The two processes are therefore linked components of a way of making knowledge.

Additionally, we should also be careful that post-structuralism does not paradoxically become the new hegemonic discourse of knowledge, displacing constructionism altogether, and ultimately deconstructing itself out of existence. Bryman (1988) offers a list of ways that quantification can enhance qualitative work, suggesting that the two methodologies can facilitate each other. For example, quantitative analyses can help to prevent researcher anecdotalism (Silverman 1993: 163), taking multiple approaches (or triangulation) can increase the chances that one's findings or claims will be accurate and surveys can help the researcher to uncover hidden patterns that are unlikely to be yielded from a close analysis of a small amount of data. Chouliaraki and Fairclough (1999: 154) note that there is a 'need to combine qualitative text analysis with quantitative analysis of large bodies of text'. And coming back to corpus linguistics, Biber (1998: 4) points out the often-overlooked fact that corpus-based research depends on both quantitative *and* qualitative techniques: 'Association patterns represent quantitative relations, measuring the extent to which features and variants are associated with contextual factors. However functional (qualitative) interpretation is also an essential step in any corpus-based analysis.'

The fact that corpus linguistics and language and identities have rarely had much to do with each other is somewhat understandable, given the fact that both areas have favoured different approaches to what constitutes knowledge-making. However, what is perhaps less explicable is that discourse analysis has not made as strong an impact upon queer linguistics as we would expect. Instead, research into language and sexuality has for the past few decades considered questions that are more concerned with identity and in particular with a gay (or less frequently a lesbian, bisexual, transsexual or heterosexual) subject. For example: is there such a thing as a gay voice? How do people construct gay or lesbian identities for themselves (and each other) through language? How are sexual identities revealed/concealed/negotiated in interaction with others?

While such questions are worthwhile, they have been criticised for assuming that there is something 'universally gay' (see Darsey's review (1981) of Hayes' theory of GaySpeak, for example) or for reifying and focusing on difference at the expense of deconstruction. Social theories such as community of practice (Lave and Wenger 1991), anti-language (Halliday 1978), imagined communities (Anderson 1983) and linguistics of contact (Pratt 1987) have all been cited in order to explain why some gay people sound 'gay' (or different from heterosexual people) in certain contexts but not others (unsurprisingly, essentialism, with its empirical overtones and concept of hard-wired difference is almost always absent from such debates).

Discourse analysis and critical discourse analysis have only in the last decade or so begun to make a real impact on research into language and identities; see Litosseliti and Sunderland (2002) for discourse-based analyses of gender. Critical discourse analysis in particular is often underpinned from a Marxist or socialist standpoint and therefore tends to foreground the concept of *power* over *identity*. In some cases, it is possible to apply power relations to identity quite easily – for example, many prevailing discourses of gender exist which serve to empower men at the expense of women (Sunderland 2004). And there are plenty of discourses which exclude or denigrate people who are not traditionally heterosexual. However, when the focus is on sexuality and desire, power structures can be less straightforward. For example, Heywood (1997) describes how in some gay men's erotic narratives, to relinquish power and be abused is in itself a source of pleasure. Such a reading suggests that it is difficult to apply Marxist interpretations of power to something like sexual desire which sometimes exists outside of conventional morality. While the approach I take is one which is broadly informed by critical discourse analysis, e.g. Fairclough (1989), an analysis of the discourses surrounding the subject of gay men therefore needs to look beyond the idea that one group are simply oppressing another, and instead consider power as potentially multi-faceted or even absent in some cases. Using a range of texts which contain discourses of homosexuality should help to highlight how power sometimes occurs as a simple oppressor/oppressed binary, but in other cases is more complex.

Texts and questions

Perhaps another reason why language and identities research has shied away from corpora is due to practical, rather than ideological, considerations. Researchers have argued that discourse analysis is very labour intensive (e.g. Gill 1993: 91) and therefore 'discourse analysis, as with many other varieties of qualitative research is usually *more* difficult than positivist number crunching' (Parker and Burnman 1993: 156). However, I would argue that a corpus linguistics approach can be equally time consuming. Large numbers of texts must first be collected, while their analysis often requires learning how to use computer programs to manipulate data. Statistical tests may be carried out in order to tell whether or not a finding is significant, necessitating the requisite mathematical know-how (or access to a good statistics department). No wonder then that it is often simply less effort to collect a smaller sample of data which can be transcribed and analysed by hand, without the need to use computers or mathematical formulae.

However, there are good reasons for employing corpora in research – particularly when considering discourse. While I would agree that approaches to language and identities that focus on counting differences and reifying rather than deconstructing categories won't take us much further than descriptive (and restricted) accounts of language use, I believe that corpus data have an important and somewhat neglected role to play in uncovering discourses of identity within language. Although the D of *difference* has given way to the D of *discourse*, it is still difficult to ignore difference altogether. For example, if we are to accept that a single gendered 'subject' (e.g. working mothers, transsexuals who appear in the Eurovision Song Contest or male violence at football matches) is discursively constructed, we must also accept that different discourse positions are likely to exist around the same subject. A dominant or hegemonic discourse is likely to produce a reverse discourse – wherever there is power, there is also resistance (Foucault 1976). For example, the discourses that created the homosexual as a 'deviant' sexual category also provided a lexicon for articulating resistance: 'homosexuality began to speak in its own behalf, to demand that its legitimacy or "naturality" be acknowledged often using the same categories by which it was medically disqualified' (Foucault 1976: 101).

However, it is important to note that discourses are not discrete, fixed entities, but instead are always gradually changing, combining, dividing and shifting in a variety of ways. Therefore discourses around the same subject are likely to be multiple and interacting, depending on who is creating them. Part of the reason for the existence of multiple discourses is the complexity of language. For example, in George Orwell's *1984* attempts to remove all discourses but the dominant ideological one were carried out by the deletion of large numbers of vocabulary items and the restriction of meanings of other words. Although this is a fictional account, there is evidence to suggest that language innovation helps to shape and give power to discourse – consider how much more difficult it would be to produce feminist discourses if words such as *feminist* and *sexist* didn't exist.[5]

As discussed earlier, discourses are linked to power: 'it is in the interest of relatively powerful groups that some discourses and not others receive the stamp of "truth"' (Burr 1995: 55). However, power is not always a simple case of oppressor and oppressed. Hence there may be a dominant or prevailing discourse of a subject and numerous competing discourses. So how is it possible to determine which is the dominant discourse? One technique would be to ask a representative set of people (e.g. by focus group or survey).

Another could be to use researcher intuition about the way the world works. However, a more reliable method would be to consult large bodies of text. One indication that something might be a dominant discourse is that we would expect it to occur with high frequency as it is constantly reiterated in a variety of ways throughout society. Such 'accepted wisdom' would not only occur frequently then, but would pervade into different types of text. Take, for example, *compulsory heterosexuality* (Rich 1980), a prevailing discourse if there ever was one. We would expect to find it in private conversation (the admiring relatives who tell the new mother that little Johnny will break all the girls' hearts when he grows up), in advertising (such as a recent UK advertisement for moisturiser aimed at women which said 'If your skin was a fella you'd dump him') and in the media (such as primetime television game shows like *Blind Date* which in the UK only use heterosexual couples). Discourses of compulsory heterosexuality could also be shown by the *absence* of explicit references to heterosexuality in speech and writing, effectively normalising or unproblematising the concept. For example, in terms of frequency we would expect to encounter the terms *man*, *gay man* and *heterosexual man* in general language in the order that I have just listed them in. *Man* is generically taken to mean *heterosexual man*, which is why the latter term would appear so rarely. *Gay man* – being the marked, 'deviant' case – would therefore appear more frequently than *heterosexual man*, but not as often as *man*.[6]

Corpus data would allow us to identify dominant discourses by giving us access to a large enough body of text to confidently illustrate how frequent and pervasive such discourses are. In addition, a corpus would allow us to uncover conflicting or oppositional discourses based around the same subject – discourses that may exist, but are less likely to be uncovered from a smaller-scale analysis or reliance on intuition. As Jaworski and Coupland (1999: 9) point out, 'most texts are not "pure" reflections of single discourses'. Additionally, contradictions between discourses in a single text can be interpreted as conservative or emancipatory to different extents (see Sunderland 2004: 213–14 for further discussion).

So rather than using corpus data to compare linguistic differences between male/female or gay/heterosexual speakers, it is possible to use it in the deconstructionist sense in order to uncover different discourses based around these categories. Therefore, the analysis in this book is not concerned with questions such as 'do gay men say *fabulous* more than heterosexual men?' but is instead interested in how gay men are discursively constructed in different sorts of texts, which are the dominant, contested and minority discourses of homosexuality, and how such discourses overlap and interact with each other. While the concept of discourse is likely to presume a qualitative means of analysis, it is difficult to conceptualise discourse without considering *difference* and *frequency* – two concepts which are well-suited to quantitative approaches. Corpus linguistics is a useful way to approach discourse analysis because of the *incremental* effect of discourse. As Fairclough (1989:

24) points out: '[t]he formal properties of a text can be regarded ... on the one hand as traces of the productive process, and on the other hand as cues in the process of interpretation.' A formal property, e.g. a single word or phrase on its own, may suggest the existence or trace of a discourse. But other than relying on intuition, we can't tell whether such a discourse is hegemonic and entrenched as 'common sense' or whether it is a minority or contesting discourse. By collecting numerous supporting examples of a discourse taken from corpora, we can start to see a cumulative effect. As Stubbs (2001b: 215) concludes: 'repeated patterns show that evaluative meanings are not merely personal and idiosyncratic, but widely shared in a discourse community. A word, phrase or construction may trigger a cultural stereotype.'

However, we need to take care in placing too much reliance on rates of recurrence. Simple frequency alone is not always the best indicator of a dominant or non-dominant discourse, although it may be a *good* indicator. A majority (e.g. frequent) discourse is not the same as a hegemonic discourse. For example, a discourse may be regularly invoked in order to discredit it, by contrasting it with another discourse. Sentences that begin with 'In the past people thought that...' would have the effect of reproducing a 'dead' or discredited discourse, although it only continues to exist as a mechanism for showcasing a newer discourse, created in opposition to it. At other times, frequency may simply not be the most relevant factor in whether a discourse is dominant – the powerful identity of the producer(s) of the discourse (e.g. politicians, newspaper editors, religious leaders, celebrities, business owners) may be more important. In a similar way, approaches that focus on different discourses need to acknowledge that the concept of discourses as discrete and separate entities is problematic. Discourses are constantly changing, interacting, merging, reproducing and splitting off from each other. Therefore a corpus-based analysis of any discourse must be aware that it can only provide static snap-shots that give the appearance of stability but are bound to the context of the data set. One method of addressing this is to collect longitudinal corpora or a range of text types, as this should provide multiple snapshots (allowing discourses to appear to come to life). For example, in Chapter 5, I examine gay men's personal adverts from the same magazine during four time periods over the course of 27 years. However, it should not be assumed that it is possible to elicit every discourse in a corpus or set of corpora, just as a corpus will not provide us with every example of language use. Instead, we would hope that a corpus could tell us something about discoursal trends and patterns, as well as revealing linguistic traces of dominant discourses and some (if not all) of the less dominant ones.

So in order to uncover discourses based on categories, we must acknowledge the existence of these categories – at least in so far as they appear as imagined constructs. A quantitative analysis should take care not to unwittingly reinforce the existence of categories such as *gay*/*heterosexual* but instead reveal how such categories are constructed as oppositions, how they are shifting rather than fixed and how they are defined and reified in relationship to each other. For this reason, many of the chapters in this book are concerned with comparisons of how discourses of male homosexuality appear in relationship to discourses of some related category (in terms of its producers or the subject under examination). For example, in Chapter 2, I look at how discourses of homosexuality are constructed differently in the House of Lords depending on whether Lords chose to argue for a change to laws regarding gay male sex or to keep the status quo; in Chapter 3, I examine discourses of homosexuality from politically left- and right-leaning tabloid newspapers; while in Chapter 6, I compare discourses in gay male and lesbian erotica. I am aware that in focusing on one subject (gay men) I am unintentionally perpetuating other discourses – such as a discourse of lesbian invisibility. However, I hope that this book will instigate corpus-based research into other discursive subjects.

The corpora that I have collected for analysis in the various chapters in this book are all publicly available. I have decided to focus on *public* discourse in relation to gay men for a number of reasons. First, practically, such texts are easier to collect. In some cases I was able to gather the data directly from Internet archives, making corpus-building a less time-consuming (although not short) task. In addition, public discourses are important because they are theoretically accessible to everybody (although people may not choose to read particular texts or may not know where to find them). Public texts are therefore likely to reproduce hegemonic or mainstream discourses concerning homosexuality – and I would argue that in order to make sense of how homosexuality is constructed in our society, the examination of public discourses is essential; in essence they are more likely to represent received wisdom on a subject, or 'the way things are'. Also, perhaps public discourses are more likely to shape and be shaped by popular opinion, simply because they are available to more people and are more likely to be contested if they wildly oppose the majority position. This is not to undermine the potency of discourse in private texts (e.g. diaries, letters, personal conversations). Private discourses may be more interesting to examine (as people may feel more inclined to speak their minds when they feel they are among like-minded others and are unlikely to be challenged, sued or attacked). They are also likely to inform and be informed by public discourses. In any case, the boundaries between public and private aren't necessarily so rigid. For example, reality television programmes like *Big Brother* allow viewers to 'eavesdrop' on private conversations while public texts (such as newspapers) have been produced as a result of dozens of private discussions between editors, sub-editors and copy-writers; what is presented publicly, then, has been created via private dialogues, the content of which will be unavailable to most members of an audience.

Whilst acknowledging that the public/private dichotomy is problematic, I have chosen to focus on texts which could be broadly characterised as available in the public domain, and suggest that study into more private forms of language use concerning homosexuality would be an interesting additional research topic to undertake. In choosing a variety of texts that discuss homosexuality in different contexts and for different purposes, I aim to elicit as complete a picture of the public discourses of homosexuality as is possible. One important point to consider is that public texts must often take into account a widely heterogeneous audience. Discourses of homosexuality can therefore be sub-divided into those that are written from the perspective of a gay or non-gay point of view, and also those which are written for a gay or non-gay audience (although such divisions represent ideals, and the identities of producers or intended audiences may be multiple).

I define a gay audience as one which is not exclusively gay, but is likely to consist of more gay people than heterosexual people. Texts created for a gay audience are likely to include lifestyle magazines, erotica, sexual health documentation or sex-related advice and fiction which features gay people as the central focus. In the same way, a mainstream audience will always contain gay people, but they will exist as a minority group. Texts which reference homosexuality but are intended for a mainstream audience could include news reports, legal debates, primetime television, scientific or medical accounts of homosexuality, documentary exposés or forms of media where gay people are represented as incidental or minority characters – for example, as the gay friend or neighbour. While there is therefore a great deal of overlap or ambiguity between what characterises a mainstream or gay audience, in many cases it is possible to identify a text as being created more for one type than the other.

Identifying the *producers* of texts as being 'mainstream' or 'gay' is a more complex task. It is not often possible to know the sexual identity of a single producer of a text (they may not be available to ask, may not want to answer the question if available, or may not tell the truth). Additionally, public texts in particular are often created by multiple authors. For example, the *Will & Grace* television series (see Chapter 4) was devised (allegedly) by one gay and one heterosexual man (Max Mutchnick and David Kohan respectively), yet scripts will have been the result of collaborations of dozens of writers whose sexual orientations are difficult to ascertain. It is even more difficult to discover the identities of the authors of the gay and lesbian erotic narratives that comprised the Internet-based corpus analysed in Chapter 6. We could assume that they would also be gay, but this may not be the case – for example, heterosexual male authors may have attributed lesbian erotica to assumed female identities. In other cases, defining producers of texts is slightly less problematic – for example, we would assume that the majority of gay personal advertisements are written by gay men for the purpose of romantic or sexual contact (although there may be other motivations for placing such an advert – such as playing a joke on a heterosexual friend or carrying out academic research[7]). It is therefore not always useful to categorise texts as having a single, definable audience or producer, although acknowledging that there may be an idealised 'imagined' audience or

Table 1.1 Texts under study, categorised by differences between producers and audiences

		Possible producer of text	
		Mainstream	*Gay*
Possible intended audience	*Mainstream*	Legal debates (2) Tabloid news (3)	Television scripts (4)
	Gay	Sexual health leaflets (7)	Personal adverts (5) Erotic narratives (6)

'typical' producer may be useful in helping us to understand how discourses surrounding homosexuality (or any other subject) come into being.

Table 1.1 shows an idealised representation of the relationship between the six text types under analysis in this book, their producers and intended audiences. The numbers after each text type indicate the chapter they appear in.

This list of text types is by no means exhaustive and is, to an extent, based on subjective and practical criteria as a result of what was available to me or what I felt might be an interesting site for discourse analysis. I tried to choose texts which differed in terms of their relationship between producers and the intended audience, although some of the cells in Table 1.1 were easier to fill than others. In particular, it was difficult to find texts that were not written by gay men but were intended for a gay audience. I chose safer sex documentation although I was aware that some of the producers (the Terrence Higgins Trust) were likely to have been gay men.

One loose criterion that I held was that the public texts should be from reasonably mainstream sources. I have not, for example, used texts which I felt were written by or for a specific subculture within the gay community (e.g. the gay sado-masochist community). In addition, the texts I have chosen have assumed that a gay or homosexual subject exists (and acknowledge this as such) and are therefore biased from a western (specifically British or American) perspective. In other cultures homosexuality may be constructed differently (or not at all), so those discourses will be correspondingly diverse. And in order to remove the possibility of the passage of time being a significant factor in the production of discourses, I have tried to sample my data from the period 1998–2003 where possible (although in the chapter on personal adverts I do consider time as a main factor in the development of discourses and in the chapter on erotic discourses approximately 30 per cent of the data was from 1991–8). The discourses that I examine, then, appeared within the same culture (or thereabouts) at around the same time period. Even with these restrictions there was still a wealth of data to choose from and it is unlikely that I will be able to elicit and explain every discourse of homosexuality that currently exists during this period.

I intend to examine texts in order to ask the following questions:

- How is language used in the public domain to construct discourses of male homosexuality? What connotations do such discourses hold? In particular how are discourses of homosexuality connected to the concepts of *gender, sexual behaviour* and *sexual desire*?
- How do discourses surrounding homosexuality differ depending on the authors of the texts and their intended audiences?
- How do such discourses exist in relation to each other? How are discourses constructed as dominant or contested?

I am in danger of reifying the category of 'gay man' by assuming that it is a term which will mean the same thing to everyone who reads it. As this book is concerned with discourses surrounding how homosexuality is constructed, I am not making any claims about the way that gay men use language. However, I do make the assumption that text producers write about and construct their own category of what they mean by the term 'gay man'. Such a category is most likely to be different depending on the text producer and the meanings within it are likely to be interpreted differently depending on the reader.

Nor, in cases where gay men are the producers of texts, am I arguing that they are representative of gay men as a whole or that they can be categorised in a certain way beyond the fact that they produced certain texts. Therefore, the gay men who placed adverts in *Gay Times* (analysed in Chapter 5) are simply described as that – gay men who placed adverts in *Gay Times*. They are a group of heterogeneous individuals who are unlikely to share much in common other than the fact that they were looking for love, sex or friendship with other men in *Gay Times*. It is neither necessary nor useful to go beyond this description because I am not attempting to say anything about the way that gay men as a group use language – what I am trying to do in this book is show how gay men as an imagined group are represented differently via discourse in a variety of contexts.

However, it is useful to define the term *gay man*, even though I acknowledge that in naming the subject I engage in an act of interpretation, and as with all such acts, others will disagree. For the purposes of this book I define *gay man* as a male adult who openly self-identifies sexually and romantically, mainly or exclusively with other males. This definition may not apply to men who have sex with other men but claim not to be gay, or to people who are not classed as adults, or to non-western cultures that conceptualise same-sex relationships differently. I defend this description in that it generally places identity at a personal level, rather than imposing an identity on someone from afar (as is the case with terms like *MSM* – see Chapter 7). However, I also know people who by my definition could be classed as gay men, but say that they hate the term (or any sexuality label) or prefer to be referred to as *queer*. With a term like *gay man* I do not believe we can produce a definition that everyone will be happy with, which is one of the reasons why I believe an analysis of discourses surrounding the term will be useful.

In my own writing I mainly use the term *gay* (as an adjective) rather than *homosexual* as I feel uncomfortable with connotations of *homosexual* which have in the past defined same-sex attraction as a medical condition. I also refrain from using *gay* as a noun because I believe that sexuality should be classed as *one* aspect of a person's identity, rather than it being the only one. A phrase like *he's a gay* therefore implies that there is little more to a person than their sexual orientation, whereas *he's a gay man* or *he's gay* suggests that there are other ways of defining that person in other circumstances.

However, I use the term *lesbian* to refer to gay women. Although I am uncomfortable with the term *lesbian* (because it is also a noun), I have found it difficult to think of an adjectival alternative. *Queer* is a more general category and has not been reclaimed by the majority of gay people (in the UK at least – it seems to have had a little more success in some parts of America) and *gay* is so often associated with men that it seems a disservice to use this adjective which may contribute to lesbian invisibility by assuming that lesbian sexuality is exactly the same as gay male sexuality. Additionally, I use the term *heterosexual* rather than *straight*, which creates another inconsistency. I dislike *straight* (as a noun or adjective) because one of its antonyms is *bent* (a word which has been used in a derogatory way towards gay people), although I also dislike the word *heterosexual* because of its association with medical discourse. However, I don't feel that *heterosexual* has the same degree of negative connotation as *homosexual* (at least for me), so I choose this word over *straight*. Other phrases are in existence, e.g. *moxie, otpotss (orientation towards people of the same sex)*, but I do not feel they have gained wide enough usage to be useful here. Therefore my use of terminology is based on a series of compromises and personally subjective decisions which reflect existing inconsistencies in the ways that terms to refer to different sexual groups are currently used.

In addition to using a range of texts that specifically reference homosexuality, I have also found it useful to employ a number of larger, publicly available corpora of 'general' language, created by other linguists. Such *reference corpora* are useful because they provide researchers with accounts of linguistic occurrence that can be said to be representative of language (or a particular language variety). These accounts can be gainfully employed when attempts are made to discover salient features within a more specific text type. We can use a reference corpus to tell us what is average, expected or 'normal' about language so that we can compare this to what is unexpected, unusual or interesting in other texts. Such a corpus may initially be useful in confirming that the texts chosen for closer study are in fact likely to include discourses pertaining to homosexuality. For example, from a reference corpus (in this case the British National Corpus) we find that the word *homosexual* tends to occur about 8.41 times per million words in general British

English. This figure is 18.93 per million for the word *gay*.[8] Higher figures than this in other texts will suggest that such data concentrates on the subject of homosexuality to a much greater degree. If we find that a text contains a higher incidence of *homosexual* than *gay*, or a much higher incidence of *gay* than *homosexual*, then this tells us something interesting too. For example, in the Terrence Higgins Trust safer sex pamphlets (see Chapter 7) the word *gay* occurs 7502 times per million words while the word *homosexual* never appears. Reference corpora, then, afford the researcher a useful benchmark against which to measure their own findings.

The main reference corpus that I have used to inform the analyses in this book is the 100-million-word British National Corpus, which comprises 90 per cent written and 10 per cent spoken British English, collected in the early 1990s. As most of the corpus texts I collected were British English, it seems sensible to compare them against this norm. However, in Chapters 4 and 6, I examine texts that were mainly produced by American authors, so in these cases I have utilised the 1-million-word FROWN corpus of written American English (also collected in the early 1990s).

Corpus processes and problems

I will use the remainder of this chapter to answer the question asked in the title of this chapter, 'What can I do with a naked corpus?', by outlining some of the analytical processes and concepts that I will be using in order to investigate the presence of discourses in the different sets of corpora that I have collected. The somewhat suggestive phrase 'naked corpus' is used because the majority of corpora I examine in this book have not been annotated with additional levels of linguistic information but exist in their raw data format.

The *frequency count* is probably the most well-known and the simplest quantitative technique that can be carried out on a corpus. We can compare frequencies of individual words, lemmas, phrases or other linguistic structures either within a certain text or between texts, different speakers, authors or genres of texts. Frequency counts can also help researchers to notice aspects of language which are unusual or unexpected. For example, Coulthard (1993) in a forensic analysis of a statement made to the police by Derek Bentley (who was hanged in 1953 for his alleged involvement in the killing of a policeman), compared a frequency list of the lexis in his statement to the lexical frequencies in two reference corpora (see Table 1.2) to show that Bentley's use of the word *then* was significantly higher than expected (he used it once every 58.2 words compared to its occurrence of once every 500 words in the reference corpora). Coulthard also demonstrated that Bentley's frequency of *then* was similar to that of a small corpus of police statements (where it occurred once every 78 words) but unlike that of other witness statements (where it occurred once every 930 words), suggesting that his statement was unlikely to have been formulated in his own words.

Table 1.2 Rank-order word frequencies in Derek Bentley's statement compared to reference corpora of spoken and general English. Reproduced from Woolls and Coulthard (1998: 35)

Rank	Bentley statement	Spoken English	General English
1	I	the	the
2	the	I	of
3	and	and	to
4	a	you	and
5	to	it	a
6	we	to	in
7	Chris	that	that
8	*then*	a	is
9	was	of	it
10	policeman	in	for

Frequency counts could also be used to answer questions such as 'Do men swear more than women?' In addition we can compare the frequencies of words or other linguistic structures with other words. For example, 'Do women (or men) use certain swear-words more than others?' While frequency counts are therefore somewhat limited (and may result in generalised descriptions about language rather than explanations), they can be used as the basis of other, more complex techniques.

If we take the focus away from counts of language use based on different groups of speakers (e.g. men versus women), we can see that frequency data can be employed more gainfully in order to examine how language is used to construct a particular subject (e.g. men or women) which in turn should help to elicit discourses. The concept of *preference* is one which can be carried out using frequency information with this sort of approach. When a text is created, producers usually have some sort of choice about the language that they can use. This argument is summed up by Stubbs (1996: 107), who writes: 'No terms are neutral. Choice of words expresses an ideological position.' As Zwicky (1997: 22) points out, one contested choice is between the use of *gay* as opposed to *homosexual*. Other choices could include the use of euphemisms (*that way inclined, confirmed bachelor*, etc.), derogatory terms (*faggot, sissy*) or reclaimings of such terms (*queer, dyke*). Danet (1980) describes a case where a doctor who carried out a late abortion was tried for manslaughter. The language used in the courtroom was an explicit concern of the trial, with lawyers negotiating the different connotations of terms such as *products of conception, fetus, male human being, male child* and *baby boy*. The choice of such terms assume different frames of reference, e.g. *baby boy* suggests helplessness, whereas *fetus* expresses a medical position. However, choice need not be lexical. Another type of choice relates to grammatical uses of words: the use of *gay* as a noun or *gay* as an adjective (or more specifically, *gay* as an attributive adjective (occurring before a noun), e.g. 'the gay man', or *gay* as a predicative adjective (occurring after a link verb), e.g. 'he is gay'). Fairclough (1989: 110–11) lists ten sets of questions relating to formal features, each one indicating that a linguistic choice has been made by the author – e.g. pronoun use, modality, metaphors, agency, passivisation, nominalisation. While Fairclough frames his questions in terms of appearing within 'a specific text', there is no reason why such an analysis of linguistic choices cannot be carried out on a corpus in order to uncover evidence for preference which occurs across a genre or language variety. However, as Sherrard (1991) points out, such a view of choice presupposes that language users feel that they actually *have* a choice or are aware that one exists. She argues that speakers will always be restricted in their ways of using language – for example, people in the 1950s would not have used *Ms* because such a choice was not available to them.

Frequency counts can also be used to create word lists of corpora which can usually be sorted alphabetically or according to frequency. Such frequency lists can be useful in carrying out comparisons of particular lexical or grammatical items, and need not be at the level of a single word. For example, with the corpus analysis program WordSmith, it is possible to create a word list consisting of the most frequent two, three, four, etc. word *clusters* (what Biber *et al.* (1999: 990) refer to as *lexical bundles*) in a corpus.

Although frequency lists give researchers an indication of how often a lexical item occurs in a text, they aren't particularly useful in showing when and where the item appears. Are occurrences of the item dispersed evenly throughout the text or are they limited to a small number of clumps? An examination of the positions that a lexical item occurs in relation to a whole text may reveal clues about the importance of that item, and the extent to which a subject is introduced early or late in relation to others. WordSmith enables researchers to view a dispersion plot of any lexical item, showing a visual representation of all of the places where it occurs in a file or files. For example, Figure 1.1 shows a dispersion plot of the words *happy/happiness/happily* in eight fairy tales.[9] For each story, we are given the total number of words, the number of occurrences of the search word or phrase and the number of times it occurs per 1000 words in the text. Then each short black vertical line represents one occurrence of the search term in a file. It can be seen from the figure that, in all eight stories, the concept of happiness occurs at the end of the story, although in a few cases (files 2 and 3) it can also occur near the beginning. The dispersion plot shouldn't lead us to conclude that fairy stories tend to have happy endings (for example, theoretically the final sentence of each story could be '*Nobody* lived happily ever after'). However, we can infer that the concept of happiness is important to the conclusion of such stories.

Another statistical procedure that can be derived from frequency lists is a *keyword* list. The earliest users of this concept did not employ corpus-based methods to decide what keywords were, but instead intuitively chose words that they believed held important concepts. Perhaps the first proponent of

N	File	Words	Hits	per 1,000	Plot
1	threep~1.txt	538	1	1.86	
2	sleeping.txt	1,816	3	1.65	
3	owwh~1.txt	1,284	2	1.56	
4	duckling.txt	845	1	1.18	
5	cinder~1.txt	1,084	1	0.92	
6	rump.txt	1,222	1	0.82	
7	hansel.txt	1,233	1	0.81	
8	rapunzel.txt	1,405	1	0.71	

Figure 1.1 Dispersion plot of words indexing happiness in fairy tales.

keywords (although he did not use the phrase) was Firth, who in a paper on 'the technique of semantics' referred to focal or pivotal words, which he described as 'sociologically important words' (1935: 41). He gave examples of such words as being *labour*, *trade* and *leisure*. Williams (1976) also noted the importance of keywords, writing a series of 110 essays on words connected with society, culture and philosophy. Taking a corpus linguistics approach, Scott (1999) locates keywords as being derived from more mechanical means. A keyword is any word which occurs more frequently than expected in a corpus or text, when compared to a larger reference corpus, or an equivalent corpus of similar size. Statistical probabilities are computed by an appropriate procedure (e.g. log likelihood), and it is also possible to specify a minimum level of frequency that must occur before a word can be considered key.

So Scott's definition of keywords is less explicitly based upon concepts that are important to culture, but allows for any word to potentially be key if it is used frequently enough when compared to a reference corpus. Scott notes that three types of keywords are often found: proper nouns, keywords that human beings would recognise as key, and are indicators of the 'aboutness' of a particular text, and finally, high-frequency words such as *because*, *shall* or *already*, which may be indicators of style, rather than aboutness. However, as McEnery (2005) argues, it is sometimes these grammatical words that direct the researcher to make the most interesting discoveries. One of McEnery's keywords, the conjunction *and*, occurred extremely frequently in a series of texts about 'bad language' because it was often used to create strong associations between swearing and other negative phenomena, for example in the high number of phrases like 'swearing, drunkenness and lewdness'.

WordSmith allows a frequency list taken from one file (or corpus) to be compared against the frequency list of another corpus (either a larger 'reference' corpus, or one that is of a similar size). When two texts of equal size are compared, two corresponding keyword lists are produced, usually of a similar length. When a smaller text is compared to a larger text, only the words that are key in the smaller text appear, along with a smaller number of negative keywords (words which have appeared in the smaller text less often than would be expected from their appearance in the reference corpus[10]). An examination of the keywords that occur when two corpora or texts are compared together should reveal something about the different discourses that are present in these sets of texts – in relation to each other, both in terms of aboutness and style.

A keyword list is usually presented in order of keyness (the most statistically significant or 'strongest' keywords appearing first). It should be noted that a keyword list only focuses on differences rather than similarities between two texts or corpora. However, keywords will reveal differences in frequencies that should point to the presence of different discourses between the two texts. Again, I am concerned with the frequency or strength of a discourse, the theory being that one way of measuring discourse strength is to compare how many times that discourse occurs in one text type when compared to another. Clearly, a discourse does not necessarily have to occur dozens of times for it to be important, but I would argue that the more times it does occur, the stronger its association with a particular text type.

How do keywords work in relation to discourse? Parker and Burnham (1993: 156) point out that discourses emerge, as much through our work of reading as from the text. Keywords will therefore not reveal discourses, but will direct the researcher to important concepts in a text (in relation to other texts) which may help to signpost the process of eliciting discourse. Examining how such keywords occur in context, which grammatical categories they appear in, and looking at their common patterns of co-occurrence should therefore be revealing. For example, Johnson *et al.* (2003) investigated a corpus of British newspaper articles which all contained references to the concept of *political correctness* over a five-year period. They found that the strongest keywords in this corpus differed over time as the focus around political correctness shifted from a range of minority identities in 1994 (*women, black, gay*) to being centred around racism in 1999, and particularly the enquiry into the death of a black young man called Stephen Lawrence (see Table 1.3). Analysing the contexts that keywords appear in, then, is a useful way of shedding light on how texts discursively construct particular objects. For example, an analysis of the presence of the keywords *American* and *America* in the 1994 data revealed that political correctness was viewed at this point as a relatively new, foreign (and unpleasant) phenomenon in the UK, having been imported from America. By 1999 such terms were no longer keywords, suggesting that political correctness was less likely to be viewed by the British press as a 'foreign' way of thinking.

Another form of analysis that can be carried out on a corpus concerns *collocation*. As Firth (1957) famously wrote: 'You shall know a lot about a word from the company it keeps', and collocation is therefore a way of understanding meanings and associations between words which are otherwise difficult to work out from a small-scale analysis of a single text. Words (or

Table 1.3 Rank-ordered keywords in discourse in newspaper articles containing the term 'political correctness' for 1994 and 1999. Reproduced from Johnson *et al.* (2003: 36)

Rank	Keywords for 1994	Keywords for 1999
1	pounds	pounds
2	women	racism
3	American	Blair
4	Hackney	racist
5	culture	millennium
6	Portillo	black
7	rape	racial
8	America	women
9	Kingsmead	Macpherson
10	black	www
11	gay	Sadowitz
12	book	fhm
13	tory	Lawrence
14	Romeo	website
15	radio	comedy
16	film	Tintin
17	Wesker	Bramleys
18	sex	Irvine
19	Mamet	ethnic
20	Tarantino	books

signifiers to use Saussure's term (1974)) can only take on meaning (that which is *signified*) by the context that they occur in. So, in order to understand the meanings of words, we have to compare them in relation to other words.

> Suppose you want to know the meaning of a signifier, you can look it up in a dictionary; but all you will find will be yet more signifiers, whose signifieds you can in turn look up, and so on. The process is not only infinite but somehow circular: signifiers keep transforming into signifieds, and vice versa, and you never arrive at a final signified which is not a signifier in itself.
>
> (Sarup 1988: 35)

While we must accept that there is no final signified, it should be seen that one way at arriving at some form of meaning is to examine how words are used in context (as opposed to dictionary definitions), and also which contexts they do *not* occur in. Collocation is therefore a process whereby we can understand meaning in terms of context. For example, take the words *bachelor* and *spinster*, which refer respectively to an unmarried man and woman. A look at their collocates in the British National Corpus reveals that although the words superficially access the same concept (to be unmarried), in actual use they refer to very different ideas. *Bachelor* collocates with *eligible, days, elderly, confirmed, flat* and *party* whereas *spinster* collocates with *elderly, widows, sister(s)* and *rape*. While both words therefore share the collocate *elderly*, the term *bachelor* also collocates with a set of words that contain more positive associations: *eligible, party, flat*; whereas the collocates of *spinster* suggest a different sort of lifestyle, e.g. *widows, sisters*. It could even be argued that words that have very strong collocates will contain traces of these meanings even when they are used apart from them. For example, if *bystander* almost always co-occurs with *innocent* we may infer that the word *bystander* implicitly contains associations of innocence which may be apparent, even in the few cases where it occurs in contexts without the word *innocent*. Usually words have multiple collocates so their implicit meaning may be derived from a combination of different pairings.[11]

There are several ways of calculating collocation. The simplest is simply to count up the number of times a word appears next to (or near) another word, after specifying a particular number of words either side of the node word. For example, *sin* collocates with *forgive* on ten occasions in the BNC within a window of three words in either direction of the word (see Table 1.4 – only words which occur within sentence boundaries are included in the table).

We can also see from Table 1.4 that *forgive* tends to collocate to the left of *sin*, and its most common position here is at L2 (or two places to the left). If the frequency of the target word is relatively low and we are using a specialised corpus, then this may be sufficient in allowing us to determine the most frequent patterns of co-occurrence. However, when using larger, more general corpora, this type of calculation may not be particularly useful to us. If the word *sin* only ever occurs ten times in the BNC and always collocates with *forgive* then this fact is going to be more important than if *sin* occurs

Table 1.4 Co-occurrences of *forgive* and *sin* in the British National Corpus within a L3–R3 span

L3	L2	L1	target	R1	R2	R3
forgive	those	who	sin	against	us.	
will	forgive	their	sin	and	will	heal
forgive	others	who	sin	against	us,	protection
to	forgive	her	sin.			
can	forgive	that	sin.			
can	forgive	my	sin.			
God	can	forgive	sin.			
God	could	forgive	sin.			
came	to	forgive	sin	and	he	wanted
to	forgive	her	sin,	he	also	wanted

3000 times yet still only collocates ten times with *forgive*. In addition, we tend to find that when we base collocation on counting, it is usually grammatical words like *the* which collocate most frequently with other words (and it is not always particularly helpful to know this). A more salient measure of collocation, then, is one which focuses on words which appear together frequently but apart relatively infrequently. Such a measure is called a mutual information (or MI) score. Mutual information is calculated by examining all of the places where two potential collocates occur in a text or corpus. An algorithm then computes what the expected probability of these two words occurring near to each other would be, based on their relative frequencies and the overall size of the corpus. It then compares this expected figure to the observed figure – what has actually happened – and converts the difference between the two into a number which indicates the strength of the collocation – the higher the number, the stronger the collocation. Some measures of MI divide the score by log base 2 (such as BNCWeb – a web-based facility used for analysing the BNC, which automatically does this, and WordSmith Tools which gives this calculation as an option). For the log base 2 calculation, any score higher than three is usually deemed to be indicative of a strong collocation.

However, one problem with MI is that it can tend to give high scores to relatively low-frequency words. For example, in the BNC, *company* and *Chicago-based* have a MI score of 6.8, even though *Chicago-based* only occurs 20 times in the whole corpus (of which five are collocates of *company*). On the other hand, *shares* which occurs 8388 times (of which 341 are collocates of *company*) receives a lower MI score of 4.2. Intuitively it could be argued that *shares* is a more important collocate of *company* than *Chicago-based*, although the MI score does not suggest this. Therefore other calculations have been suggested in order to take into account the frequency of collocates. For example, the z-score (Berry-Rogghe 1973), MI3 (Oakes 1998: 171–2), log–log (Kilgarriff and Tugwell 2001) or log-likelihood (Dunning 1993) scores. Table 1.5 gives these scores for *company* with *shares* and *Chicago-based* (from BNCWeb).

In all cases apart from MI log base 2, *company/shares* receives a higher score than *company/Chicago-based*. Therefore, in this book, when BNCWeb is used,

Table 1.5 Different collocational measures for *company/shares* and *company/Chicago-based*

	Company/shares	Company/Chicago-based
MI (log base 2)	4.24	6.86
MI3	21.0	11.5
Log-likelihood	2568.69	56.87
Log–log	35.7	15.93
Z-score	76.1	23.9

collocations are given as log–log scores, whereas collocates calculated via WordSmith, which doesn't have this option, are given as MI (log base 2).[12]

However, while collocates can be useful indicators of the meanings of words, as with word lists, the fact that they appear out of context can mean that information is obscured. So looking back at an earlier example, why did *bachelor* collocate with *days* in the BNC? When we examine how these words actually occur together, they are often in sentences where men fondly look back upon their 'bachelor days', suggesting that such a period was a happy one and adding further weight to the positive associations of *bachelor*. Therefore a *concordance analysis* is often necessary in order to uncover subtleties of meaning in a text or corpus. A concordance, also referred to as a 'key word in context' or KWIC, is simply a list of all of the occurrences of a word (or phrase or other linguistic feature) in a text in the context that the feature occurs in. Concordances can usually be sorted alphabetically (e.g. on the word to the left or right of the node word) which makes patterns easier to uncover.

For example, in the BNC the strongest collocate of the word *daylight* is *broad*. The *Oxford English Dictionary CD-ROM* gives one of the meanings of *broad* as an adjective as being 'Of day, daylight'. However, upon examining a list of all the cases where these two words co-occur, it appears that they regularly appear in constructions that describe something bad happening, usually connected to crime or violence, e.g. 'abducted on motorway in broad daylight', 'stabbed in broad daylight', 'snatched off a bus in broad daylight' (see Table 1.6). A concordance of *broad daylight* therefore tells us about a very specific use of the two words in this context, which is linked to the unexpectedness of a crime or shocking incident occurring when people could be around to witness it. Concordances and collocations can therefore be extremely helpful in uncovering discourse patterns. Stubbs (2001b: 215) notes:

> Evaluative meanings are conveyed not only by individual words but also by longer phrases and syntactic structures, and by co-occurring node and collocates. Repeated instances of collocation across a corpus provides objective, empirical evidence for evaluative meanings.

Collocations can be particularly important when examining the meanings of sexuality labels like *gay*, *homosexual*, etc.[13] And it is in discourse – the use of language in specific contexts – that words acquire meaning. Collocations are not the same thing as discourses, but they can act as useful indicators of what discourses might be.

It is also possible to create collocational *networks*, in the form of diagrams which show multiple links between sets of collocates in a text. For example, McEnery (2005), in his analysis of seventeenth-century British texts produced by the Society For the Reformation of Manners, showed how a network of collocates created associations between concepts such as *lewdness*, *drunkenness*, *swearing*, *vice*, *blasphemy* and *profaneness*.

Table 1.6 Sample concordance of 'broad daylight' from the British National Corpus

sewers. Woman abducted on motorway in	broad daylight	while phoning AA. Later murdered.
, having been abducted and then stabbed in	broad daylight	, the prosecution alleges.
's brother, was snatched off a bus in	broad daylight	while travelling with his family. The
, a "Mirista" who was captured in	broad daylight	and stripped to his underwear back in
. Socialists stab each other in the chest in	broad daylight	.
want; at other times, however, as in	broad daylight	, "it is not in my power to . . . determine
gave no hint of anything amiss and, in	broad daylight	, the events and the disturbing stories
that would be risky, because it would be	broad daylight	, and there would be plenty of people
they split up and simply walked through in	broad daylight	. All of them made it back to the rende
way with driving among enemy vehicles in	broad daylight	. But that was what the SAS was all ab

A related concept to collocation is the concept of *colligation* (Stubbs 2001b: 65):

> Colligation is the relation between a pair of grammatical categories or, in a slightly wider sense, a pairing of lexis and grammar. For example, the word-form *cases* frequently co-occurs with the grammatical category of 'quantifier', in phrases such as *in some cases, in many cases*.

And the notion of collocation can be extended even further, to include *semantic preference*. This is a term similar to Louw's (1993) and Sinclair's (1991) concept of *semantic prosody*. Semantic preference is, according to Stubbs (2001b: 65), 'the relation, not between individual words, but between a lemma or word-form and a set of semantically related words'. For example, in the British National Corpus the word *rising* co-occurs with words to do with work and money: e.g. *incomes, prices, wages, earnings, unemployment*, etc. Semantic preference also occurs with multi-word units. For example, *glass of* co-occurs with a lexical set of words 'drinks': e.g. *sherry, lemonade, water, champagne, milk*, etc. Semantic preference is therefore related to the concepts of collocation and colligation, but focuses on a lexical set of semantic categories rather than a single word or a related set of grammatical words.

Semantic preference is related to the concept of *discourse prosody*, although the difference between the two is not always clear-cut. Stubbs (2001b: 65) says it is partly a question of how open-ended the list of collocates is. So it may be possible to list all of the words for 'drinks', indicating a semantic preference, but a more open-ended category such as 'unpleasant things' might be seen as a discourse prosody. For example, we could say that *broad daylight* possesses a negative discourse prosody. Stubbs (2001b: 88) later notes that even a category of semantic preference will be open-ended, but will contain frequent and typical members.

In addition, semantic preference denotes aspects of meaning which are independent of speakers, whereas discourse prosody focuses on the relationship of a word to speakers and hearers, and is more concerned with attitudes. Semantic preference is therefore more likely to occur in cases where attitudes are not expressed. However, even the absence of an attitude can be significant, for example, by showing a speaker's desire to remain 'on the fence'.

It can be seen, then, that with the discussion of keywords, collocation and semantic preference, we have moved away from the notion of simple categories based on frequency and onto more complex forms of analysis which require qualitative interpretations of data in order to provide explanations for patterns. Processes in corpus linguistics, then, should provide both a basis for creating structures and the means to deconstruct them.

Finally, one process that can be carried out on a corpus is by enhancing it with additional levels of linguistic annotation. For example, texts can be annotated in terms of parts of speech, to allow the grammatical functions of words to be taken into account during analysis. Such annotations allow researchers to distinguish between different uses of the same word. Granger (2002: 17–18) points out that French learners of English tend to use the word *to* with about the same frequency as native English speakers. However, while these learners use *to* as a particle with a similar frequency to native speakers, they tend to under-use the prepositional use of *to*. Semantic annotation can also be carried out (e.g. Wilson and Thomas 1997) which could theoretically aid the identification of semantic or discourse preference. In Chapter 4, I carry out a keywords analysis of scripts from the television series *Will & Grace*, not on words, but on key semantic and grammatical categories within a corpus.

There are, however, a number of issues which should be taken into account when using corpus data, which are worth addressing here before moving on. All methodologies have weaknesses, which do not automatically mean that a technique should be discarded, just that the researcher should be aware of and honest about its limitations. First, corpus data are usually only language data (written or transcribed spoken), and discourses are not always confined to verbal communication. By holding a door open for a woman, a man could be said to be performing a communicative act which could be discursively interpreted in numerous ways – a discourse of 'the gallant man' versus a discourse of 'male power imposing itself on women' for example. In a similar way, discourses can be embedded within images – for example, pictures of heterosexual couples often occur in advertising, helping to normalise the discourse of compulsory heterosexuality while photo spreads of women in magazines aimed at men reveal dominant discourses about what constitutes an attractive woman by male standards. Caldas-Coulthard and van Leeuwen (2002) investigate the relationship between the visual representations of children's toys (in terms of design, colour and movement) such as The Rock and Barbie and texts written about them, suggesting that in many cases discourses can be produced via interaction between verbal and visual texts.

The fact that discourses are communicated through means other than words indicates that a corpus-based study will be restricted – any discourses that are uncovered in a corpus will be limited to the verbal domain. Some work has been carried out on creating and encoding corpora of visual materials, e.g. Smith *et al.*'s corpus of children's posters (1998), although at the moment there doesn't appear to be a standardised way of encoding images in corpora.[14]

In addition to this, issues surrounding the social conditions of production and interpretation of texts are important in helping the researcher understand discourses surrounding them (Fairclough 1989: 25). Questions surrounding production, such as who authored a text, under what circumstances, for what motives and for whom, in addition to questions surrounding the interpretation of a text – who bought, read, accessed, used the text, what were their responses, etc. – cannot be simply answered by traditional corpus-based techniques, and therefore require knowledge and analysis of how a text exists within the context of society and social practices.

A third problem with corpus data is that they will not tell us what is *absent* in a corpus. For example, if we compare the number of times that different words referring to homosexuality appear in a text, we may be tempted to only focus on the words that appear rather than the words that don't. So if *gay* appears 50 times and *faggot* appears once, we may point this out, but omit to mention that other words, such as *queer, homosexual*, etc. never occur. Prior awareness or intuition about what is possible in language should help to make us aware of such absences, and often comparison with a larger normative corpus will reveal what they are. Hunston (2002: 22–3) also warns that corpus analysis cannot tell us if something is possible, only that something is frequent.

A fourth problem is the existence of numerous processes, statistical measures and tools which can be applied to text, suggesting that there is no single set way to approach analysis. For example, would a keywords analysis be the best way (or fairest way) to uncover discourse patterns? Would investigating concordances in order to uncover semantic preference be useful? Or would looking at the collocations of words be preferable? And if collocations are used, which measure should be employed – log–log, log-likelihood, MI3, z-score, etc.? To an extent, the use of particular processes of combinations of processes should be aided by the research questions that are being asked, but the point should be made that the direction that corpus analysis takes (as with other methodologies) is not a foregone conclusion, but subject to researcher choice.

We must also be careful about placing too much reliance on corpus data as the *only* way of interpreting the meaning of a text or lexical item. For example, in Chapter 2, members of the House of Lords often collocate the word *commit* with terms involving sexual acts (*buggery, anal sex*, etc.). In the British National Corpus, *commit* collocates with a semantic set of terms to do with crime. Therefore, we could argue that the Lords who use phrases like *commit anal sex* are implicitly constructing gay men as criminals. However, such an interpretation rests on the fact that we all have a similar kind of (subconscious?) understanding of the way that the English language works. Would someone who has English as a second language interpret *commit anal sex* in the same way as a native speaker, a corpus linguist or a gay rights activist? If the Lords' choice of this phrase *is* subconscious, and our understanding of it is also subconscious, then how can we ever ascertain that a message about gay men as criminals has actually being passed from the sender to the recipient? And even if the corpus interpretation is valid, different people will respond to the message in a variety of ways. Therefore, the corpus interpretation is one possible interpretation out of many. It is an interpretation based on norms and frequent patterns within language. But just as the subject of this book is concerned with a sexual practice which is sometimes considered 'against the norm', so can there be interpretations of language that go against the 'norms' of corpus data.

Similarly, corpus data do not interpret themselves – it is up to the researcher to make sense of the patterns that are found, postulating reasons for their existence or looking for further evidence to support hypotheses. However, a problem with researcher interpretation is that it is still a form of interpretation and open to contestation. Such concerns, however, suggest that corpus analysis shares much in common with forms of analysis thought to be qualitative, and at least with corpus analysis the researcher has to provide explanations for results and language patterns that have been discovered in a relatively neutral manner. Unlike more qualitative forms of analysis, the corpus linguist does not act as judge and jury over the process (e.g. by choosing to analyse smaller samples of texts that may support his/her hypothesis). Corpus data therefore frame explanations, setting the parameters by which they can exist. With a smaller-scale qualitative analysis, the results themselves may be interpretative as well as their explanations. Of course, it is the corpus researcher who chooses which texts she will examine (and which ones she won't), although I have tried to address this by using a range of different text types from a range of sources.

Therefore, it is something of a myth to conceptualise corpus linguistics as a completely empirical, objective approach to language analysis, particularly when performing discourse analysis. Would my findings be any different, for example, if I decided to approach them from a position which viewed homosexuality as morally wrong, or as somehow superior to heterosexuality? I imagine they would. While the computer has no bias, the researcher cannot make the same claim to impartiality. At least by stating my position at the beginning, readers can interpret my own interpretations accordingly. In writing this book I did not work from a hidden agenda (not consciously at least), nor did I know the outcome of this study before I undertook it (some of what I found was surprising). However, my own biases will certainly have influenced the discourses I uncovered, the way I wrote about them and the way I presented them to the reader.

My findings are therefore based on the corpus-assisted interpretation of discourses of gay men, mediated by my own researcher bias (what I looked for, where I looked for it and how I interpreted it). I don't think this negates the analysis. All forms of discourse analysis are interpretative, and corpus-based norms at least suggest that the interpretations are going to have some degree of validity – because the language-based phenomena under discussion occurs in regular, repetitive patterns.

So it is with these riders in mind that I turn now to the analysis of discourse I have performed on different corpora pertaining to homosexuality. I consider each text type on its own in the following six chapters. I begin by considering public texts that have not been written by gay men, nor have them as their main audience. Chapters 2 and 3 examine a series of debates about the age of consent for gay men in the House of Lords and uses of the word *gay* and other related terms in tabloid newspapers. In Chapter 4, I look at scripts from the television situation comedy *Will & Grace*, intended for a mainstream audience, but written from a gay perspective. Then I consider texts that have been written for gay audiences by gay men. Chapters 5 and 6 examine personal 'lonely-hearts' adverts and erotic narratives respectively. Then, in Chapter 7, I look at sexual health documentation written for gay men by the Terrence Higgins Trust – a group which provides pamphlets for numerous groups other than gay people. In the concluding chapter I draw together the different strands of discourse in order to uncover a wider picture of the way that different discourses interact with each other in society.

2   Unnatural Acts

The House of Lords debates on gay male law reform

Introduction

I begin by considering two contexts which contain public discussion and commentary about gay men from a generally non-gay perspective. As in most cases where authorship is multiple, it is not always possible to state conclusively that all of the people who contributed towards the creation of the data examined in the following two chapters are not gay – in this chapter for example, one speaker, Lord Alli, *does* identify himself as gay and there may be others who are gay but choose not to be forthcoming with the information. However, for the most part, the following two chapters consider discourses of homosexuality that are imposed by others. As the discourses of homosexuality that can be traced to the late nineteenth century were similarly applied by a powerful external body (the medical profession) rather than by the people who claimed homosexual identities, it is fitting to examine two similarly powerful external bodies who, to a greater or lesser degree, are able to influence the attitudes and behaviours of the rest of the population. Chapter 3 considers the tabloid press, who reach millions of readers on a daily basis, whereas this chapter examines British Parliament – which ultimately has had the power to decide whether gay people should be classed as criminals or not.

The House of Lords, reform and debates on homosexuality

Three elements make up Britain's 'Crown in Parliament': the monarch, the House of Lords (consisting of hereditary peers, life peers, Law Lords, Anglican archbishops and bishops) and the House of Commons (consisting of elected representatives). For legislation to become law, it must be passed by all three elements. In practice, however, it is the House of Commons which produces and passes laws. The monarch has given royal assent automatically for over 280 years,[1] while the Parliament Act of 1911 removed the House of Lords' power to reject legislation. Instead a power of delay was substituted, which was further curtailed by the Parliament Act of 1949. Since then, the

House of Commons has been able to present any bill previously rejected by the Lords (except one to prolong the life of Parliament) for Royal Assent one year after its rejection, in a new session of parliament. In addition, the 'Salisbury' convention means that the Government's manifesto commitments in the form of Government Bills may not be voted down by the House of Lords at their second reading (House of Lords 2002a). The role of the House of Lords, therefore is to play:

> an important part in **revising legislation** and keeping a check on Government by **scrutinising** its activities. It complements the work of the Commons, whose members are elected to represent their constituents. Members of the Lords are not elected and are unpaid. They have a wide range of experience and provide a source of **independent expertise**. The House also has a **judicial role** as the final Court of Appeal.
>
> (House of Lords briefing 2002b: 1, bold print reproduced)

Recently, constitutional reforms have attempted to reduce the power of the House of Lords further. In December 1998, the Lords had 1297 members, of whom 1166 were eligible to attend Parliamentary sessions and vote in divisions. The largest proportion of these members were hereditary peers (59 per cent) of which 55 per cent were eligible to attend and vote. This figure breaks down further to approximately 47 per cent Conservatives, 4 per cent Liberal Democrat and 3 per cent Labour. The House of Lords had been criticised as a 'long-stop' for the Conservatives, wherein Conservative defeats in the Commons can be reversed by the permanent Conservative majority in the Lords and Labour legislation can be blocked (Bell 1981: 1). There is some evidence to support this view – since 1970–1, Labour Governments had 63 legislative defeats in the Lords per session, whereas this figure was eight per session for Conservative Governments. Tony Blair's Labour Government suffered more defeats in the Lords during 1997–8 than any government since 1979–80 (Cracknell 2000: 12).

On November 11, 1999, more than 660 hereditary peers lost their right to sit and vote in the Lords, as the Government's reform bill was given Royal Assent. The following spring, the House of Lords was reformed further, although 92 of the 758 hereditary peers were allowed to remain in the Lords, after being elected by their colleagues. In order to help decide who should remain, each candidate produced a 75-word manifesto. Some manifestos received scathing attention by British journalists. For example, the BBC (2001) noted that Lord Monckton of Brenchley argued the case for muzzling cats to preserve Britain's wildlife, while Baroness Strange wrote that she had brought flowers to the House of Lords. The Baroness was elected to remain with 53 votes. Lord Monckton was not elected.

One area in which the House of Lords has traditionally opposed the government concerns legislation to change the UK's laws relating to homosexuality. A contested issue that has been debated by the Lords was the age of consent for gay men. While the age of consent for heterosexual inter-course is 16 (except for heterosexual anal sex, which is only legal at 18), the age of consent was set at 21 for homosexual intercourse (including both anal and oral sex as well as mutual masturbation, the latter two generally referred to under law by the phrase 'gross indecency') on July 27, 1967.[2] On Febru-ary 24, 1994, Members of Parliament voted to lower the age of sexual consent for gay men to 18, although the question of equalisation (e.g. making the age of consent to 16 for everyone) returned to Parliament in 1998. During three debates, which took place on July 22, 1998, April 13, 1999 and November 13, 2000, the House of Lords rejected a Bill to equalise the age of consent for heterosexual and homosexual sex to 16 years. During its third reading, a 'compromise'[3] amendment, tabled by Baroness Young, attempted to reduce the age of consent for all sex acts to 16, except for anal sex (both heterosexual and homosexual), which would remain at 18. The Bill (without Baroness Young's amendment) was eventually passed by the House of Commons on November 30, 2000.

The House of Lords debates on the age of consent are of particular interest because the powerful status of the Lords as 'a source of independent exper-tise' and their ability to delay or modify proposed government reforms in a public arena will have implications for the ordinary lives of gay people in the UK, and will also influence both private and public discourses of homo-sexuality by setting an example to the rest of the country. If a Lord says on record that homosexuality is wrong or unnatural, for example, this will rep-resent a powerful validation of such a discourse to the rest of the country.

This chapter examines the language that was used in these debates, focus-ing on how discourses of homosexuality were constructed by the particip-ants, in particular by concentrating on lexical items that were most frequently used by opposing groups.

Data

The data under study consist of three electronic transcripts of House of Lords debates, from the 1998, 1999 and 2000 debates on the age of consent, consisting in total of 119,830 words.[4] Utterances in these texts were annot-ated with a code of 1–4 according to the stance of the speakers on law reform related to homosexuality. The first two debates resulted in a vote so, for almost all of the speakers, it was possible to determine their position in the debates (whether for (1) or against (2) law reform), either by checking how they voted, or by looking at the content of their speeches for phrases such as 'I will vote for/against reform'. However, even within these two opposing camps a wide range of attitudes could be expressed. For example, not everyone who supported law reform had the same attitude towards homosexuality. Lord Alli, the only openly gay Lord, spoke from his own experience:

For me this debate tonight is not an academic, intellectual or even theological one. Between the ages of 16 to 21 I suffered under this law. I was made to keep my relationships secret from my employers, friends and even my family. To create that level of fear in anyone so young is unforgivable and I do not believe that we should put any more young people through it.

(Lord Alli, April 13, 1999)

On the other hand, Lord Rowallan, who also supported reform, was more equivocal:

I do not like the open, camping, overt sexuality of Peter Tatchell[5] and his ilk. I do not approve of men or women kissing in public another person of the same sex. Nor do I like to see heterosexual sex in public places. But it happens everywhere. I am not a prude.

(Lord Rowallan, April 13, 1999)

Another category (3) was created for people who were undecided about law reform or who abstained from voting, although this group was relatively small (their speech consisted only 937 words of my corpus). A final category (4) was applied to parts of the debate which were not related to discussing law reform but touched upon procedural matters, such as who should get to speak next or how long should be spent debating the reform. Again, this type of meta-discussion constitutes only a small part of the debate (3383 words). Therefore, the majority of text under analysis focused on the presentation of positions that were either for (1) or against (2) law reform regarding homosexuality. Of these two stances, 50,476 words consisted of pro-reform debate, while 56,705 words were spoken by the anti-reformers.

Analysis of discourses

Using WordSmith Tools, the text which contained speeches from those who were opposed to law reform was compared to the speeches from the pro-reformers (see Chapter 1 for a fuller discussion of keywords).[6] A keywords comparison was carried out, in order to ascertain which words appeared significantly more often in one side of the debate, as opposed to the other (the p value was set at 0.0005).[7] Forty-one words were found to be keywords – 16 of which were more frequently used by the pro-reformers and 25 of which occurred more often in the speech of those opposed to reform (see Tables 2.1 and 2.2 which give the keywords for pro-reform and anti-reform speech respectively – the words are presented in order of keyword strength).

An analysis of these keywords reveals the different ways that the debaters chose to frame their arguments, to either argue for or against reform. Although these keywords act as pointers towards some of the most frequently accessed (and therefore significant) discourses associated with

Table 2.1 Keywords in the pro-reform speeches. Numbers in brackets show relative frequencies per 1000 words

Word	Frequency in pro-reform speeches	Frequency in anti-reform speeches	Keyness
law	218 (4.32)	93 (1.64)	67.5
she	89 (1.76)	22 (0.39)	51.6
baroness	174 (3.45)	82 (1.45)	45.5
criminal	78 (1.55)	24 (0.42)	36.8
harm	31 (0.61)	3 (0.05)	30.2
convention	22 (0.44)	2 (0.04)	21.9
rights	61 (1.21)	24 (0.42)	21.3
sexuality	42 (0.83)	14 (0.25)	18.1
reform	11 (0.22)	0 (0)	16.6
nothing	20 (0.40)	3 (0.05)	16.1
association	28 (0.55)	7 (0.12)	16.1
her	64 (1.27)	31 (0.55)	15.9
tolerance	10 (0.20)	0 (0)	15.1
orientation	30 (0.59)	9 (0.16)	14.5
sexual	123 (2.44)	82 (1.45)	13.7
human	60 (1.19)	32 (0.56)	12.2

homosexuality and law reform, it is necessary to carry out a closer analysis of how these words occur in the context of the debate in order to understand how they contribute towards such discourses.

Identities or acts?

Although the words *gay* and *homosexual* occurred frequently in the debates, they were not keywords in either set of texts. However, as they were important concepts it is useful to begin the analysis by an examination of how they were commonly used. Within the debates as a whole, the word *gay* occurred 115 times (*gays* occurred four times), while *homosexual* occurred 305 times and *homosexuals* appeared 81 times. As Table 2.3 shows, while *homosexual(s)* tended to occur more than *gay(s)* overall, this phenomenon was more marked in the language used by the anti-reformers.

Some anti-reformers specifically noted that they disapproved of the current use of *gay*:

> I have never liked the use of the word 'gay' in this context. It is an old English girl's name. I do not mind 'homosexual'.
> (Lord Selsdon, April 13, 1999)

> Public opinion is being manipulated by insistent use or misuse of euphemisms. One speaks about 'gays'. I like to think of myself as a gay

Table 2.2 Keywords in the anti-reform speeches. Numbers in brackets show relative frequencies per 1000 words

Word	Frequency in anti-reform speeches	Frequency in pro-reform speeches	Keyness
buggery	60 (1.06)	8 (0.16)	39.2
age	354 (6.24)	186 (3.68)	35.6
lowered	25 (0.44)	0 (0)	31.8
anal	84 (1.48)	23 (0.46)	30.3
subsection	18 (0.32)	0 (0)	22.9
indecency	23 (0.41)	1 (0.02)	22.5
at	303 (5.34)	179 (3.55)	19.6
vaginal	15 (0.26)	0 (0)	19.1
act	84 (1.48)	32 (0.63)	18.5
per	45 (0.79)	11 (0.22)	18.4
cent	45 (0.79)	11 (0.22)	18.4
compromise	14 (0.25)	0 (0)	17.8
blood	14 (0.25)	0 (0)	17.8
intercourse	83 (1.46)	33 (0.65)	16.9
gross	18 (0.32)	1 (0.02)	16.6
Wolfenden	17 (0.30)	1 (0.02)	15.4
commit	12 (0.21)	0 (0)	15.3
lowering	43 (0.76)	12 (0.24)	15.1
lining	11 (0.19)	0 (0)	14.0
page	11 (0.19)	0 (0)	14.0
demand	11 (0.19)	0 (0)	14.0
sensitive	11 (0.19)	0 (0)	14.0
condom	10 (0.18)	0 (0)	12.7
greatly	10 (0.18)	0 (0)	12.7
girls	77 (1.36)	34 (0.67)	12.5

Table 2.3 Frequencies of *gay(s)* and *homosexual(s)* in the House of Lords debates. Numbers in brackets show relative frequencies per 1000 words

	Pro-reform	Anti-reform
gay(s)	58 (1.1)	61 (1.0)
homosexuals(s)	166 (3.2)	214 (3.7)

fellow. I enjoy gayness. I object to others appropriating that term. Similarly, 'lifestyle' is being abused these days. Even the word 'partner' which once had a very innocent meaning is abused.

(Lord Jakobovits, July 22, 1998)

A collocational analysis reveals some of the most common ways that *gay* and *homosexual* were used in the context of the speeches. Overall, the most frequent collocates of *homosexual* at R1 (one place to the right of the target word) in the House of Lords texts are *acts* (30), *activity* (22) and *consent* (28), while for *gay*, the most frequent right-hand collocates are *people* (20) and *men* (16). Therefore, in these debates, *homosexual* seems to be framed more often as a behaviour, whereas *gay* is an identity or trait. Other collocates of *homosexual* include *act* (8), *sex* (7), *behaviour* (7), *offences* (4), *practices* (4) and *intercourse* (4).

Returning to look at the keywords, of the keywords used by those who were against reform, a number of them are linked to sexual acts: *intercourse*, *buggery*, *gross* and *indecency* (the latter two occurring together in the phrase *gross indecency*). In addition the keywords *anal* and *vaginal* both collocated with *intercourse* and *sex* almost every time they are used, making them also refer to sexual activity. The keyword *act* is also used to refer to sex, although in 20 out of a possible 84 cases, this word refers to Government Acts. The phrase *act of buggery* occurs 11 times in the anti-reform speeches, *act of gross indecency* occurs ten times and *act of sodomy* occurs four times. Buggery and sodomy are both used to mean 'anal sex'.

The phrase *homosexual act* also occurs four times. One Lord explicitly states that homosexuality is an act (rather than, say, an orientation):

> Many believe the act of homosexuality to be unnatural and say that it should not be permitted at all.
>
> (Lord Davies of Coity, November 13, 2000)

Therefore, a discourse that the anti-reform Lords have accessed is one that links homosexuality to external *acts* or *behaviours*, rather than being an internal part of one's identity. We could refer to this as a 'homosexual *acts* define homosexuality' discourse. On the other hand, the pro-reform Lords, in linking the more recently coined term *gay* with keywords like *sexual orientation* or *sexuality*, do not focus on sexual acts, and instead reference a discourse of 'internalised gay identity'.

Pro-reform: a discourse of tolerance

One discourse accessed by the pro-reformers is based around the keywords *convention*, *rights* and *human*:

> In my view the Government are acting wisely in trying to put beyond doubt the outcome of this issue before the United Kingdom is exposed to the ridicule of a court decision requiring it to comply with the European Convention on Human Rights. All that has been taking place while this Parliament passed the incorporation of the European Convention on Human Rights into the Human Rights Act. If we do not pass this legislation, when the Human Rights Act is brought into operation

we will be required by British courts in all probability to comply with the legislation.

(Lord Warner, April 13, 1999)

This discourse presents an ostensibly neutral view of homosexuality, although reference to 'human rights' via Europe implicitly makes the point that the current laws are in violation of them (at least as far as Europe is concerned). However, Warner (and others) argue that reform may as well go ahead because it is going to be imposed upon the UK in any case – the word *required*, although not a keyword, collocates with both the keywords *convention* and *rights*.

However, looking at other pro-reform keywords, interestingly the words *criminal* and *law* tended to occur together. The fact that the current law criminalised gay men who were aged 16 and 17 is often used as one of the main arguments for reform:

We do not ask Members of the Committee to approve of homosexuality or homosexual acts, or even to understand why they happen, but to remove the weight and penalty of the criminal law from those young men aged 16 and 17 who consent to have sex with other men. Surely, except for those on the very extreme of this debate, no one believes that we should criminalise 16 and 17 year-olds for having consensual sex.

(Lord Alli, November 13, 2000)

The pro-reform speeches also contain the keywords *reform*, *rights* and *tolerance*. They point out that a number of expert groups or *associations* (also key) have supported the Bill (notably the British Medical Association and the Family Welfare Association). The words *sexuality*, *sexual* and *orientation* are key (the latter two usually collocating together as in the phrase *sexual orientation*), again suggesting that the pro-reformers are more concerned than the anti-reformers with constructing people in terms of their identity instead of their behaviour. The keyword *harm* occurs in the pro-reform speech because it is used to argue against one of the anti-reformers' points about homosexual law reform, that homosexual acts are likely to cause harm to the people who engage in them.

There might, however, be stronger arguments about self-harm and harm to others, but I doubt it. I do not wish to deny that self-harm and harm to others can constitute strong arguments for treating one group differently from another. What I am saying is that I do not think the empirical case in relation to such harm has been made.

(Lord Plant of Highfield, April 13, 1999)

The pro-reformers' use of the keyword *nothing* occurs 45 per cent of the time as part of the phrase 'nothing to do with'. This is used to negate anti-arguments that connect lowering the age of consent to other issues such as political correctness, morals, age, or liking/disliking people who are gay.

> The fact that we do not much like what someone else is doing is not a ground for preventing him or her from doing it in a free society unless it harms others. Liking and disliking has nothing to do with it.
>
> (Lord Plant of Highfield, April 13, 1999)

The keywords *baroness*, *she* and *her* were most often used to refer to Baroness Young, who tabled amendments to the Bill that the House of Commons were trying to pass, and again were used in speeches that set out to directly counter her arguments. Therefore, in addition to creating a unified discourse of homosexuality which emphasises equality in society, tolerance and human rights, a number of the pro-reform speeches are concerned with challenging a set of connected discourses put forward by the anti-reformers. It is these discourses, and their associated keywords, that I wish to examine in more detail, as they reveal a more varied and complex set of attitudes towards homosexuality than those of the pro-reformers.

A criminal behaviour

If the pro-reform speakers drew on discourses of human rights and equality to support their argument, what opposing discourses were accessed by the anti-reform speakers?

Referencing homosexuality as an act rather than an identity is essential for those who are anti-reform in that it disassociates criminality from a particular identity group but instead focuses it around the behaviour. It is easier to base definitions of criminality around behaviours or acts rather than social groups.

During the debates there are references to *anal intercourse* (78), *buggery* (68), *gross indecency* (19), *anal sex* (19) and *sodomy* (8). The phrase *gross indecency* was used in the 1885 Criminal Law Amendment Act which states:

> Any male person who, in public or in private, commits, or is party to the commission of, or procures, or attempts to procure the commission by any male person of, any act of gross indecency shall be guilty of misdemeanour, and being convicted shall be liable at the discretion of the Court to be imprisoned for any term not exceeding two years, with or without hard labour.[8]

The labelling of sexual activity between two men as *gross indecency* therefore accesses a criminalising discourse from over 100 years ago and implies that there is still something criminal about a decriminalised act. Of the 19 references to gross indecency, 18 of them were made by the anti-reformers. What is notable is that the phrase *gross indecency* is not used by some of the anti-repeal Lords to refer to criminal sex acts (such as rape or a man exposing himself in a public place) but to refer to gay male sex itself.

> I do not accept that acts of anal intercourse or gross indecency of a homosexual kind are as natural as normal heterosexual relations.
>
> (Lord Cope of Berkeley, April 13, 1999)

Therefore, the language used to talk about gay male sex suggests that those who are against reform have already judged it to be wrong. *Gross indecency* is both a euphemism and a dysphemism. It euphemistically acts as a vague phrase which does not directly reference sex or homosexuality, yet it dysphemistically refers to gay sex as being *indecent* (a word which collocates in the 100-million word British National Corpus with *buggery, assault, obscene, rape, offence, guilty* and *accused*).

In the House of Lords debates, all 12 uses of the keyword *commit* refer to sex, and in ten of these specifically to gay sex. For example: *commit buggery* and *commit anal intercourse* both occur three times, *commit sexual activity* occurs twice, while *commit sexual acts, commit acts of gross indecency, commit an act of buggery* and *commit an act of gross indecency* all occur once. The lemma COMMIT collocates strongly in the British National Corpus with the words *atrocities, suicide, arrestable, crimes* and *offence*. Therefore, although the word *commit* does not necessarily mean *crime*, when we look at how it is widely used in society, we find that it shows a *semantic preference* for criminality (see also Stubbs 2001b: 64–6). So to commit buggery is implicitly associated with being a criminal, even though the 1885 Act was partially overturned in 1967 with the Sexual Offences Act which decriminalised homosexual sex acts (for men aged over 21). However, some Lords still choose to refer to anal sex in terms of a criminalised discourse:

> As regards human rights, I do not believe that there is any human right to commit buggery.
>
> (Baroness Young, April 13, 1999)

Lord Selsdon draws on a discourse from the 1940s, when buggery was still a crime:

> I was brought up on a farm at the end of the war ... I had the doubtful privilege of learning about life in the raw, all the activities of the animals, and that two bulls might try to do something to each other. On a shelf in the library one of the books was called *The Police Constable's Guide to his Daily Work* ... The first item was 'The abominable crime of buggery'. I did not know what buggery was. I consulted the farmworkers and they explained to me that this was an unnatural act, either between two men or between a man and an animal. It was effectively bestial.
>
> (Lord Selsdon, April 13, 1999)

This speech makes an explicit link between sex between men (homosexuality) and sex between men and animals (bestiality). It also draws a conclusion from the latter type of sex and applies it to the former 'bestial'. The word *bestial* has two meanings, one which refers to animals and a more evaluative one which means something less than human. Lord Selsdon goes on to say that buggery is an 'abominable act' and 'in general, it is brought about by lust, not by love'. In addition, buggery is something that people can be 'subjected to' (Lord Davies of Coity, April 13, 1999) and it is a 'dangerous practice' (Baroness Blatch, November 13, 2000).

Ruined for life

A related discourse to that of homosexuality as an act, rather than an identity, is linked to the anti-reformer's belief that the act most commonly associated with homosexuality, anal sex, will lead to danger and ruin. For example, the guidelines on giving blood are quoted several times as a reason why anal sex is dangerous (the word *blood* being a keyword in the anti-reform texts):

> the UK blood transfusion service leaflet states categorically: 'If you are a man who's had sex with another man, even "safe sex" using a condom, you should never give blood'. Those . . . examples certainly convince me that we should take no steps that could increase the health risk to young people.
>
> (Lord Davies of Coity, November 13, 2000)

Another aspect of the dangers of anal sex is HIV/AIDS (referred to 40 times by the anti-reformers and 23 times by the pro-reformers). The word *condom* is a keyword in the anti-reform speeches, and is almost always used to refer to the possibility that condoms can break during sex (or that people won't wear them):

> Safe? There is not such a product as a safe condom for those who indulge in anal sex.
>
> (Baroness Seccombe, November 13, 2000)

> 'we are designed with a nearly impenetrable barrier between the bloodstream and the extraordinarily toxic and infectious contents of the bowel. Anal intercourse creates a breach in this barrier for the receptive partner, whether or not the insertive partner is wearing a condom.' The suggestion is that the ultra tough condom will suit the bill. Everyone knows that the ultra tough condom will not be worn. No condom is often the case because, as has been said, some people delight in taking the risk.
>
> (Lord Ackner, November 13, 2000)

Condom failure has become the leading cause of unwanted pregnancy, according to the *British Medical Journal*, 1996, vol. 312 at page 1059. There are, of course, inherent flaws in latex condoms and those flaws are at least 50 times larger than the AIDS virus. Incidentally, the AIDS virus is 450 times smaller than human sperm, so it is no surprise that the effectiveness of condoms for AIDS prevention is much worse than for contraception.

(Lord McColl of Dulwich, November 13, 2000)

It is unexpected to see the word *girls* appear as a keyword in the anti-reform speeches, particularly as the age of consent Bill is primarily concerned with bringing the age of consent for gay *males* in line with everybody else. *Boys*, which is not key, occurs 119 times in the debate (51 times by pro-reform speakers and 68 times by anti-reform speakers). *Girls*, on the other hand, occurs slightly less frequently across the debate, but significantly more frequently in the speech of the anti-reformers (see Table 2.2). There appear to be two main reasons why girls are mentioned frequently by the anti-reformers, both of which are linked to different types of danger.

First, there is the assertion that the Bill involves the lowering of consent for anal sex for females aged 16 as well as males. Note that the anti-reformer's use of the word *girls* is particularly emotive, accessing ideas about children having sex, whereas in fact the debate concerns people aged 16 and 17 who are considered old enough under British law to get married, have heterosexual sex and smoke tobacco.

By referencing females, those who position themselves against a change to the age of consent argue that they are against anal intercourse, rather than being against gay people per se.

It is not a question of homophobia; it is a question of people having a differing view. I believe that we should continue to protect young people between the ages of 16 and 18 from being seduced into what is undoubtedly an unnatural practice and one which may have an enormous and possibly detrimental effect on them for the rest of their lives. It is surely not unreasonable to be concerned about that... It is not homophobic to want to protect young people between the ages of 16 and 18.

(Lord Stoddart of Swindon, July 22, 1998)

Both teenage boys and girls will now be exposed to all the risks of anal intercourse; they will be far more likely to run the risk of AIDS.

(Baroness Young, April 13, 1999)

This Bill would reduce from 18 to 16 the age at which men can legally commit acts of gross indecency with boys and acts of buggery, an unnatural, unsanitary and dangerous act, on both boys and girls.

(Lord Ashbourne, April 13, 1999)

A number of other words are also connected to this discourse of danger to girls and boys. For example, the keyword *lining* is an important concept within this discourse, being used in an argument against lowering the age of consent, because of the apparent damage that anal sex can cause.

> As the noble Lord, Lord Quirk, pointed out in a previous debate, the rectum is lined with a delicate gut epithelium, or lining, which is only one cell thick, measuring a very small fraction of a millimetre. That is in marked contrast to the lining of the vagina, which is a tough skin-like structure many cells thick. As the rectal lining is so delicate, it is frequently damaged by intercourse and therefore infected with a variety of hostile germs, the most severe being AIDS, hepatitis and a virus leading to anal cancer, together with the usual venereal diseases of syphilis, gonorrhoea and other infections... In addition to the damage to the lining of the rectum, the tight and powerful muscles that sur-round the anal canal can also be damaged and those subjected to persis-tent damage can even become incontinent.
>
> (Lord McColl of Dulwich, November 13, 2000)

Anal intercourse is described as something that has 'appalling' and 'frighten-ing' 'health risks' and 'medical dangers' associated with it. It is also some-thing that became legal for men and women to 'indulge in' from the age of 18 since 1994. An analysis of *indulge, risk* and *danger* shows the negative concepts associated with anal sex by the anti-reformers. Forms of the lemma INDULGE occur 15 times in the debates, and in all cases but one, refers to anal sex (the exception refers to blackmail). In the British National Corpus, INDULGE strongly collocates with *whims, idle* and *luxury*, suggesting that it carries with it a semantic preference for unnecessary pleasure.

The lemma RISK, although not key, occurs 94 times in the debates, with almost all of the 61 cases of use by anti-reformers referring to anal sex. Sim-ilarly, forms of the lemma DANGER occur 75 times in the debates, always referring to gay sex in the 53 cases where it is used by the anti-reformers. The pro-reformers never use it in this way, except on a couple of occasions to deny or play down the extent of the danger. The 'danger' of anal sex is also compared to the dangers of other activities such as smoking tobacco:

> A dispute arose between my noble friend Lord McColl, who made an extremely important speech on the medical dangers of anal intercourse – the statistics he gave on smoking and anal sex and the shortening of young people's lives as a consequence of those activities should be remembered by us all.
>
> (Baroness Young, November 13, 2000)

So far, we have seen that the discourse of the dangers of anal sex is used to apply equally to boys and girls – which enables the anti-reform stance appear to be not homophobic. Hence, the use of *girls* is important in this discourse. However, a second discourse which also involves the use of the keyword *girls* states that boys need to be protected because they are less mature than girls:

> There is no doubt that girls mature much earlier than boys. Boys very often are only just coming to terms with their sexuality at 16. Consequently, I accept that there is more of a case for the age of consent for girls to be lower than for boys.
>
> (Baroness Seccombe, April 13, 1999)

> Boys in particular are often less mature than girls at 16, and not infrequently ambivalent about their sexuality. Good parents do not want their sons to be encouraged to take up homosexual relationships at such an early age.
>
> (Baroness Young, April 13, 1999)

In addition, one Lord, arguing from a 'feminist' standpoint, claims that boys are 'ruined for life' by being seduced, but girls are not:

> . . . if someone seduced my daughter it would be damaging and horrifying but not fatal. She would recover, marry and have lots of children (as some such people do). On the other hand, if some elderly, or not so elderly, schoolmaster seduced one of my sons and taught him to be a homosexual, he would ruin him for life. That is the fundamental distinction. I must repeat my conviction: as regards rent boys (about which I know, not from first-hand but second-hand experience) one can ruin a person for life by treating him as a homosexual object when he is in his teens. I draw a distinction. There is no doubt about that distinction. I am sorry if the feminists – I always call myself a feminist – say there is no distinction. There must be a distinction because of the point I made. A girl is not ruined for life by being seduced. A young fellow is. That is the distinction.
>
> (Lord Longford, July 22, 1998)

Therefore, not only is the anal lining in danger of being 'ruined' by anal intercourse (leading to incontinence), but also the lives (of boys) can be ruined as well. Incidentally, Lord Longford does not mention the gender of the person who hypothetically seduces his daughter. So either he is suggesting that a woman who is seduced by another woman will 'recover' and go on to live a heterosexual life (ergo lesbian seduction does not have the same long-term consequences as gay male seduction), or he assumes that the only people who carry out seductions are male.[9]

The two discourses of ruin based around girls do not sit comfortably with each other. On the one hand, anti-reform is justified as not homophobic because it will result in danger to girls as well as boys. But on the other, girls aren't seen as being as much at risk because they are 'more mature' and not 'ruined for life' if 'seduced'.

The thin end of the wedge

Finally, the keyword *demand* is used in a 'thin end of the wedge' discourse by those against reform, to imply that the more 'rights' gay people acquire, the more they will want. Such a discourse therefore implicitly acknowledges that other areas exist where there is inequality in the law between heterosexual and homosexual people.

The *Oxford English Dictionary* makes a number of distinctions in its coverage of the word *demand*. It can mean to ask for a thing peremptorily, imperiously or urgently. But it can also mean to ask for something with legal right or authority, to claim something one is legally or rightfully entitled to. Yet in the British National Corpus, strong collocates of forms of the lemma DEMAND include *menaces, imperiously, ransom, indignantly, unlawfully, kidnappers, irritably* and *angrily*. So while the semantic preference of 'imperiousness' seems to occur in actual language use as the dictionary definition suggests, the claim that DEMAND typically occurs when someone has a legal right to make a demand is actually refuted by corpus data. Instead we find that it occurs with words like *unlawfully, kidnappers* and *ransom* – words that imply a complete *lack* of a legal right for something.

> To continue, a lowering of the age of consent will lead to the demand to lower it still further. In 1994 we debated, and Parliament agreed, the lowering of the age from 21 to 18. Five years later the demand is to lower the age to 16. This is the thin end of the wedge.
>
> (Baroness Young, April 13, 1999)

> I believe that this is the thin end of the wedge. I know that many homosexual organisations say that they are not in favour of lowering the age of consent to 14, but some are. It will lead to a demand for gay and lesbian marriages and for the right for such couples to adopt children. I understand that the Government are already considering repealing Clause 28...
>
> (Baroness Young, November 13, 2000)

This argument is linked to what is called the 'penumbrae effect':

> It is intended to reduce to 16 the age of consensual homosexual sex for boys. Many of us have been in this argument since the age of consent was 21. After the operation of the penumbrae effect, as it is called, the effective age is 14, because there will be no prosecutions of people aged 16 or 14 for any kind of sexual act.
>
> (Lord Stally, April 13, 1999)

Therefore, if anal sex is legalised, while that in itself will be dangerous in terms of ruining boys for life, it will also lead to further 'demands' for equality. The consequences of reform are therefore framed as affecting more than just 16 and 17 year olds who want to have anal sex. Therefore, the 'thin end of the wedge discourse' comes into conflict with the discourse that locates the debate as just being about the act of anal sex, in that gay people are seen as wanting 'rights' such as being able to marry or adopt children.

Collocational networks

In order to present a clearer picture of how the keywords interact with each other, a collocational network was created, showing the major links between different words. This network is shown in Figure 2.1 (keywords used by the anti-reform Lords) and Figures 2.2 and 2.3 (those used by the pro-reform Lords). Each collocational network was created by calculating mutual information scores (calculated with log base 2) for each of the keywords, using WordSmith, applying a similar technique to that of McEnery (2005). Collocational links are shown between different keywords (shown in square boxes) with lines. The direction of collocation is indicated by arrow heads. For example, *vaginal* has an MI score of 5.68 with *intercourse*. However, *intercourse* has an MI score of 5.30 with *vaginal*. Therefore, *vaginal* is more likely to be found near *intercourse* than *intercourse* is to be found near *vaginal*. Where MI scores were the same in both directions, no arrow head is shown. Any collocational pairs of less than 3 were not included in the network, as Scott (1999) indicates that an MI score below this is considered to be tenuous.

In addition to showing keywords, the networks in Figures 2.1, 2.2 and 2.3 also show non-keywords in cases where more than one keyword collocates with the same non-keyword. These non-keywords are shown in ovals. In Figure 2.1, the keywords *gross* and *indecency* were combined together, as their collocational patterns were identical, and the two words almost always occurred together as the phrase *gross indecency*. In addition, some lemmas of word forms are shown – so AGE refers to *age* and *aged*, DANGER refers to *danger* and *dangerous*, COMMIT refers to *commit*, *committed* and *commission* and MAN refers to *man* and *men*. Keywords which did not collocate with any other keywords are not shown in the diagram.

Figure 2.1 shows how the network of anti-reform discourses of homosexuality link together. For example, the discourse of danger and ruin is signified by the links between the words in the top left-hand part of the diagram: *blood*, *hiv*, *infection*, *intercourse*, *lining*, *vaginal*, *anal* and DANGER. The discourse of homosexuality as a criminal behaviour is shown by the group of words at the bottom of the diagram: COMMIT, *legally*, *gross indecency*, *buggery*, ACT and *private*. The 'thin end of the wedge' discourse is shown in the top right-hand part of the diagram with the words: AGE, *consent*, LOWER and *demand*.

Interestingly, although the debate is supposed to be about the age of consent for anal intercourse, the words *age* and *consent* appear to be less

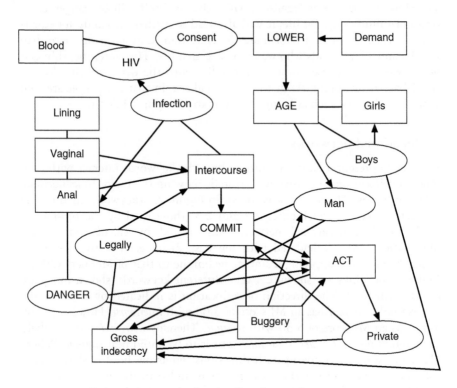

Figure 2.1 Collocational network of anti-reform keywords.

central concepts in the collocational network, than the words *anal* and *intercourse*. However, the words with the most connections are those towards the bottom of the network: *gross indecency*, COMMIT, ACT and *buggery*.

In Figures 2.2 and 2.3, two collocational networks for the pro-reform Lords are shown. What is interesting here is that two separate sets of discourses are accessed, each of which uses a distinct lexis. Figure 2.2 uses a smaller set of lexis based around references to the European Convention of Human Rights.

While this discourse takes a non-judgemental stance on homosexuality, the other collocational network presents a set of related discourses which are more concerned with moral issues (Figure 2.3). There is the linking of equality and tolerance (middle of the diagram), and references to criminal law. There is the conceptualisation of homosexuality as sexual orientation, fixed at an early age – an identity rather than a behaviour – and the argument that change to the law will not cause harm (bottom of the diagram). Finally, there are references to the anti-reformers (top right of the diagram) and their intentions.

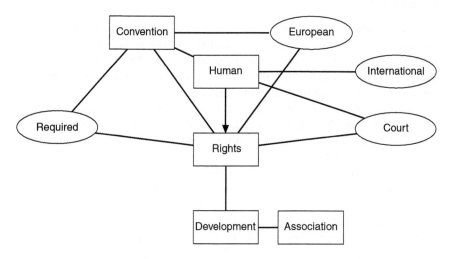

Figure 2.2 Collocational network of pro-reform keywords: Europe lexis.

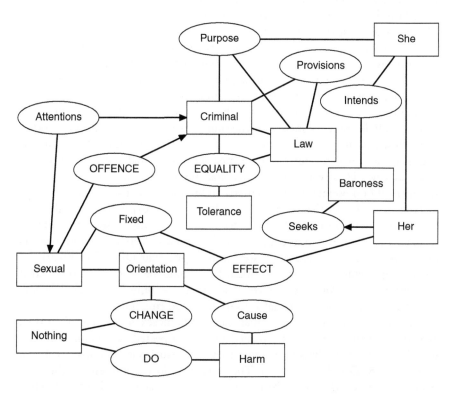

Figure 2.3 Collocational network of pro-reform keywords: moral lexis.

Conclusion

Perhaps we should not be surprised that there are so many references to anal sex during the debate. The proposed Bill is not to legalise gay male sex per se, but to change the age of consent for anal sex from 18 to 16. However, we need to closely examine the link between the ways that acts and identities are represented in relationship to homosexuality.

The term *homosexual identity*, as Cass (1983: 108) notes, is often used in a haphazard fashion, having (at least) five possible meanings.[10] Gleason (1983: 918) points out that the more general term *identity* is relatively new, emerging in social science literature in the 1950s and made popular by the psychoanalyst Erik Erikson.[11] For Gleason, most definitions of *identity* tend to fall into one of two opposing conceptions. In one sense, identity can be called 'intrapsychic' in that it comes from within, is fixed and stable and is what people speak of when they talk about 'who we really are'. For example, John is male because he possesses a penis. On the other hand, identity can be 'acquired' in that it is a conscious or internalised adoption of socially imposed, or socially constructed roles. Therefore, it could be argued that having a male identity involves much more than possessing a penis – it involves how people act, walk, talk, what they wear, etc. In addition someone can be said to identify as 'a medical doctor' because they have been to medical school and now work as a GP. A doctor is still a doctor, however, even when she is not at work – the identity may not be 'active', but it is still there, although latent. When such a person is asked about their occupation, they will answer 'I'm a doctor' even when they are not at work. So an activity or behaviour does not have to be carried out constantly for it to constitute an identity.

One trait unites all gay men together – perhaps it is the only trait that they can all be said to share – attraction (physical and romantic) to other men. How this attraction manifests itself can vary across individuals. Not all gay men have anal sex (and not all men who have anal sex identify themselves as gay). However, despite this, anal sex has become one of the main signifiers of homosexuality, particularly in homophobic discourses.

Homosexual identities have never been made explicitly illegal, only homosexual acts, and specifically a set of acts relating to sex or arranging sexual contacts ('gross indecency', 'buggery' and also 'soliciting' and 'procuring') were illegal. For example, we might argue that talking in Polari – a form of 'gay language' (Baker 2002a, b) – could be seen as a homosexual (speech) act. Yet Polari was never made illegal – only homosexual behaviours based around actual sexual activity have had this status.

However, in practice the criminal status of homosexual acts has often been extended towards anyone who owned or was suspected of owning a homosexual identity, regardless of whether they had sexual relationships (see Jivani 1997: 137–8, David 1997: 165). Therefore, it is in the interests of the anti-reformers to stress that the debate is only about the 'dangers' of anal sex, while downplaying the fact that in the past the criminalisation of sexual acts have had far-reaching consequences on the main group of people who have been associated with such acts, including people who never have anal sex. By disassociating the link between behaviour and identity, the Lords do not acknowledge that, for a large proportion of society, the two are inextricably linked.

Because of the use of nineteenth-century phrases such as *gross indecency*, and the fact that the Lords were debating the change of a law which was passed in 1967, many of the discourses of homosexuality that were used by the anti-reformers could be classed as pre-liberation discourses, where gay men were criminalised and viewed as dangerous deviants. The average age of a Lord at the time of the last debate was 67 years, while this figure was 52 for Members of Parliament (Cracknell 2000: 10). Indeed, only a few years after the debates, a number of the peers who had taken part in them had died (including Lord Longford who talked about 'homosexual objects' and Baroness Young who many people viewed as the driving force behind the anti-reform movement). While old age does not equal old ways of thinking, the age of the House of Lords was criticised by gay rights groups who characterised them as being out of touch with society.

The arguments used by the anti-reform debaters could be said to form a chain which justifies opposition to reform as not homophobic:

1   Homosexuality is an act, rather than an identity.
2   The prototypical act of homosexuality is anal sex.
3   Anal sex is a dangerous and criminal indulgence.

These three arguments are strongly linked. For example, the idea that gay male sex is a criminal behaviour hinges on the assumption that one is dealing with a practice or act rather than a social identity.

Also, by constructing the subject in terms of acts, the anti-reform debaters are able to broaden the scope of the debate to include heterosexual women (e.g. the presence of *girls* as a keyword). Ergo,

4   Both boys and girls can be ruined by anal sex.
5   Opposition to anal sex is therefore not homophobic.

However, certain anti-reform arguments did not fit into the chain as well – e.g.

6   Boys are more at risk than girls (which did not match the arguments in 4 and 5) and
7   Lowering the age of consent is the thin end of the wedge leading to demands for rights for gay people (which did not match the arguments in 1 and 5).

On the other hand, the discourses used by the pro-reformers were more straightforward and did not require an inter-related yet contradictory chain of argumentation. They either argued for tolerance and equality, or warned that the government would be forced to make the change in order to fall in line with European human rights conventions.

The debates on the age of consent also attracted a great deal of coverage by the media and political groups. For example, the House of Lords was decried by gay rights groups such as Outrage and Stonewall, as well as the gay press. The BBC News service carried a debate on its website in July 1998, asking 'Are the Lords in touch with the people?'[12] Respondents were divided over the issue. Some posted comments such as 'The House of Lords is digging its own grave', calling the House of Lords 'anachronistic non-sense', 'out of touch with modern day issues' and claiming it espoused views that reflect 'ignorance, bigotry and superstition'. Other respondents pointed out that while the Lords showed a 'lack of contemporary thinking, they still have a basic understanding of morality', 'that it is not the role of the House to slavishly represent the views of the people' and 'throughout history, socie-ties have deferred to the reason, wisdom, and experience of their elders in matters concerning society'. Perhaps we should note again that the House of Lords describe themselves as 'a source of independent expertise', and while they no longer have the power to prevent Government Acts from being passed, their opinions, which are widely reported, represent hegemonic, if not majority, discourses. Although many hereditary Lords have been removed since 1999, the House has continued to delay legislation designed to make the status of homosexual people equal to that of heterosexuals (for example, the repeal of Clause 28).

Postscript

A final incident reveals both the anti-reformers' dedication to keeping the status quo, and also the power of discourses to influence people's perceptions of actual language use. In January 2001, after the age of consent was reduced to 16 for both homosexual and heterosexual sex in the UK, it was reported that Baroness Young had opened a website called www.ageofconsent.org.uk which was designed to determine public opinion with respect to the age of consent issue.[13] The website asked Internet users 'Do you want to keep the age of consent for anal intercourse for both girls and boys at 18?' The 'yes' option read 'Please vote here if you are in favour of keeping the age of consent for anal intercourse at 18' while the 'no' option read 'Please vote here if you are against keeping the age of consent for anal intercourse at 18'.

As shown earlier, one of the discourses associated with the pro-reform debate was that of equality, which was indexed through keywords such as *rights*, *reform* and *tolerance*. Therefore, because the wording of the question included the phrase 'both girls and boys' a number of people mistakenly voted 'yes', thinking that this would result in equality for gay people. As a result, there were complaints that the wording of the poll had been mislead-ing (Smithard 2001: 15). The website reported that of 51,675 votes cast by October 2001, 45 per cent had voted 'yes' and 55 per cent had voted 'no'.

It is perhaps too simplistic, though, to accuse Baroness Young of directly borrowing the discourse of equality which was associated with the pro-reformers in a deliberate attempt to mislead. As seen in the analysis of the keyword *girls*, the anti-reformers also used a discourse of equality, by focusing on the fact that both boys *and* girls would be in danger from anal sex (and both should therefore be protected from it). For example, the phrase *boys and girls* occurs five times in the pro-reform speeches and 21 times in the anti-reform speeches, whereas these figures are one and six times respectively for the phrase *girls and boys*. Therefore, the Baroness' use of language in the poll was in keeping with the anti-reformer's use of language throughout the debate.

However, it is unlikely that the majority of people who voted in the poll would have followed the three House of Lords debates closely. Baroness Young's discourse of 'equality at age 18 for boys and girls to have anal sex' was one discourse among many that the anti-reformers utilised – whereas for the pro-reformers, their discourse of equality for all tended to be the primary one, and was much more heavily linked to them. So by referencing a discourse of equality, which was primarily associated with the pro-reform debaters, the Baroness, perhaps inadvertently, may have gained additional support for her cause. This concluding note to the Age of Consent debate shows the power of discourses – by phrasing an argument using aspects of a discourse that has been previously used by people who put forward a different or oppositional point of view, one can increase the likelihood that people will misinterpret it as one that they support.

3   Flamboyant, predatory, self-confessed homosexual

Discourse prosodies in the British tabloid press

Introduction

In 1963, four years prior to the decriminalisation of homosexuality in the UK, the Soviet spy John Vassall was discovered to be gay. The British tabloid newspaper the *Sunday Mirror* published an article entitled 'How to Spot a Possible Homo', which listed a number of folk stereotypes about gay men:

> It is high time we had a short course on how to pick a pervert... Basically homos fall into two groups – the obvious and the concealed... THEY are everywhere, and they can be anybody... I wouldn't tell them *my* secrets. 1 The Middle-aged man, unmarried... 2 The man who has a consuming interest in youths... 3 The Crawler... 4 The Fussy Dresser... 5 The Over-clean man.
>
> (*Sunday Mirror*, April 1963)

It could be argued that, since decriminalisation, and particularly over the last ten years, social attitudes towards homosexuality have changed, and it is unlikely that mainstream newspapers today would consider printing this kind of story. For example, the *Mirror* now publicises events at the London nightclub G.A.Y., and it successfully campaigned for a gay air steward called Brian Dowling to win the popular reality television gameshow *Big Brother* in 2002.

However, qualitative work by linguists like Morrish (2002) and Chirrey (2003) suggests that newspapers have continued to produce discourses of homosexuality which are often negative. Morrish reports how broadsheet newspapers including the *Guardian* and *The Times* covered the travails of Peter Mandelson, a gay (former) government minister for Labour. She notes that he was portrayed as effeminate through the use of a nickname, *Mandy*; there were coded references to homosexual acts and sensibilities, e.g. 'What Peter Mandelson did was the political equivalent of bare-backing'; and he was described as camp, hedonistic and narcissistic. Morrish concludes: 'The most remarkable thing about the press representation of Peter Mandelson is the way in which the above strategies are effected by a deployment of the linguistic resources of camp' (Morrish 2002: 4). Such strategies are subtler than the *Sunday Mirror*'s references to gay men as 'perverts' or 'homos' in the 1960s. They rely on a well-placed word or phrase, an insinuation, or a pairing of the concept of homosexuality with something else. In addition, by writing about a particular gay man, rather than gay men en masse, it becomes more difficult for complaints of discrimination to be levelled at a newspaper. For example, it could be argued that the media's negative treatment of Peter Mandelson is restricted to Peter Mandelson, not about gay men in general. This contrasts sharply with the 1963 'How to Spot a Possible Homo' article, which targets anyone with a gay identity. In addition, what is *not* articulated may be as important as what is. For example, Henley *et al.* (2002), in their study of reports of violent attacks, found that the *Washington Post* used fewer, less specific nominals when referring to anti-gay violence than other types of violence. This contrasted with the *San Francisco Chronicle* which, based in a more gay-friendly community, did not differentiate significantly by sexual orientation. In addition, Gough and Talbot's (1996) examination of 'problem pages' in the *Mirror* found that, despite the fact that the agony aunt, Marje Proops, was a proponent for gay rights, her advice to one writer who was worried about homoerotic experiences he had had while young reinforced conventional notions about sexuality:

> Many heterosexual men have a passing curiosity about homosexuality, and that isn't a bad thing. It compels you to make choices ... You made [your choice] many years ago when you began to pursue women.
>
> *(Sunday Mirror*, January 17, 1993)

Tabloid discourses of homosexuality are therefore more subtle and complex than they were in the 1960s and it is unlikely that a newspaper's editorial would openly declare gay men to be 'perverts'. However, the overall effect of the more careful use of language pertaining to homosexuality in contemporary news reporting may mean that negative discourses are not always noticed or subsequently challenged. A single edition of a newspaper may not include any reference to homosexuality, or only positive ones – as in the *Mirror*'s reviews (and publicisation) of the G.A.Y. nightclub. Even if a single, questionable word or phrase is embedded within a mostly positive article, this may be excused or overlooked by the reader. As Bell (1991: 232) points out, people's recall of news stories is very low: rarely more than 30 per cent, and sometimes as low as 5 per cent.

However, newspaper reporting has a cumulative effect. Day after day, many people purchase and read the same newspaper, absorbing its news and also the way that it reports world events. Newspapers are therefore ideal sites where the incremental effect of discourse can take place. A negative or ambiguous word, phrase or association may not amount to much on its own, but if similar sentiments appear on a regular basis, then the discourse will become more powerful, penetrating into society's subconscious as the given way of thinking. As Fairclough (1989: 54) observes:

> The hidden power of media discourse and the capacity of ... power-holders to exercise this power depend on systematic tendencies in news reporting and other media activities. A single text on its own is quite insignificant: the effects of media power are cumulative, working through the repetition of particular ways of handling causality and agency, particular ways of positioning the reader, and so forth.

But audiences are not passive: as McIlvenny (1996) suggests, meaning is created from interaction between a text and its readers. Texts can only take on meaning when consumers interact with them. For example, Hermes (1995) shows how readers of traditional women's magazines viewed them as a marker of low-status, e.g. 'You forget as soon as you've read it' but used them as an activity that filled time and did not require much attention. The readership of a newspaper also has the opportunity to respond, via its letters page, although only a small proportion of letters are published, and the newspaper has the capacity to veto, edit or prioritise those which it decides to print. Readers may also refuse to buy a newspaper if they disagree strongly enough with the discourses it regularly employs. For example, the *Mirror*'s circulation fell to below two million for the first time in 70 years during its coverage of the 2003 war on Iraq, which was linked to its anti-war stance (Gibson 2003).

Therefore, stereotypically, mainstream popular newspapers need to at least reproduce some hegemonic or 'popular' discourses in order to remain in business – large numbers of people will not buy what they do not agree with. However, at the same time, newspapers are able to influence their readers by producing their own discourses or helping to reshape existing ones. Such discourses are often shaped by citing the opinions of those in powerful and privileged positions. Becker (1972: xx) calls this the 'hierarchy of credibility' whereby powerful people will come to have their opinions accepted because they are understood to have access to more accurate information on particular topics than everyone else. Hall *et al.* (1978: 58) say: 'The result of this structured preference given in the media to the opinions of the powerful is that these "spokesmen" become what we call the primary definers of topics.'

Discourses within newspapers are usually the result of collaboration between multiple contributors. For example, while each newspaper generally has an over-arching political stance, within a single edition of a newspaper, different articles may express a variety of views on the same subject (particularly among newspapers which aim to represent a 'balanced' coverage of an event). So, some writers might be chosen specifically because they hold unpopular or controversial views. In addition, a single story is unlikely to have been 'written' by just one person. Articles may be cropped or changed by numerous copy-writers, sub-editors and editors before they are published (Bell 1991: 33–55).

Also, newspapers can alter their stance on different subjects over time, so we would particularly expect discourses within newspapers to be conflicting and shifting over any given period. While there may be gay people who work for tabloid newspapers, we don't usually know the sexuality of journalists, nor are tabloids aimed specifically at gay people. Therefore, like the House of Lords, tabloid newspapers are sites of mainstream discourses of homosexuality. However, unlike the House of Lords, such discourses are governed to a large extent by market forces and acknowledgement of the opinions, preoccupations and fears of its readership.

A tale of two tabloids

Because newspapers offer mainstream and popular discourses of homosexuality that can influence large numbers of people, and/or reflect current attitudes, it is the intention of this chapter to look at how contemporary discourses of homosexuality are constructed in two daily British tabloid newspapers, the *Daily Mail* (also including the *Mail on Sunday*) and the *Mirror* (also including the *Sunday Mirror*). The distinction between tabloid and broadsheet news is not always easy to make and stems back to the development of new printing techniques in the early 1970s. These techniques allowed publishers to produce and sell more newspapers by making them easier to handle and read. The tabloids, being half the size of broadsheets, have large, short headlines (particularly on the front pages) and focus more on easy-to-read celebrity gossip. The broadsheets are larger and more difficult to handle, with colour often restricted to photographs and the front page title lay-out. They focus more on political news at both the national and international level and use a more sophisticated style of writing.[1] However, as Keith Waterhouse (1993) points out, the simplistic style of tabloid reporting disguises how difficult this genre is to create: 'Although the tabloids are reckoned to need a reading age of around ten, understanding them needs a high degree of sophistication.'

During the period 2001–2, the *Daily Mail* and the *Mirror* were each read by approximately 5.5 million people every day, with figures almost reaching 6 million for the Sunday editions.[2] (The only daily newspaper which was more popular in the UK was the *Sun*, which was read by about 9.5 million people in the same period.[3]) It was therefore decided that an examination of the discourses surrounding homosexuality within the *Daily Mail* and the *Mirror* would be suitable for analysis, as they had large, roughly equal readerships. In addition, these two newspapers differed in terms of their political affiliations. From 2001–2 the *Mirror* was more supportive of the Labour Government than the *Daily Mail*. The *Mirror* could also be classed more prototypically as a tabloid newspaper or a 'red top' (so-called because its name appeared in red print at the top of the front page). However, shortly after September 11, 2001 there was an effort to take a more politically involved stance on news reporting, and the words 'the *Mirror*' were printed in black, rather than red.

The *Daily Mail*, on the other hand, was generally unsupportive of the Labour Government during the period under study and tended to have a more conservative worldview. Julie Burchill, a columnist for the *Guardian* (a liberal broadsheet newspaper), wrote that the *Daily Mail* is a

> dark, nihilistic number ... I think of it as The Daily Hell... What is the Daily Hell scared of? How long have you got? On one day last week, you could have chosen from the abortion pill, gay rights, police, dogs, white people having black babies, taxes, single mothers, career women, exams, teachers, doctors, taxi drivers, unions, drugs, compensation, Big Brother, HRT, sugar, vitamin pills, foreign beer and girls who go on holiday to Greece.
>
> (Burchill 2002)

A final, more pragmatic criterion made the *Daily Mail* and the *Mirror* attractive sources of data. The text from these two newspapers had been stored on a searchable Internet archive called *NewsBank Infoweb*. This made searching for and collecting articles about homosexuality much easier than anticipated. However, the process of downloading and collecting a corpus of over 3000 articles individually still took several days. In the case of the *Daily Mail*, the archive stretched back to 1998, while with the *Mirror*, electronic archiving had commenced in 2000. However, when looking closer at the archive, the number of articles that were available from 2000 and earlier appeared to be much smaller than those available after 2001, indicating that not all of the articles had been archived before 2001. The presence of the Internet news archive, and the availability of articles within it, therefore dictated, to an extent, the newspapers and time periods that could be studied.

For each newspaper, over the two-year period from January 1, 2001 to December 31, 2002, every article from both newspapers which contained at least one reference to the words *gay*, *gays*, *homosexual* and *homosexuals* was examined. In some cases, articles were excluded from the corpus because they did not refer to sexual identity. For example, the word *gay* occasionally occurred as a Christian name. One way of making sense of a discourse of something is to compare it to a discourse of what it is not, so it was also decided to look at articles which contained the words *heterosexual* and *heterosexuals* as well.

The remit of this corpus is therefore restricted, in that the articles only tell us how journalists refer explicitly to homosexuality. For example, as with Morrish's analysis, an article about a gay person such as Peter Mandelson may never use the word *gay* or *homosexual*, but can still produce discourses that reference his sexuality, e.g.: 'Mandy's disco dancing skills were clearly delighting several young members dancing around him in Brighton' (the *Guardian*, June 5, 1996, quoted in Morrish 2003). This suggests a potential drawback of corpus analysis – it is easier to collect the more obvious linguistic phenomena. But this is also true of any form of language analysis. This limitation of the data has not resulted in a dearth of articles to analyse, although it does mean that any claims about discourses of homosexuality are being made about on-record citations of the words, rather than a less-easily argued 'guilt by association' stance, such as when journalists write about Peter Mandelson without referring to his sexuality. However, it is also likely to be the case that more ingenious ways of creating discourses of homosexuality that exist in the tabloid press can be uncovered by other means (for example, by examining articles which contain references to well-known gay figures).

In addition, I have not specifically collected articles which contain derogatory words for homosexuality such as *faggot*, *pansy* or *puff*, or articles which reference the word *queer* (which is sometimes used in a derogatory way, but can also be used in positive, reclaiming or academic contexts). These words certainly occurred (although infrequently) in the newspapers, often with distancing quotes around them. By concentrating on the words *gay* and *homosexual*, I am therefore looking at the two words that most members of mainstream society would associate with people who have sexual and romantic relationships with members of the same sex. They are also the words that are most likely to be used by members of that same group. And because these are such well-known and widely-used words, employed by different groups in society, their meanings are extremely contestable.

Table 3.1 shows the breakdowns of *gay(s)* and *homosexual(s)*, for the total number of articles the word occurred in, the total occurrences of each word (a word could appear in an article more than once), and the total number of words in the articles.

While both newspapers favoured using *gay* rather than *homosexual*, this preference was much more marked for the *Mirror*. The word *heterosexual* was

Table 3.1 Frequencies of sexuality words in tabloid newspapers

	Search term gay(s)		homosexual(s)		heterosexual(s)	
Newspaper	*Daily Mail*	*The Mirror*	*Daily Mail*	*The Mirror*	*Daily Mail*	*The Mirror*
Articles	812	1560	421	237	135	117
Occurrences of word	1684	2942	637	266	174	149
Number of words in articles	754,811	848,762	411,068	130,270	146,800	77,533

used much less often than *homosexual*, although possibly because an alternative to heterosexual, i.e. the word *straight*, was used more frequently instead. The word *straight* was not examined, due to time constraints – although this word occurred many more times than the other words examined, only a proportion of those were to do with sexuality (e.g. most were used in phrases like *straight line* or *straight away*). However, phrases such as *straight relationship* have been examined and are described below.

Although there is disagreement over the percentage of people in a given population who are gay or lesbian (for example, Kinsey 1948: 651, said that 4 per cent of people were exclusively homosexual, although this figure is disputed by groups like *The Family Research Institute*, e.g. Cameron 1993), it is interesting that homosexuality is referred to explicitly more often than heterosexuality. As stated in Chapter 1, a reason for this could be that as a minority identity, it is more unusual and/or problematic and therefore more likely to be remarked upon. In addition, heterosexual identities may not be explicitly referred to, because they are assumed to be present anyway, or they are referred to by other words. For example, for many people, the word *doctor* tends to implicitly mean 'male doctor', hence the use by some people of phrases like 'lady doctor' to mark what they view as the minority case.[4] In the same way, when newspapers talk of a 'three-in-the-bed romp', it will be assumed that such a romp will be heterosexual in nature, meaning that the phrase 'three-in-the-bed gay romp' will need to be used, to mark it as exceptional.[5]

We therefore find that, in tabloid journalism, some gay people are almost always referred to in terms of their sexual identity. As noted earlier, the winner of the reality game show *Big Brother* in 2001 was a gay man called Brian Dowling. An article in the *Mirror* (March 5, 2002) entitled 'I want people to stop calling me gay says Big Brother Brian' outlines this phenomenon:

> CHILDREN'S TV presenter Brian Dowling ... has admitted he's sick of the gay tag he earned from his camp behaviour on Big Brother. The former Ryanair steward said he is delighted with his success but wishes he could be just Brian. He added: 'Why do they keep having to say gay Brian? Everyone knows I'm gay. "Gay Brian Goes To The Shops, Gay Brian Buys Milk, Gay Brian Bleeds If You Cut Him. What's wrong with just Brian? It does get a bit much."'
>
> (The *Mirror*, March 5, 2002)

Ironically, the *Mirror* was one of the newspapers who had contributed to this labelling, referring to Brian Dowling as gay 51 times in phrases like *gay Brian*, *gay air steward Brian Dowling*, *gay Irish Brian* and *gay Big Brother star*. This case demonstrates the complexity of discourse surrounding a single subject in newspapers, multiple voices resulting in an overall stance that often appears conflicted, hypocritical or ambivalent. In addition, the fact that Brian's 'gay tag' has been reportedly earned from his 'camp behaviour' reveals a common way in which sexuality and gender are conflated in discourse.

Discourse prosodies

It was first decided to examine the immediate left- and right-hand collocates that surrounded the words *gay(s)*, *homosexual(s)* and *heterosexual(s)* to see the most common contexts in which these words were used. Table 3.2 shows the ten most frequent (where they exist) left- and right-hand collocates for *gay(s)* and *homosexual(s)*. Only collocates that occurred five or more times are given. The table consists of mainly function words: articles, prepositions, pronouns, conjunctions and auxiliary verbs. This is not surprising. As Scott (2000: 111) points out: 'collocation listings generally throw up an apparent relationship of colligation. The most frequent collocates of any node item in English will generally be *the, of, was*, etc.'

However, there are a few content words: *openly, repressed, closet, lesbian, couples, rape, rights, sex, acts, experiences, relationships* and *steward*. A closer examination of these words may reveal something about the most common discourses used, but it will not give us a complete picture. For this, we need to consider *discourse prosodies*.

To recap from Chapter 1, an examination of discourse prosodies is a way of moving beyond the lexical level by considering that different structures may have the same meaning. For example, single-word units may express a similar or related semantic concept: *hot, burning, boiling, scorching, searing*, etc., or phrases that are grammatically different may carry out a similar

Table 3.2 Most common immediate left- and right-hand collocates of *gay(s)* and *homosexual(s)*

Left-hand collocates	Daily Mail	Right-hand collocates
a 167, the 164, of 73, and 72, was 63, for 46, is 43, openly 38, to 36, be 26	gay(s)	and 91, in 69, the 52, to 36, he 34, who 31, lesbian 26, a 25, I 23, but 20
a 80, of 40, for 38, and 34, the 26, was 19, repressed 14, that 13, to 12, his 10	homosexual(s)	couples 34, and 30, rape 16, rights 14, sex 13, in 11, acts 10, experiences 9, relationships 9, who 9
Left-hand collocates	*The* Mirror	*Right-hand collocates*
a 342, the 209, was 188, of 94, is 72, and 68, for 63, I'm 59, not 58, be 50	gay(s)	and 147, in 115, the 99, he 53, to 51, I 46, who 38, but 36, are 34, steward 34
a 29, of 17, and 13, for 12, was 11, the 10, closet 6	homosexual(s)	the 17, and 12, in 8, but 7, he 7, of 6, his 5

function: *he admitted he was gay, his admission was that he was gay, he confessed to being gay*. Therefore, it may be the case that a word may occur next to *gay* or *homosexual* only once or twice, and will therefore not appear in the above table. Such low-frequency combinations of words are not normally considered to be collocates of each other.

However, when taken into consideration with other, similar low-frequency pairs of words we may see an overall pattern forming. Such patterns, or discourse prosodies help to shed light on the prevailing discourses surrounding homosexuality in these texts. In addition, if a particular word occurs frequently next to *homosexual* or *gay*, then it may be useful to see what other words this word collocates with – for example, by examining how it is used in other corpora such as the British National Corpus.

In only examining the words which appear immediately one place to the left and right of *homosexual(s)/gay(s)*, this places a limitation on discourse prosodies that will be found. Because of this, in some cases where a single word appears to be part of a noun phrase or multi-word idiom, the whole phrase has been included in the analysis. Also, it should be noted that words within a discourse prosody should not be taken at face value. For example, if *stupid* occurred frequently next to *homosexual*, we might have jumped to the conclusion that people were referring to gay people as unintelligent. However, when looking at how this phrase actually occurred in context, it might have been apparent that people were referring to gay people as *not* stupid. In other cases, a writer may be reporting an opinion that someone has given, and then go on to disagree with it. Yet even in these cases, a continual pairing of the words *homosexual* and *stupid* might serve to associate the two concepts together in people's minds, even if that is not what is directly intended.

In addition, particular care needs to be taken when examining terms which appear to the left of *homosexual(s)* and *gay(s)* to take into account the fact that these words may be part of a longer noun phrase. For example, if *notorious* collocates with *homosexual*, we may jump to the conclusion that a newspaper is writing about a notorious homosexual person. However, when looking at the full sentence, we may find a phrase such as 'he frequented a notorious homosexual drinking establishment'. So, in this case, homosexuals are not explicitly being described as notorious, although a place where they visit does have this association, and homosexuality per se is therefore implicitly tarred with the same brush.

Tabloid discourses

The 'one of many problematic minority groups' discourse

From Table 3.2 it can be seen that one of the most common collocates of the words pertaining to homosexuality was the word *and*, occurring 187 times as a left-hand collocate and 280 times as a right-hand collocate. The word *and* is a co-ordinating conjunction, connecting words, phrases or clauses that are of equal importance or have the same grammatical structure in a sentence. In the corpus data, *and* is used to connect noun phrases which have a similar value together, for example, in sentences like: 'The nation is not possessed by an overwhelming urge to fill the Shadow Cabinet with 25-year-old black lesbians and homosexual asylum-seekers' (the *Mail on Sunday* reporting on Lord Tebbit warning Iain Duncan Smith of the dangers of wooing minorities at the expense of core Tory values, August 4, 2002). Table 3.3 shows which other groups are connected to gay identities by examining terms which appear around the phrases 'gay(s)/homosexual(s) and' or 'and gay(s)/homosexual(s)'.

Table 3.3 Groups associated with *homosexual(s)* and *gay(s)*

Left-hand terms	Daily Mail	*Right-hand terms*
Asians 2, Aussies 1, blacks 15, cohabitees 2, ethnic minorities 6, females 1, lesbian(s) 36, Nazis 1, one-parent families 1, unmarried 1, women 10, women bishops 1	gay(s)	bisexual 18, black(s) 9, cohabiting 3, disabled 1, ethnic/minorities 7, heterosexuals 5, lesbian(s) 40, prostitutes 1, single women 1, straight 4, unmarried couples 14, women 5
black lesbians 1, cohabiting partners 1, ethnic 2, feminist 1, lesbians 1, heterosexuals 9, unmarried couples 4	homosexual(s)	asylum seekers 2, ethnic minorities 1, heterosexuals 1, lesbians 2, single people 1, 'straight' 1, transsexual 1, transvestite 1, unmarried couples 4, women 1
L1 terms	*The* Mirror	*R1 terms*
black(s) 17, drug users 1, ethnic minorities 1, feminists 1, girls 1, Jews 3, lesbians 22, pensioners 1, straight 10, unmarried 4, women 3, women bishops 2	gay(s)	Arabs 3, bisexual 32, black(s) 7, drug abusers 1, ethnic minorities 2, heterosexual 5, lesbian(s) 54, Nazis 2, straight 12, transgendered 3, transvestites 1, women 2
abortionists 2, adulterers 1, black people, 1, unmarried couples 2, divorcees 2, heterosexuals 4, immigrants 1, Jews 1, Muslims 1, refugees 1, trades unions 1, social workers 1, liberals 1, whites 1, unmarried mums 1, single mums 1	homosexual(s)	bisexual 2, Christians 1, civil liberty activists 2, criminals 1, divorcees 1, drug users 2, feminists 1, lesbians 1, liberals 1, prostitutes 1, social workers 1

Therefore, the word *and* appears to be used to connect homosexuality to other minority groups. The most common group associated with *gay(s)* and *homosexual(s)* is *lesbians*, occurring 156 times overall. This word collocates most often with *gay(s)* rather than *homosexual(s)*, suggesting that *homosexual(s)* is more likely to be a hypernymic semantic category, incorporating both male and female sexual identity within it. *Bisexual* and *straight/heterosexual* occur next most often, being referenced 52 and 51 times respectively. Other sexual identities include transgendered people and transvestites, occurring six times. Homosexuality is therefore linked most often with other sexual identities, and particularly those which possess a minority status. In fact, it should be noted that all of the other types of identities connected to homosexuality, other than *heterosexual/straight* (and one case each of *Christians* and *whites*), are viewed by the newspapers as minority or problematic identities in some way.

A number of other terms are used to refer to unmarried people or people who have sex but are not married to each other: *adulterers, cohabitees, cohabiting, unmarried couples, unmarried mums, single mums, divorcees, single people* and *one-parent families* (occurring 41 times collectively). These words occur more often in the *Daily Mail* than in the *Mirror*. What homosexuality has in common with these identities is sex occurring outside of the boundaries of an institutionalised (heterosexual) relationship. *Abortionists* (2) are loosely linked to this group, again being people who may be seen to be a threat to the traditional nuclear family.

It is less easy to find direct links between other identity collocates and homosexuality, other than the fact that a minority or stigmatised status is shared. For example, another set of collocates refer to ethnicity: *asylum seekers, Arabs, asians, Aussies, blacks, ethnic minorities, immigrants, Jews, Muslims* and *refugees* (occurring 83 times collectively). The most common collocate from this list refers to black people. There are also a number of collocates related to criminal identities (*criminals, drug users, Nazis* and *prostitutes* (occurring nine times)) and those connected to politics, and particularly those traditionally associated with liberal stances (*civil liberty activists, feminists, liberals, social workers, trade unions* (occurring 10 times collectively, and only in the *Mirror*)). As well as feminists, references to women tend to be frequently mentioned, e.g. *women, girls, lesbians, single mums, black lesbians*.

The use of *and* to connect homosexuality to other, problematised, minority groups based on unmarried, ethnic, criminal and political identities is typical of features of *moral panics*. Moral panics can be defined as the efforts of a particular group to exert collective moral control over another group or person. They are characterised by the identification of a 'problem' which is perceived as a threat to a community or section of a community's values or interests (sometimes reflecting political or religious beliefs), e.g. pornography on television. There is a rapid build-up of public concern focused on the supposed problem, and often numerous solutions are proposed, until the panic recedes or results in social change (Thompson 1998: 98).

Hall *et al.* (1978: 222) describe how moral panics can result in *signification spirals*, whereby convergence takes place – two or more activities or events are brought together in ways that suggest there are parallels between them. Hall *et al.* note how it is not uncommon to find a mapping together of moral panics into a general panic about social order. Jenkins (1992: 10) describes this as *symbolic politics*, whereby attention is drawn to a specific problem because it symbolises another issue, which cannot be attacked directly.

So why are gay people often linked to other minority groups in the tabloid press? In some cases it is because the news story is focusing on concerns which are shared between two or more groups (e.g. adoption or rates of HIV infection). For example, the *Daily Mail* (April 2, 2002) reports: 'The Labour Party chairman has declared that gay and unmarried couples should be allowed to adopt children.' The *Mirror* (September 2, 2001) attempts to dismiss HIV as just a problem experienced by two minority groups, although still links the groups together: 'Those who have ignored the threat of HIV may think that the virus is mainly confined to drug users and the gay community.' In other cases, the link is more tenuous – it is simply there because these groups are all minorities:

> The failure of William Hague's rather unconvincing lunge to the Right has strengthened the arguments of self-styled modernisers. They – as we disclose today – are plotting to cull plummy white males from the Parliamentary candidates' list, and replace them with pastel-suited women, members of ethnic minorities and declared homosexuals.
>
> (The *Mail on Sunday*, October 6, 2002)

An article by the *Mirror* (July 18, 2002) shows how homosexuality is worked into a discourse of collective negative minorities. The newspaper has traced the actors who played roles in the American television series *The Waltons*:

> THEY were the all-American family whose simple life on Walton's Mountain entranced a generation of TV viewers ... But in reality the cast were a million miles from their clean-cut characters, as revealed in a programme which brings the stars back together after 21 years. One was an alcoholic, another a homosexual with extreme pro-communist views, while another posed for Playboy.

Here homosexuality is defined in opposition, 'a million miles', to a 'clean-cut' identity, and also linked to alcoholism, extreme pro-communism and posing nude for a magazine. Homosexuality is therefore newsworthy, being defined as problematic and shocking because it is linked with other identity traits that also hold these characteristics, when contrasted with the 'clean-cut characters' of Walton's Mountain.

Transiency

Gay relationships are frequently described in ways that imply they are transitory and unimportant. For example, a phrase like *gay crush* (see Table 3.4) implies an attachment that is immature, or one associated with being at school. Taken together, other words suggest that the form of a particular gay relationship is fun or hedonistic: *fling(s)*, *romp(s)*, *frolics* and *adventures*. The strongest log–log collocate of *romp* in the British National Corpus is *sex*, whereas *fling* (as a noun) collocates in the BNC most often with *final*, suggesting that a fling often occurs before settling down into a relationship. The strongest collocates of *adventures* in the BNC are *wonderland*, *Alice* (both from the C. S. Lewis novel *Alice's Adventures in Wonderland*), *romantic*, *military* and *sexual*. *Frolics* collocates with *fun* most often in the BNC. It should be noted that many of the R1 words in Table 3.4 occur as plurals. A gay person does not have a single affair, but many. This further implies that their relationships are unstable and transitory, and that gay people are promiscuous (see also Table 3.10).

In addition to these 'fun' words, other terms suggest relationships that are sexual, rather than being based on commitment: *affair*, *encounter*, *liaisons*, *romance*, *boyfriend* and *lover*. In the BNC, *liaisons* collocates with *romantic*, *dangerous* and *sexual* most strongly. *Affair* in the BNC collocates with words like *extra-marital*, *sordid*, *adulterous*, *satanic* and *secret*, whereas *encounter* collocates with *brief*, *sexual* and *chance*.

While the phrase *gay/homosexual lover(s)* occurs 100 times in the tabloid texts, this is not the only way that relationships can be represented. Table 3.5 shows how often the words *couple(s)*, *relationship(s)*, *partner(s)* and *lover(s)* are used to explicitly refer to homosexual and heterosexual people.

As noted above, homosexuality is remarked on more often than heterosexuality for all of these types of words – probably because heterosexual relationships are unmarked as the norm. The word *couple* is used most often

Table 3.4 Terms which suggest gay relationships are transient

L1 *terms*	Daily Mail	R1 *terms*
	gay(s)	affair(s) 6, crushes 1, lover(s) 33
casual 1, experimenting 1, former 1, occasional 1	homosexual(s)	affair(s) 1, encounter(s) 2, flings 1, liaisons 2, lover(s) 3, relations 1

L1 *terms*	*The* Mirror	R1 *terms*
casual 2	gay(s)	affair(s) 12, boyfriend 2, crush 2, encounters 3, fling(s) 4, frolics 1, lovers 61, romance 2, romp(s) 7
former, one-time 1	homosexual(s)	adventures 2, encounter 1, flings 1, lovelife 1, lover 3

Table 3.5 Frequencies of relationship words, related to sexuality

	couple(s)	*relationship(s)*	*partner(s)*	*lover(s)*
homosexual(s)/gay(s)	151	49	25	100
heterosexual(s)/straight(s)	21	8	3	1

when identifying people as being in a heterosexual or homosexual relationship. However, if we look at the ratios of the words *couple/relationship/partner/lover* depending on whether they are used to refer to gay or heterosexual people, we find a difference. With *relationship*, the ratio is 49:8, suggesting a bias of about 86 per cent towards gay people. For *couple*, the bias is about 88 per cent in favour of gay people. This figure is 89 per cent for *partner*. However, for *lover* the bias is even higher: 99 per cent for gay people. So while both heterosexual and homosexual people in relationships are most likely to be referred to as couples, if a word like *lover* is used in conjunction with a sexuality identifier, it is much more likely to be referring to homosexuals rather than heterosexuals, and this is more pronounced than other words like *couple*, *relationship* and *partner*. The word *lover* places an emphasis on romance and sex rather than commitment and stability.

The left-hand terms in Table 3.4, *casual*, *experimenting*, *former*, *occasional* and *one-time*, all have a discourse prosody of impermanence: e.g. 'The allegations against him are that he had casual gay sex and he let cannabis be smoked and stored in his flat' (the *Sunday Mirror*, March 24, 2002). While these words don't occur often with overt sexuality markers like *gay* and *homosexual*, they do occur more frequently with other words. For example, the phrase *casual sex* in reference to gay men occurs nine times, *casual sexual encounters* occurs three times, *experimenting with sex/love* occurs three times and *occasional yearning* occurs once.

It's a behaviour not an identity

Related to the discourse of gay transient relationships is one which attempts to frame homosexuality as a (sexual) behaviour, rather than an identity, as also found in Chapter 2, used by the anti-reform debaters in the House of Lords. The emphasis is on homosexuality as an act – so, as with the House of Lords data, we find words like *act(s)*, *activity/activities*, *behaviour*, *encounter* and *practices* occurring as right-hand collocates with *gay(s)* and *homosexual(s)* (see Table 3.6). However, the use of plural nouns (gay experiences versus gay experience) again suggests that repetition is involved – a recurring (yet vague) behaviour which serves to identify someone by what they do over and over again.

Sexuality is also constructed as a matter of taste, for example, in the same way that someone might have a taste for a certain type of cheese. Words such as *tendencies*, *proclivities*, *tastes* and *feelings* again serve to diminish the

Table 3.6 Terms which associate homosexuality with acts or tastes

L1 terms	Daily Mail	R1 terms
experienced 1	gay(s)	background 1, experiences 3, tendencies 2
active 1, consenting 1, engage in 1, practising 2	homosexual(s)	act(s) 13, activity/s 9, behaviour 3, experience(s) 12, feelings 2, inclinations 1, intercourse 3, passions 1, practice(s) 5, proclivities 1, tastes 1, tendencies 1

L1 terms	The Mirror	R1 terms
	gay(s)	encounter 2, experience 2, feelings 1, goings-on 2, tendency/s 4
consenting 1, practising 1	homosexual(s)	act(s) 2, activity/s 6, experience(s) 3, practices 1

notion of gay identity. Interestingly, many of these collocates are plural. People are not said to have a tendency to be homosexual or a homosexual tendency, but instead are described as having *tendencies* – the pluralisation of the word suggests a complex of associated behaviours or acts, which require specification via existing shared knowledge. The word *tendencies* collocates strongly with the following other words in the BNC: *suicidal, depressive, anti-social, aggressive, violent, criminal* and *dangerous*. Tendencies are clearly not a good thing to have.

In addition, there are references to *consenting homosexuals* and *practising homosexuals*. The former phrase echoes the 1957 Wolfenden Report which stated that 'homosexual behaviour between consenting adults in private should no longer be a criminal offence'. Collocates of *consent* in the BNC are *informed, without, refusal, coercion* and *unreasonable*. The fact that consent for something *must* be given before it can happen, and that this is enshrined in law, suggests that consent relates to an unpleasant or inconvenient activity. *Practising* also has legal connotations; common collocations in the BNC being *barristers, solicitors, lawyers, doctors, teachers, christians, catholic* and *homosexual*. If people are going to practise an activity, it is likely to be law, medicine, religion, teaching or homosexuality. So being gay is likened to a career or job, or a religion – the important point here being that a practice is an extrinsic activity or behaviour, rather than an intrinsic identity trait (such as gender or race) as such. If we can refer to a 'practising homosexual', then theoretically a 'non-practising homosexual' can also exist. The difference being that the practising homosexual engages in sexual activity, whereas the non-practising homosexual does not. As with *consenting*, the word defines homosexuality solely in terms of having sex.

Crime and violence

Another set of terms relate homosexuality to crime, and particularly violent crime, as Table 3.7 shows.

In some cases, these collocates are used to refer to a small number of individual cases. For example, the phrase *gay ripper* which occurs 23 times, always refers to William Beggs who was jailed for the murder of a teenager. *Gay slasher* also refers to the same man, whereas *gay slayer* refers to another killer, Peter Moore. The phrase *gay serial killer* is used to refer to other murderers, Allan Grimson and Dennis Nielson, as well as William Beggs. Perhaps it could be argued that there is nothing particularly objectionable about noting the sexuality of a serial killer. However, the pairing of *heterosexual/straight* and *serial killer* does not occur in these newspapers (perhaps because it is assumed to be the default case). An unfortunate consequence of making the sexuality of a serial killer explicit only when he (and in the cases discussed above they are all male) is gay is that a link is made in the minds of the readers between homosexuality and murder. Because gay identities do tend to get remarked on (e.g. 'Gay Brian'), whereas heterosexuality is simply assumed, discourses of homosexuality possess a high saliency.

Sexual violence is also connected to homosexuality, with the words *rape* and *rapist* occurring 50 times immediately to the right of *gay(s)* or *homosexual(s)*. Another term, *male rape*, can be used to acknowledge that men may rape other men, but the perpetrators do not necessarily identify as gay. However, the phrase *male rape* only occurs 30 times in the period under

Table 3.7 Terms related to crime and violence

L1 terms	Daily Mail	R1 terms
violent 7	gay(s)	rape 8, inmates 3, paedophile 1, prisoners 3, rape 9
convicted 1, dangerous 1, murderous 1, murdering 1, murdered 1, guilty of 3, violent 4	homosexual(s)	assault(s) 3, killer 1, Nazi 1, offences 4, paedophile(s) 3, prisoner(s) 3, rape 16, rapist 1

L1 terms	*The* Mirror	R1 terms
brutal 1, convicted 1, violent 4	gay(s)	attack(s) 5, bashing 5, fraudster 1, killer 5, killing 3, prisoners 1, rape 8, rapist 1, ripper 23, serial killer 3, slasher 1, slayer 1
convicted 1, murdering 2, guilty of 1	homosexual(s)	conviction 1, offences 1, rape 6, rapist 1, serial killer 1, victim 1

study in the two newspapers (while *male rapist* occurs once), suggesting that these sorts of rapes are more likely to be talked about in terms of sexual identity, rather than the gender of those involved.

The words *offences, convicted* and *conviction* tend to occur most often with the word *homosexual*, and are most often used to refer to events that have happened in the past, or in more recent situations where homosexuality was illegal (such as the armed forces):

> There were rumours of Mr Fry having gay tendencies (not accepted at all in those days) and, eventually, confirmation that he had a homosexual conviction against him.
>
> (The *Mirror*, February 11, 2002)

> Lexel was a convicted homosexual who left the Nazi party only after many of his gay Brownshirt colleagues were assassinated during the Night of the Long Knives.
>
> (The *Mail on Sunday*, June 23, 2002)

> The crewmen involved, nine of whom were later found guilty of homosexual offences, ranged in rank from able seaman to petty officer.
>
> (The *Mail on Sunday*, November 11, 2002)

However, these vague-sounding legal phrases are not explicit about what such homosexual 'convictions' or 'offences' actually are, nor do the articles acknowledge that there was anything unfair about criminalising homosexuality in this way. I would therefore argue that continuing to use phrases like this is a way of extending the 'homosexual as criminal' discourse, beyond the period in which this was sanctioned by governments. This reference to historical discourses is similar to the use of phrases such as *sodomy, buggery* or *gross indecency* in the House of Lords (see Chapter 2).

From Table 3.2 it can be seen that common left-hand collocates of *gay(s)* and *homosexual(s)* are the verb forms *is* and *was* – often occurring in phrases such as 'X is gay' where X is the name of a person – and usually someone whose homosexuality is being revealed as newsworthy. Looking at who is actually being named as gay here reveals another way that homosexuality is linked to discourses of crime and violence. For example:

> AMERICAN investigators believe that terrorist ringleader Mohamed Atta and at least five others among the 19 suicide hijackers who attacked New York and Washington were secretly gay.
>
> (The *Mail on Sunday*, November 4, 2001)

> British soldiers in the Second World War knew there was something not quite right about the Fuhrer. 'Hitler has only got one ball,' went the well-known song. Now a German professor of history, Lothar Machtan,

has gone one better: Hitler was a homosexual, he claims, and all previous biographies of Hitler will have to be rewritten to take account of Hitler's shady, gay past.

(The *Mail on Sunday*, October 21, 2001)

In addition, Osama Bin Laden is described by the *Daily Mail* (November 21, 2001) as having passionate male friendships described as 'gay crushes'. By reporting stories that some of the world's worst war criminals were gay, the tabloid newspaper links atrocity to homosexuality. Homosexuality is therefore further linked with crime and deviance.

Shame and secrecy

In the section above, we saw how homosexuality was linked to the identities of people who had committed atrocities. Such articles are justified as 'newsworthy' because this is new information. An important aspect of the identity of the criminal is to do with deceit and lying. I now want to consider in more detail an opposing pair of discourses which relate homosexuality to secrecy and shame. A number of words suggest a discourse prosody of shame and secrecy (Table 3.8). Homosexuality is something that is *repressed* or *suppressed*. It is *secret*, *secretive*, *hushed-up* or *denied* (*not gay* is one of the most frequently occurring phrases in the corpus). People may have a gay *past* or *background*, or be involved in a homosexual *underworld*. The *Daily Mail* (September 30, 2002) refers to the 'tortured homosexual' as a 'comfortable stereotype'. However, the secret can also be discovered. People can be *outed* and *revelations* are made about their sexual identities.

To be gay is also likened to being a criminal. In Table 3.8, there are 28 instances of people *admitting* to being gay or homosexual. They also *confess* or *self-confess*, are *alleged* to be or *accused* of being gay and they may have 'harboured homosexual passions' (the *Daily Mail*, October 15, 2002).

In addition there are gay *scandals*, *slurs*, *smears*, *rumours*, *jibes* and *taunts* (all mainly occurring in the plural, suggesting repetition or recidivism). To be referred to as gay is an insult for people who claim to be heterosexual:

TV BRAWLERS Lennox Lewis and Hasim Rahman were sensationally at it again last night with police in Las Vegas forced to intervene. Trouble flared when Lewis, still outraged at 'gay' slurs uttered by Rahman during their first bust-up in Los Angeles on Thursday, jumped to his feet during an address by his opponent.

(The *Mirror*, September 11, 2001)

The *Mirror* also reproduces the discourse of shame and secrecy in a regular gossip column called *Wicked Whispers* where they allude to a famous person's secret homosexual identity, without naming them:

Table 3.8 Terms related to secrecy and shame

L1 terms	Daily Mail	R1 terms
admitted a 3, admittedly 2, admit/ted he's 2, came/come out as 7, closet 5, not 14, repressed 1, secret/ly 2	gay(s)	allegations 1, confession 1, past 8, rumours 1, slur(s) 2, smears 1
accusations of 1, admission of 3, admitted to 2, allegations of 3, alleges 6, closet 6, former 1, harboured 1, not 4, secrets of 1, suspected of 1, past 1, private 1, repressed 14, secretive/secret 3, self-confessed 2, suppressed 1, tortured 1	homosexual(s)	backgrounds 1, past 1, rumours 1, scandal(s) 1, underworld 1

L1 terms	*The* Mirror	R1 terms
admitted 2, admitted he's 1, admits he's 2, admitted to 1, admitted he was 10, alleged 4, came out as 4, outed as 2, closet 4, self-confessed 1, confesses 1, denied 1, reveals he's 1, revealed he was 4, rumours he is 1, denies he's 3, not 57, probably 3, really 4, hushed-up 1	gay(s)	slurs 11, jibes 1, past 4, rumours 2, secret 3, taunts 1
outed as a 1, alleged/ing 3, allegations of 2, closet 6, confession to 1, revelations of 2, repressed 3, secret 3	homosexual(s)	past 1

WHICH brand new pop star who can't stop bragging about his new-found luck with the ladies is actually hiding a little secret? Despite his recent (short-lived) fling with a female he is actually gay – but bosses don't want the fans to know . . .

(The *Mirror*, December 9, 2002)

WHICH soap star has a gay secret? Off screen, this actor likes to pretend he is as straight as they come. But during a spell living in America, he shacked up with another man.

(The *Mirror*, August 7, 2002)

These articles usually refer to a man who 'pretends' to be heterosexual – therefore, he is doubly tainted – by being gay and by lying about it. However, in reproducing such discourses, it could be argued that the newspaper is contributing to the social stigma of homosexuality, ensuring that famous people will continue to hide their sexual identities. The newspapers don't acknowledge that in the past people have had to hide their sexuality or face prison and that, even now, being openly gay can be problematic. As Chirrey (2003: 32) notes in her discussion of the mainstream media's response to British pop star Will Young's 'coming out':

> The lexis that they select, such as 'confession', 'admission' and 'admits', resonates with a sense of acknowledging criminality, sinfulness and blame, while phrases such as 'his secret' and 'in hiding' suggest that being gay is characterised by clandestine activity, presumably due to its supposedly shameful nature.

Shamelessness

But while some gay people are ashamed of their sexuality and conceal it, a related discourse exists – one in which another set of gay people have *no* shame. As Table 3.9 shows, when some people come out, they don't *confess* their sexuality, but they *declare* or *proclaim* it, like a town-crier with a piece of important news. Such people are *infamous*, *visible* and *famously* homosexual. Their sexuality is *well-known* by everyone and prefaced by adverbs that suggest that the person being talked about purposefully seeks attention. Such people have no compunction not just in being *openly* gay but *flagrantly, flamboyantly, outrageously* or *unbelievably* gay. Interestingly, phrases like *proudly gay, happily gay* or *assuredly gay* never occur in the tabloid corpus. The emphasis on these types of people is not to do with pride, but to do with showing off.

In addition, sometimes such people are constructed as being unable to hide their sexuality and are viewed via adverbs of scale as *obviously, really, so, clearly, very* or *totally* gay. This discourse also competes with the idea of homosexuality as just a sexual behaviour, associating it with manner, style and gender performance. *Flamboyant*, for example, collocates most strongly in the BNC with the word *style*.

> Certainly, if Pim Fortuyn had been around in Nazi Germany in the 30s, this flamboyant homosexual would have been among the first to hear the midnight knock on the door.
>
> (The *Mirror*, May 13, 2002)

> Elton John ... Rock megastar, alltimegreat [sic] songwriter, much-loved public figure, world-class tantrum-chucker and flamboyantly out homosexual.
>
> (The *Daily Mail*, June 14, 2002)

Table 3.9 Terms related to shamelessness and obviousness

L1 terms	Daily Mail	R1 terms
declare he's 1, definitely 1, explicit 1, famously 1, flagrantly 1, flamboyantly 1, graphic 1, hideously 1, notorious(ly) 2, proclaimed himself 1, obviously 1, openly 38, outrageously 1, prominent 1, really 1, so 3, totally 2, very 2, visible 2	gay(s)	
acknowledged 1, clearly 1, crass 1, declared 1, devoutly 1, flagrantly 1, flamboyantly out 1, high profile 2, notorious 1, openly 1, well-known 3	homosexual(s)	

L1 terms	*The* Mirror	R1 terms
definitely 1, famous 3, flamboyant 1, notorious 4, obviously 2, well-known 5, openly 31, outrageous 2, outwardly 1, publicly 1, unbelievably 1, remarkably unflamboyant 1	gay(s)	
confirmed 1, crude 1, explicit 1, flamboyant 1, infamous 1, well-known 1	homosexual(s)	

Negative connotations are associated with some of these words. For example, *notorious* which occurs seven times with *gay(s)/homosexual(s)* also collocates strongly in the BNC with *criminals*, *estate* (as in 'rough council estate') and *prison*. We also find that people are described as *hideously gay* and there are references to *crass* and *crude homosexuals*.

Interestingly, flamboyancy is seen by one journalist as a gay norm, in an article in the *Mirror* about a drag queen contest in Wales.

> At 9pm the first people – remarkably unflamboyant gay punters – step into the darkened Nova Centre's Starlight Suite, a cavernous mirrored ballroom with sticky floors that may have been fashionable in 1979.
>
> (The *Mirror*, September 15, 2001)

Here, the fact that the punters *aren't* flamboyant is seen as remarkable.

The phrase *devoutly gay* suggests another orientation to homosexuality. Although there aren't enough occurrences of *devoutly* in the BNC to warrant an analysis of its collocates, the word *devout* collocates with *Catholic(s)*, *Anglican* and *Christian* most strongly. As with the phrase *practising homosexual*, there is a metaphor that homosexuality is a religion (or cult), something which will be examined more closely later in this chapter.

The phrase *confirmed homosexual* suggests two things – someone who is openly and unwaveringly gay. This phrase most likely developed from the older euphemism *confirmed bachelor*, showing a change in the way that homosexuality is now reported. So *confirmed bachelor* was a way of being coy about naming someone as gay, but *confirmed homosexual* is a way of being explicit about someone's sexuality.

Another term used as part of this discourse is *declare*, which can be adjectival, as in *declared homosexual*, or as part of a verb phrase 'he declared he's gay'. The strongest five collocates of the lemma DECLARE in the BNC (using log–log) are *bankrupt, unconstitutional, void, war* and *illegal*. What is declared has negative semantic prosody.

Sometimes writers access the discourses of secrecy and outrageousness at the same time, as in the following article:

> As if the characters ensconced in the Big Brother house were not outrageous enough, Channel Four is about to bring in a controversial new housemate. Viewers are being asked to choose between grandmother Anne Edgar, closet homosexual Josh Rafter6 and part-time model Natasha Simpson.
>
> (The *Daily Mail*, June 1, 2001, my italics)

Promiscuity

Closely related to the discourses of notoriety, crime, relationship transience and 'sexual behaviour rather than sexual identity' is another discourse which frames homosexuality in terms of sexual obsession and in particular aggression and sleaze.

In Table 3.10, gay men are described as *frequenting, cruising* and *prowling* places where sexual activity may take place. As with words like *proclivities, tendencies* and *experiences*, the verb usage of the adjective *frequent* again suggests an activity which is continually repeated. To frequent a place is to return to it again and again, an addictive pattern of behaviour. *Cruising*, which is a vernacular term used by gay people, occurs several times in quotes, suggesting that the authors want to distance themselves from association with the subculture. What places or things are described as being gay or homosexual at the R1 node? *Saunas, brothels, bordellos, chat-lines, meeting spots, hang-outs, pick-up spots* and *knocking shops*.

Gay people also *indulge in* or *solicit for* sex. As discussed in Chapter 2, if we indulge in something then we yield to it in order to gratify or pleasure

Table 3.10 Terms related to promiscuous sex

L1 terms	Daily Mail	R1 terms
frequenting a 1, frequented by 1, brothel for 1, 'cruising' for 1, prowling for 1, soliciting for 1, frequent(s)/(ed) 3, group (sex) 3, grubby 1, promiscuous 2	gay(s)	conquests 1, 'cruising' 1, predator 3, group sex 2, haunt 1, prostitutes 2, saunas 3
indulge in 1, lecherous 1, predatory 1, promiscuous 1, rampant 2, voraciously 1	homosexual(s)	advances 3, bordello 1, brothel 1, craving 1, 'cruising' 1, excess 1, group (sex) 1, orgy 5, prostitute(s) 2, saunas 1, soliciting 1

L1 terms	The Mirror	R1 terms
three-in-a-bed 3, frequented by 1, cruising 2, cruising for 1, hangout for 1, haunt for 1, lap-dancing for 1, indulged in 1, persistent 1, promiscuous 1, sleazy 1	gay(s)	advances 3, chat-line 4, cruising 1, predator 5, haunt 7, massage parlour 1, meeting spot 1, orgies 5, pick-up spot 4, prostitute 1, sauna/s 9
meeting place for 1, pick-up point for 1, indulging in 1, promiscuous 2, rampant 1, soliciting 1	homosexual(s)	advance/s 2, haunt 1, knocking shop 1, tourists 1

ourselves. The phrase *homosexual excess* has a similar semantic pattern, suggesting over-indulgence. The word *haunt* (as a noun) occurs ten times with *gay(s)/homosexual(s)*. As with *frequent*, this word suggests a place that is often visited.

Homosexuality is also written about in conjunction with words that suggest a large sexual appetite: *lecherous, promiscuous, predatory, persistent, rampant* and *voraciously*. *Rampant* is a negatively loaded word which collocates strongly in the BNC with *inflation, individualism, corruption*. It also collocates with *lion* and *lions*. In a similar vein, *predatory* collocates with *fish, birds, animals* and *species*. These words link homosexuality to a metaphor of gay men as animals, unable to control their sexual urges.

> DAY-BY-DAY, the image of the Windsors has been blackened by each twist, from the widespread flogging off of royal gifts to the rampant promiscuousness of gay palace staff (yesterday a retired senior police officer said servants had compromised security by bringing suspected male prostitutes into all the London royal palaces).
>
> (The *Daily Mail*, November 11, 2002)

In addition, the words *grubby* and *sleazy* taint homosexuality with the notion of sex-as-filth. Finally, there are references to *orgies*, *lap-dancing*, *three-in-a-bed*, *group* (sex), *prostitutes* and *tourists*. While other discourses of homosexuality may view it as a form of deviancy in itself, the way that gay sex is sometimes reported to occur makes it even *more* deviant – so money changes hands or more than two people are said to be involved.

Ubiquity

While the previous discourses have been concerned with propagating negative stereotypes of homosexuality (e.g. gay men lie about their sexuality or they're blatantly shameless about it, they're sexually aggressive and their relationships are casual and irrelevant), another set of discourses are more concerned with a different aspect of creating a moral panic about gay people. This relates to them becoming more powerful. As Table 3.11 shows, one of the easiest ways to achieve this is to suggest that there are lots of gay people in existence, and that they do not function as individuals, but rather as a unified group. So a pop star will be said to have a *gay following*, or be supported by *legions* or *armies* of fans (the military metaphor here hints at possible danger – these legions of fans are currently only interested in pop, but they might become interested in other things, such as gay rights).

A particular place will be said to be *dominated by*, *full of* or *packed with* gay or homosexual people, and there will be references to a gay *village*, *district*, *quarter*, *metropolis*, *community* or *culture*. Some of these phrases (notably

Table 3.11 Terms related to collective groups

L1 terms	Daily Mail	R1 terms
	gay(s)	circle/s 2, clientele 1, community 25, cult experience 1, culture 1, district 2, environment 1, fraternity 1, mafia 3, mob 1, 'village' 1, quarter 2
dominated by 1, crowded 1, thriving 1	homosexual(s)	community 2, coterie 1, population 1, society 1
L1 terms	*The* Mirror	R1 terms
close-knit 1, packed with 1	gay(s)	capital 3, community 42, crowd 4, following 8, metropolis 2, population 1, village 5
cult 1, full of 2, legion of 1, thousands of 5, army of 1, hundreds of 1	homosexual(s)	community 4, following 1, ring 1

community, *culture* and *village*) don't contain negative connotations (note again the *Daily Mail*'s distancing quotation marks around *village*), but others suggest that something more sinister is afoot. For example, the *Daily Mail* reports allegations that there is a 'gay mafia' at Buckingham Palace. Meanwhile the son of Princess Michael of Kent is described as mixing 'with a louche set and has allied himself to a gay fraternity ... with growing frequency, he chooses to entertain many male friends "at home" and staff have found themselves stepping over young men's bodies in the morning' (the *Daily Mail*, November 22, 2002). The *Mirror*, in an article entitled 'Gay orgies, sex in saunas and drinking binges' (June 22, 2002), describes how 'Trainee priests at the Catholic Church's top college in Ireland held boozy gay orgies and sexually abused younger students'. The article ends with the following sentence: 'Monsignor Michael Ledwith left St Patrick's College in Maynooth, in 1994 amid allegations that a homosexual ring was operating there.' A *ring* implies a closed or secret group and is often used to refer to people who are engaged in illegal activity, particularly sexual activity – we find phrases like *child sex ring* and *paedophile ring* in the BNC. *Circle* is used in a similar way to *ring*. The *Daily Mail* (November 29, 2002) describes Lord Byron's 'gay circle' at Cambridge, for example.

Therefore, this discourse has two main facets to it – that there are legions or armies of gay people, but also that they exist in a private world, which is closed off to members of mainstream society.

Proselytising children

So if there are armies of gay people who exist as a mafia or have their own secret rings or circles, then what are they trying to do? There are two discourses which explicitly reference gay people's supposed attempts to gain power. As Thompson (1998: 43) points out: 'No age group is more associated with risk in the public imagination than that of "youth" ... Youth may be regarded as both at risk and a source of risk in many moral panics.' So we find a discourse of homosexuality that is associated with their alleged attempts to influence children and is strongly linked to one of the most controversial and long-running ideological battles over homosexuality: Clause 28.

Clause 28 was introduced by Margaret Thatcher's Conservative Government in 1988, and stated that a local authority should not 'promote homosexuality or publish material for the promotion of homosexuality ... promote the teaching in any maintained school of the acceptability of homosexuality as a pretended family relationship by the publication of such material or otherwise.' The *Daily Mail* has therefore reproduced the negative discourse of homosexuality that was reified within the wording of Clause 28, by referring to the *promotion* of homosexuality 19 times, see Table 3.12 (the *Mirror* does not make use of this discourse). For example, the *Daily Mail* describes Clause 28 as a 'ban on local authorities promoting gay sex in schools' (July 13, 2001), an ambiguous phrase which makes it sound as if

Table 3.12 Terms related to gay people influencing children

L1 terms	Daily Mail	R1 terms
adoption by 5, extolling 1, promotion of 5, preach 1, promote/ing 7	gay(s)	adoption/ing/s 35, dad 1, 'families' 1, literature 2, parents 2, propaganda 8
promotion of 1, preach 1, promote/ing 5	homosexual(s)	families 2, material 1, parents 1, propaganda 7

L1 terms	*The* Mirror	R1 terms
	gay(s)	adoption 3, child/ren 4, dads 12, fathers 2
	homosexual(s)	dad 1

local authorities had been encouraging children to have gay sex while in the school grounds! The exact meaning of *promote* is difficult to elucidate. The *OED* gives it as 'to further, advance, encourage'. In the BNC it collocates strongly with words like *regeneration, equality, awareness, efficiency, welfare, health* and *stability*. It therefore has a semantic pattern associated with positive outcomes. So the phrase 'should *not* [my italics] promote homosexuality' makes sense if we understand that homosexuality should not be promoted because promotion is associated with good things, *ergo* homosexuality is not a good thing.

The *Daily Mail*'s frequent referral to Clause 28 and the promotion of homosexuality is due to the fact that Tony Blair's Labour Government had unsuccessfully tried to over-turn the Clause during the period under analysis. The word *extolling* has a similar semantic pattern, as does *preach* – a word which collocates in the BNC with *sermon, gospel* and *Jesus*. As with the words *devout* and *practising, preach* accesses a discourse of homosexuality as a religion – and one where its worshippers seek converts, e.g. 'New Code For Teachers "May Force Schools To Preach Gay Propaganda"' (the *Daily Mail*, July 13, 2001)

One of the ways that homosexuality can be promoted is via homosexual *propaganda, literature* or *materials*. The use of a word like *propaganda* frames the discourse of homosexuality as being a war rather than a religion. *Propaganda* (which did not feature in the original Clause 28 wording) collocates strongly in the BNC with the words *Nazi, Hitler, enemy, weapon, war* and *barrage*. The following excerpt of an article from the *Daily Mail* employs a number of war metaphors (shown in bold) in an article entitled 'Labour's stealth war on Clause 28'.

LABOUR is planning a new **assault** on the law banning homosexual **propaganda** in schools – this time by **stealth**. Following a series of

bruising defeats in the Lords on the issue, Ministers have conceded it would be pointless to **launch** a second **head-on attack** on Clause 28. But they are hoping to **neutralise** the clause by drawing up legislation to be brought in if their party wins the next General Election which bolsters the rights of 'Minorities' in the workplace, including gays and the disabled.

(The *Daily Mail*, December 26, 2000[7])

For the discourse of 'homosexual propaganda' to be effective, a related discourse, which assumes that sexual identities can be unstable, and therefore changed, must be accessed. It is mainly children who are seen as having unstable identities. For example, the *Daily Mail* (July 11, 2001) reports the Chief Rabbi Dr Jonathan Sacks as saying:

There is a real danger that the abolition of Section 28 will lead to the promotion of a homosexual lifestyle as morally equivalent to marriage. Not only will this confuse many young people whose sexual identities are still fluid. It will frustrate any attempt to educate children in the importance of marriage as the basis of a stable and caring society.

Another way that gay people are seen as potentially influencing children is by procreating or adopting. The *Daily Mail* refers to gay people adopting children 40 times, again with reference to parliament debates about allowing gay and unmarried couples to adopt children. The *Daily Mail* is generally against the idea, e.g. columnist Melanie Philips writes 'all children need a mother and father – which is why gay adoption is not a good idea' (January 24, 2002). In addition, the newspaper quotes members of the House of Lords or Parliament who are against gay couples being allowed to adopt:

The Government are still voicing serious concerns about the proposal. Lord Campbell Savours said he was particularly concerned that gay men would adopt vulnerable boys. 'It is not about abuse, it is about what could happen in the minds of these boys,' he said. 'Could boys in these circumstances become sexually confused?'

(The *Daily Mail*, December 6, 2002)

Tony Blair will back moves to allow unmarried and homosexual couples to adopt children, Downing Street signalled yesterday ... Baroness Young ... argued that taking children out of care and putting them in 'homes where relationships are fundamentally unstable is wrong'.

(The *Daily Mail*, May 9, 2002)

In addition to these discourses, children are shown to be particularly at risk from gay people in other ways. For example:

In a moving article, Vanessa Feltz described the agony her daughter faces on turning 16. She listed all the modern horrors – everything from gay chat rooms to over-developed thumbs from text messaging – that the kid must face as she becomes a young woman.

(The *Mirror*, March 28, 2002)

ALANIS Morissette has pretty peculiar expectations for her future children. The long-haired American warbler either wants one girl or six boys and, if it's the latter, she says: 'Hopefully one of them would be gay. Then I could support his feminine side.' How lovely.

(The *Mirror*, September 5, 2002)

Wanting to have a gay child is constructed as 'peculiar' and therefore sarcastically 'lovely', whereas a 16-year-old girl must be warned about the 'horrors' of gay chatrooms (but not presumably the horrors of heterosexual ones).

The gay lobby

While gay people are characterised as trying to influence children via propaganda or adoption, a related discourse suggests that they are attempting to gain political power through collaboration with the government and by campaigning for rights. The *Daily Mail* reports that the government is 'so obsessed with gay issues' (February 6, 2002) and that Tony Blair seems 'obsessed by gay rights' (October 2, 2002). They also talk about 'New Labour's contempt for marriage and Blair's continuing love affair with homosexuals' (February 25, 2001). This sexual relationship metaphor is echoed by the *Daily Mail*'s description of Lord Tebbit's attack on the Conservative Party: 'The former Conservative chairman launches a blistering attack today on the party's obsession with wooing ethnic and homosexual voters and demands a return to its core values' (August 1, 2002). Therefore, the government are also characterised as being gay, because they are wooing, obsessed by and have a love affair with gay people.

People who want gay rights are described as *activists*, *campaigners*, *pressure groups*, *protesters* and *demonstrators* (see Table 3.13). But they can also be *radicals* and *militants*. There are *demands* for gay rights and *pickets* are carried out. There is a gay *lobby*, and a gay *agenda*. Campaigners can be *strident* and *vociferous*:

At the heart of the vociferous activist gay lobby is the desire to prove that within every male there lurks strong homosexual tendencies. That after six pints of lager each one of us is capable of taking a partner at the other end of the ballroom.

(The *Daily Mail*, April 14, 2002)

Table 3.13 Terms related to political power

L1 terms	Daily Mail	R1 terms
activist 1, allow/s/ing 16, banned/ing 5, ban on 4, campaign/s/ing for 5, demands for 1, encourage(s) 3, equality for 3, give 3, influential 1, laws on 3, legalise 3, legal for 1, militant 3, obsessed by 1, obsession/ed with 7, outlawed/s 2, picketed by 1, recognition of 2, right(s) of 4, strident 1, support/s/ing 7, vociferous 1	gay(s)	activist(s) 10, agenda 1, campaign/er/s 4, debate 1, equality lobby 1, rights 2, issue(s) 8, lobby 23, marriage(s) 25, radicals 1, rights 67, wedding 9
advocates 2, allow(ing) 6, criminalising 1, decriminalise 2, equality for 1, forbidding 1, give/giving 4, governing 1, legalise 1, love affair with 1, let 1, make/making 2, militant 4, outlaws/ing 3, puts 1, radical 1, rights for 2, rights of 1, wooing 1	homosexual(s)	agenda 1, campaigner 1, equality 1, law reform 1, lobby(s) 2, marriage 12, movement 1, organisation 1, pressure group(s) 2, reforms 1, rights 1, unions 1 vote, 1, voters 2

L1 terms	*The* Mirror	R1 terms
allow(ing) 4, enabling 1, rights to 2	gay(s)	activist(s) 10, campaigner 1, cause 1, demonstrators 1, group(s) 4, issues 3, law 8, marriage 14, protesters 1, rights 33, vote 1, wedding(s) 17
	homosexual(s)	marriage 1, rights 5, weddings 1

Strong collocates of *lobby* in the BNC are *strong* and *powerful*. Collocates of *agenda* are *hidden* and *secret*.

One of the political advances that the gay 'lobby' appear to want is equal rights with heterosexual people. This would include the legal recognition of gay relationships and the decriminalisation of gay sex in public places to bring it in line with heterosexual sex in public places. The verbs *allow*, *enable*, *encourage*, *let*, *put*, *give* and *make* appear in the *Daily Mail*'s references to equality (my italics):

> This effectively *puts* homosexual couples on the same footing as married heterosexuals.
>
> (The *Daily Mail*, May 15, 2002)

The Pink Paper, which serves the homosexual community, greets the death of courageous, principled Lady Young with the headline: 'Activists delighted by death of bigoted baroness.' They say she'd have attempted 'to derail the bills which *give* gays partnership and adoption rights, protection against discrimination, and equalised indecency laws.' Charming world we live in, isn't it?

(The *Daily Mail*, September 17, 2002)

Colin Hart, director of the Christian Institute, warned that despite Mr Blunkett's assurances, the relaxation of the law could *encourage* gay men to have sex in public places.

(The *Daily Mail*, June 20, 2002)

In future our Government proposes to *let* gay couples adopt. How very New Labour. How politically correct. And how deeply depressing.

(The *Daily Mail*, May 8, 2002)

Another example of the 'gay lobby' discourse is shown in articles which suggest that gay men are receiving special rights or treatments at the expense of other sectors of society. For example, in an article entitled 'Care-Home Closures to Worsen the Trolley Crisis' (the *Daily Mail*, September 10, 2001), we are told that the NHS is paying for a country weekend break to help gay men to come to terms with their sexuality. A Tory MP is quoted as saying: 'To spend £3,000 in this way is an insult to people who are on the waiting list for vital treatment at hospitals throughout the country.' This emphasis on the 'opportunity cost' of gay equality has been shown as a favourite argument to other forms of 'political correctness' in tabloid newspapers (Johnson *et al.* 2003).

Discourses of heterosexuality

Before concluding, it is useful to compare the above discourses with the ways in which heterosexuals are discussed or framed in the tabloid newspapers. As already noted, the words *heterosexual* and *heterosexuals* occur comparatively fewer times than the words to do with homosexuality, suggesting that is the unmarked, normative case. In a large proportion of cases, heterosexuality is referred to alongside homosexuality, e.g. 'Existing law makes no distinction between heterosexual and homosexual adoptive parents' (the *Mirror*, May 8, 2002), although as shown above, the reverse is not true. That is, if homosexuality is discussed, it does not follow that heterosexuality will also be mentioned. This further validates heterosexuality as the normative, preferred status – only needing to be discussed in relationship to something that is not viewed as the norm.

There are also discourses which appear to mirror some of those related to homosexuality, although on a much smaller scale. For example, heterosexuals are described as *undeniably, supremely, confirmed* and *'blatantly'* (referencing the shamelessness discourse described above). They can also be *voraciously, rampant, dominant, aggressive* or *fearsomely* heterosexual (similar to the sexually aggressive discourse of homosexuality). Or they can be *repressed, closet, secretly* or *supposedly* heterosexual (similar to the secrecy discourse). However, I would argue that these discourses are comedic parodies which actually imply homosexuality rather than equivalent heterosexual reproductions of discourses based around homosexuality:

> John Bercow, 39, who resigned as Tory pensions spokesman because he supports gay adoption, parades his gorgeous leggy girlfriend, Sally Illman. Until his engagement to the ... advertising executive, his mother Brenda accompanied him to parties. A lady of my acquaintance told him: 'How sweet to bring your mother!' Mr Bercow replied: 'I'm a rampant heterosexual, you know.'
>
> (The *Daily Mail*, November 8, 2002)

> I think Oscar Wilde was a repressed heterosexual.
>
> (The *Daily Mail*, March 4, 2001)

Finally, a number of more straightforward terms occurring next to *heterosexual(s)* reference 'normality': *solidly, robustly, normal, monogamous, red-blooded, hot-blooded, merely, basically, jolly, strait-laced, happily married, purely, sober, thoroughly, strictly, beautiful* and *good-looking*. Again, these terms occur as part of the discourse of homosexuality as shameful, in sentences which aim to deny that a person is gay:

> Mr Smith stresses that he is solidly heterosexual and has never experienced gay tendencies.
>
> (The *Daily Mail*, November 10, 2002)

Interestingly, the only lexical collocate of *red-blooded* in the BNC is *male*, suggesting that a red-blooded heterosexual is one who is also defined by his masculinity.

Discussion

While both newspapers reproduce a range of connecting negative discourses surrounding homosexuality, there are also some differences in their underlying attitudes. The *Mirror* engages less often with the more politically based discourses, whereas the *Daily Mail* is more concerned about the consequences of equality and the effect of 'gay propaganda' on children (see Table 3.14 which summarises the frequencies of all of the discourses found). The *Daily Mail* also represents homosexuality as a behaviour more than the *Mirror*. I would argue that both newspapers still view homosexuality as

Table 3.14 Frequencies of terms which reference particular discourse types found

Discourse	Daily Mail	*The* Mirror
other minority groups	219	226
transiency	54	105
behaviour not identity	63	25
crime and violence	75	80
shame and secrecy	107	151
shamelessness	76	59
promiscuity	53	67
ubiquity	49	84
proselytising children	86	22
the gay lobby	294	107

something problematic, but to different degrees – with the *Daily Mail* being more openly hostile, using negative discourses of homosexuality in order to criticise the Labour Government. The 'gay lobby' discourse is the one which the *Daily Mail* engages in most often, suggesting that this is where their concerns are most focused. On the other hand, the *Mirror* is more focused on the shame and secrecy discourse, which appears to be a part of sensationalistic journalism, often concerned with reporting on the lifestyles of celebrities.

Tabloid newspapers now have to be more careful about the ways that they represent homosexuality than they did in the 1960s before decriminalisation, or in the 1980s, when AIDS was closely linked to gay men. What the current tabloid discourses therefore reveal are attempts to revive or prolong an older moral panic about homosexuality, particularly on behalf of the *Daily Mail*, by referring to older forms of language (e.g. more reliance on words like *homosexual* than in the *Mirror*) and legal language (e.g. terms like *consenting* and *promoting*). By relating homosexuality to sexual aggression, deviancy and impermanence, and creating a pair of discourses associated at the extremes of either secrecy/scandal and shamelessness/flamboyance, homosexuality is continually problematised – there is no middle way. Homosexuality, where it is found or suspected, must be commented on – whereas heterosexuality is passed over or assumed because it is not newsworthy. While homosexuality is seen as being against the norm, this view is enhanced by the fact that gay people are frequently associated in tabloid news with violence, crime, sleaze, promiscuity, prostitution or group sex. Tabloid reporting of homosexuality therefore contains a degree of prurience – shocked outrage in salacious tones.

The *Daily Mail*'s discourses of gay men as powerful, ubiquitous, secretive and proselytising suggests an underlying fear and anger – that a change is occurring which they are powerless to prevent. While the *Daily Mail*'s adherence to a long-standing moral panic on homosexuality makes sense if we take into account both its and the Labour Government's opposing political stances, the *Mirror*'s attitude appears more ambivalent. While there is acceptance that equality is necessary and a good thing, some journalists in the *Mirror* can't help commenting on difference, perhaps because it is there, and because it affords a quick joke:

> The gay community are to get their own Garda squad to help them cope with violence. It's nice to know they will have somebody to turn to in time of trouble. Just as long as they don't plan to walk the beat with their police chums – holding hands.
>
> (The *Mirror*, December 14, 2001)

Perhaps with the *Mirror*, we are seeing the final stages of the moral panic that peaked in 1963 with the 'How to Spot a Homo' article. Or perhaps moral panics over minority groups never completely die; they just adjourn for a few years or decades, with the media still continuing to present negative stereotypes, but in a more diffuse way, and without so many political references, until a major event or scandal brings them back. There are commercial motivations for tending the dying embers of a moral panic – newspaper sales do well from reviving them. Certainly, while the negative discourses continue to exist and are casually reported on an almost daily basis, it is easier for a moral panic to be resurrected if tabloid newspaper editors feel it necessary.

Although tabloid discourses of homosexuality may be thought of as being predictable to summarise, the results of this chapter suggest that, in fact, homosexuality is constructed in complex ways that are sometimes conflicting, frequently ambivalent and often insensitive. Although the political stance of the newspaper has some bearing on the focus of discourses around homosexuality, even the *Mirror*, with its more tolerant views, frequently accesses negative discourses to represent gay people. There are other ways that corpora could be used to identify discourses of homosexuality in the tabloid press (for example, by carrying out concordances of notable gay figures and examining the language used about them, or by focusing more on grammatical patterns, e.g. issues of agency, modality or passivisation). In addition, there are many more sites where negative discourses of homosexuality are accessed by and for mainstream groups. However, it is time now to turn away from the obviously negative, and instead focus on the ways that gay people are represented under different situations. We keep with mainstream audiences for the moment, but the next chapter focuses on representations of gay identity where at least one gay man had a considerable amount of input in their creation – the American situation comedy programme *Will & Grace*.

4 'True Man' and 'McFairyland'

Gay identities in an American sitcom

Introduction

Along with fast food, music, film and fashion, television is one of the most salient and abundant forms of American culture and, because of its popularity in many other parts of the world, such exports have been critically referred to as forms of *cultural imperialism*, a term proposed by Schiller in 1976, in order to explain the way in which the large multinational corporations, including the media, of developed countries, dominated developing countries. For example, Graddol (1996: 215) suggests that American gameshow formats, even when translated into other languages, still reproduce the behaviours and values associated with American society. Television therefore has the potential to transmit discourses far beyond the remit of a single nation.

The situation comedy (usually shortened to *sitcom*) is one of the most popular genres in American television, dating back to the 1950s with early incarnations like *I Love Lucy* (1951–61) and *Leave it to the Beaver* (1957–63) focused around patriarchal family units. Sitcoms generally fill a half-hour time slot of programming (with advertising) and usually feature a small cast of recurring central characters who react to and interact with each other in humorous ways, often while attempting to resolve a series of conflicts. Some sitcoms appear to be static, in that the 'situation' of the characters never appears to change from one episode to another – for example, only relationships between central characters are permanent. However, with other sitcoms, particularly those that are successful (and hence long-running), characters age and change, or new characters replace actors who leave the programme.

Sitcoms can be described as reflections of family life and are often linked to societal events, changes and issues, which are shaped by and/or may help to shape societies themselves. For example, in the 1970s, sitcoms such as *The Brady Bunch* and *Diff'rent Strokes* reflected the presence of non-traditional families in American society, and also helped to legitimate such families. In the 1980s, as well as showing traditional 'middle-class' households, sitcoms began to be more representative of a variety of identities or groups –

Roseanne featured a working-class family, *The Cosby Show* was set in a black household, while *The Golden Girls* featured a group of women aged over 50 living together. However, it has been argued that, ideologically, sitcoms fulfil an inherently conservative function, with almost every decade reconfiguring and updating the concept of the nuclear family (Caldwell 1995: 18). Taylor (1989) demonstrates how the 'myth' of the nuclear family on network television remained resilient in conservative 1980s sitcoms, whereas Hamamoto (1990) argues that even in its liberal manifestations, the sitcom has worked to preserve the mainstream, white status quo by eliding racial and ethnic issues. Marc (1989: 24) in his comparison of sitcoms and stand-up comedy, argues that 'experiments notwithstanding, the sitcom has generally upheld the sanctity of the proscenium, and producers ... have taken pains to respect the age-old tradition of grafting humor to moral suasion. . . . Sitcoms depend on familiarity, identification and redemption of popular beliefs.' Therefore, a sitcom tends to 'establish a range of comfortable emotions and familiar logics in whatever subject matter it addresses' (Marc 1989: 26).

In the 1990s, some American sitcoms moved away from the focus of the family, and instead placed characters in other (mainly urban) settings such as the workplace (e.g. *Veronica's Closet, Spin City, Caroline in the City*) or have concentrated on unrelated groups of friends (*Friends, Ellen, Sex in the City*) who act as each other's surrogate families. In the United States, the number of adults living alone rose from 17.1 per cent of all households in 1970, to 25.5 per cent in 2000, whereas married couples with their own children had fallen from 40.3 per cent in 1970 to 24.1 per cent in 2000 (Fields and Casper 2001: 3). With more adults remaining single than in previous decades, contemporary sitcoms have therefore foregrounded even more non-traditional concepts of the family. However, until the 1990s, gay and lesbian characters in sitcoms were under-represented, especially within core casts of characters. In 1997, a lesbian character was revealed in the sitcom *Ellen*. Both the title character, Ellen Morgan and the actress who played her, Ellen DeGeneres, 'came out' after the series had been running for three years. As a result of the decision to explore Ellen's sexuality, the series attracted criticism from right-wing groups and the media. For example, the magazine *Entertainment Weekly* put a picture of actress Ellen DeGeneres on its cover with the caption, 'Yep, she's too gay.' The programme was eventually cancelled.

In 1998, a second sitcom featuring gay characters was shown in America. This programme, *Will & Grace*, focused on a close long-term friendship between a gay man and a heterosexual woman living in Upper West Side Manhattan. In addition to these characters, Will had a gay friend called Jack, and Grace, who worked as a designer, had an assistant named Karen. These four characters appeared in the opening credits after the third series, establishing them as the core group. Holleran (2000: 65) refers to *Will & Grace* as the first 'gay sitcom', describing its content as 'not merely gay, but hard-edged, LA circuit-queen gay'.

The notion of 'success' within American television programming can be understood in a number of ways. For example, a programme can receive critical acclaim in the media, or it can attract a small number of fans who watch the programme regularly and help to publicise it via websites or fanzines. However, television executives generally measure 'success' by the Nielson rating system of audience viewing figures – a successful show will attract large audiences and enable the television network to charge higher prices to advertisers during the programme's commercial breaks.

While audiences found *Ellen* to be 'too gay' after the title character identified as a lesbian, *Will & Grace* proved to be more popular, usually gaining a 10–20 per cent share of the television-watching audience, and being particularly liked among viewers aged 18–25,[1] a group who are viewed as important to advertisers because they are more likely to have disposable incomes, are style-conscious (and style-leaders) and may have recently left home for the first time, requiring the purchase of commodities for their new living circumstances. As well as being popular among the 18–25 age group, *Will & Grace* was also well received by critics, as the following press release suggests:

> 'Will & Grace' has enjoyed both critical acclaim and ratings success. Since its debut, the show has been honored with an Emmy Award nomination for Outstanding Comedy Series, a People's Choice Award as Favorite New Comedy Series; a Golden Globe nomination for Best Comedy Series; an American Comedy Award nomination for Funniest Television Series; a GLAAD Media Award for Outstanding TV Comedy Series; Television Critics Association nominations for Outstanding New Program and Outstanding Achievement in Comedy; a TV Guide Award nomination for Favorite New Series and a Founders Award from the Viewers for Quality Television.
>
> Last year in its second season, 'Will & Grace' emerged as one of the biggest appointment programs on television. The show built on its lead-in by 63 per cent and ranked among the 1999–2000 season's top 20 series with a 6.2 rating and 16 share in the key adult 18–49 demographic.[2]
>
> (NBC, *Will & Grace* Press Release, August 2, 2000)

While *Will & Grace* has been critically acclaimed by gay groups (as the GLAAD Media Award suggests), its high viewing figures indicate that it is watched by a mainstream (i.e. mainly heterosexual) audience. As further evidence of its popularity, NBC producers moved the sitcom into their Thursday night 'Must See television' primetime slot during the 2000–1 season. Therefore the characters and storylines within *Will & Grace* can be said to have been accepted by a sizeable proportion of the American television-watching population. In addition, the export of *Will & Grace* to countries such as Sweden, Portugal, France, Finland, Germany, Austria, Britain and Turkey, and its subsequent overseas popularity, suggests that its discourses of homosexuality are at least accepted within contemporary western societies.[3]

It is the intention of this chapter to discover and analyse discourses pertaining to homosexuality within *Will & Grace* using a corpus-based analysis of the scripts. One potential problem with examining transcripts of spoken language data (whether real-life or scripted) is that paralinguistic and non-linguistic aspects tend to be over-looked (Hunston 2002: 23). For example, a character's tone of voice, their actions, facial expressions, personal attire and posture can be important in determining their mood or personality and will therefore give greater meaning to their speech. A reading of scripts of *Will & Grace* tends to confirm this – the programme makes more sense and is funnier when it is watched, rather than read. A corpus-based approach focusing only on linguistic aspects of human interaction will therefore be limited, and conclusions about discourses should be confined to the sphere of linguistic communication.

With that stipulation in mind, an analysis of the language of the characters should help to elicit some of the discourses of homosexuality that have helped to make *Will & Grace* acceptable to a large, western mainstream audience. I wish to focus on three aspects of the language: first, the use of words relating to sex and sexuality by all of the characters in the programme. Second, the speech of the two central gay characters, Will and Jack, in order to determine whether gay identity is constructed in a homogeneous way or whether they represent different 'types' of gay men (will their language use be similar or different, and in what ways?). Finally, I wish to examine the language of Grace and Karen, the central female characters in *Will & Grace*. An investigation of their roles and relationships to the other characters should enable a fuller understanding of the programme's overall structure and discourse types within it.

The data used in this chapter consists of written transcripts of 107 episodes of *Will & Grace*, representing all of the episodes from the first four seasons (a single season consists of between 20 and 25 episodes), and the first fifteen episodes of the fifth season (additional episodes had not been shown at the time the analysis was carried out). In total this consisted of 310,316 tokens. Stage directions, pauses or other paralinguistic information and the names of speakers were indicated by using adapted opening and closing sgml tags, but were not included in word counts or when calculating frequency data, e.g.:

<STAGE> Jack enters and leans back against the door. </STAGE>
<JACK> Ohh. Look at this. </JACK>
<STAGE> JACK pulls up his shirt revealing his stomach. </STAGE>
<GRACE> Aah! </GRACE>
<WILL> Jack, warn people before you do that. </WILL>

In order to make the speech more readable, any further examples from the scripts are quoted without sgml tags. As the speech was scripted, it was much more fluent than the speech of spontaneous conversation. Phenomena such as false starts, hesitations, self-corrections and inaudible or unclear speech were almost non-existent. It was therefore not difficult to represent utterances in a way that approached grammatical sentences, with appropriate punctuation marks. Clearly, with the high level of scripting in this data, it should not be concluded that the ways that Will and Jack talk are going to be representative of how 'real' gay people use language. Instead the data should reveal how the scriptwriters have accessed existing or created new discourses about homosexuality, filtered through the unreal yet uniquely moral medium of the television sitcom.

Discourses of sexuality and desire

While two of the four central characters in *Will & Grace* are gay men, the speech of *all* of the characters, including those who are not gay, can be said to contribute towards discourses about homosexuality, to a greater or lesser degree. To begin the analysis, concordances of the words *gay* (and a range of other terms referencing sexuality), *sexuality*, *sex* and *love* were carried out on the whole corpus, as it was hypothesised that these words would focus as sites around which discourses of sexual identity would openly appear in the scripts. The frequencies of words relating to sexual identity labels and their speakers are shown in Table 4.1. Only word senses which relate to sexuality

Table 4.1 Characters' use of words relating to sexuality

Word	Will	Grace	Jack	Karen	Other	Total
bi	0	2	0	1	0	3
breeders	0	0	0	0	1	1
fag	1	0	4	1	1	7
fairy	3	0	1	2	3	9
gay	143	84	119	42	90	478
hetero	0	0	3	1	1	5
heterosexual	1	1	3	0	2	7
homo	6	6	9	4	0	25
homosexual	3	1	2	1	2	9
lesbian	0	3	10	5	1	19
lez	0	0	2	2	0	4
lezzy	0	0	0	1	0	1
mary	2	1	3	7	0	13
queen	6	7	5	1	2	21
queer	5	3	6	3	2	19
sissy	1	1	2	2	1	7
straight	17	14	24	11	21	87
straightie	0	0	1	0	0	1
Total	188	123	194	84	127	715

are included in this table – so, for example, cases of *fairy* which do not refer to gay men have not been counted.

Of the four central characters in the sitcom, Will speaks the most (78,925 words), followed by Grace (76,610), Jack (51,839) and Karen (43,881). Proportionally, Jack's use of sexuality words is therefore higher than the table suggests – 0.37 per cent compared to Will's 0.23 per cent. However, what should be clear from the table is that all of the four central characters use a range of words relating to sexuality, including a relatively small proportion of pejorative words such as *sissy* and *homo*.

Of the 478 uses of the word *gay* in the *Will & Grace* corpus, only a small percentage of them refer directly to sex, so the phrase *gay sex* occurs twice, while *gay porn* occurs five times. The most common two-word phrases involving the word *gay* are *I'm gay* (31), *gay guy* (26), *gay man* (26), *you're gay* (22), *he's gay* (21), *gay bar* (19), *gay men* (14) and *gay guys* (12). The most common immediate collocates of *gay* therefore imply identity rather than behaviour. Less frequent collocates relate to notions of gay community: as well as *gay bar*, there is *gay men's chorus* (7), *gay scene* (6), *gay club* (6), *gay cabaret* (3), *gay group therapy* (4), *gay community* (2), *gay culture* (2), *gay sensitivity seminar* (2) and *gay disco* (1).

A number of the IS *gay* and *gay guy/man* constructions refer to the relationship between the two central characters in the sitcom, which is frequently problematised, particularly by the supporting character Karen. Grace is viewed as having a long-standing inability to form relationships with heterosexual men:

KAREN: Well honey, I figured that since he's gay and she's a handlebar moustache away from being gay herself. . .

(Episode 4.25)

KAREN: Oh Lord. There's a lot of gay guy–straight girl couples. It's like a hologram of your past relationships.

(Episode 4.20)

KAREN: Oh honey, how's she ever gonna get married if she's playing house with a gay guy?

(Episode 1.2)

WILL: [to Grace] I can't believe you ended up with another gay guy, it's so sad.

(Episode 3.1)

GRACE: What happens if I never meet anybody? Shouldn't I at least get first dibs? Isn't that one of the privileges of the 'straight girl gay guy' relationship? Shouldn't you be my fallback sperm?

(Episode 2.11)

The word *homosexual* only occurs nine times in the data, and appears to be used in a more self-conscious or ironic way than *gay*. For example, Will parodies the 'scientific' discourse of homosexuality as a medical condition by using it to explain why he owns so many boxer briefs: 'The homosexual is the leading exponent of the underpant hybrid.' In addition, another character who has recently 'come out' and is going on a date with Will says awkwardly, 'I'm sorry I'm late, I didn't know what to wear for our second homosexual date.' Will replies: 'Oh traditionally, whatever's hanging on your homosexual chair in your homosexual bedroom.' The notion of labelling a date as 'homosexual' is made to appear as inappropriate or unnecessary as a 'homosexual chair'.

Will & Grace also contains a number of words which appear to be more pejorative about homosexuality. These include *homo* (25), *queer* (19), *fag* (7), *sissy* (7) and *lez* (4). In addition *gays* as a collective noun occurs 12 times.

Queer is used in both pejorative and reclaiming senses. For example, when Grace says that Will came back from Europe early to go to the Barney's sale, Will responds with: 'Grace, you say it that way, you make it sound so queer' as if *queer* is something to be ashamed of. However, in another episode Grace echoes a political slogan to Will: 'We're here, we're queer, and he better get used to it.' Other uses show a sense of ambivalence or ambiguity, and often involve rhymes or puns. For example, in episode 5.14, Karen tells a rival for her friendship with Jack: 'You may have taken my steer, but I'll be damned if you're gonna take my queer.' While in episode 4.3 she sarcastically tells Will: 'OK I get it now, you're coming in loud and *queer*.'

The same sorts of structures apply to the word *homo*. Will says 'homo on the range' instead of 'Home on the Range'. Jack says 'Homo, I don't think we're in Barney's any more', punning on the Judy Garland line from the Wizard of Oz: 'Toto, I don't think we're in Kansas any more.' Will calls Jack 'Homo Wan Kenobi' and 'a homo without a home'. However, at other times *homo*, like *queer*, can be used when characters insultingly want to point out stereotypically 'gay' behaviour. During a word game Grace says, 'Broad?' and Will replies with, 'Way.' She responds with: 'No not Broadway you homo. Broad shoulders.' During an argument, Jack and Will trade insults, calling each other 'blouse wearing fairy', 'girl', 'eye-brow plucker' and 'homo'.

Karen typically uses *gay* as a plural noun when she wants to criticise or comment on Will or Jack by claiming that their behaviour is stereotypically representative of all gay people: 'You gays and your discipline', 'The gays love their presents. Just wave something shiny in front of their faces, you can get whatever you want', 'Wow. The gays really love their rules.' The word *gays* is marked as being pejorative or insensitive in other episodes. For example, in episode 3.4, during a gay sensitivity seminar Will is hosting for the police, the following exchange occurs, showing why the need for such a seminar exists:

OFFICER KIRK: Alright, let's get started. Everybody take your seats. OK, welcome to the Caribbean sensitivity seminar.

WILL: Uh, actually, officer, we're, uh . . .

OFFICER KIRK: Oh, yeah, right. Sorry. Today we're doing the gays. Let's, uh, give 'em a warm welcome.

WILL: Thank you – Ahem – Very much.

However, homophobia is not limited to heterosexual characters. For example, in the same episode, Jack makes several stereotyping and insulting references to lesbians. He also pejoratively uses the word *straightie* twice to refer to heterosexual characters, which is perhaps an attempt by the scriptwriters to show that prejudice about sexuality isn't limited to homophobia or made by heterosexual people. His comments about heterosexuality sometimes parody negative attitudes towards heterosexuality, e.g. 'Politically, I'm tolerant of the heterosexual lifestyle, but the actual act is rather revolting' (episode 1.20), 'Heterosexual marriage is just wrong. I mean, if God had intended man and woman to be together he would have given them both penises' (episode 2.19), 'Suffering is a state of mind – quite like heterosexuality or the Mid West' (episode 4.13).

Additionally, a storyline relating to Will's internalised homophobia is addressed in episode 1.19 when Will is embarrassed in public by Jack and tells Grace: 'Sometimes he's such a fag.' Jack overhears and in a later scene acts stereotypically and offensively masculine:

JACK: Did you catch the Knicks game last night? It rocked, huh?

WILL: It can't be National Butch Day, 'cause the banks are still open . . .

JACK: [to a woman] Hey, Betty. Nice rack.

WOMAN: You're an idiot.

JACK: Thanks. Probably a lez, huh?

WILL: You just spat on your shoe. What are you doing?

JACK: Well, you know the old saying – a rolling *fag* gathers no moss.

WILL: What?

JACK: Yeah, you can lead a *fag* to water, but you can't make him drink. A penny saved is a *fag* earned.

WILL: Jack, you –

JACK: I heard what you called me the other day . . . I'd rather be a fag than afraid.

However, the longstanding friendship between Will and Jack is demonstrated in episode 2.8, when Will tries to convince Jack to tell his mother he is gay:

WILL: Remember that time at Matt Stokes' party where we met for the first time, and I was in such deep denial about being gay, I think I was 20 pounds overweight?

JACK: 30.

WILL: Maybe 25.

JACK: Maybe 35.

WILL: Anyway . . . You came up to me. We didn't know each other that well. You pulled me aside, and you said, 'Aren't you tired yet?' And I was tired. Tired of actually reading *Playboy* for the articles. Tired of keeping my Bette Midler albums in Led Zeppelin sleeves. So you took me to clubs and introduced me to people, made me realise what I'd been missing by not being myself. And I'm thankful for that.

JACK: I – I also taught you how to dance without pointing all the time.

WILL: And I'm thankful for that. Now here's my secret: I admire you, Jack. Because you are more yourself than anyone else I have ever known.

JACK: Will, look, I appreciate what you're trying to do, but. . . This is different. My mother will fall apart. She's –

WILL: Jack, Jack, Jack, Jack, Jack. Aren't you tired yet?

Therefore, an over-arching discourse of homosexuality in *Will & Grace* could be described as a 'be yourself', moral discourse. There is a focus on sexuality as identity rather than behaviour and an emphasis on the importance of 'coming out' in order to 'be yourself' in addition to accepting that gender performances which are honest are preferable to those which are seen as traditionally acceptable yet dishonest. Being yourself is seen as preferable to the alternatives: being *tired* or *afraid*. Finally, this discourse stresses the importance of accepting *all* forms of sexual identity, not simply gay identity.

However, the positive representation of homosexuality in *Will & Grace* is not allowed to detract from the humour of the sitcom, nor does it allow the characters to become too comfortable with each other – happy endings or scenes where characters resolve their problems or differences are frequently punctured by a final ironic remark. For example, at the end of the 'are you tired yet?' scene, Will and Jack hug. Jack's final comment to Will, 'Hmm, somebody needs to go back to the gym', serves to diffuse any sexual tension caused by the men hugging, and also reminds the audience that despite the 'message' of acceptance, morality comes secondary to humour. One of the aspects of *Will & Grace* which defines it as different from earlier sitcoms is its reflexivity. In episode 2.14, for example, Jack is furious because a gay kiss is cut from a sitcom called *Along Came You*. While *Along Came You* doesn't exist outside of *Will & Grace*, this episode acknowledges that in real life such kisses have been withdrawn from American programmes so as not to offend the 'viewing American majority' or commercial television sponsors (see Hantzis and Lehr 1994: 119–20, Hubert 1999: 35). Will isn't overly concerned about the withdrawal of the kiss, although Jack encourages him to complain to the television network. After their complaint isn't taken seriously, Will unexpectedly kisses Jack during a live television broadcast of *The Today Show*, as a political statement:

JACK: Anyways, um, the reason we're here. Um, I don't know if you're aware, but on this week's episode of *Along Came You*, there was supposed to be a kiss and there wasn't.

TV PRESENTER: You know, Jack, sometimes a kiss is just not a kiss. Do we have any annivers –

JACK: Whoa, whoa, whoa, back to Jack. We went to complain, and this
   closet case upstairs – cute, in an offbeat way, got his number – totally
   gave us the brush off. And I just want to know how long I'm going to
   have to wait until I can see two gay men kiss on network television.
WILL: Not as long as you'd think. (He kisses Jack).

While the kiss between Will and Jack could be read as an authentic, taboo-
shattering incident (Holleran (2000: 66), for example, writes: '[the charac-
ters] seemed so free, so believable all of a sudden, out in the open air. There
was spaciousness about their world, and suddenly the possibility of their
interaction with real life, the real city, and real emotions, rose up'),
Provencher (2004) argues that the context of the kiss

> illustrates the lack of affection between two same-sex characters that
> continues to persist on primetime commercial television ... So many
> layers of artifice now exist between the spectator of *Will & Grace* and the
> two characters (Will and Jack) that the kiss remains virtually impossible
> to read as an authentic form of expression between two gay men.

The fact that Will and Jack have become actors in a television broadcast
(*The Today Show*) within another television show (*Will & Grace*) means that
the kiss occurs as a play within a play (Forestier 1981) and the television
audience are separated from it, particularly by the displacement of viewing
pleasure – the audience gets to witness the reactions of other characters
watching the kiss (Grace, Karen, Rosario, etc.).

There are 656 occurrences of the word *love* in the scripts, of which 115 of
them consist of the phrase *I love you*. This is the most popular three-word
phrase containing the word *love* (the next most common is *in love with*,
occurring 29 times). An analysis of *I love you* shows that many of these cases
are not straightforward declarations of romantic love but are often ironic,
cases of reported speech, exaggerations or expressions of happiness, friendship or familial love. The phrase *in love with* reveals much more about the
network of desire which exists between the main characters. It is apparent
that Grace is in love with Will, which is the reason why she is unable to
form relationships with other (heterosexual) men:

GRACE: Come on, help me. I need a good lie.
KAREN: Oh, I know. Honey, come on, that's easy. Just tell him you're madly
   in love with Will. Of course, I don't know where the lie part comes in,
   but... Now, I think it'll work.

(Episode 2.14)

WILL: Whenever [Grace] hits a real low point, she breaks out the slide projec-
   tor and spends a few days trying to figure out 'where it all went wrong'.
JACK: I'd say it was the day she became a gay man and fell in love with you.

(Episode 4.7)

In episode 1.6 Grace points out that when Will told her he was gay 'everything changed' and ever since she has been waiting for him to 'change her world' with his next big secret. During episode 3.8, in a 'flash-back' sequence where we see this event occur, we learn that Will and Grace were engaged to be married while at college. At the point where they are about to have sex, Will tells her: 'I don't think I really knew for sure until we were in bed together. You know? And I took one look at you in your sexy underwear, and I just went . . . "Whoa. I am gay." You know? I mean, do you know what I mean?' Grace responds with 'You bastard! I'm in love with you, and you're treating me like some sort of test drive!' So, in addition to positive discourses that emphasise tolerance, equality and self-expression, a somewhat competing discourse which is some- times found in *Will & Grace* is a 'What a shame (that all the eligible men are gay)' discourse, referring to the fact that Will would be an ideal partner for Grace if only he were heterosexual. This discourse, being similar to those found in the films *The Object of My Affection* (1998) and *The Next Best Thing* (2000), is positioned from the heterosexual female character's point of view.[4]

Also in the flashback episode, Jack confesses that he's in love with Will while they are shopping:

WILL: Should we do sweet potatoes or mashed?

JACK: Mashed, and I'm in love with you.

WILL: Ahem. What?

JACK: Will, why are we pretending? We spend every second together. We call each other a hundred times a night. I saw the way you were looking at me the other day when we were at that place shopping for shoes.

WILL: Look, Jack. I owe you everything, you know? I mean, this past year, coming out. You've been like my shepherd through the Himalayas of – Of him-a-laying. But I just don't feel that way about you, you know? I love you the way you love a cherished family pet. That you never want to have sex with. We're meant to be girlfriends, not boyfriends, you know? It's better that way.

Will is therefore positioned as the ideal partner for both Grace and Jack although he does not return either of their affections because Grace is a woman, and Jack is too much like a 'girlfriend' or a 'pet'. The fact that a romantic reso- lution can never be reached for these three central characters is in keeping with the sarcasm and ambiguity of the concluding lines of the more serious scenes, which prevents any moral message from over-riding the humour.

There is only one occurrence of the word *sexuality* in the *Will & Grace* corpus, although its use is enlightening in that it indicates a major dif- ference between Will and Jack: '*Will*: Maybe I don't wear my sexuality like a sash and a tiara the way Jack does, but I am willing to put my gayness up against anybody's.' Another difference between Will and Jack is found by examining a concordance of the word *sex* (135 occurrences). Will is often characterised as celibate:

JACK: We are in the apartment that sex forgot.

(Episode 4.16)

GRACE: When was the last time you had same-sex sex?'
WILL: I'm choosy!

(Episode 4.8)

Jack, on the other hand, is constructed as having a more seasoned and body-conscious attitude towards gay sexuality:

JACK: (at the gym) Come on! Let's go, let's go! Push! Remember: No pecs, no sex!
BARRY: This all seems so superficial. Are gay guys only about bodies and faces?
JACK: Absolutely not. They're only about bodies. Faces you can cover up with a cute hat or leather hood.

(Episode 5.13)

JACK: Sex is a drug, Karen. I should know. I'm a licensed dealer.

(Episode 5.1)

Therefore, while Will and Jack are both gay men, their sexual identities are constructed differently. Will's homosexuality is not as 'obvious' as Jack's, and he is characterised as having fewer relationships, whereas Jack is viewed as more sexually confident, to the point of being promiscuous.

Will and Jack

So far an analysis of sexuality-related words in *Will & Grace* has demonstrated how attitudes towards homosexuality and homophobia are presented via the character's speech as well as showing the existence of a network of unrequited love within the sitcom, centred around Will. However, in order to examine discourses of homosexuality further in the sitcom, it is necessary to further consider the ways that the characters are constructed in relation to each other. Why, for example, is Grace attracted to Will and not Jack? What are the major differences between Jack and Will's language use? In what other ways are they represented as being *gay*? And why is it necessary to include a fourth (heterosexual, female) character, Karen, in the sitcom?

As suggested by the fact that Will speaks more than the other characters in the sitcom and has his name in the title of the programme, he is the lead male character, with Jack acting as a supporting male lead. In order to focus on differences or similarities between Will and Jack based on their language use, I wish to analyse the most common differences between the two characters. Using all of Will's speech across every episode in the corpus as a single 'text', it is possible to compare it against Jack's speech. As seen in Chapter 2 with the examination of the two sides of the House of Lords debate on the age of consent, this should result in a list of lexical keywords, or words which occur in one text proportionally more often than expected when compared with the other. This approach to dramatic texts has been carried out successfully by Culpeper (2001) who analysed keywords in the language of six characters from the play *Romeo and Juliet*. Culpeper justifies comparing the speech of the characters against each other as follows:

> Characters are partly shaped by their context. Thus, it makes little sense to compare, say, the characters of Romeo and Juliet with the characters of Macbeth or Antony and Cleopatra, since the fictional worlds of Italy, Scotland and Egypt provide very different contextual influences. Furthermore, characters, like people, are partly perceived in terms of whom they interact. Indeed, linguists have argued that interaction itself can reveal personality. Brown and Levinson put it thus: 'an understanding of the significant dimensions on which interaction varies should provide insights into the dimensions on which personality is built, as well as social relationships' (1987: 232).
>
> (Culpeper 2001: 16)

However, while Culpeper looked at lexical keywords, it is also possible to focus on differences at the grammatical or semantic rather than lexical level. A potential problem with deriving and examining lexical keywords is that differences based upon semantic prosody or colligation may be overlooked. For example, if Jack uses a group of similar words like *fabulous, fantastic, super* and *terrific* more than Will, none of these words may be revealed as key because each one occurs too infrequently to be taken into consideration. However, if we consider these words as a category in itself – say, of 'positive intensifiers' – and compared the total frequency of words in this category for Will and Jack, we may find that the category itself is key in Jack's speech. The same kind of process could be carried out on grammatical categories. For example, if Will uses 2000 modal verbs overall, and Jack only uses 1000 modals, a log-linear test could be carried out to determine whether Will's use of modal verbs is 'key' when compared to Jack's. Therefore, in this chapter, ways of considering keywords beyond the lexical level are examined.

However, in order to examine key semantic and grammatical categories, it is necessary to carry out additional levels of encoding upon the *Will & Grace* corpus. Such a list will still only give categories that are based on single words (although in some cases multi-word units are labelled as occurring as one category – for example *sort of* is usually tagged as an adverbial idiom) – but by examining concordances based on these categories, it should be possible to uncover more complex grammatical or semantic patterns.

Therefore, the scripts were run through a web interface developed at Lancaster University called Wmatrix (Rayson 2001). This interface was created in order to annotate corpora by assigning part of speech and semantic tags to raw text data. It accessed a program called CLAWS (Constituent Likelihood Automatic Word-tagging System) to carry out the grammatical tagging; the same program had been used to part-of-speech tag the British National Corpus (see Garside and Smith 1997). The tag set consists of 18 main part of speech categories that are then sub-divided into a further 137 grammatical tags. For example, the category 'verb' contains 31 different types of verbs to show modality, tense and lexical versus auxiliary verbs. The full tag set is shown in the Appendix. As shown in the example below, a word containing cliticisation can be split into its grammatical components in order to receive more than one tag (e.g. *I've* becomes I_PPIS1 've_VH0), while a set of words that form an idiomatic phrase are each tagged as if they are a fractional part of a single tag (e.g. the prepositional idiom *outside of* becomes outside_II21 of_II22). An example of a grammatically tagged section of the corpus is shown below:

> <WILL> Oh_UH,_, Grace_NP1,_, I_PPIS1 'm_VBM sorry_JJ._.
> I_PPIS1 could_VM n't_XX control_VVI myself_PPX1._. It_PPH1
> 's_VBZ just_RR ..._... outside_II21 of_II22 a_AT1 circus_NN1 contor-
> tionist_NN1,_, he_PPHS1 's_VBZ the_AT only_JJ man_NN1 I_PPIS1
> 've_VH0 ever_RR met_VVN that_CST can_VM actually_RR blow_VVI
> smoke_VV0 up_RP his_APPGE own_DA ass_NN1._. </WILL>

This grammatical tagging system also allows distinctions between uses of words based on different grammatical functions to be taken into consideration: e.g. gaze_NN1 (noun) versus gaze_VVB (verb).

A second program called USAS (UCREL Semantic Analysis System) (Wilson and Thomas 1997) accomplished the semantic tagging. The semantic tag set was originally loosely based on Tom McArthur's *Longman Lexicon of Contemporary English* (McArthur 1981). It has a multi-tier structure with 21 major discourse fields, sub-divided and with the possibility of further fine-grained sub-division in certain cases. In some cases, tags can be assigned a number of plus or minus codes to show where meaning resides on a binary or linear distinction. For example, the code T3 refers to 'Time: Old, new and young; age', so the word *kids* is assigned T3− placing it at one end of a linear scale, whereas a word like *pensioner* would receive T3+. In addition, when words can fit into more than one semantic category, they may receive more than one semantic tag, shown by a forward slash sign. So *kids* is also tagged as S2mf which places it in the category of 'People'. The full tag set is shown in the Appendix. An example of a semantically tagged section of the corpus is shown below:

> <JACK>_PUNC Why_Z5 is_A3+ n't_Z6 there_Z5 any_N5.1+
> coffee_F2 ?_PUNC </JACK>_PUNC
> <KAREN>_PUNC Same_A6.1+++ reason_A2.2 you_Z8mf do_Z5
> n't_Z6 have_A9+ a_Z5 wife_S4f and_Z5 three_N1 kids_T3-
> /S2mf._PUNC It_Z8 's_A3+ the_Z5 way_X4.2 God_Z4 wants_X7+
> it_Z8._PUNC </KAREN>_PUNC

After the corpus was tagged grammatically and semantically, WordSmith was used in order to obtain frequency lists of the number of grammatical and semantic tags used by each character in the corpus. These frequency lists were then compared against each other in order to reveal key semantic and grammatical categories that were distinct for different characters. The results are discussed below, beginning with a comparison of Will and Jack.

Semantic comparison (Will/Jack)

Table 4.2 shows the semantic categories which were key in Jack's speech, when compared against Will's speech, at the level of $p < 0.001$ (using log-linear tests), while Table 4.4 shows categories that were key in Will's speech when compared to Jack's. Because Will's speaks much more than Jack in the scripts, the best indicator of difference is by comparing the two columns marked '%' rather than comparing raw frequencies with each other.

The strongest semantic category which occurs more often in Jack's speech when compared to Will's is that of female names. The majority (68 per cent) of these names refer to Karen, one of the other recurring characters on the sitcom, who Jack has a close friendship with. However, a number of the other female names used by Jack refer to actresses or celebrities: *Cher* occurs 18 times while *Farrah Fawcett-Majors, Jennifer Love Hewitt, Jennifer Jason Leigh, Joan Van Ark, Lara Flynn Boyle, Sarah Jessica Parker, Penelope Cruz* and *Rosemary Clooney* are also referenced. This preference of mentioning actresses with three names serves a particular communicative function for Jack, who states their names as exclamatives, e.g.: 'Wait a minute. Farrah Fawcett-Majors! I've got it!' Jack also uses the name *Mary* seven times in a way

Table 4.2 Key semantic categories in Jack's speech, when compared to Will's

Label	Semantic category	Will's speech		Jack's speech		Keyness
		Frequency	*%*	*Frequency*	*%*	
Z1F	names: female	246	0.12	284	0.21	42.5
B1	anatomy/physiology	658	0.32	567	0.42	22.9
Z99	unmatched	3056	1.50	2241	1.68	16.9
O4.3	colours	70	0.03	87	0.07	16.1
X2.5	understand	95	0.05	109	0.08	16.0
Z4	discourse bin	4848	2.37	3461	2.59	15.5
T1.1.2	time, present, simultaneous	341	0.17	296	0.22	12.5
S3.2	relationship: intimate/sexual	404	0.20	343	0.26	12.5
S4M	kin: male	107	0.05	111	0.08	11.5
K4	drama, theatre, showbusiness	275	0.13	242	0.18	11.2

which tends to be exclamative. *Mary* is described as a gay vernacular word (Rodgers 1972: 131) being used as a general exclamation, e.g. 'Oh Mary!', although any gay man can also be referred to as a Mary. Jack uses Mary as an exclamation by invoking the name of the 1970s pop group Peter, Paul and Mary (in the same way that Farrah Fawcett-Majors is used): 'Well Peter, Paul and Mary, you are fabulous!' or the names of Mary-Kate and Ashley, teenage twins who have their own television show 'Mary-Kate and Ashley! It's beautiful!' Here Mary-Kate stands in as two names. Jack's exclamative use of Peter, Paul and Mary is a variant on Montagu's 'profane' category of swearing (1967: 105) by uttering the names of religious figures, e.g. 'Oh Jesus, Mary and Joseph' or 'Jesus H. Christ!' In Jack's worldview, his deities are not traditional religious figures, but female stars from the entertainment world.

Therefore, Jack uses a sequence of three proper nouns (most usually the names of female celebrities) in order to show surprise or emphasis, a trait that none of the other characters share. Stylistically, lists of three items have particular discourse significance; for example, in political speeches, points are sometimes made in groups of three for rhetorical effect, whereas Jack's 'name-dropping' of famous people who have middle or hyphenated names could be a strategy that links him to an ironic notion of high culture or importance.

In addition, Jack uses *Mary* to refer to Will in an insulting way: 'Put the kettle on Mary, we're going to the gym' or by calling him 'Mary Fat-Jeans'. In episode 3.8, he refers to an incident in the past when Will and Grace were dating, which he labels 'When Mary met Sally', a parody of the film *When Harry Met Sally*.

Jack's use of female names, and in particular his use of *Mary*, can therefore be characterised in terms of Harvey's descriptive framework of verbal camp (see Table 4.3). A parody of femininity is achieved by the use of female names as exclamations, but in other cases there is inversion of gendered proper nouns (referring to Will as Mary), while ludicrism is achieved by the punning of 'When Mary met Sally'.

The next strongest key semantic category in Jack's speech involves words connected to anatomy or physiology, in particular *hair, eyes, face, back, head, heart, body, feet, eat, hand, teeth, boobs, nose, shoulders* and *drink*. Taken individually, none of these words (other than *eyes*) would have been lexical keywords, but collectively as a semantic field, they suggest that Jack talks about body parts and bodily processes significantly more frequently than Will. Jack's more frequent use of colours and colour-related terms could be seen as an aspect of Lakoff's 'women's language' (1975: 8–9), particularly his use of rare colour shades (Jack refers to *tangerine, lemon* and *powder blue*). This category is often linked to body parts in Jack's speech, e.g: 'I guess maintaining the shades of red in your hair keeps you so busy.' Jack's use of body and colour words therefore suggests a preoccupation with physical appearance. A lexical keyword that Jack uses is *fat*, which is almost always used to criticise Will's weight.

Table 4.3 A descriptive framework for verbal camp, reproduced from Harvey (2000: 243)

Strategy	Surface features
1 Paradox through	incongruities of register
	explicitness and covertness
	'high' culture and 'low' experience
2 Inversion of	gendered proper nouns
	grammatical gender markers
	expected rhetorical routines
	established value system
3 Ludicrism by	
a) heightened language awareness through	motivated naming practices
	puns/word-play
b) pragmatic force through	double-entendre
4 Parody of	
a) aristocratic mannerism by	use of French
b) femininity by	innuendo
	hyperbole
	exclamation
	vocatives

Jack also uses a relatively high number of words which were unfamiliar to the semantic tagger and therefore tagged as 'unmatched' (Z99). At this stage it is hypothesised that Jack's speech contains a more unpredictable or creative use of language than Will's, something that we will examine more closely when looking at the key grammatical categories.

A category described as 'understand' also occurs more often in Jack's speech. This reveals a higher number of cognition verbs such as *realise* and *understand*, or verb phrases which orient to cognition such as *got it*, *figure it out* and *makes sense*.

This semantic category can be represented via a variety of grammatical patterns. For example, the speaker (Jack) can refer to his ability to understand (or lack of it), or someone else's understanding (or lack of). In addition, Jack can orient to the subject of understanding by asking a question, e.g., 'Do you realise what's happening?' or using an imperative, 'You figure it out'. These two forms can imply that the speaker thinks that the hearer does not understand something, although this is not always the case. For example, a question form like 'Did you understand that?' may simply indicate the speaker's uncertainty about the hearer's understanding. In addition, use of tense and modality can position the speaker's impressions of the hearer's ability to understand in different ways: 'You'll understand eventually' implies the hearer doesn't understand at the moment, but will at some unspecified future date.

The most common grammatical pattern within this category that Jack uses takes the form of first person positive, e.g. 'I understand', occurring 28 times whereas he expresses understanding in the first person negative eight times. When talking about other people, this pattern is reversed – the second/third person positive occurs five times, whereas the second/third person negative occurs on 15 occasions. Therefore, Jack is constructed as claiming to have more knowledge about situations than the people around him. Will is more likely than Jack to use the first person negative (e.g. *I don't understand*) with this semantic category (14 times), although is still more likely to use the first person positive overall (15 times). He also tends to conclude that other people do understand something (13 times) rather than not (ten times). Will also tends to express doubt at other people's understanding by hedging an utterance as a question (15 times as opposed to three times for Jack). Jack's speech therefore appears to be more confident and assured, while Will is more hesitant.

Another key semantic category used more frequently by Jack is the 'discourse bin', consisting of discourse markers, e.g. greetings (*hello, hi*), agreement/disagreement (*yes, no, obviously, I know, mm, right*), exclamations (*oh, wow, aha, damn, god*), politeness (*please, thanks*), apologies (*sorry*) and fillers (*um, uh*). This category is associated with spoken, rather than written, texts (Stenström 1990) and is one of Biber's (1988: 102) features of an involved, rather than informational style of language (although Biber only cites five discourse particles in his study: *well, now, anyway, anyhow* and *anyways* (1988: 241)).

Category T1.1.2 refers to the time: present, simultaneous. Jack uses more words such as *now, currently, today, tonight* and the phrases *right now, so far* and *these days*. The most frequent word in this category that Jack uses, *now* (occurring 172 times or 58 per cent of this category), has two main functions in his speech. It can be used to strengthen an imperative: 'Now be gone, before someone drops a house on you!' (see the sample concordance of Jack's uses of *now* in Table 4.4). And it can also refer to a change from previous events: 'Now I know why Evita was such a bitch.' It could be hypothesised that Jack's orientation to the present simultaneous suggests that he is more likely to 'live in the present' than Will, although it is difficult to be certain about this explanation as the present simultaneous has a wide range of meanings.

Jack also talks more about intimate relationships, using words like *boyfriend, couples, kiss, love, romance* and phrases like *blind date, go out with* and *sleep with*. He also talks about male relatives more frequently than Will – in particular using the words *father, dad* and *daddy*. There appear to be two reasons for this. A long-running storyline concerns Jack's search for his real father, whereas a humorous expression that he commonly uses is 'who's your daddy?', where *daddy* is used as gay slang to refer to a dominant sexual partner. The final semantic category which Jack uses more often is to do with drama, the theatre and showbusiness but this is probably because Jack's ambition is to be a successful actor.

There are six semantic categories that occur more often in Will's speech

Table 4.4 Sample concordance of Jack's use of *now*

by gets here. That's not what she needs	now	. And I should know. I am a mother.
adverse to that. I'll take that present	now	.
eah, vell, the law sucks, darling. Oh,	Now	I've gone and worked up an appetite.
	Now	be gone before someone drops a house o
n't I? Now, back to zero. Your date is	now	becoming very bored with you. You ca
ds arrive to mourn his sudden passing.	Now	!
t of things I'd like to do to you right	now	. I just need a yes or a
was good. I was too good, I think. And	now	I'm plagued with doubt. Should I com
ipe and took my candy cigarettes … But	now	I want out.
you on oyster Tuesdays? Me. It was me.	Now	, I want my $500,000 in 50s! 50s with
m typecast! Pigeon-chested! Corn-holed!	Now	I'll never get a chance to play the
Ugh. This is so tight.	Now	I know why Evita was such a bitch. W
It's not for us.	Now	, Will just had the floors redone, so
umé. I've updated my special skills. I	now	know stage combat, banjo, and, as of
igned to grace us with his presence, we	now	have enough waiters to do ballet ser
more! Before it used to be World, Jack.	Now	it's Jack, World.
I used to have multiple personalities.	Now	I'm only dating one guy. Oh, and if
irable is visual-eye-zation, all right?	Now	, it's the end of the evening, and Ka
? I just kind of want to be alone right	now	.
ou, okay? We are discussing Barry right	now	.

when compared to Jack (see Table 4.5). The strongest – negatives – consists of the morpheme *n't*, as well as the words *not*, *never*, *nothing* and *no*. This category is discussed in more detail in the section on grammar.

Will uses more food-related vocabulary than Jack. This includes words that refer to meals (*dinner*, *lunch*, *breakfast*) as well as types of food (*cheese*, *candy*, *nuts*, etc.), other food-related objects (*restaurant*, *waiter*) and verbs of consumption (*eat*, *feed*). The setting which appears most often in *Will & Grace* is Will's apartment – an open-plan space consisting of a living area and kitchen where characters are often seen eating or preparing food. Will's food-related utterances include: 'Here taste this. Is there enough curry?', 'That's the last time I cook something out of a magazine' and 'OK guys, dinner's ready'. As well as appearing in this domestic setting, Will is also associated with dining out, using phrases such as: 'We could all have lunch together in Soho', 'You called me out of a business lunch to fix your fax?' and 'Last night at the restaurant he tried to say I love you in sign language'. Therefore Will's association with food represents two facets of his identity – domesticity and urban sophistication.

Will also refers to speech more directly than Jack, using words such as *voice*, *tell*, *say*, *talk*, *speak*, *chat* and *mention*. Two other related semantic categories used more often by Will are general communication, including words like *mean* and *message*, and participation, covering words like *party*, *meeting* and *conference*. These categories suggest that Will is more linguistically aware or other-oriented than Jack. Finally Will talks more about crime, law/order, which is unsurprising, given that he works as a lawyer.

Grammatical comparison (Will/Jack)

Only four grammatical categories were key in Jack's speech when compared to Will's (see Table 4.6). The strongest difference was in the use of foreign words. While foreign words aren't particularly frequent in either character's speech, Jack uses them nine times more often than Will. Most of these foreign words are in French (23 out of 36), with Spanish also being used (ten

Table 4.5 Key semantic categories in Will's speech, when compared to Jack's

Label	Semantic category	Will's speech		Jack's speech		Keyness
		Frequency	%	Frequency	%	
Z6	negative	2043	1.00	1110	0.83	25.8
F1	food	547	0.27	260	0.19	18.4
Q2.1	speech: communicative	835	0.41	427	0.32	17.7
Q1.1	communication	206	0.10	86	0.06	13.0
G2.1	crime: law/order	202	0.10	85	0.06	12.3
S1.1.1.3	participation	57	0.03	15	0.01	11.5

Table 4.6 Key grammatical categories in Jack's speech, when compared to Will's

Label	Semantic category	Jack's speech		Will's speech		Keyness
		Frequency	%	Frequency	%	
FW	foreign word	36	0.03	4	0.00	44.8
FU	unclassified word	89	0.08	46	0.03	38.2
APPGE	possessive pronoun, pre-nominal	1192	1.09	1476	0.88	29.0
PPIO1	1st person singular objective personal pronoun *me*	647	0.59	800	0.48	15.9

occurrences). Jack's use of French and Spanish is idiomatic, including words like *oui, gracias, pied de terre* and *pomme de terre*, e.g.: 'Ooh and for moi, ooh a postcard from mama!' Jack's use of French is therefore similar to the camp performances of 1960s radio characters Julian and Sandy, who spoke a British language variety used by gay men called Polari (Baker 2002a: 57). Julian and Sandy, like Jack, were struggling actors. Harvey notes how use of French fits into his framework of camp, by parodying aristocratic mannerisms:

> It is typical in English camp for a speaker to sprinkle his/her speech with elements of the French language. I would like to argue that the use of French grows out of an appropriation of aristocratic gestures which has a long history in camp. Its signalling of the values of refinement is merely the contemporary avatar of a longer tradition that reaches back into the class politics of pre-modern Europe.
>
> (Harvey 2000: 251)

Jack also combines two of Harvey's categories together, using French as parody and ludicrism in the form of a pun: 'I'm fat, je suis fatty gay.' Jack's use of Spanish is perhaps less concerned with aspirations of aristocracy but a desire to construct himself as worldly and sophisticated via a sense of cosmopolitanism or exoticism.

As with the semantic comparison, the category 'unclassified' occurred more frequently in Jack's speech. These were words which the grammatical and semantic taggers were unable to annotate, because they were either unfamiliar or non-standard uses of language.

One aspect of Jack's 'unclassifiable' language involves onomatopoeia: for example, saying 'ding' to emulate the noise of an egg timer, or using 'doot' when pretending to be a 'meddle detector' (a pun on metal detector): 'Let's put Will through the meddle detector shall we? Doot doot doot doot doot.' Jack also uses rare exclamative expressions: 'whoop-de-damn-doo!', magical spells: 'Now for my first trick, I will turn everyone in the audience gay. Ala-kazam ala-kum-hot, ala-kum-dum. Poofter!' and singing: 'La la la la la la. A doobie doobie do.' Therefore, this use of 'unclassifiable' language often occurs as part of a playful performance.

The final two grammatical categories used more often by Jack are both pronouns – the possessive pronoun pre-nominal, which includes *my*, *our*, *your*, *his*, *her* and *its*, and the first person singular objective personal pronoun: *me*. The most common possessive pronoun that Jack uses is *my*, comprising 56 per cent of this category. Compare this to Will, who uses *my* as 44 per cent of his total possessive pronouns. Jack's most common use of *my* is in the exclamation *my god* (115 times). He also refers to *my life* (26 times), *my mother* (12 times), *my father* (11 times) and *my name* (10 times). With *me*, the most frequent verbs appear as part of imperative constructions: *let me* (41 times), *excuse me* (41), *tell me* (25), *help me* (21) and *give me* (17).

On the other hand, Will's speech contains more cases of the second person pronoun *you*, and the inclusive first person pronoun *we* (see Table 4.7). Will's speech therefore appears to be more focused on others, in particular the hearer, whereas Jack's use of first person pronouns *me* and *my* suggests that his language is more self-involved. Fowler and Cress (1979: 203) suggest that the frequent occurrence of the second person pronoun in a person's language is a measure of 'the speaker's consciousness of, care for, or, most often, desire to manipulate the addressee'.

Will uses the word *that*, both in its conjunction and determiner form, more often than Jack. Taking the conjunction form first, notable patterns include: SAY *that* (17 times), KNOW *that* (15 times), *the fact that* (ten times), *it's just that* (seven times), [determiner] + *guy that* (7) and *I'm (not) the one that* (five times). For Will, *that* as a conjunction often appears in conversations that involve confrontation or confession: 'It's just that Sam can't have you 'cause you're mine!', 'So now I'm so lonely and pathetic I can't even handle the fact that my best friend is seeing someone, is that it?', 'You'll be

Table 4.7 Key grammatical categories in Will's speech, when compared to Jack's

Label	Semantic category	Jack's speech		Will's speech		Keyness
		Frequency	%	Frequency	%	
CST	*that* as conjunction	171	0.16	372	0.22	15.3
DD1	singular determiner	923	0.84	1666	1.00	17.0
PPY	2nd person personal pronoun *you*	2127	1.94	3671	2.20	20.8
XX	*not, n't*	941	0.86	1741	1.04	23.1
PPIS2	1st person plural subjective personal pronoun *we*	341	0.31	718	0.43	24.8

happy to know that Paul and I aren't seeing each other', 'It's just, I'm the one that always has to clean up the mess', 'we've always said that one day we'd have a baby.' Will also uses *that* more often as part of a category of singular determiners, including *this* and *another*. These determiners occur 31 per cent of the time before the verb to BE.

Biber *et al.* (1999: 159) point out that negative forms tend to occur more frequently in spoken, rather than written, discourse, and are linked to the higher number of verbs that are used in speech. However, Will does not use a significantly higher number of verbs than Jack.

Negation is used most often by Will to pre-modify forms of DO (762 times), IS (398) and HAVE (33 times). Will's negation also often occurs with the modal verb CAN (172 times). Finally, negation is also often used by Will to refer to himself: the form I + verb + negator occurs 591 times, whereas you + verb + negator occurs 208 times. In contrast, other modifying pronouns/determiners appear less frequently: *it* (96), *that* (47), *this* (31), *we* (67), *he* (48), *she* (32) and *they* (13). Will's use of negation therefore seems to be most often focused around himself, and with the noun DO: the most common pronoun + verb + negator pattern that Will uses is *I don't* occurring 267 times, with *I'm not* occurring 106 times, and *I can't* at 94. The most frequent verbs following negation are *know* (113), *have* (71), *want* (49) and *think* (43). The phrase *I don't know* occurs 80 times. Will's use of negation, then, seems to be more focused around his own abilities, and particularly knowledge, than with labelling others or restricting their behaviour. In light of the fact that a main semantic difference between Will and Jack's language is Jack's use of words connected with understanding (particularly demonstrating his own or the lack of others), we could conclude that Jack's use of language helps to construct him as more self-assured, self-absorbed, playful and camp than Will (see Table 4.8 for a summary of the main linguistic differences between the two characters).

Grace

The ways that Will and Jack are constructed as gay characters only reveals one aspect of the discourses of homosexuality in *Will & Grace*. In order to

Table 4.8 Main differences between Jack and Will

Jack	Will
Self-absorbed	Other-focused
(Overly-)Confident	Sometimes unsure
Uses language to be playful	Uses language reflexively
Camp	Not camp
Sexual	Domesticated
Pseudo-sophisticated	Sophisticated

make more sense of the ways that characters inter-relate to each other, it is therefore useful to look more closely at the language of the other two central characters – Grace and Karen. With this in mind, key semantic and grammatical categories were derived for the female characters, using a similar technique to that described above. However, rather than comparing Grace with Karen, it was decided that it would be more useful to compare Grace's speech with that of everybody else's in the scripts, and then to carry out the same technique for Karen's speech. It was decided to only focus on positive key categories here, as the negative categories tended not to show up what was distinctive about a person's speech, but what was distinctive about the speech of others. For example, the negative grammatical key categories in Karen's speech when compared to everyone else's included *that* as both a determiner and a conjunction, the negator *not* and the first person plural pronoun *we* (in other words, almost all of the grammatical categories that were key in Will's speech – see Table 4.7).

Grace uses more pronouns than any of the other characters and particularly more male pronouns (see Table 4.9). Her use of male pronouns mainly involves referrals to Will, Jack and also a number of romantic relationships with men that she forms throughout the series: 'He dumped me and found someone else!', 'He gave me his sweatshirt', 'Leo told me that he loved me.' Grace's search for 'true love' is one of the main themes of *Will & Grace*, highlighted over the other characters.

Table 4.9 Key semantic categories in Grace's speech, when compared to everyone else's

Label	Semantic category	Grace's speech		Others' speech		Keyness
		Frequency	%	Frequency	%	
Z8	pronouns	6507	2.76	18,225	2.44	74.2
Z8M	male pronouns	907	0.39	2283	0.31	33.5
A5	evaluation	2132	0.91	5846	0.78	32.5
Z8MF	pronouns, non-gendered	7684	3.26	22,705	3.04	29.1
Z6	negatives	1926	0.82	5288	0.71	28.8
S6	obligation and necessity	722	0.31	1801	0.24	28.7
X2	mental actions and thought	1674	0.71	4582	0.61	26.1
Z5	grammatical bin	15,853	6.73	48,154	6.45	23.3
A14	exclusivers/particulisers	663	0.28	1723	0.23	18.4
Z1F	personal names – female	351	0.15	847	0.11	17.8
T1	time	2565	1.09	7390	0.99	17.4
A3	being	3626	1.54	10,630	1.42	16.6
A1	general and abstract terms	1750	0.74	4951	0.66	16.6
N4	linear order	377	0.16	957	0.13	13.0
Q2	speech acts	1309	0.56	3714	0.50	11.8
A13	degree	925	0.39	2569	0.34	11.7
A8	seem	272	0.12	673	0.09	11.5

Although Grace uses more female names than any of the other characters, the majority of these refer to her employee Karen (213 occurrences) and her friend Ellen (36). Unlike Jack, Grace does not normally refer to actresses or call gay men by female names. Therefore her use of this semantic category contains none of the camp strategies employed by Jack, but is more conventional.

Another semantic category that Grace uses often is 'obligation and necessity'. This includes the words *need* (142 times), *should* (119), and phrases like *have to* (121) and *supposed to* (35). The most common pronoun associated with this category is *I*, with the phrase *I need* being common in Grace's speech.

Grace also uses more words of degree (*really, very, even, little*), exclusivers (*only, just*) and words of evaluation (*OK, well, fine, good, great, fantastic*) than other characters – this is discussed in more detail below.

Three of the grammatical categories that are characteristic of Grace's speech are also found in Will's speech (when compared to Jack): the conjunction *that*, negators and singular determiners (see Table 4.10). Grace uses these parts of speech in a similar way to Will – for example, the most common pattern involving a negator is *I don't know*. Grace's use of the semantic category of 'speech acts' is also similar to Will's. However, Grace's use of the singular first person pronoun makes her speech more self-centred and therefore more similar to Jack's. Grace's use of *was* is often preceded by *I* (156 times).

Two categories that Grace makes use of more than other characters are general adverbs and wh-adverbs. In terms of general adverbs, Grace most often uses words that are common to spoken conversation: agreement, intensifiers, hedges and politeness markers: *OK* (525 occurrences), *just* (591), *so* (306), *really* (235), *well* (239), *right* (143), *please* (82), *maybe* (84), *never* (104), suggesting that her speech is more reactive than that of the other characters.

Table 4.10 Key grammatical categories in Grace's speech, when compared to everyone else's

Label	Grammatical category	Grace's speech		Others' speech		Keyness
		Frequency	%	Frequency	%	
VBDZ	was	543	0.34	1205	0.24	36.2
CST	conjunction: that	418	0.26	895	0.18	34.0
RR	adverbs	3468	2.15	9434	1.92	32.9
DDQ	wh-determiner	951	0.59	2427	0.49	21.1
PPIS1	I	3995	2.47	11,295	2.30	16.9
XX	negator	1656	1.03	4513	0.92	15.1
DD1	singular determiner	1614	1.00	4414	0.90	13.8
PPH1	it	1545	0.96	4234	0.86	12.7
RRQ	wh-adverb	596	0.37	1530	0.31	12.4
VVGK	going to	382	0.24	938	0.19	12.3
VHG	having	71	0.04	127	0.03	12.2

This claim is supported by Grace's high use of wh-adverbs, particularly *why* (228), *how* (212), *where* (84) and *when* (73). Grace's speech therefore appears to be somewhat contradictory – while a number of features suggest that she is focused towards others, her high use of the first person singular pronoun also marks her speech as being more self-oriented than anyone else in the sitcom. This is something that Will remarks on in episode 1.13:

WILL: You have a tendency. . . . You kind of need to be the star of your rela-
       tionships, you know. I mean it's all about your stuff. Your boyfriends
       are like gardeners, and you're sort of. . .
GRACE: No, no, no. No, no, no, no. Do not call me a flower. I am not a
       flower. I am a gardener. I do plenty of hoeing.

Grace could therefore be constructed as 'high maintenance' or needy, although this kind of insecurity could be directly a cause of her inability to form a romantic attachment to Will (the 'what a shame' discourse), as shown above.

Karen

The central relationship in *Will & Grace* is the friendship between the two title characters. Will is constructed as professional, yet caring and sensitive – he would therefore be an ideal romantic partner for Grace, were he not gay. Jack provides a contrast to Will, and much of the programme's humour, as his more theatrical friend. However, the fourth character, Karen, is a role that is less obvious than that of the others. She works as Grace's 'assistant' and develops a close friendship with Jack. The first reference to Karen is in episode 1.1:

GRACE: I'm looking for tissues.
WILL: Have your assistant get them for you.
GRACE: She's late again.
WILL: Oh! Fire her already.
GRACE: I'm not going to fire Karen. Her social contacts keep my business
       afloat.
WILL: Why does she even work? I mean, isn't she worth, like, a gazillion dollars?
GRACE: She feels working keeps her down to earth.

Unlike the other characters in the sitcom, Karen has a life and relationships which occur off-screen. She is married with step-children, and while these characters are often referred to, they never appear. In episode 3.4, it is explained that Karen works because she hates 'being home with Stan and the kids'. However, Karen notes that she chooses to work for Grace when there are 'tons of places [she] could be away from them'.

One possible reason for the presence of Karen in *Will & Grace* is that two male and two female characters act as a gender balance. Three central gay male characters may have made the programme less appealing to a mainstream audience. Also, the decision to make Karen heterosexual provides a sexuality balance: there are equal numbers of core heterosexual and gay characters. However, carrying out an analysis of Karen's key semantic and grammatical categories should provide a more illuminating view on her role in the sitcom.

Semantic comparison (Karen/everyone)

The greatest semantic distinction between Karen and other characters in *Will & Grace* is her more frequent use of food-related words (Table 4.11). However, a closer analysis of this reveals that this is, in fact, due to her use of the word *honey*, which occurs 682 times, compared to the rest of the cast who only utter *honey* 105 times collectively. Karen uses *honey* not to refer to food, but as a general term of endearment used on everyone she interacts with. Karen's use of the word *honey* is viewed as such a defining aspect of her character that, in episode 3.4, an intern who starts work at Grace's office starts to emulate Karen by dressing and talking like her. After Karen points out that this is inappropriate, the intern asks: 'Can I still use the word "honey"?'

There is an inherent ambivalence in using such a linguistic strategy: a word like *honey* suggests that the speaker is being affectionate. However, when used indiscriminately as Karen does, the word loses its affective power, suggesting that instead the speaker has forgotten whom she is addressing. In an analysis of the gay language variety Polari (Baker 2002a: 45–6), it was found that similar words, *dear*, *ducky*, *heartface* and *girl*, were also often over-used by Polari speakers as a kind of exclamation mark, occurring at the end of utterances.

As with Jack's speech, Karen also makes use of the 'discourse bin' category of speech often. However, Karen's use of discourse markers tends to be

Table 4.11 Key semantic categories in Karen's speech, when compared to everyone else's

Label	Semantic category	Karen's speech		Others' speech		Keyness
		Frequency	%	Frequency	%	
F1	Food	921	0.80	1736	0.24	731.7
Z4	Discourse bin	3732	3.25	17,584	2.46	228.1
M1	Moving, coming, going	952	0.83	4362	0.61	68.4
X3.2	Sensory: sound	162	0.14	559	0.08	38.8
B5	Clothes and personal belongings	238	0.21	982	0.14	29.5
L2MFN	Living creatures generally	114	0.10	438	0.06	19.0
M3	Vehicles and transport on land	49	0.04	144	0.02	17.9
N3.2	Measurement: size	179	0.16	796	0.11	15.2

limited to fewer types than Jack. Karen's most frequent discourse markers are *oh* (807 occasions), *ha* (478), *no* (253) and *yeah* (247). *Oh* is an interjection, used to introduce utterances or to respond to those of others. Biber *et al.* (1999: 1083) note that 'its core function appears to be to convey some degree of surprise, unexpectedness or emotional arousal'. However, when looking at Karen's use of *oh*, it tends to be used to show emotional arousal more than surprise. As Harvey (2000: 241) points out: 'exclamations are identified as "feminine" because they are essentially *reactive.*'

Other discourse markers that Karen uses, which are lexical keywords, when compared with the speech of everyone else, include: *hmm, hell, yeah, huh, mm, lord* and *devil*. As Jack invokes the names of female actresses as his deities, it is interesting that Karen occasionally uses *devil* as an exclamative, e.g. 'Oh devil!', perhaps suggesting that her religious views are somewhat unorthodox. As a strategy of camp, this could fall under the 'inversion of established value system' category.

Ha occurs during laughter, e.g. *ha ha ha*, which was encoded as separate syllables in the transcription of the scripts. It's clear that Karen laughs more than the other characters, and that this laughter usually occurs as a response to something she, rather than another character, has said:

> Enjoy your journey . . . to hell! Ha ha ha ha!
>
> (Episode 1.9)

> Oh I know. He's miserable. He doesn't know who his father is. It's terrible. Ha ha ha!
>
> (Episode 2.13)

> Oh Jack. It warms my heart to hear you say that. Or maybe it's just the gin rickey I had in the car. Ha ha ha ha! Even on skid row I'm funny.
>
> (Episode 2.13)

> Hey, this is a place of business! We are trying to get some work done in here, and we don't need you just barging – OK, I'm saying it and I don't even buy it. Ha ha!
>
> (Episode 2.16)

The category M1 refers to 'movement: coming and going'. Karen's frequent use of this category in her speech can, however, largely be explained by her use of the phrase *come on*, which occurs 184 times. *Come on* is the most common intransitive phrasal verb used in conversation (Biber *et al.* 1999: 411) and is used as an exhortation to act ('Come on honey! You can do it!'), as a pre-departure summons to move ('Come on honey! Let's go shopping'), or as meaning to start or be activated (e.g. 'The heating didn't come on this morning'). However, Karen only uses *come on* in the first two senses. Her use of *come on* could be said to be an attempt to impose her will or control over other characters. In a similar way, the category X3.2, which refers to 'sensory: sound', appears to be key in Karen's speech because of her use of the word *listen* (occurring 95 times). All of Karen's uses of *listen* occur as part of an imperative clause, e.g.: 'Oh my god, listen to me!', 'Listen, get your ass over to Bergdorf's', 'Listen, Ben is a catch and for some reason he's crazy about you.' Therefore, Karen's use of *listen* is primarily for giving out advice or commanding others.

Karen also talks about clothing more than the other characters, using words like *wearing* (16 occurrences), *wear* (13), *shoes* (16), *pants* (ten), *blouse* (eight) and *suit* (six). Several of these citations are used in order to criticise the clothing or taste of others: 'Oh honey, change that blouse. You work in an office, not a pirate ship', 'These lips don't touch anything in a track suit', 'Honey, we talked about this blouse', 'Oh honey, did you really think you could get into heaven wearing body glitter?', 'Lord, you are as simple as that blouse you're wearing.' In addition, Karen often refers appreciatively to expensive brands or items of clothing: 'Just a maid? That's like saying Pradas are just shoes', 'I got my $700 custom-made shoes on', 'What have you done with my shoes? They're one of a kind.' Karen's talk about clothing therefore suggests she is critical of others but also is wealthy enough to know about and afford better clothing than those around her. Her frequent use of category M3 (vehicles and land transport) is also explained by her wealth. The main word she uses here is *driver*, referring to her personal chauffeur.

Karen also refers to more 'living creatures generally' (category L2MFN). However, a close look at this category reveals that many of the creatures she refers to are not literally animals, but instead refer to pet or insulting names that she has for others. In particular, she refers to *pigs* 12 times (generally as people who she views as greedy, dirty or sexual), e.g. 'This place is a pigsty and you're a dirty pig boy!' Karen's affectionate name for Jack is *poodle*, which she uses 29 times. She refers to her breasts as *puppies* twice, but also uses *puppy* in a similar way to *pig* nine times.

Another aspect of Karen's predilection for insults, along with references to clothing, or animal names, is her use of words that relate to 'measurement: size', and particularly her use of *big* (50 occurrences) and *little* (97 occurrences), which make up 82 per cent of this category. These words have the effect of strengthening an insult: 'you big lez', 'Your boyfriend's a big flaming, feather-wearing, man-kissing . . .', 'You're chewing like a big cow', or emphasising a body part: 'She's got big feet', 'He thinks you've got big melons', 'Was her nickname "Slutty Big Boobs"?' *Little* is used as a more affectionate insult: 'You listen to me, little missy!', 'You dirty little monkey', 'You're a filthy little piggy.' *Little* is also used by Karen in a litotic way, to down-play the importance of a statement which has far-reaching consequences or could be viewed as insulting. For example, when revealing important news: 'I've got a little gossip', when terminating a friendship: 'Well I have a little joke for you. Knock Knock. I'm not there', and when insulting another person's clothing: 'Kicky little blouse.' As Harvey (2000: 255) notes, camp is expressed through hyperbole: 'Of the set of features that elaborates the emphatic style of camp, two (hyperbole and exclamation) parody a stereotype of femininity that is effusive and buffeted by extreme affective states – not the site, in other words, of the putative calm rationality of maleness.' Karen's use of *big* achieves this function. But in addition to hyperbole, the litotic understatement signified by words like *little* is also an important stylistic feature of camp. For example, when Karen tells another character: 'I think you have a little addiction problem.' In episode 2.3, Karen tries to convince Jack to accompany her to her step-children's parent–teacher conference, by first offering him a spa day, and down-playing the length of time the meeting will take:

KAREN: So, honey, how would you like to have a spa day with me Monday?
JACK: Jack happy! Jack happy!
KAREN: That's right, we'll do a little mud, a little seaweed, totally detox. Then we'll get plastered, and go over to my stepkids' school for a little parent–teacher conference.
JACK: School! Why don't you take, and I'm just gonna throw this out at you . . . their father?

By linking *little* first to pleasant events 'a little mud, a little seaweed', Karen also attempts to create an association between them and an unpleasant event 'a little parent–teacher conference', although this strategy is not successful.

Polari speakers expressed litotes through use of the suffix *-ette* (Baker 2002a: 59–61). By down-playing tragic circumstances and over-playing the importance of the mundane, camp allows its speakers (often, although not always, gay men) to re-establish an alternative value system, whereby subjects considered important to mainstream hegemonic society are viewed as inconsequential, while trivial (e.g. feminine) matters are prioritised. Hyperbole can therefore only function as a strategy of camp if its opposing linguistic function, litotes, is also taken into account.

Grammatical comparison (Karen/everyone)

Only three grammatical categories occurred in Karen's speech more often than in the combined language of the rest of the cast (see Table 4.12). The first, prepositional adverbs, involves the words *on* (253 occurrences), *up* (140), *out* (124), *down* (67), *back* (55), *off* (48), *over* (44), *around* (36), *in* (36) and *about* (7). As pointed out in the discussion of semantic differences, Karen's use of the imperative phrase *come on* accounts for 184 uses of the word *on*. However, even if Karen's use of *come on* was reduced to make it comparable to the frequency that others employ it, she would still use more prepositional adverbs than the other characters.

Karen's use of prepositional adverbs tends to be used in conjunction with

Table 4.12 Key grammatical categories in Karen's speech, when compared to every-one else's

Label	Grammatical category	Karen's speech		Others' speech		Keyness
		Frequency	%	Frequency	%	
RP	Prepositional adverb	819	0.88	3844	0.69	40.8
DD2	Plural determiner	91	0.10	321	0.06	18.5
NNU2	Plural unit of measurement	19	0.02	42	0.00	11.4

verbs in order to give commands. To give a small sample, she tells people to *sit down* (ten occurrences), *shut up* (five), *get out* (three) *stick around* (two), *come back* (two), *ease up, hurry up, crank up the heat, wrap 'em up, put 'em up, back up, pull over, hand it over, fork it over, go over there, come over to my place, figure something out, work something out, don't poop out on me, pick out a dog, come on out, count me out, look out, check it out, fan out, break out, get back out* and *put on a happy face*. As with her use of *listen*, Karen's use of these phrasal verbs tends to be mainly concerned with controlling the behaviour or movement of others.

Examining a concordance of Karen's prepositional adverbs, one phrase which stands out as being highly frequent is *what's going on*, occurring 23 times. This question often occurs as part of a longer sequence, consisting of several parts:

What's going on? What's happening? What's with the TV?

(Episode 2.7)

What's going on? What's happening? What's the emergency?

(Episode 4.20)

What's going on? What's happening? What's with all the man-candy in the hallway?

(Episode 3.15)

What's going on? What's happening? What's with the geisha hand?

(Episode 3.9)

What's going on? What's happening? Why is it talking to me?

(Episode 3.4)

This sequence of three questions – acting as a rhetorical triplet – serves an emphatic purpose. The first two questions usually follow the same pattern and can be applied to most circumstances because they are so general. Only the last question of the sequence refers to the specificity of a particular situation. This style of question asking is seen as such a central part of Karen's way of speaking that, in episode 2.6, Grace references it by imitating her while they are shopping. Karen, however, fails to recognise the imitation, and responds with the same set of questions:

GRACE: Come on. Karen, you got to get into the spirit of it. I've found some really cute outfits here. I wear them to work, and you tell me how much you hate them. [Imitating Karen] Honey, what's going on? What's happening? What's all this about?
KAREN: Honey, what's this? What are you doing? Who's that supposed to be?

The second grammatical category that Karen frequently uses is the plural demonstrative determiner, consisting of the words *these* (33) and *those* (60). Of the two words, *those* occurs as a lexical keyword in Karen's speech, suggesting that it is her use of *those* which is the more distinctive aspect of her language. *Those* is generally used in order to signify that something is distant in relation to the speaker, either in terms of its location, or to demonstrate emotional detachment. Karen's use of *those* regularly signifies her emotional detachment or disapproval:

I'm not putting my mouth on this thing. Who knows what <u>those</u> paramedics use these dolls for while they're sitting around.

(Episode 1.21)

Martini honey, and don't waste any space with <u>those</u> olives.

(Episode 1.13)

God didn't give you <u>those</u> meat packer hands so you can eat finger sandwiches.

(Episode 3.22)

Come on! I know what guilt is. It's one of <u>those</u> touchy-feely words that people throw around when they don't really mean anything. You know, like 'maternal' or 'addiction'.

(Episode 3.1)

Finally, Karen uses more plural units of measurement than other characters (although this is a grammatical category that nobody uses particularly frequently). Half of Karen's references to units of measurement involve money, and often relate to the wealth of her husband: 'For my first anniversary I got ... a million dollars in cash', 'Stan pays deaf immigrants 12 cents an hour to make tube socks', 'There are thousands of children in the third world who rely on the 11 cents an hour my husband pays them.' Karen's wealth (through her marriage to Stan) is therefore seen as doubly undeserving – she doesn't work for it, and her husband obtains it through unethical work practices. At the same time, this wealth contributes to the detachment of the character.[5] Karen also uses units of measurement as part of hyperbolic statements: 'All you have to do is run a lousy marathon. Stan weighs 5000 pounds. It's miles just circling him', 'You know what I think speaks gallons about you.'

Karen's identity is therefore constructed via uses of language which access aspects of Harvey's features of camp, but in a way that is different from Jack. While Jack's language is self-oriented and playful, using foreign language and the names of divas to create the appearance of sophistication, Karen's use of language underscores the fact that, unlike Jack, her cultural capital is not a façade. Karen's use of commands and insults, and her rather dismissive attitude towards other characters, result in a form of camp which is witch-like or queenly (in the sense that it is imperious), whereas Jack's use of camp is more based on the distance between his self-presentation and his actual circumstances.

Discussion

The critical and ratings success of *Will & Grace* can be attributed to the fact that the programme writers have accurately judged the discourses that mainstream audiences are ready to accept when it comes to showing gay characters on television.

An over-arching discourse in *Will & Grace* is that sexuality is part of a person's identity and that it is important to 'be yourself'. This discourse rests well with the theory that sitcoms are inherently moral forms of media. However, due to the presence of camp humour within the programme itself, there is a strong element of ambivalence running alongside the more humanistic aspects of the sitcom. Will and Grace's relationship is often depicted through the eyes of other characters as dysfunctional or unhealthy, whereas the two supporting characters, Jack and Karen, are also seen as delusional as well as selfish and self-absorbed.

Another aspect of the sitcom's ambivalence is demonstrated by the homophobic language which is occasionally used by both gay and heterosexual characters in order to humorously insult or stereotype gay people. The employment of terms like *fag*, *homo* and *queer* acknowledges the existence of homophobia as complex and context-related, with subtle shades of interpretation. When Karen is annoyed at Will for pointing out that they're playing poker not gin, she says: 'The gays really love their rules.' It could be argued that the writers are showing her to be homophobic or stereotyping of gay people. Yet at the same time, Karen's best friend is Jack – a gay man. Karen's response, and the ambivalent homophobia in the programme, is therefore often situational and directed at a single person. As described earlier, many of the pejorative terms are employed as a form of humorous linguistic wordplay, 'Knock knock, anybody homo?', 'Homo wasn't built in a day', rather than to directly insult gay people. In contrast, there are very few overtly homophobic statements in *Will & Grace*, and where they do exist, they tend to be challenged, as when Will calls Jack a fag. Therefore the programme acknowledges the existence of homophobia and attempts to defuse it, by making a joke or pun of it, by framing it as a situational response, or by exploring and exposing more deep-rooted attitudes. Additionally, Jack's 'heterophobia' is presented as a parody of homophobia, showing that the same arguments used on gay people can be just as easily made on heterosexual people. This widens the focus of storylines about discrimination in order to educate viewers that the 'be yourself' discourse relates to all forms of sexuality, not just homosexuality.

However, while audiences are considered 'ready' to consider homophobia, it appears that they are not yet ready for gay sex. In spite of its emphasis on sexuality, *Will & Grace* is an inherently sexless sitcom. As Provencher (2004) writes:

> many commercial primetime television series still continue to avoid the candid treatment of gay characters and their stories by portraying them as 'de-sexed' and 'uncoupled' second-class citizens who must participate in heteronormative settings to find a sense of 'normalcy' or 'belonging'.

The fact that unrequited love has resolved into friendship for both Grace and Will, and Jack and Will, means that the central relationships in the sitcom are not grounded in requited sexual desire. For example, the gay kiss between Will and Jack in episode 2.14 is inspired not by romance but by politics. Interestingly, in the first four seasons the only long-running heterosexual sexual relationship in the programme is between Karen and Stan, although it happens off-screen as Stan is never seen.[6] Therefore, it could be argued *Will & Grace* rests well with earlier theories of sitcoms as being 'inherently conservative' by reconfiguring and updating the concept of the nuclear family. *Will & Grace*'s success suggests that large proportions of mainstream western society are ready to expand the concept of the nuclear family to include gay male characters, as long as their sex lives remain backgrounded.

However, we also need to examine what sort of gay male characters Jack and Will are, how their sexual identities are constructed, and how they relate to other characters in the sitcom. Jack's faux sophistication (namedropping, French, show-business) is contrasted with Will's authentic sophistication associated with his dining out and professional legal career. We can also contrast Jack's use of discourse markers with Will's orientation to verbs associated with communication and interaction, or Jack's confidence ('I got it!') with Will's use of negatives to indicate introspection and a willingness to admit when he doesn't understand something. Jack uses a more playful, performative form of language, utilising aspects of camp such as parody and ludicrism. He talks more openly about relationships and the body, while his use of colour terms, exclamation and female names is reminiscent of the stereotypical so-called 'female register'. Finally, Jack's use of first person singular pronouns, contrasted with Will's second person and first person plural pronouns, suggests that Jack is self-absorbed, while Will is attentive to others.

The programme therefore represents a wider view of gay men, giving the audience two 'flavours' to choose from, which act as counter-balances to each other. On the one hand, Jack is a camp, self-regarding show-off. His language and behaviour fit the stereotype of the 'flamboyant gay man', similar to the constructions found in the *Daily Mail* (see Chapter 3). However, any power that Jack has to offend is diminished, because the audience recognises the character as being delusional and relatively powerless. The 'flamboyant gay man' stereotype isn't particularly new. For example, in the UK, sitcom characters like Mr Humphreys in *Are You Being Served*, Gloria in *It Ain't Half Hot Mum* or roles played by Charles Hawtrey and Kenneth Williams in the *Carry On* films or Hugh Paddick and Kenneth Williams in the radio series *Round The Horne* all utilised similar camp comedian roles. In America, a similar role was performed by Paul Lynde who played Uncle Arthur in the sitcom *Bewitched*. However, what distinguishes Jack from these earlier camp constructions is that in the past their homosexuality was often left unstated or only implicitly referred to. Jack, on the other hand, is camp and outspokenly gay. He is more political about his sexuality than Will (for example, he protests about the missing gay kiss in his favourite sitcom). Where Mr Humphreys and Uncle Arthur attempted (perhaps in vain) to be ambiguous about their sexuality, Jack is loud and proud.

Will, on the other hand, is a successful lawyer who does not display any of the camp traits associated with Jack. His relationship with Grace (referring to her as *honey* and *sweetheart*) is akin to a sexless marriage, and unlike Jack, he does not tend to have romantic relationships. Will's gender performance is closer to that of the masculine hegemonic stereotype – incidentally, his surname is Truman – or True Man. Jack's surname, McFarland, is occasionally pronounced 'McFairyLand'. The qualities that Will possesses are similar to those which are found to be desirable in gay personal advertisements (*professional, masculine, attractive*) discussed in Chapter 5, whereas he could also function as an idealised character from the gay erotic stories examined in Chapter 7 – if it were not for the fact that he does not have sex.

So Will's restrained sexuality, combined with his domesticity and caring other-centred personality, also serve to remove any threat that he will challenge heterosexual hegemony. However, if the qualities embodied by Will and Jack were combined into one character, the result would be something that *could* be potentially threatening – a successful, masculine, sexually confident, politically active gay man. By dividing these traits among two characters, the threat to heterosexual hegemony is removed – Jack is a sissy and Will is Grace's non-sexual 'husband', ostensibly neutered. With that said, the sitcom, in portraying two gay men who perform their gender very differently, breaks with the stereotype that *all* gay men are sissies. Instead, it presents a discourse of homosexuality as consisting of different types of gender performance: some gay men are camp, but others are more masculine.

It would be over-simplifying the analysis, however, to conclude that Will is constructed as completely masculine while Jack is totally feminine. For example, Will is constructed as possessing some 'feminine' traits, e.g. he is positioned as carrying out domestic tasks such as cooking, shown as using more uncertain language and being more aware of others.[7] Jack, on the other hand, is more self-concerned, sexually predatory and uses non-standard language – features often associated with masculinity. Therefore, I would suggest that one way that gay men are constructed in the sitcom is by combining stereotyped masculine and feminine traits together in different ways. Will is therefore positioned as more attractive because he is shown to possess the best of both types of gender traits (career-focused, caring, domesticated), whereas Jack displays more negative qualities from both genders (bitchy and frivolous but self-centred and sexually voracious).

However, what both Jack and Will have in common is the context within which they live out their lives as gay men. The sitcom's urban setting: Upper West Side Manhattan, the professions of the main characters: interior designer, lawyer, actor, wife of millionaire; their lifestyles and their witty *bon mots* all point to a construction of gayness that is socially upward-looking. As Harris (1997: 8–10) describes, as a young gay man growing up in a working-class American community, he acquired a clipped British accent from watching movie stars like Joan Crawford, Bette Davis and Katherine Hepburn:

> This strange act of ventriloquism ... is the direct outcome of my perception in my youth that, as a homosexual, I did not belong to the community in which I lived, that I was different, a castaway from somewhere else, somewhere better, more elegant, more refined, a Little Lord Fauntleroy marooned in the wilderness.

The world of *Will & Grace* offers a similar refined ideal. Will's witty, rich friends, his large, beautifully decorated urban apartment, his career – all are presented as an aspirational ideal – a good way of being gay. Whether we consider Jack's shallow attempts to appear cultured (his use of French, for example) or Will's more credible sophistication, the important point to note is that refinement is a large part of the gay identity of both characters.

While Will is contrasted with Jack, the two gay male characters are themselves counter-balanced against two heterosexual female characters – ensuring that the programme does not become too gay or too male, and therefore opening up its potential to a wider, mainstream audience. Grace's speech contains aspects which construct her as being stereotypically 'feminine' – her high use of discourse markers, intensifiers, hedges, etc. Her speech also appears more other-centred – with a high number of pronouns (especially male pronouns orienting to her relationships with men). However, Grace's high use of the first person pronoun and her use of words like *need* also suggest a side of her personality that is more neurotic and self-centred. Grace is therefore constructed as a 'needy woman'. She takes the role of the 'fag-hag', the heterosexual woman who desires Will but can never have him – her relationships with other men are therefore set up to fail because no one can live up to the ideal of Will. It is in this way that the sitcom's status quo can be maintained.

However, the fourth character, Karen, acts as more than a female balance. Karen does not talk or behave like a stereotypical heterosexual female. Many of the linguistic strategies that she uses can be more commonly attributed to 'camp talk', for example, her exclamation, hyperbole, litotes and the use of the same affective pet name for everyone.[8] Her dominance is demonstrated through insults concerning the clothing sense of others and her frequent imperatives, particularly *come on* and *listen*. She is therefore part stereotypically feminine – emotional and reactive – and part aggressively masculine. Many of the traits that Karen displays could be viewed as being more camp than any of the other characters in the programme. Karen's role is therefore reminiscent of a drag queen's gender performance – an exaggerated parody of femininity: superficially reactive and affectionate yet detached and self-assured. The unreal, performative aspect of Karen's character is further demonstrated by the fact that none of her family are ever seen, and by the character's voice – a high-pitched falsetto. Karen's affinity with drag queens is shown further in episode 1.5 when she meets a group of real drag queens on Halloween and instructs them with advice on applying make-up: 'Well, all right, girls, gather around. It's makeup-tip time. OK, first off, a blanket note about base. Don't forget the neck, because they won't. Those Adam's apples don't just cover themselves, now, do they, girls? No, they don't.'

I'd suggest two possible explanations for Karen's gender performance. First, as work by Barrett (1997) indicates, linguistic forms associated with one group can also be used by other people, for a range of reasons. Karen's use of camp could therefore demonstrate to audiences that camp is a strategy which can be employed by people other than gay men, eroding a discourse which associates gay men with camp (although still associating camp with femininity). However, Jack and Karen's uses of camp are not the same. Karen's performance is more imperious (critical and commanding of others) whereas Jack's appears more self-absorbed (talking about himself). A more complete examination of how camp strategies combine together in order to create different kinds of gender performance for male and female, heterosexual and gay speakers is therefore necessary.[9]

A second possible reason for Karen's camp performance is that she is constructed symbolically as a drag queen. Yet, if that is the case, then why was the character not written as an actual man in drag? Perhaps it was feared that such a character would change the gender/sexuality balance of the programme, resulting in three gay male characters and one heterosexual female character – which may be unappealing to a wider audience. Writing Karen as a bona fide drag queen may have been viewed as too exotically gay for mainstream American audiences.

In a sense then, using a female character to play a drag queen is similar to a theatrical device used in Shakespearean times, when women were not allowed to act on stage, and therefore boys or young men took female roles (Hov 1990, Brockett 1991). In order for a drag queen to be accepted by contemporary mainstream audiences (and advertisers), she must be played by a woman. Karen is therefore doubly in drag – a female female impersonator. As Holleran (2000: 66) and Kanner (2003: 34–5) argue, Karen is the 'queerest' character in *Will & Grace*. Karen also contributes to the 'sophisticated' discourse of homosexuality in the sitcom by the fact that she is by far the richest character in the programme. She opens up the possibility of a life of extravagance and opulence to the other characters.

Therefore, both of the female characters in *Will & Grace* are crucial in allowing us to make sense of the success and mainstream acceptance of the sitcom, and also in offering an understanding of how discourses of homosexuality are evolving in western society. The presence of heterosexual female characters suggests a discourse of integration, but one that is not without problems. Grace can never have a sexual relationship with Will. However, this problem is seen as being a shame and disappointment for her. It is framed in terms of 'If only Will was heterosexual', rather than 'If only Grace was a gay man'. For example, when Will and Grace hug after an argument, Grace's mother, who is watching asks: 'You two feel something when you hug? Anything? Because, Will, if you did, it would make my life so much easier.' While the problem is therefore seen as Grace's (or her mother's!), rather than Will's, it is at least shown in a way which absolves Will of blame. However, gay men are still represented as a potential pitfall for heterosexual women. The 'what a shame' discourse warns heterosexual women that gay men are nurturing, attentive and well-groomed, but can never offer a woman what she *really* wants. Interestingly, *Will & Grace* tends not to feature the same sort of discourse from a gay perspective – where gay men need to be wary of friendships with unattainable men as this may lead to years of heartache. Jack's unrequited love for Will is only made apparent in one episode and is not commented on again. Viewers are made to feel sympathy for Grace much more often than for Jack – it is seen as more of a shame that a gay man cannot be a partner for a heterosexual woman than for another gay man.

Will & Grace therefore amply demonstrates how far American audiences have come since the patriarchal sitcom families of the 1950s ... and that they still have some distance to go.

5 'No effeminates please'

Discourses of gay men's personal adverts

Introduction

> Attractive looking, late forties, mature, fit, non-scene, non-smoking, straight-acting seeks similar or younger (21+) masculine guys for uncommitted friendship. Any country, no effeminates please.

The history of the magazine stretches back to the late seventeenth century. In 1693 the periodical *The Ladies' Mercury* was launched with the aim of providing entertainment and education in a morally uplifting way for literate, leisured women. Other journals which followed in the eighteenth century (*The Ladies' Magazine*, *The Lady's Magazine*, *The Lady's Monthly Museum*) were similarly aimed at upper-class women. By the nineteenth century, economic prosperity and higher standards of literacy (due to the Education Act of 1870) ensured that the target audience changed – middle-class women, who were expected to show little interest in world affairs and were instead grounded in issues of domesticity, personal appearance and family life were the new readers of titles like *The Englishwoman's Domestic Magazine*. In the last two decades of the nineteenth century, 48 such magazines were launched, being generally less expensive than previous journals and making profit from advertising revenues (Ferguson 1983: 16).

With the advent of good-quality, cheap printing technology, the twentieth century saw the birth of the magazine mass market, with magazines aiming to attract both middle- and working-class women. Middle-class monthlies were joined by working-class weeklies and as the market flooded, editors resorted to a number of strategies to attract an audience. One such strategy involved targeting specialist audiences (e.g. younger or older women, or people with specific interests). It has been argued that such magazines have not only defined their readers as women, but have helped to create the women they have addressed (Beetham 1996). Since the 1950s, the magazine industry became engaged in a competitive struggle, with ensuing cycles of expansion and contraction as more and more women's magazines attempted to gain hold of increasingly slimmer slices of audience loyalty. As Ferguson (1983: 25) points out:

the launch of new titles in the 1950s was exceeded only by the zeal with which others were launched, merged or killed in the 1960s, the caution with which their successors were launched in the 1970s . . . and the distinct reticence displayed . . . in the 1980s.

Magazines aimed solely at either gay or heterosexual men can often contain more similarities than differences. Both tend to include features based on health, fashion, exercise, consumer goods and sex, an ironic, irreverent style of writing is frequently applied, and they often use attractive semi-clothed male models in advertising or other features. However, for gay men such images can play a dual role. As with heterosexual men, they present aspirational ideals of consumption, grooming, fitness and masculinity which invite the reader to identify with, reject or compare himself to, but gay men may also find the same representations of masculinity to be sexually desirable. The depiction of 'ideal' or new masculinities in gay lifestyle magazines is therefore doubly compelling for the target audience – object cathexis (the desire to possess) merges with object identification (the desire to become).

One of the most significant differences between magazines that are aimed at heterosexual men and those marketed towards gay men is that the latter are likely to include a section for personal adverts, allowing its readership to engage socially, romantically or sexually with each other. In the west, the personal advert represents a quest for a romantic partner or perfect mate (Nair 1992) with partner selection being anticipated via descriptions of the self, other and desired relationship (Erfurt 1985). Personal columns are a kind of 'colony text' (Hoey 1986) made up of numerous separate entries which may be categorised in different ways (e.g. men seeking women versus women seeking men) although the meaning of each entry is not affected by the order in which they appear. The personal advert is a minimalist genre (Nair 1992), often with non-essential items such as function words being omitted (Bruthiaux 1994). They tend to have an informal, spoken style, often featuring lexical vagueness (Crystal and Davy 1975: 111–14), e.g. imprecise references to age or approximations via the suffix -ish (tallish, youngish, etc.).

The lonely hearts advert has always been a popular feature of gay magazines, and for decades has been one of the ways that gay men have made contact with each other, sometimes meeting another openly gay man for the first time. While Shalom (1997: 187) notes that people feel ambivalent about using personal adverts as it brings their personal world into the public sphere, this is not usually the case with gay men, whose minority status in society has meant that they have had to use less mainstream means to make romantic and sexual contacts.[1]

Harris (1997) gives a historical overview of gay personal adverts in America from the 1940s onwards. His qualitative analysis focuses on the ways that advertisers became more specific about the qualities of their prospective partners over time, as well as increasingly drawing upon narratives of gay pornography. He notes that the history of the assimilation of gay men into mainstream society can be charted by the fact that euphemisms such as 'special friend', which were common to adverts of the 1950s, were replaced by terms such as 'husband' in the 1990s. Thorne and Coupland carried out a study of 100 gay male and 100 lesbian personal advertisements, noting that gay male advertisers prioritise appearance over personality while the reverse was true for lesbian advertisers (1998: 240). They also analyse four types of gay male adverts in some detail, each constructing a different discourse type with specific goals and identities being referenced (e.g. ex-forces bloke, Hollywood iconography, a sexually explicit hard-sell, and older men seeking younger men in exchange for domestic security). Leap (1996: 150–8) looked at *responses* to personal ads in reference to safer sex, finding that when the advertiser specified that he didn't use condoms, the respondents wrote about their own interests and physical attributes. However, when the advertiser specified that condoms were obligatory, respondents focused on the advertiser's attributes and interests, and minimised discussion of their own personal details.

Other approaches to personal adverts have involved a quantitative analysis of a larger set of adverts, sometimes using a corpus linguistics approach. Shalom (1997) carried out a corpus-based analysis of personal adverts in London's *Time Out* magazine. Her data were taken from a five-month period in 1995. While ambitious, in examining the most frequent lexis of four groups of advertisers (gay and heterosexual men and women), only 155 adverts were placed by gay males. Shalom also found that gay advertisers were more likely to specify physical attributes and also tended to use the words *similar* and *masculine* more than other advertisers. Marley (2002) also used a corpus of personal advertisements to examine issues concerning questions and modality, although all her advertisers were heterosexual.

The aim of this chapter, then, is to carry out an analysis of gay male personal adverts which combines Shalom's corpus-based study, using a larger sample, with the diachronic analysis used by Harris in order to look at how gay men use language to construct identities in the personal ad genre, and how such identities have changed over time.

I chose to focus on personal adverts from a single magazine (*Gay Times*, formerly *Gay News*), as it has not particularly changed its focus – providing a balance between reporting on political developments concerning the legal and social status of gay men, as well as acting as a lifestyle magazine, giving information about gay-related media (films, television, books and latterly websites, etc.). It is also the longest-running gay magazine in the UK, and perhaps the most mainstream, being available in many newsagents. *Gay News* was founded in 1972 as a bi-monthly newspaper, connected to the emerging Gay Liberation movement in the UK[2] and relaunched in 1983 as a magazine. By 1985 it had become the monthly *Gay Times*, and it survives to the present.

While a corpus-based approach to personal adverts will not explain why gay identities have (or have not) changed over time, they will at least provide a representative set of linguistic snap-shots, and it is my intention to link the longitudinal patterns found in the corpus to other types of socio-cultural data such as attitudinal data and an analysis of representations of homosexuality and masculinity in the media over time. This multidiscipli-nary approach will enable hypotheses about changing constructions of gay identity to be explored more fully.

Once the corpus had been collected and annotated, it became clear that there were numerous ways of approaching the analysis – for example, by examining patterns relating to the age of the advertiser and the age of the desired partner, or by looking at the ways that ethnic identities were con-structed in the adverts. However, for the purposes of this chapter, I chose to focus on the ways that advertisers negotiated gendered gay identities, both for themselves and in the sort of person they desire to meet.

Masculinity, as a gendered practice, is often stereotypically associated with heterosexual men. While Meinhof and Johnson (1997: 19–21) note that there are many ways of being masculine and we should therefore think in terms of masculinities rather than there being a single masculine identity, Connell (1995: 76) stresses the importance of recognising relations among masculinities, pointing to hegemony, subordination, complicity and mar-ginalisation as four of the practices and ways of regulating the main patterns of western masculinity. Masculinity is often viewed as a desirable trait by gay men, yet stereotypically, gay men have been represented as camp or effeminate via folk myths and in the media over the twentieth century.[3] Thus the relationship between homosexuality and masculinity is potentially complex. Gay male personal adverts would therefore function as a possible site where desires and fantasies surrounding masculinity are fore-grounded, negotiated and contested. As Connell (1995: 41) states: 'Gay men's collect-ive knowledge ... includes ambiguity, tension between bodies and identi-ties, and contradictions in and around masculinity.'

Methodology

One problem with studying personal adverts over a long period of time is that different magazines cater for different audiences, or the same magazine may 'rebrand' itself, deliberately deciding to change its target audience over time. Therefore diachronic change in adverts may be a result of a magazine attempting to attract different sorts of people, rather than any wider social factors. In order to address issues of data representativeness, it would have been useful to build a larger corpus which sampled dozens of different maga-zines, but due to constraints of time this was not an option.

Because the corpus data used in this chapter are only derived from *Gay News/Times* it is therefore important to note that any findings should only relate to the readers of this magazine who placed adverts and not be gener-alised to all gay men in the UK. However, the mainstream and popular status of this magazine suggests that these findings can be more credibly generalised as being representative of gay men in the UK than adverts in, say, a gay magazine which caters for a more specialist audience such as *bears*.[4] Possibly the magazine's emphasis on current events, social issues and arts reviews may mean that it attracts a more mature audience than youth-oriented publications such as *Attitude* and *Boyz*. It should also be noted that, in 1973, *Gay News* was one of the few options for gay men who wanted to place a personal advertisement. By 2000 there were many more sites that carried gay personal ads in the UK: numerous gay magazines, mainstream publications such as *Time Out* and the *Guardian*, websites and telephone dating. So it should be taken into account that some of the men who placed an advert in *Gay Times* in 2000 would have done so because they did not have access to, or preferred not to use, other types of advertising. This may possibly make the 2000 dataset a more homogeneous sample than those who posted adverts in 1973, where less choice was available.

Although *Gay News* was founded in 1972, the earliest issues I could obtain were published in 1973. The data was therefore sampled over four equal nine-year periods, from 1973, 1982, 1991 and 2000. As Harris (1997: 44–5) notes, the personal advert is a continuously evolving form of discourse. One reason for this could be that when people engage in writing an advert they are likely to emulate what they find desirable in those that they have already read. Therefore certain phrases or words will become increasingly popular, while others become moribund. Evidence for this is suggested by the fact that when terms become popular they are often replaced with an acronym. This abbreviation of a longer phrase such as *good sense of humour* is both convenient and cost-effective – it is cheaper to post an advert saying *GSOH* than one which writes out the phrase word by word. So, by taking a 'snapshot' of the state of personal adverts from the same magazine at nine-year intervals, it should be possible to see how constructions of gay identity within *Gay News/Times* have changed over time.[5]

For each year that was sampled, four issues of the magazine were used, although adjacent issues were not sampled in order to prevent the likelihood of repetitions of the same advertisement. Approximately 2000 words of adverts were collected from each issue. In this way almost 8000 words of adverts were collected for each year, resulting in a total corpus of 31,788 words (1350 adverts in total, with a mean advert length of 24 words). In terms of modern corpus building, this is a relatively small size. However, the personal advert is characterised by a high degree of repetition which allows patterns to be observed even with a small sample of data.

So that the description of the advertiser could be analysed separately from the description of the sort of person the advertiser was looking for, the corpus was marked up in the following way:

> <advertiser>London. Professional guy (30) slim fair short hair</advertiser> seeks <target>similar active guy over 21</target> for a real relationship. Photo please. Box 255.30

The adverts should not be read as revealing any 'truths' about the advertisers, but instead can tell us the ways in which gay men chose to present their identities to potential partners, by constructing the most attractive possible image of themselves in order to ensure an optimal number of responses from people whom they considered to be desirable.[6] As a result, the constructions, both of the advertiser and of what he desires, are likely to be fuelled by ideals and fantasies, which are possibly embodied within the pages of the magazine, for example via images of the attractive men used in commercial advertising.[7]

Analysis

About 60 per cent of the advertisers used an identity-based noun, usually to describe either themselves or the sort of person they were seeking. Often these nouns were preceded by a list of adjectives. Table 5.1 shows the most frequently used noun labels in the corpus.

Overall, the most popular noun used was *guy*, followed by *male* and *man*. These terms were often preceded by adjectives such as *young, professional, active, slim* and *masculine*. The terms *guy, male* and *man*, being so popular, were relatively neutral or 'default' descriptors of identity. In contrast, *gent* or *gentleman* were paired with words like *mature, elderly, refined* and *retired*. A chi-squared test on this data, as described in Kilgarriff (1996a, b), showed a difference between frequencies of these words over time at the 5 per cent level of significance – suggesting that particular words were more likely to be used at certain time periods than others. For example, in 2000, *blokes* and *lads* had become more popular than in previous years, suggesting a more masculine, working-class identity, with words like *skinhead, horny, muscular* and *rugby* occurring as common left-hand collocates.

Overall, the most frequent adjectives used in the adverts were *slim* (305), *similar* (284), *young* (217), *attractive* (176), *active* (155), *sincere* (155), *professional* (147), *genuine* (133), *non-scene* (133) and *tall* (119). However, descriptions of the self differ somewhat from descriptions of the other, as Tables 5.2 and 5.3 reveal.

Table 5.1 General male identity-based nouns

	1973	1982	1991	2000	*all*
bloke	1	1	1	8	11
chap	3	5	0	0	8
fellow	1	0	0	1	2
gent(leman)	3	7	6	6	22
guy	86	169	144	151	550
lad	1	0	4	17	22
male	68	15	5	30	118
man	38	19	19	32	108

Table 5.2 The most popular adjectives used to refer to the self

1973	1982	1991	2000	all
1 young (52)	slim (74)	slim (52)	slim (71)	slim (244)
2 slim (47)	attractive (47)	non-scene (49)	professional (53)	attractive (146)
3 attractive (33)	young (33)	straight-acting (40)	caring (34)	professional (132)
4 good-looking (24)	tall (32)	professional (34)	attractive (31)	young (116)
5 lonely (23)	non-scene (30)	attractive (33)	tall (30)	tall (105)
6 active (22)	professional (30)	good-looking (27)	good-looking (26)	non-scene (100)
7 tall (19)	active (22)	tall (24)	fit (25)	good-looking (93)
8 professional (17)	quiet (18)	young (23)	affectionate (24)	active (55)
9 sincere (15)	good-looking (16)	intelligent (22)	non-scene (20)	caring (55)
10 affectionate (13)	sincere (16)	sincere (18)	GSOH (19)	sincere (55)

Table 5.3 The most popular adjectives used to refer to the desired other

	1973	1982	1991	2000	all
1	similar (61)	similar (73)	similar (80)	similar (62)	similar (276)
2	active (47)	active (26)	young (30)	younger (20)	active (96)
3	sincere (31)	younger (24)	younger (26)	active (17)	younger (91)
4	younger (21)	sincere (22)	slim (17)	slim (14)	sincere (71)
5	non-camp (13)	young (22)	straight-acting (17)	young (13)	slim (61)
6	attractive (10)	slim (20)	smooth (13)	non-scene (12)	genuine (46)
7	non-effeminate (10)	genuine (15)	cleanshaven (11)	caring (11)	non-scene (34)
8	slim (10)	discreet (12)	genuine (11)	genuine (11)	non-camp (31)
9	genuine (9)	non-camp (12)	non-scene (10)	sincere (10)	attractive (30)
10	masculine (8)	non-scene (12)	black (9)	intelligent (9)	intelligent (28)

While advertisers were much more likely to refer to themselves as *slim, attractive, professional,, tall* or *young*, they tended to be seeking someone who was *younger, genuine* or *similar*. Shalom (1997: 195–6) also notes that *similar* was the most popular word used in her corpus of personal adverts. However, while Shalom concludes that in her corpus of male, female, gay and straight adverts, *similar* could often be used to refer to *parts* of the advertiser's self-description, particularly sexuality in the case of gay male advertisers, I would argue that in the case of adverts placed in a more specialist magazine where it is already assumed that all of the advertisers and readers are gay, then *similar* is more likely to be used in conjunction with other, non-sexuality-based adjectives.

The most frequent adjectival collocates occurring within four places to the left or right[8] of *similar* were: *non-scene* (19), *sincere* (17), *genuine* (15), *straight-acting* (13), *younger* (12), *gay* (11), *attractive* (10), *discreet* (10), *slim* (9) and *young* (9), suggesting that these terms tended to be generic attributes which many advertisers claimed to both possess and desire. One way of constructing an appealing or attractive identity, therefore, is to create one based on a cluster of generic qualities, which explains the high level of repetition between different advertisements.

From Tables 6.2 and 6.3, it can be seen that different lexical strategies were used at different times to refer to masculine identities: *straight-acting, non-camp, non-effeminate* and *masculine* occur at different periods as popular adjectives. An analysis of all of the adjectives in the data revealed that there were other, less frequently occurring words or phrases that referred to masculinity. Table 5.4 shows the ways in which the uses of these words changed over time, across all of the data.

A chi-squared test carried out on this data (Kilgarriff 1996a, b) revealed that there were differences in the ways that masculinity-based words were used over time at the 0.001 per cent level of significance.[9] In 1973, advertisers were most likely to refer to masculinity by using *anti-types* – words which stated a lack of a particular trait. So terms such as *non-camp, non-effeminate* and *not camp* were most commonly used (comprising about 56 per cent of overt masculinity lexis in this year). By 1982, three differing strategies fought for dominance: *non-camp* was still used, as was *masculine*. However, comparisons to stereotypical male heterosexual gender norms (e.g. *straight-looking*) were also beginning to be used more frequently. In 1991 the situation had changed again. *Straight-acting* had become by far the most dominant term, used in 47 per cent of cases where men wanted to overtly refer to masculine gendered behaviour. In 2000, *straight-acting* continued to be the most frequently used marker, having been acronymised as *SA*. However, the term was not as popular as it was in 1991, with the older terms: *masculine* and *non-camp*, although also declining over time, taking up a larger proportion of terms relating to masculinity.

In some cases, advertisers may only construct the desired 'other' as masculine:

Table 5.4 Adjectives referring to masculinity

	1973	1982	1991	2000	overall
butch	3	0	1	1	5
manly	0	0	2	0	2
masculine	15	21	19	18	73
no camp	2	0	0	0	2
no campers	1	0	0	0	1
no effems/effeminates	3	2	2	0	7
no fem	1	0	0	0	1
non-camp n/camp	20	19	8	5	52
non-fem non-fm	0	1	1	0	2
non-effeminate	15	3	2	0	20
not camp	8	0	0	0	8
outwardly straight	0	1	0	1	2
real man	0	0	1	0	1
straight-acting	0	1	57	19	77
straight type	1	1	1	0	3
straight appearance	1	2	2	0	5
'straight'	0	0	3	0	3
straight	1	0	3	0	4
straight life(style)	0	0	4	0	4
straight-living	0	1	0	0	1
straight looks	0	1	0	1	2
straight-looking	6	14	14	2	36
straight-talking	0	1	0	0	1
SA	0	0	0	20	20
SL	0	0	0	9	9
ungay	0	0	1	0	1
total frequency	77	68	121	76	342
total % of sample	0.96	0.85	1.54	0.94	1.07

> Older man searching for young man 20s. Me, semi-retired, time to fill. Interests theatre, ballet, opera, dining out, international travel. Kind and caring. You non-scene, drugs, smoking, masculine, clean-shaven, slim, good muscles, straight-acting. Box 7100

However, in other instances, *straight-acting* is offered as an exact exchange:

> Good-looking, 32, 6' tall, slim, straight-acting. Interests: keep fit, weights, badminton, squash, other sports and interests. Non-scene, genuine person, wanting to meet similar, straight-acting with similar interests. 21–34. Photo please. ALA. Box 9333

Lest it be assumed that none of the advertisers specified camp identities in themselves or their desired others, it should be noted that there were a small number of cases (11 out of 1350 adverts) where this happened (two which used the word *feminine*, three which used *camp* and six which used *effeminate*). One of the advantages of working with corpora is that they are often large enough to highlight exceptional cases, which a more qualitative analysis of a smaller text would miss. The analysis of exceptions can be fruitful in understanding how a particular linguistic phenomenon is used. For example, Stubbs' (2001b: 48–9) analysis of collocates of CAUSE showed that the term tended to occur with negative events: *cause anger, cause an accident*, etc. One important exception to this was the phrase *cause amusement*. However, when Stubbs examined the word *amusement* in a corpus, he found that it occurred most often in a negative sense, to signify that someone was amused by another's misfortune. Therefore, *cause amusement*, although appearing as an exception, still supported the main semantic pattern of CAUSE.

The two advertisers who used *feminine* were both from masculine or 'outwardly straight' men who were looking for transvestites, e.g.:

> Convincing TV? Over 21? Feminine? Non-smoking? Attractive masculine guy 34 could be very interested in friendship! Photograph please. North West/Midlands/anywhere. Box 255.25

Some of the uses of *effeminate* or *camp* were also used by men who considered themselves masculine but were seeking a more feminine partner:

> Businessman, mid 40s, seeks young effem/gay to act as his secretary/PA and share his home etc. Nice lifestyle, good prospects, possibility of lasting 1 to 1. Only honest, sincere and trustworthy guys need apply with photo.

> Young male (Over 21) perhaps shy, effeminate. Sought by guy 30s-straight appearance, told not bad looking. Own modern flat London, car, active. Hopes for lasting friendship. Possibly Share flat Photo phone number appreciated ALA Box 37/142 L

In both cases, this is a case of a financially viable, older, masculine man seeking a younger, more passive man – with the implication that a relationship almost akin to 'man and wife' would be formed. However, not all references to effeminacy seek to replicate heterosexual gender norms:

> Lonely, frustrated student (22), disabled, seeks long-term mate (21–29) for caring, loving, non-casual relationship. Effems welcome. Write with photo, phone number soon. Box 231.19

In this case, it seems possible that one set of attributes which could be viewed as less-than-perfect for some people – 'lonely, frustrated, disabled' –

are offered in exchange for another which could be seen as having an equally low market rate – 'effems welcome'. Finally, referring to campness could be used as a way of constructing a negative yet 'honest' identity, a strategy also noticed by Thorne and Coupland (1998):

> Not quite devastating to look at, occasionally camp, 25 lazy, thin, brown hair, sometimes drunk in Manchester. What butch beauty will sweep me off my feet. Box 37/45

Here *camp* collocates with other negative qualities – 'not devastating to look at', 'lazy', thin hair', 'sometimes drunk'. Such a strategy employs reverse psychology, by emphasising negative points and ensuring that the advert will stand out as different and humorous. Therefore, while there are exceptions to the rule, which specify campness or effeminacy, they consist of an extremely small minority, and to a large extent tend to reinforce the discourse that masculinity is actually preferable to most people.

However, what is perhaps most interesting and unexpected from Table 5.4 is that the figures for overt masculinity lexis in 1991 are much higher than in the other three time periods that were sampled (this relationship between time period and identity construction is examined in more detail later in the discussion section). In 1991 the idealised connection between heterosexuality and masculinity resulted in adverts such as the one below:

> Normally straight? Just happened to be looking at these pages? Clean-shaven, non-smoking young-looking guy (21+) wanted by straight-acting totally non-scene male 28. Fun/friendship. London Box 6611

The main adjectival collocates of the words which refer to masculinity (taken as a whole) in Table 5.4 are: *non-scene, slim, similar, attractive, professional, active, tall, clean-shaven, intelligent* and *young*. There appears to be a recursive relationship between these adjectives and masculinity – the adjectives not only refer to masculinity (or at least a recognisably mainstream type of masculinity) but they also help to bring it into being. A discussion of the strongest collocate, *non-scene*, is perhaps useful here. The term *gay scene* roughly refers to the commercial side of gay culture: particularly bars and nightclubs but also incorporating cafés, restaurants, saunas, shops, charity and sporting events or specialist clubs relating to hobbies or sexual fetishes. To be *non-scene* is therefore to claim to have either minimal contact with other gay people or to only meet gay people in non-gay establishments. The term *non-scene* is not present in the 1973 data, occurs 42 times in 1982, rising to 59 times in 1991 (when explicit references to masculinity are also highest) and decreases to 32 times in 2000. The pairing of *non-scene* and terms such as *straight-acting* is interesting, perhaps implying the belief that social contact with other gay men is emasculating. *Non-scene* also collocates strongly with the terms *totally* (MI score 3.86), *ambitious* (3.28), *healthy*

(3.19) and *down to earth* (3.02), although overall these terms occur relatively infrequently.

Linked to the concept of masculinity is the word *active*, which is the second most common word used to describe the desired other overall. The meaning of *active* is somewhat more difficult to define than a term like *non-scene* or *straight-acting*. It can refer to someone who has a great deal of energy and enjoys participating in sport. However, I would argue that the high frequency of *active* in gay personal adverts suggests it is being used as a code to indicate someone who is active sexually (particularly in terms of someone who is sexually dominant or takes the inserter role during sex). *Active* was most popular in 1973, occurring 71 times, decreasing to 48 times in 1982, and then 13 times in 1991, but by 2000 had regained ground slightly with 23 occurrences. However, the word appears to be used in different ways over time. In all but one of the uses of *active* in 2000, the word appeared as part of the phrase *active type*, e.g.:

> S/A, unpretentious, domesticated professional, 41, seeks sharing interests (sitcom, music, travel, food, drink) and more with masculine, active type, non-scene mate (30–45), Sussex, Box 6552

Active is therefore often linked to masculinity – suggesting that for some advertisers gender identity is performed by a person's sexual behaviour or role in addition to other characteristics.

The phrase *active type* did not occur at all before the 2000 data. Interestingly, the word *passive* occurred 14 times in the 2000 data, of which 12 of these were of the form *passive type*. *Passive* only occurred once in the 1991 data, and not at all before that. The use of *passive* in the 2000 data suggests more evidence that *active/passive* refer to sexual roles rather than levels of activity.

While *active* appears to have been the only word which referred to sexual roles in 1973, by 1982 the euphemisms *school-master* and *strong-minded* had both started to be used by advertisers. Interestingly, both terms have the acronym *S/M*, suggesting that they could have been a code for sadomasochism:

> London/anywhere. Good looker, 26 6', slim seeks to meet strong-minded guy school-master type same age. Photo helps. Box 255.22

As Table 5.5 shows, by 1991 words like *submissive* and *dominant*, which are more sexually suggestive, had become more popular, whereas 2000 saw a return to *active*, but this time with the previously unmentionable half of the binary pair, *passive*, being used. Interestingly, overall words that refer to sexual roles were lowest in the 1991 data, suggesting that advertisers during this period were less likely to be explicit about what they wanted sexually. The word *fun*, which is used as a euphemism for sex, is highest in 1991,

Table 5.5 Frequencies of terms referring to sexual roles

	1973	1982	1991	2000
active	71	48	13	23
dominant	0	0	5	3
daddy/father	1	2	5	3
masterful	0	0	3	1
master	0	0	1	2
nephew	0	2	3	8
passive	0	0	1	14
school master	0	8	2	3
slave	0	0	0	1
strong minded	0	8	2	1
son	0	0	0	2
sub/submissive	0	0	10	6
uncle	0	3	5	1
versatile	1	4	1	4
total	73	75	51	72

occurring 81 times. It did not occur in the 1973 data, appeared twice in 1982 and 74 times in 2000. The strongest collocate of *fun* in the corpus is *safe*.

However, a concept which did occur most frequently in 1991 is that of discretion. In 1991 the words *discreet* or *discretion* occurred 37 times, while this figure appeared 30 times in 2000, 29 times in 1982 and only seven times in 1973, six years after the decriminalisation of homosexuality. Perhaps, because old habits die hard, many older gay men still required or were expected to be discreet in 1973, so there was less need to state it as a requirement. For example, research which looked at gay men who grew up in the 1950s and 1960s (Baker 2002a, Baker and Stanley 2003) found that many of them did not align themselves with the values of Gay Liberation. Additionally, the new Gay Liberation movement (Power 1995) may have made discretion unfashionable in favour of a sense of openness and pride, particularly for younger gay men.

However, the higher number of references to discretion in 1991 (when compared to 1982 and 2000) again suggests a desire to be covert about gay identity during this period. *Discreet* occurs relatively infrequently in the corpus, although when it does occur it collocates strongly with the words *bi* (MI score 3.62), *uncomplicated* (3.31), *straight* (3.10) and *down to earth* (3.10).

Discretion is often linked to adverts where the advertiser seeks to engage in sexual practices that he considers to be somewhat unconventional (by his perceived societal standards). So this may include outwardly heterosexual, bisexual or masculine men wanting to find male partners, or men who wish to find escorts, much younger partners or transvestites:

Gwent/Glamorgan. Mid 30s, company director, totally non-scene, seeks manly men in the first stages of middle-age spread for evenings in and evenings out. Married/bi's welcome, but definitely discreet, non-camp. Photo please. ALA Box 4600

Exforces rugby fan/player, 29 non-scene, discreet, genuine, down to earth, frustrated, seeks long lasting similar mates, 121 relationship Box 4602

Professional guy, 40, stocky build, seeking white, compliant, horny lad under 21 as occasional escort/companion, all expenses paid. Write with horny letter/photo for instant reply. Discretion assured. Box 6556

Running shorts, jocks, crickets briefs etc. Sports lover seeks frank penpal. Athlete, coach, gay, bi or TV very discreet. ALA. Box 7292

One of the most obvious ways to construct a masculine identity is via references to the body, particularly by emphasising muscularity, definition and size. The following advert from 1991 emphasises physicality both in terms of the advertiser and the person he is seeking:

Black guy. Tall, muscular build, broadminded, good humour, seeks tall dominant heavyweight bodybuilders/rugby guys for fun and friendship. All nationalities welcome. Photo with letter ensures quick reply. Box 6405

Words which suggest a masculine body (e.g. *well-built, athletic, muscular, fit, trim, strong, hunk*) were lowest in 1973 (with fourteen occurrences) and increased over time, rising to 69 in 2000. Also, references to traditionally male sports such as *wrestling*, *rugby* and *football* slowly rose over time, from six in 1973 to fifteen in 2000.

Bourdieu (1978) conceptualises the body as a form of commodification or physical capital in modern societies, a theory which has particular resonance with the genre of personal adverts. Indeed, the personal advert becomes a part of the commodification process of gay identity, with its descriptors converging on ideals of masculinity and muscularity. Whereas in the past, muscular male bodies were a form of physical capital, exchanged via manual labour for wages (Bourdieu 1986: 246), or when middle-class gay men paid working-class 'trade' for sex, what is now on offer in exchange for a muscular male body is simply another muscular male body – a non-financial 'trade', in what seems to be an increasingly competitive market.

The other popular body type which is often mentioned in the adverts is *slim*, which had a sharp rise in occurrences between 1973 and 1982. Even in 2000, *slim* was used more often than all of the other muscularity words combined together, but it is definitely the case that descriptors of mesomorphic bodies are catching up (see Table 5.6).

Table 5.6 Terms relating to physical build

	1973	1982	1991	2000
rugged	2	1	0	0
well-built	0	3	0	0
athletic	1	8	3	12
muscular	2	7	16	12
muscle	0	2	2	0
fit	0	6	22	30
trim	0	1	4	1
strong	2	1	2	2
gym-trained/toned	0	0	1	3
sturdy	0	1	0	0
body-builder	4	0	0	0
good/nice/firm/physique	3	10	4	6
good/nice body	0	1	0	2
defined body	0	0	0	0
masculine body	0	0	1	0
hunk	0	0	1	1
total	14	41	56	69
total % of sample	0.17	0.51	0.71	0.86
slim	58	93	82	86
total % of sample	0.72	1.16	1.04	1.07

Words which collocate frequently with *slim* in the corpus include: *smooth*, *boyish*, *clean-shaven*, *affectionate*, *caring* and *sincere*, while words which collocate with the muscularity words in Table 5.6 include: *hairy*, *straight-acting*, *masculine*, *similar*, *mature* and *handsome*. These collocates define two poles of desirable masculinity. Slimness in the adverts is therefore associated with youth, a lack of body and facial hair and a softer, caring personality, whereas muscularity is linked to age, body and facial hair and masculinity:

> Central Londoner, attractive, masculine, strong minded, thickset, intelligent, articulate, fifty, seeks slim, younger, boyish companion over 21. Box 231.13

> You (28–40) active type, shy, competitive, you like to win and you're genuinely into sport football, golf etc. You're looking for opposite type, me, 35, passive boyish type, slim, cheerful, affectionate, London based Irish guy who can knock a laugh out of people the odd time. I will relocate if necessary. Box 6262

> Oxford Hairy muscular 35 year old seeks smooth boyish guys for

cycling, wine tasting, theatre, music (all types), hiking, good conversation and quiet weekends with lots of hugging. Box 9163

Another way in which masculinity is constructed through some personal adverts is via reference to hair (see Table 5.7). This occurs either by referring to hair colour[10] or to the length or amount of hair a person has (or would like their prospective partner to have). References to hair (in terms of its quantity) are also highest in 1991 – both for terms which refer to the presence of hair (particularly male hair – *hairy chests, beards, moustaches*) and for terms which refer to a lack of hair (e.g. *smooth, skin, clean shaven, shaved*).

In 1973 and 1982, terms which refer to presence of hair are slightly more frequent than terms which refer to removal or shortening of hair. This trend is reversed in 1991 and 2000. However, overall references to both presence and non-presence of hair are highest in 1991. If, as is suggested by the analysis so far, 1991 was a year in which masculine identities were particularly popular, then perhaps it is the case that the maintenance of body hair is

Table 5.7 Presence or absence of body hair

	1973	1982	1991	2000
Presence of body hair				
long hair	3	0	0	0
hirsute	6	8	6	2
beard(ed)	2	9	10	0
moustache	1	5	2	0
tache	0	0	2	0
hairy	4	8	11	4
hairy chest	1	0	4	3
sub total	17	30	35	9
Lack of body hair				
clean shaven	6	13	20	11
skin(head)	4	2	4	6
smooth	2	8	22	9
crop	0	0	3	1
bald	0	2	0	1
short hair	0	1	0	3
shaved	0	0	3	0
sub total	12	26	52	31
totals				
combined total	29	56	87	40
% of sample	0.36	0.70	1.11	0.49

one way in which gay masculinity can be indexed. Removal of body hair allows a muscular body to be more clearly seen, whereas shaving the head (*skin head* or *zero crop*) has had associations with working-class masculinity since the 1970s. A lack of body hair may also signify youthfulness. However, the presence of body hair emphasises males as being different from females – being able to grow a beard or moustache or possessing a hairy chest are also signifiers of masculinity. The following advertiser from 1991 uses *manly*, *hairy*, *muscular* and *non-scene* – all indicators of the masculine identity he is trying to project:

> South Wales. Manly 28 year old, 5'10", dark, hairy and muscular, non-scene, professional, seeks taller, straight-acting, very hairy guy 25–35 with good physique for companionship and maybe more. Sense of humour as valid as hairy legs and chest! Box 9356

Blachford (1981:192) points out that one way in which gay men came to construct masculinity during the 1970s was via *expressive artefacts* and *concrete objects*. This refers to particular types of clothing – work boots, tight jeans, chaps and leather – as well as tattoos, handle-bar moustaches, cropped or short hair, uniforms or objects associated with masculinity such as pipes and motorbikes. Such references actually pre-date the 1970s, although it may be argued that it was with the advent of Gay Liberation that they became entrenched as symbols of gay masculinity. As other references to masculinity appear to have increased since the 1970s, perhaps we would expect to see even more of these types of words appearing in gay personal adverts, particularly in 1991.

However, sexual fetishes relating to masculinity such *as leather*, *denim* and *sportswear* have become increasingly unpopular since 1973 (see Table 5.8).

Table 5.8 References to expressive artefacts and concrete objects

	1973	1982	1991	2000
tattoo	1	1	1	1
leather	31	14	17	4
denim	17	5	2	0
sportswear	0	9	2	0
jocks	0	1	2	1
briefs	0	11	4	2
boots/booted	2	1	5	0
breeches	0	2	0	0
cigarettes	0	0	3	0
pipes	0	0	1	0
motorbike	0	0	1	1
total	51	44	38	9
% of sample	0.63	0.55	0.48	0.11

We could argue that perhaps the reason for this is because such identities had become so popular that they had been subsumed by a hypernymic word such as *clone*, which implies a uniform gay identity based around symbols of masculinity such as cropped hair, moustaches and denim. However, the word *clone* only appears in the corpus three times in 1982 and 1991.

While references to masculine clothing and artefacts decreased over time, the fetishisation of masculine identities, especially those which relate to 'real-world' traditionally male occupations (e.g. *fireman, police, ex-army, trucker*) was at its highest in 1991 (Table 5.9).

> Hairy active type and horny professional, 40, seeks younger skin or labourer type. Can accommodate, East Anglia. Box 6924

> W Midlands Ex-army NCO 46, seeks police/fireman or ex-forces for disciplined relationship Box 6596

Perhaps another way in which masculinity can be expressed in personal advertisements is by reference to a successful career or material possessions (e.g. *car, home*). Traditionally it has been the male who has been the 'breadwinner' in the past, so it could be theorised that by demonstrating financial security, an advertiser is implicitly making a statement about his 'success' at being a man. O'Kelly (1994: 23) quotes Dunbar as saying that people indicate wealth by 'identifying what job they do, whether they are educated, or what kind of car they drive'. Shalom (1997: 200) notes that in her corpus of personal adverts, *professional* was one of the three most commonly occurring

Table 5.9 References to masculine occupations and roles

	1973	1982	1991	2000
biker	0	7	6	2
ex(forces)	0	0	4	1
ex(services)	0	0	3	0
fireman	0	0	2	0
police	0	0	3	1
security guard	0	0	1	1
soldier	0	0	2	0
(ex)navy	1	0	2	2
(ex)army	0	0	1	1
construction	0	0	1	0
sailor	0	0	2	1
labourer/builder	0	0	1	2
truck(er)	1	2	2	2
total	2	9	30	13
% of sample	0.002	0.01	0.03	0.01

adjectives used, and it was gay men and heterosexual women who were most likely to include it in their adverts. In Chapter 4 it was seen that the character of Will in *Will & Grace* was depicted as having a desirable gay identity. Will possesses masculine traits as well as owning a large apartment in a fashionable part of Manhattan and holding down a successful career as a lawyer. So, would it be the case that in the *Gay News/Times* personal advertisement corpus, references to aspirational, class-based ideals, similar to those possessed by Will, would also occur as indicators of masculine success?

> Uncle type, 45, tallish, slim, intelligent, caring, solvent, with own home and successful business, seeks young guy 21–25. ALA with picture. Box 9362

> Surrey. Gay professional couple 40s, 50s, slim, attractive solvent WLTM couple or single guy for fun friendship. ALAWP. Box 6975

> Aberdeen area. Forties, slim, genuine, professional guy, average looks OHAC, seeks younger slim guy for friendship, hopefully 1-2-1 ALAWP. Box 6952

Claims about holding down particular 'professional' jobs (*doctor, lawyer, executive, director*, etc.) peaked in 1973 (see Table 5.10), while references to owning a car and/or home were highest around 1982 (during a decade of high unemployment) and decreased thereafter, possibly because home/car ownership was becoming increasingly taken for granted due to the relative prosperity of the country since the 1990s. Interestingly, the inclusion of the words *solvent* and *professional* gradually increased over time, being most common in the 2000 data. However, taken as a whole, references to a successful career or material possessions are highest in the 1982 data and lowest

Table 5.10 Indicators of success

	1973	1982	1991	2000
successful	1	4	2	3
solvent	0	1	1	11
professional	17	32	36	62
car	19	18	7	2
own business	0	3	3	0
home/pad/flat/house/place	44	61	20	5
doctor/lawyer/executive/director/graduate	20	8	14	9
OHAC (own home and car)	0	0	0	3
total	100	127	83	95
% of total	1.25	1.59	1.01	1.11

in the 1991 data (although this difference was *not* statistically significant) – a finding which is at odds with the fact that other ways of expressing masculinity are highest in 1991. Perhaps it is the case that in 1982, with UK unemployment at a high level, career status became a more relevant issue for advertisers.

Discussion

Why were advertisers more concerned with certain markers of masculinity in 1991 and why had their definition of gender at this time converged upon *straight-acting* and related collocates, a term which ties masculinity to heterosexuality, implying an association between effeminacy and homosexuality?

One way to provide an explanation for this observation is to examine the ways that gay and heterosexual men in the UK during 1991, and the years leading up to it, were perceived by mainstream society, including the government and the media.

During the 1980s in the UK, gay men had been blamed for the spread of HIV and consequently AIDS by a number of tabloid newspapers, including the *Sun*, who consistently stated that AIDS is a 'gay disease', the *Daily Mail* and the *Daily Express* who followed the line that homosexuals were to blame for the appearance and spread of HIV (Sanderson 1995: 46). The introduction of Clause 28 in 1988, which stated that a local authority should not 'promote homosexuality or publish material for the promotion of homosexuality ... promote the teaching in any maintained school of the acceptability of homosexuality as a pretended family relationship by the publication of such material or otherwise' placed a further legal stigma upon gay lifestyles. Unsurprisingly, negative attitudes towards homosexuality rose during the 1980s,[11] peaking in 1987 (see Table 5.11), the year before the introduction of Clause 28.

However, while gay men were increasingly represented negatively during the 1980s, images of heterosexual masculinity had begun to be increasingly represented as sexually attractive in the media and advertising (Bronski 1998: 105). For example, a 1985 television advertisement for Levi's 501 jeans which featured the model Nick Kamen undressing to his boxer shorts

Table 5.11 Percentage of respondents answering 'always wrong' to the question 'What about sexual relations between two adults of the same sex?' Data derived from *British Social Attitudes* 9th, 13th, 16th and 17th reports (Jowell 1996: 39, Jowell *et al.* 1992: 124, 1999: 348, 2000: 112)

Year	1983	1984	1985	1987	1989	1990	1995	1998	2000
%	50	54	59	64	56	58	55	38.5	37.5

increased sales by 800 per cent (Simpson 1994: 97). While it could be argued that these images had been appropriated from ideals of male beauty in the gay media, it was the first time that such directly sexualised images of the exposed male body had been widely used on mainstream audiences. Physical fitness also became more mainstream over the 1980s, represented in film by body-building actors such as Sylvester Stallone and Arnold Schwarzenegger. At the same time, some gay men turned to body-building as a response to AIDS (Harris 1997: 93–4). The gay media has been increasingly likely to employ images of unclothed muscular (and therefore, by implication, masculine) men in a variety of advertising and other features (Dotson 1999: 135–40), particularly since the 1980s.

During the 1980s, as male homosexuality became more stigmatised and male heterosexuality became eroticised, it is possible that gay men felt the need to distance themselves from appearing obviously 'gay'. This would have led to an emphasis on 'discretion' and a gender performance most usually associated with heterosexual men – stereotypically masculine, or 'straight-acting'. It would also have led to a focus on the shape of the male body; since the 1980s the mesomorph is increasingly defined as an ideal body shape for males, both heterosexual and homosexual. Hair is also seen as an important signifier of gay masculinity – either by shaving the head and body (in order to make muscles more defined), or by possessing hair characteristics associated with males (hairy chest, beard, moustache) – both being ways of emphasising the masculine body. With the emphasis on masculine constructions being overtly concerned with appearances – the body and the gender performance – at the same time the association of masculinity with success is downplayed in 1991, perhaps because it is not as easy to demonstrate (or manufacture) as other indicators of masculinity.

In conflict with the above findings, identities based around leather and denim were relatively unpopular in 1991, although masculine occupational identities such as fireman and ex-army were at their most popular at this time. However, as Blachford (1981) notes, the leather and denim identities had gained ground in the 1970s. Perhaps by the 1990s they were seen as unfashionable by mainstream gay men, or too 'obviously gay', a theory which holds with the idea that gay men wanted to distance themselves from appearing explicitly gay in 1991. On the other hand, identities connected to stereotypically masculine occupations were possibly seen as more authentic and therefore attractive because of their association with masculinity but not specifically homosexuality. Masculinity is therefore connected to a cluster of interacting factors which change over time, including physical appearance, sexual role and occupation. Finally, allusions to specific types of sexual activity were also lowest in the 1991 data. Again, this may have been linked to concerns about HIV transmission via sex, leading advertisers to play down references to sex, instead preferring a vague phrase like *safe fun*.

There is no such thing as an average gay man or an average advertiser. A wide range of ages, professions and locations were represented in the *Gay*

Times data. It is also unlikely that the advertisers would have viewed their sexuality in the same way. What I think is interesting, however, is that despite the fact that the advertisers were not a particularly homogeneous group, the ways that they chose to represent themselves and what they were looking for resulted in patterns of re-occurrence. This heterogeneous group – an 'imagined' society in a sense – *chose* to represent itself in similar ways, by referring to quite a narrow set of ideals based around particular notions of masculinity.

However, one factor which was discussed earlier is that, as the twentieth century progressed, the number of possible sites for placing personal ads for gay men in the UK increased (particularly with the popularity and availability of the Internet). So it could be the case that the apparent decrease in interest of *Gay News/Times* advertisers in 'expressive artefacts and concrete objects' (Table 5.8) by 2000 is the result of such interests being catered for by niche magazines and websites which concentrate on particular fetishes or different constructions of gay masculinity. Such men may advertise elsewhere, feeling that *Gay Times* is too mainstream or its advertisers place the wrong amount of emphasis on physical appearance and mainstream conceptualisations of masculinity for their tastes. The source of the corpus was limited in order to concentrate only on the construction of identities within the relatively unchanging and long-running *Gay News/Times*, but a larger corpus of personal adverts, which is both longitudinal and takes samples from multiple sources, might have resulted in different findings. It could be argued that we may be able to generalise the patterns found in the *Gay News/Times* personal adverts over the last 30 years to other representations of identities found in the (mainstream) gay media, particularly as personal adverts are often expressions of idealistic desire. However, the patterns elicited from the personal advertisement data may not reveal the range of possible identities that are constructed by gay men away from the media, or they may foreground certain constructions of gay masculinity at the expense of others.

So it may be the case that other factors can explain the preoccupation with the appearance of heterosexual masculinity in the early 1990s by the advertisers in *Gay Times*. However, if the above theory holds, then a significant proportion of gay men, feeling stigmatised as disease spreaders and potential proselytisers by a hostile government and media, suffered an identity crisis, becoming increasingly fixated on the idea of stereotypical heterosexual masculinity. Therefore, this research suggests that the negative treatment of a minority group by mainstream society can have far-reaching consequences in the ways that members of the minority group perceive themselves, ultimately attempting to appropriate and exaggerate alternative identities that are viewed as more acceptable by mainstream society.

6 As big as a beercan

A comparative keyword analysis of lesbian and gay male erotic narratives

Introduction

> My partner, the veteran cop know [sic] he has me now. His strong arms pull my body into his, and then his hairy paws start grouping [sic] my uniform-clad body as his mouth closes over mine. His rough tongue pushed its way down my throat. His hard hungry hands work over me until I'm writhing uncontrollably in his grasp.
>
> 'Rookie Cop' (the *Nifty Erotic Stories Archive* – Gay Adult Friends section)

> We started to kiss again while Angel moved her hands down past my shoulders and to the bottom of my shirt. She slowly went under my shirt and touched my delicate skin. Her very touch made me tingle all over. She started kissing me on my neck and slowly moved down my chest. I could hear myself breathing harder as she felt me tremble with excitement.
>
> 'Beautiful Love: Angel Eyes' (the *Nifty Erotic Stories Archive* – Lesbian Adult Friends section)

While personal advertisements offer one site of desire for examining discourses surrounding the construction of gay identity, another possible area involves stories about gay people having sex. Such narratives can either be fictional or 'true-life' accounts of sexual experiences, and will differ from the personal advertisement genre in that they are even more liable to be based around ideals. While people who write personal adverts are likely to try to construct themselves and their potential partners in the best possible light, a balance still must be maintained between fantasy and realism. Erotic narratives, on the other hand, can be allowed to disregard realistic accounts of sex because their main purpose is to sexually arouse its audience. Therefore, erotic narratives tend to feature descriptions of the best, most exciting sex possible.[1] They are important sites in revealing discourses of idealised sexual relationships between ideal participants of a particular gender or sexual orientation. An examination of gay male erotic narratives should tell us a number of things:

- the identity constructions and language use of those who are viewed as ideal sexual partners;
- important themes or narrative patterns within the texts which reveal the discourses of sexuality that the authors have accessed;
- the language that gay consumers/creators of erotic texts find to be sexually arousing.

There are several possible approaches to take in order to examine discourses of gay identity in erotic narratives. For example, a researcher could focus on a single text or carry out a more quantitative study on a number of texts, looking at frequencies of particular lexical items or grammatical structures. However, it is also possible to carry out a comparative study, which should reveal what are the most important differences between two (or more) types of narratives. After carrying out a small-scale pilot study, where I compared gay male narratives with other types of texts, I decided that comparing gay male erotica with an equivalent set of lesbian erotica would yield the most relevant and interesting results.[2]

The decision to compare gay male narratives with lesbian narratives, rather than with heterosexual male (or female) narratives, makes the main focus of this chapter not on differences between homo- and hetero- but on gender differences within the homo- category. It could be argued that gay male sexuality represents a more 'pure' type of male sexuality, showing what men are like when in the absence of women. For example, Edwards (1994: 95) writes: 'Cruising sexuality, as instrumental, unemotional and orgasm-oriented is indeed male sexuality *par excellence*.' However, it is not always possible to ascertain the sex or sexuality of the authors of erotic texts. It should not be assumed, therefore, that gay male texts are always written by gay men, or lesbian texts by gay women. For example, one form of gay erotica known as slash fiction (often based on fictional accounts of gay male sex between television characters) is often written by heterosexual women (Plotz 2000). And it perhaps should not also be assumed, then, that the 'intended audience' of the gay male narratives is always going to be gay men, although it is likely that many gay men will find gay male narratives more arousing than other types of erotic narratives. When working with Internet texts, it is usually difficult to ascertain the identities of individual authors. However, while this may affect the sorts of questions or conclusions that we can make about such texts, it should not preclude research into this area.

Defining what is meant by an erotic narrative is not an easy task. The word *erotica* is often confused with, conflated with, or used as a euphemism for *pornography*. Bright (2001: 42) points out that there is rarely agreement over what the two terms mean: 'It's simply impossible to find two people who agree straight down the line as to what is in the E section and what belongs under P.'

For some, the difference between the two is a matter of taste or personal preference. The Meese Commission of 1986 defined pornography as 'any depiction of sex to which the person using the word objects'. Erotica was viewed as sexually explicit material but the committee found that the term was used to refer to material 'of which the user approves'. The relationship between pornography and erotica is further complicated by conflicting feminist critiques. Some feminist perspectives of pornography cast it in terms of unequal gender relationships. Brownmiller characterises it as 'the undiluted essence of anti-female propaganda' (1975: 394), whereas Longino (1980: 42) defines it as 'the degrading and demeaning portrayal of the role and status of the human female'. On the other hand, Steinem (1978: 37) describes erotica as 'a mutually possible, sexual expression between two people who have enough power to be there by positive choice ... It doesn't require us to identify with a conqueror or a victim.' Bright (2001: 44) notes that porn has come to be defined as pictorial rather than textual, whereas Dworkin (1981: 9) suggests that the only difference between erotica and pornography is in terms of production values: 'Erotica is simply high-class pornography; better produced, better conceived, better executed, better packaged, designed for a better class of consumer.'

So choosing to categorise a text in terms of pornography or erotica forces a person to make a value judgement, and also to reveal their own political or moral stance in relation to it. I refer to the specific texts under analysis in this chapter as erotica rather than pornography, because that was the collective heading under which they were initially described in the place they were archived. The majority of the texts feature consensual adult relationships. However, this definition may not satisfy all readers of these texts, some of whom may find them to be pornographic or obscene. The fact that gay and lesbian narratives generally do not (directly) involve men exploiting women may mean that they are inconsistent with some feminist definitions of pornography. However, because they involve explicit details of same-sex intercourse, the narratives may be viewed by some readers as *more* pornographic than similar stories featuring heterosexual sexual activity.

The small amount of previous work on gay male erotica has tended to focus on professionally published literature. For example, Bolton (1995) carried out a quantitative study of ten books containing gay male erotica published between 1981 and 1992, looking at the frequencies of body parts and descriptors applied to them. He found a pre-occupation with penis size, although he concluded that such narratives were important in that they 'instruct us in knowledge which can help us promote a sexuality that is rich and satisfying' (Bolton 1995: 205). One consequence of this could be in the design of health promotional materials (see also Chapter 7). Harris (1997: 158) tracks the evolution of commercial gay erotica throughout the twentieth century, noting that it has resulted in the 'active suppression of the gay sensibility, a process in which manufacturers divest us of our subcultural identity'. Heywood (1997), who also looked at similar texts, focused more on the construction of transgressive anonymous encounters as erotic, particularly focusing on the interplay between sexual role and masculine identity.

However, because professionally published written erotica is often subject to editorial guidelines which may restrict its final form, it was concluded that an analysis of this genre may produce differences depending on the intended audience, but these differences may be the result of the guidelines, rather than the writing style of the authors. For example, a publisher or editor may require a text to be of a certain length or have criteria about what may or not be written about. Therefore, it was decided to focus on the genre of 'amateur' erotica (e.g. narratives that were written for the pleasure of the author and potential readers, rather than narratives written for financial profit), as this would be more likely to reflect the authors' own fantasies, and be less likely to be subjected to editing practices, or tailored to a specific set of guidelines.[3] Amateur erotica may be viewed, therefore, as a more complete reflection of the original authors' desires and identity constructions.

The source of amateur erotica that I chose to study was from a public Internet archive at www.nifty.org. This site, which is updated daily, contains emailed stories from across the world (although most of the authors tend to be based in North America). It is classed into a number of categories including gay, lesbian, bisexual and transsexual. Within these categories are sub-categories such as 'adult friends', 'celebrities', 'military', 'first time', etc. It was decided to collect two million words of gay male and lesbian erotic narratives, and these would all be from the 'adult friends' sub-category. Only one sub-category was chosen, in order to avoid overlap as some stories appeared in more than sub-category. The 'adult friends' category was also the most general of all of the categories, focusing on a variety of adult sexual relationships. Therefore, I examined 342 texts containing lesbian narratives (1,010,837 words total) and 354 texts containing gay male narratives (1,013,527 words total). This data was 'cleaned' by removing headers which gave extraneous information such as email addresses, date of publication and disclaimers. As a result, the final word counts were 985,331 words for the gay texts and 991,189 words for the lesbian texts. The gay narratives were therefore slightly longer on average (the mean length being 2898 words versus 2775 words). An examination of the standardised type token ratio, average word length and average sentence length also showed the two sets of data to be remarkably similar.[4] All of the texts were submitted to the archive between 1991 and 2002 with over two-thirds of them occurring during or after the year 2000.

Before proceeding, there is also an issue which needs to be addressed about comparing 'differences'. As described in Chapter 1, early studies of language and gender tended to focus on comparisons between males and females, for example, Lakoff (1975). Later, this theoretical perspective was refined into a *dominance* model, whereby differences were reinterpreted as to do with males asserting power over females. More recently, a model which has focused on *discourses* has replaced earlier constructs. So does this quantitative comparison of two sets of data, nominally labelled as male and female data, signify an unwelcome return to the difference model?

One concern that I have about a model that *just* focuses on discourses is that it could be in danger of erasing the notion of differences between the ways that gendered identities are represented. A criticism of the earlier models of gender and language was that they tended to report data quantitatively, without explaining what the results meant. Also, the early difference/dominance studies tended to focus on spoken language, usually involving transcribed conversations of relatively small numbers or few participants. It was therefore impossible to generalise findings from these studies to say that they were representative of the speech of males and females on a wider scale.

The data in this chapter, however, are not concerned with differences in the way that real men and women use language. Any speech in the texts is uttered by fictional characters. There is no point in making any claims that such fictional characters are representative of how real people speak. In any case, erotic narratives often detail idealistic, surreal events that are unrepresentative of most people's experience. Of course, the language of the fictional characters *was* written by someone and one line of inquiry therefore could be: 'Do male and female writers of erotica use language differently?' However, while we can make guesses about the identities of Internet erotica writers, we cannot be certain our assumptions are correct. As the writers made their email addresses available, we could email them to ask who they are, but again we cannot be certain that we will receive an honest answer. So I make no absolute claims about the identities of the authors who created the texts. Instead, I am interested in how identity is constructed differently for each of the erotic genres, and the discourses that the authors draw on, in order to create recognisably (or not!) gendered characters. Differences in the vocabulary of these texts are therefore not reflective of 'real life' differences in how people really talk, but are more indicative of how people *believe* they should talk in erotic same-sex situations.

In choosing a method of comparing the two genres of erotica with each other, I have decided to focus again on *keywords*. Exploring the keywords that occur when two corpora are compared with one another should reveal something of the different discourses that are present in these sets of texts, in relation to each other, both in terms of aboutness and style. Keywords themselves will not reveal discourses, but they can be used as signposts for them. Examining how such keywords occur in context, which grammatical categories they appear in, and looking at their common collocational and phrasal patterns should reveal something about discourses of homosexuality, if they exist.

While it is almost impossible to build a corpus that claims to be fully representative of a particular genre of language, the fact that this dataset consists of just under two-million words means that it can hopefully circumvent the criticisms of the earlier difference studies that focused on small samples of data.

Keywords analysis

In order to compare the two text types, a keywords analysis was carried out, using WordSmith Tools (Scott 1999). As described in Chapter 1, this is a form of analysis which creates frequency lists for both sets of data, and then compares the two lists together. Log-likelihood tests then determine whether a particular word has occurred statistically more frequently in one list than another, given the overall size of the texts and their frequencies in both lists. The 'cut-off' point for determining whether a word was a keyword was whether the difference in frequency between the two files was significant at a level less than $p = 0.000001$. Even at this extremely high level, a total of 1055 keywords were found, 504 which occurred significantly more often in the gay texts, and 551 which occurred significantly more in the lesbian texts. An analysis of these keywords should reveal differences between the two types of texts, which should shed light on how erotic discourses are constructed around gay male and lesbian subjects.

Before starting the analysis, some issues concerning the analysis of two sets of keywords should be noted. First, the comparison of the two sets of files will not elicit a list of keywords which are typical of erotic narratives per se. So, for example, it is likely that words such as *sex* or *came* would be keywords in most types of erotic texts when compared to general language use, but they will not be revealed as such in this analysis as we would expect both the lesbian and gay texts to use these sorts of words about equally. The analysis is therefore not so much concerned with delineating the sorts of words which make erotic narratives distinctive from other types of language, but just those keywords which reveal evidence of distinction between gay and lesbian narratives. However, in order to determine which words *are* key in both sets of texts, when compared to written language in general, keyword comparisons of both sets of erotic narratives were also made with the Frown corpus (a one-million word corpus of American written text from 15 genres, collected in the early 1990s).

Second, as with other forms of corpus analysis, a list of keywords may reveal differences at the lexical level, but will not explain why these differences exist. It is therefore necessary to go beyond such lists, looking at how keywords are used in the context of individual narratives, which will necessitate the examination of concordances or collocational data. We should not assume that a word is always used in the same way, particularly across different genres of text. For example, the word *sessions* occurs significantly more in the gay texts than the lesbian texts (35 versus 3). In the gay texts, *sessions* is often used as a way of referring to a particular kind of sex – one with little emotional commitment: e.g. wanking session. We could therefore conclude that this sort of term is used more often in gay texts than lesbian texts. That certainly is the case, but it is not the full story. When we look at the lesbian texts, *sessions* is *never* used to refer to sex, but instead refers to workout sessions or sessions with a psychiatrist. The difference between the two genres is therefore greater than we had originally suspected. In other cases, a word will be used in a similar way in both genres of texts – for example, there isn't much of a difference in the way that *sweat* occurs in both gay and lesbian texts, although it is a keyword in the gay narratives. Where there are major differences in the uses of keywords across genres, this has been pointed out. It's therefore the case that a word can be key because it occurs in a text or genre with high frequency and has a particular meaning or association that is important. In contrast, when a word is not key, it will occur less frequently than expected and in less predictable ways.

Unfortunately this sort of keywords analysis would not be able to distinguish between different uses of the same word – so if the phrase *wanking sessions* occurs 30 times in the gay texts while *workout sessions* occurs an equal number of times in the lesbian texts, *sessions* would not appear as a keyword, even though there is a difference in the way that it is used. The keywords analysis is therefore limited to the lexical level (although, as shown in Chapter 4, it is possible to carry out keywords analyses on grammatical or semantic categories, or on multi-word units).

Third, a keywords analysis operates by comparing expected/unexpected frequencies rather than small/large frequencies. Therefore, words that appear a relatively small number of times can still be key, as long as there is a significant difference in their expected frequencies. For example, a word like *bloated* that occurs only 18 times in the gay texts, but zero times in the lesbian texts, would be classed as a keyword (this was one of the weakest keywords that was found, with a keyness of 24.9. At the other end of the scale was the word *his*, which occurred 25,543 times in the gay texts and 874 times in the lesbian texts, and had a keyness of 27,843.5).

And finally, keywords don't necessarily reveal differences across a range of texts. For example, if *bloated* only ever occurs in one gay narrative, does that make it worth pointing out as an interesting and general language distinction between gay and lesbian narratives, or is it simply the result of something about that specific narrative?

In order to address this issue a key keywords analysis was first carried out on the data. A key keywords list tells us how many texts a keyword appears in as key. For example, in the lesbian texts the word *herself* is a keyword. It occurs 1168 times across 216 texts, although when each lesbian text is analysed separately against the gay texts as a whole it only occurs as a keyword in 91 of them. Table 6.1 shows the top 30 key keywords for the lesbian and gay male texts. While the lists reference similar concepts: pronouns, body parts, clothing, people, many of the key keywords are gendered as we would expect and don't reveal much about discourses of homosexuality beyond this fact. So there is clearly a problem here. Individual keywords may occur too infrequently to be of use to us, whereas the key keywords tend to only reveal the most obvious differences. One solution then is to focus on groups of keywords which have similar semantic properties or functions within the texts. On their own these keywords may occur relatively infrequently, but taken as a group they lend more weight to the presence of a particular discourse. For example, we could combine the analysis of *bloated* to consider other keywords such as *fat, thick, huge, massive* and *bulging*. Rather than carrying out a semantic tagging of the texts (as occurred in Chapter 4), it was decided to put them into groups by hand based first on an analysis of their part of speech (e.g. all of the nouns were categorised as one group, the verbs put into another) and then categorising them where necessary according to semantic themes, e.g. for nouns: parts of the body, clothing, types of people, etc. And because a word may be key and only occur within a small number of texts (therefore not being particularly representative of the corpus), it was only decided to consider gay keywords which occurred in 25 gay texts or more, with the same cut-off point also applying to lesbian keywords.

When discussing the different discourses which arose from an analysis of the keywords, it was more useful to consider words which stretched across different semantic or grammatical boundaries, but were thematically linked

Table 6.1 Top 20 key keywords in the lesbian and gay erotic texts when compared against each other

Lesbian key keywords			Gay key keywords		
Word	Key in number of texts	Overall frequency	Word	Key in number of texts	Overall frequency
her	327	33,708	his	334	24,516
she	320	23,224	he	328	20,647
breasts	136	1339	him	249	7574
pussy	123	2021	cock	203	4914
clit	109	747	dick	109	1834
herself	91	1168	I	103	36,975
woman	61	1433	balls	87	1059
panties	54	649	my	83	20,826
bra	48	468	ass	51	2151
cunt	44	531	himself	43	657
skirt	42	283	man	37	1262
the	41	39,861	load	35	490
breast	34	431	guy	33	777
my	32	16,398	we	31	5158
girl	32	789	cum	31	1404
dildo	31	328	shaft	28	521
she'd	30	497	he'd	26	437
you	29	8448	hole	24	717
lesbian	26	320	me	21	10,190
girls	26	501	penis	21	396

in other ways. Such thematic links were only discovered by close analysis of concordances and collocations of each keyword in the list.

Discourses

Sexuality

One discourse that both the lesbian and gay narratives seem to share is concerned with the fact that many of the characters in the stories have not considered themselves to be gay or lesbian in the past. Therefore the stories utilise a discourse of compulsory homosexuality – that everyone is latently gay or lesbian and that the same-sex experiences they have in the narratives will be more pleasurable or fulfilling than the heterosexual sex they have previously been used to.

As part of this discourse, many stories employ an 'initiation' narrative whereby heterosexual characters experience gay or lesbian sex for the first time. For example, one keyword in the gay texts is the word *weird* (Table 6.2). This adjective is generally used to describe the feelings of men who have suddenly found themselves in a sexual relationship or attracted to another man: '*I hope this doesn't sound weird but I've had a hard-on since you called today*' ('Ted and the Jacuzzi'); *It felt a bit weird to be lying like that with another guy clinging onto me* ('The Photo Opportunity'). *Weird* occurs more often with down-toners, e.g. *a bit weird* (4), *a little weird* (5), *kinda weird* (4), *sorta weird* (1) than with maximisers: *really weird* (1), *incredibly weird* (1), *fucking weird* (2), suggesting that the strangeness of the situation isn't too overwhelming, certainly not enough to prevent sex from occurring. Therefore, *weird* helps to express a discourse of gay male sexual initiation.

Strange, unusual, odd and *peculiar* (which aren't keywords) also fulfil the

Table 6.2 Keywords suggesting a discourse of compulsory homosexuality

	Keywords	Frequency	
		Gay texts	Lesbian texts
Gay keywords	weird	70	23
	something	731	976
	nobody	68	21
	dad	172	41
	wife	223	77
	father	171	56
Lesbian keywords	husband	28	303
	mother	103	241
	mrs	28	219

Table 6.3 Frequencies of words that indicate strangeness in gay and lesbian erotic texts

Words	Overall frequency	
	Gay texts	Lesbian texts
weird	70	23
strange	85	95
unusual	21	18
odd	33	32
peculiar	3	2

same function and occur about the same amount of times in both sets of texts (see Table 6.3). Therefore experiencing unusual feelings isn't just limited to the gay texts. *Weird* possibly occurs as a gay keyword because it is more colloquial or non-standard than words like *unusual* or *strange*, a phenomenon which will be considered in more detail later. *Nobody* (key in the gay texts) is also usually used in narratives involving initiation or secrecy: *Nobody, and I mean nobody ever even suspected I had a double life* ('Symbiosis'); *Through my fogged brain I heard Kelly say, 'Come on man. Nobody has to know'* ('Kelly').

Something (key in the lesbian texts), is often used to refer to feelings, relationships or speech: *as she could plainly distinguish . . . this was something different* ('Beth and Shannon'); *I bet there is something going on between Rai and Tonet* ('Haven'); *I need to tell you something. I love you too* ('Sammy's Revelation'). Words that appear directly after *something* in the lesbian texts include: *wrong* (16), *special* (11), *different* (10) and *new* (6). *Something* appears to be used as part of the compulsory homosexuality discourse in the lesbian texts, which often acts as a precursor to sex, e.g. *'Gretchen, there's something you should know. I've been a lesbian for most of the last 10 years'* ('Princess Reunion').

In addition, the heterosexuality of characters in the novels is made explicit by the number of gendered keywords in the texts that suggest traditionally heterosexual relationships (*father, dad, wife* in the gay texts and *husband, mother* and *mrs* in the lesbian texts): *She was safely home and I was in bed with her panties long before my husband came home* ('Mildred'); *The two men stood naked before each other: my dad with his cock hard and glistening from Steve's saliva* ('Babysitting Discovery Part 7'). Therefore, although different sets of keywords occur in the two genres of narratives, both are used, in slightly different ways, to construct a discourse of compulsory homosexuality.

Gender

Closely linked to the discourse that casts characters as possessing heterosexual identities but engaging in homosexual behaviour is one which also defines them as hyper-gendered. So men are extremely masculine and women are extremely feminine. As noted earlier, it is unsurprising that many of the keywords are gendered (see Table 6.4). For example, there are numerous words to describe male genitalia and male underwear in the gay narratives, and words for the female equivalents in the lesbian narratives. Perhaps what is more interesting are words for body parts that are *not* traditionally associated with a particular gender. For example, *sweat* occurs as a keyword in the gay texts almost always occurring as a noun 295 times, compared to 138 times in the lesbian texts. The politer word, *perspiration* (although not a keyword) occurs 32 times in the lesbian texts, and 17 times in the gay texts. Sweat has several functions in the erotic narratives. It is used to show that someone is aroused: *I could see the sweat he worked up moving around me as I posed for him!* ('Car Wash Man'). The presence of sweat helps to eroticise human bodies, which *shine, gleam* or *glisten* with it, while its smell or taste is *sweet, musky, fresh, pungent* and *manly*. Sweat is also a sign of exertion or 'hard work' during sex: *He was thrashing his head on the sweat drenched pillow* ('Two Way Marriage'); *Glen ground his hips into me, writhing like some fuckin' dogs, sweat pouring from our foreheads* ('Will Fuck for Grass').

In terms of clothing, again the presence of keywords involving gender-specific items are to be expected. The occurrence of *socks* as a gay keyword is partly attributed to one narrative, entitled 'Sock Tied and Tickled', which has 26 references to this item of clothing, and as suggested from the title, socks play an important role in the story. However, even with this story excluded, there would still be 76 other references to socks in the gay narratives, compared to 16 in the lesbian narratives, and when keywords are recalculated without this file, *socks* is still a keyword for the gay files. So why are

Table 6.4 Keywords suggesting discourses of gender in gay and lesbian erotic narratives

Discourse	Keywords	Frequency	
		Gay texts	Lesbian texts
Gay men are brutes	socks	102	16
	sweat	295	138
	beer	273	33
	football	66	14
	towel	232	118
	team	76	18
Lesbians are ladies	stockings	14	68
	glass	93	216
	wine	49	293
	tea	12	87

socks relatively seen as more important in the gay narratives? In the lesbian texts socks are most often used as part of an overall description of what someone is wearing, along with other items of clothing. While this also occurs in the gay texts, socks are subjected to a wider variety of uses: *'Did you listen to them and see if the guys had socks stuffed in their bathing suits?'* ('Somewhere Along the Way'). As with sweat, the smell of socks is seen as erotic: *a smelly, strong smell of just removed socks was superb* ('My Smelly Friend'). Socks are also often described as being removed, along with underwear, so that a character is completely naked. The words *pulled* and *off* are strong collocates of socks in the gay texts. Other collocates, which involve removing both shoes and socks include *kicked off, tugging, removed, stepping out of* and *slipped off*. However, perhaps the reason why *socks* occur so infrequently in the lesbian texts is because the alternative *stockings* occurs more often (68 times). Semantically, *socks* is a term that is perhaps more gender-neutral than words like *pants* or *dress*. However, in written erotica, clothing is far more likely to be gender-stereotyped, so women will wear stockings more often than socks. Therefore, at this stage, it could be theorised that when a choice exists between a gender-neutral term and a gender-stereotyped one, the erotic narratives are likely to select the stereotype.

Moving on to look at other nouns, predictably the gay texts feature keywords that indicate orientation towards safer sex: *condom, condoms, sheath, lube. Beer(s)* is a common keyword, occurring in over a quarter of the gay male texts, functioning as a masculine beverage, and acting as a precursor to the sexual activity that takes place. The introduction of beer into the narrative signifies an informal, matey situation (with one's *buddies* – also a gay keyword in the singular). In most of these cases, drinking beer occurs in private, domestic situations, usually involving watching sports on the television or getting drunk at home, rather than in bars: *I arrived before the game, grabbed a beer and made myself comfortable in front of the television* ('Football'); *His brother, my brother, and a few guys that played hockey together all got together for the Grey Cup game, ordered some spicy pizzas, ate junk food and drank lots of beer* ('The Day after the Grey Cup'). Beer therefore enables masculine camaraderie, being associated with competitive drinking (while watching competitive sports). The presence of alcohol in the bloodstream in these stories often helps to remove inhibitions, or to mitigate sexual behaviour between men, which is the result of inebriation; the characters are often unable to recall exactly what happened the next morning.[5] For example, in 'Meeting at the Beach', where *beer(s)* occurs seven times, during military training in Panama, two soldiers have 'perhaps a few beers too many' and become 'past sobriety'. They become sleepy, remove their clothes and climb into their tent. Then one soldier is woken up by his friend performing oral sex on him. Their sexual encounter is never discussed between them.

In contrast, the drink of choice in the lesbian texts is *wine*, often occurring as part of the phrase *glass of wine*, which explains the occurrence of *glass* as a lesbian keyword. Wine serves a similar function to beer, although it is used more often as an accompaniment to conversation, rather than watching television. Wine also contains connotations of sophistication and culture. For example, in 'Awakenings', Yolanda invites Kathryn back to her flat and presents her with a tray containing three types of cheese and wine. However, wine is also used as a narrative device in order to relax inhibitions: *'Well if you don't like what you hear I will blame it on the wine. But I have seen the way you look at me sometimes'* ('One for the Night'). *Tea* also occurs as a keyword in the lesbian texts, which is again used in domestic 'at-home' contexts, sometimes occurring as part of breakfast, the morning after a sexual encounter: *'I have to say last night was incredible,' Kathryn said as she took a sip of tea* ('Awakenings'). Tea also has soothing qualities: *I went to make us some tea to calm her nerves* ('Melanie's Seduction'); *Olivia left her to go to the kitchen to put some hot water on for tea to soothe her nerves* ('The Friendship of Lovers'). The way that the drinks are handled by the participants in the narratives also reveals gender differences. For example, while tea is *sipped* and wine is *drunk*, beer is *downed*, *guzzled*, *swigged* and *gulped*. Tea is *made* and *poured*, whereas beer is *grabbed*, *popped open*, or even thrown from one character to another, as if a ball in a sports game: *He threw me a beer, while he snapped his own* ('Porno Booths, Teachers and Italian Sausage').

Football is a keyword in the gay texts, serving several purposes. First, as already described, football is the sport that is watched prior to gay sex, establishing the masculine/heterosexual credentials of the characters in the narrative. But also, a number of the narratives involve football players: *Frank never considered sucking a dick but since he and his football buddies had jerked each other off, he never minded giving me a hand* ('Boys Next Door'). In addition, male characters' physiques are admiringly compared to those of footballer players in other narratives: *He had shoulders like a football player, massive and mounding up to the neck* ('Cyclist'); *He was in his early twenties, sported a very beefy outta-shape ex-football player look* ('Chunky Bodybuilder'). The gay keyword *team* also suggests a sports theme, with strong collocates being *football*, *wrestling* and *swim*. The keyword *towel* is also often used in sports narratives. Showering together after a sports game acts as a way of revealing the characters' naked bodies. Towels are often worn, then removed or allowed to casually fall open to reveal a character's arousal: *He just looked at me and grinned as he pulled the towel apart to reveal what had to be one of the most beautiful hardons* ('My Lover's Brother'). Towels also have a secondary function in a number of the narratives, being used to clean the body after sex: *'Now get me a towel and a wash-cloth so I can clean this shit up'* ('UPS'). Towels therefore signify the need to clean up after some form of physical exertion, either sport or sex.

Some of these differences reveal similar strategies. For example, beer and wine both serve the same narrative device in the gay and lesbian texts respectively – to loosen inhibitions so that sex can occur. However, they also perform another function, to establish gendered situations and identities, which are designed to enhance the reader's understanding and enjoyment of the story.

A class discourse also appears to run through the different narratives – masculinity is strongly related to working-class male identities – shown through the emphasis on non-standard language (see below), work metaphors, beer drinking and sports watching. On the other hand, femininity is constructed as more middle-class – for example, using polite language (see below), sipping tea or drinking wine (with three types of cheese).

Are there any references to non-masculine identities in the gay texts or non-feminine identities in the lesbian texts? *Effeminate* occurs four times in the gay texts, *camp* occurs twice, as does *sissy*, and *feminine* occurs seven times. However, a number of these terms are used to deny effeminacy: *I was determined he was NOT gonna see a 'sissy' side of me* ('Somewhere Along the Way'); *The cheeks were well-rounded without being feminine* ('Cutting Expenses'). *I liked watching the expression on his face when I explained that the idea of a gay man having to be some limp wristed, effeminate fop was a great American myth* ('Zeke's Come Undone').

In two cases, men's eyelashes are described as feminine, while in another, a character is described as effeminate in his mannerisms, but this is countered by the fact that he is married with children ('My Friend Brian'). Finally, in 'The Fantasticks', a character is described in the following way: *This compact hunk was something to look at but when he opened his mouth, he destroyed all the fantasies. The poor guy had this feminine, nasally voice that just didn't match the body.* Effeminacy is therefore not generally presented as a desirable trait in the gay male texts.

In the lesbian texts *butch* occurs 23 times, *masculine* occurs seven times, *manly* occurs twice and *mannish* and *macho* occur once each. However, although these terms also occur relatively infrequently, they are often used in a more descriptively neutral way: *Tracy Conway was a somewhat masculine woman in her thirties who also worked in the Mall at a sporting goods store* ('One For All'). In a few other cases, masculinity is seen as a positive trait: *And Mal is so butch. So deliciously butch* ('Celebration'); *God, butch women are gorgeous* ('Shameless in Chicago'). Butch lesbians, while marginalised, are at least occasionally presented as sexually attractive, whereas camp gay men are not.

Sex

A number of verb keywords in the gay texts function as machine metaphors, when used in conjunction with parts of the male body (Table 6.5). Just like a car engine, a penis can be *lubed*. It can also *leak* or *throb*, and it can be *jacked*, as a car is when it needs a tyre changing. Another metaphor likens the penis to a machine that digs for oil: it can *drill*, *pump* or *spurt*. Interestingly, the words *work* and *worked* also function as gay keywords. While *work* can refer to actual paid work in the texts, it is also often used to refer to physical exercise, e.g. *to work out*, but it also occurs in a sexual sense: *We work even faster and suck harder* ('A Surprise Visit'). In the lesbian texts, *work* is only used in a sexual sense 6 per cent of the time as opposed to 17 per cent

Table 6.5 Keywords suggesting discourses of sex in gay and lesbian erotic narratives

Discourse	Keywords	Frequency	
		Gay texts	Lesbian texts
Gay men are emotionless machines	lubed	47	4
	jacked	35	3
	leaking	58	5
	throb	45	7
	throbbing	232	50
	spurt	44	8
	spurts	35	2
	pumped	142	28
	pumping	168	42
Gay sex is work or action	sweat	295	138
	work	776	553
	worked	357	234
	action	136	63
	job	303	145
Gay sex is unrelated to the rest of life	sessions	35	2
For lesbians love and emotion are strong elements of an erotic narrative	love	693	1150
	passion	112	223
	relationship	64	138
	lover	97	380
	laughter	27	76
	song	21	53
Lesbian sex occurs after a long build-up of desire for a person	many	256	392
	been	1505	1911
	how	1275	1550
Age is wisdom	older	118	245

for the gay texts. Sex, for gay men, is more often likened to work, and bodies or body parts function as machines. As Talbot (1998: 192) points out in her discussion of masculinity: 'Bringing in the family wage is deeply entrenched as masculine in a wide range of discourses. Work is part of being a "real man".' Other (non-keyword) gay verbs which liken sex to work are *milked*, *plowed* and *plumbed*. It's interesting that the word *job* occurs within phrases that are to do with sex involving men: e.g. *blow job*, *hand job*.

Sex itself is often referred to as *action* in the gay texts, either to literally describe what is happening: *I continue working his ass with my piston action* ('Chris'); or as a more vague euphemism for sexual activity: *I'm still looking for some action* ('Boys Next Door'). Another word to refer to gay sex is *sessions*: *as we get to know each other's sexual tastes, later sessions included full nudity and mutual sucking sessions* ('Good Wanks'). In 42 per cent of the uses of this word, it is used to delineate particular types of sexual activity: *jerkoff sessions, massage sessions, licking sessions,* etc. In 31 per cent of cases it refers to sexual activity in general (the remaining cases are non-sexual). The use of *sessions* implies a delineated period of time where *only* sexual activity is happening, and has the effect of compartmentalising sex or setting it aside from other activities. Gay male sex therefore is represented as not occurring as an activity with fuzzy boundaries – for example, being the result of a romantic build-up – but simply occurs, as a *session*.

While physicality discourses of 'sex as work' and 'men as machines' suffuse the gay narratives, the lesbian texts contain keywords which indicate *emotional* feelings. For example, the variants of the lemma MAKE occur more often with *love*, as a euphemism for sex, occurring 212 times. This contrasts with gay words to refer to sex, like the euphemism *action*, or an openly literal phrase like *jack-off session*. *Love* has many other functions, however. It can be used to refer to a partner (*my love*), as a verb (*I love you*), or to describe the status of feeling (*they were in love*). The lesbian keyword *passion* serves similar functions to the feeling status of love, but are more uncontrolled expressions of sexual desire: *She had risen to the height of her passion and I knew she was close to orgasm* ('Perfectly Pampered Payback'). On the other hand, *relationship* is similar to uses of *love* that concentrate on affection and commitment, whereas *lover* focuses on the object of that affection.

Many (key in the lesbian texts), usually occurs in phrases which indicate periods of time, appearing before *months, minutes, moments, years, times, nights* and *occasions.* It is used within these phrases to show the strength of feeling that one character has experienced. This can occur during descriptions of sexual activity: *we were there on the bed for many minutes licking and savouring each other* ('Mrs Jackson – The Seduction'); however, it is most often used to show that one character has had feelings that have stretched back over much longer periods of time: *And she couldn't help thinking how many times she wanted to just walk up to her and kiss her* ('Untitled 4'). *Many* therefore often indicates depth of feeling and desire. In a similar way, the adverbial keyword *how* is often used in the lesbian texts to refer to time, e.g. *how long* (59), *how many times* (15). Sex between men, on the other hand, is constructed as more spontaneous or opportunistic; it simply happens without reference to a long-standing build-up of desire.

Another lesbian keyword is *been*. In 40 per cent of its occurrences, it is preceded by the word *had*. *Been* therefore implies past actions or feelings: *She couldn't wait to see what else she had been wrong about* ('The Love Boat'); *I was still a virgin and had never been penetrated* ('Princess Reunion'). Within the context of the narratives, then, *been* is often used in order to indicate that a change or development has taken or is taking place, linking it to the discourse of compulsory homosexuality.

Older occurs 245 times and appears in 70 of the lesbian texts (compared to 118 times in the gay texts and in 61 individual files). The phrase *older woman* occurs 97 times in the lesbian texts. *Younger*, which is not a keyword in either of the sets of texts, occurs 136 times in the lesbian narratives and 102 times in the gay texts. At a first glance, it looks as if the lesbian texts contain more older characters, but this isn't necessarily the case. For example, if one character is older than another, then it follows that the second character must be younger. Rather than writing 'Mary is older than Kate', the same relationship could as easily be expressed with 'Kate is younger than Mary'. What is happening in the lesbian texts, then, suggests two things: first, that age differences are noted more often in these texts, and second, they are expressed in terms of one person being older, rather than younger than the other. Why is this the case? Age is often used in the erotic narratives to indicate experience, wisdom or the initiation of one character into a sexual relationship by another: *'Not so fast Anna,' Jessica chided. 'I like it soft.' The teenager flushed with embarrassment to the roots. She immediately changed tactics, letting the older women guide her* ('The Librarian and the Lolita'); *'It isn't my place, but if you will listen I will give you some advice,' the older woman offered* ('A Night at the Jefferson'); *Jeanette being the older one she took charge and made love to Sabrina all night* ('Horse Backing WV').

The lesbian keyword *laughter* has two main functions in the lesbian texts: either to show that characters are happy, or to indicate a shared joke. *Song* is also a lesbian keyword, not referring to characters singing, but almost always used when characters listen to romantic or sexy music together. *Song* therefore acts as a scene-setting word, like *beer* and *wine*, suggesting that auditory stimulation is important in lesbian erotica.

Physicality

As well as casting male bodies as machines, and sex as work, another discourse likens male bodies to weapons and sex as violence (Table 6.6). For example, keywords like *shoot* suggest that the penis is used as a weapon: *As the first wave shot out Patrick pulled his mouth away and aimed the rapidly shooting rod at Jack's backside . . .* ('Jack Black and the Pizza Boy'). In the lesbian texts, *shot* is used in a much less sexual way, occurring in a range of phrases; *her eyes shot open, my nerves were shot*, etc.

Other gay keywords suggest violence: *shoved, grabbed, jerk, jerked, jerking, slapping. Slapping* most often occurs when someone's penis thrusts into someone else's anus, mouth or face: *Their bodies were loudly slapping together* ('Wedding Bell Blueboys'). *Shoved* occurs when a penis or finger penetrates another person: *I shoved myself in deeper, telling him to take it all the way* ('Only One Way to Go'). *Jerk* and *jerk off* are colloquialisms for masturbation, whereas *grabbed* in 75 per cent of 479 cases is used when one person takes hold of another's clothes or body: *His right hand reached across and grabbed the zipper on Bill's flight suit* ('Three Times in the County Seat'); *He grabbed my*

Table 6.6 Keywords suggesting discourses of physicality in gay and lesbian erotic narratives

Discourse	Keywords	Frequency	
		Gay texts	*Lesbian texts*
The penis is a weapon	shot	321	86
	shoot	200	21
	shooting	125	20
Gay men are animals and	grunted	61	6
gay sex is violent	groaned	163	41
	grabbed	479	276
	shoved	112	26
	jerk	92	24
	jerked	106	34
	jerking	86	19
	slapping	54	13
	pain	230	121
Lesbians are tender and	kiss	470	920
gentle	kissed	467	913
	kisses	58	182
	kissing	245	469
	parted	54	173
	touch	277	489
	traced	18	84
	pressed	256	407
	softly	156	312
	soft	397	695
	gently	460	673
	gentle	97	182
	lightly	150	248

cock and in one motion empaled {sic} his mouth on it ('Roommate') The following list of verbs used in the gay texts are not keywords, but taken together are indicative of a semantic prosody which views penetration as metaphorical violence: *ached, assaulted, attacked, banged, battered, blasted, captured, clamped, crashed, crushed, erupted, exploded, fired, flared, flashed, hammered, hauled, impaled, jousted, launched, moaned, plowed, plunged, pounded, probed, pulled, pushed* and *yelled.* Harris (1997: 147–8) suggests that the occurrence of such high-impact verbs in gay pornography is a relatively recent development, related to gay men's post-Stonewall self-confidence. However, it could also be argued that such words suggest a desire to experience and inflict pain on others. Rough sex can be a traditional expression of machismo, but it can also be an expression of masochism.

Another gay keyword is *pain*, and is almost always used to refer to unpleasant sensations which initially occur during anal sex. Interestingly, the noun which collocates most often with *pain* is *pleasure* (occurring within a 5L–5R span in 26 out of 508 cases) in phrases like: *Lee moaned in a mixture of pleasure and pain* ('Firm Friends'); *he gasped, partly in pain, partly in pleasure* ('Desk Job'); *Mat gasped to the mixes of pleasure and pain I was causing him* ('Moonlight in the Eastern Townships'). Pain is also described as *beautiful, erotic, luscious* and *sweet*, as well as *agonizing, blinding, excruciating* and *unthinkable*, revealing a somewhat ambivalent attitude towards it. However, the focus on pain in the gay male texts is another way in which the masculine identities of the characters are negotiated. Enduring pain (particularly as the passive partner during anal sex) is a way that a masculine identity can be sustained during a sexual act which is normally associated with taking a feminine/passive role, as Zeeland notes:

> Some marines I have known claim that Marines view being penetrated not at all as female, but as a *manly* test of endurance that, successfully withstood, leaves the bottom with *more* power.
>
> (Zeeland 1996:10, italics reproduced)

The lesbian sexual verb keywords are more literal and affectionate by comparison. Rather than the act of penetration, KISS occurs much more often, whereas other contact words include *touch, traced* and *pressed*: *Tortuously, I traced around her hard nipples* ('Kailen'); *Brandy pressed her exploration of Julia's pussy with her tongue* ('Cabin Fever').

Three lesbian adverbial keywords – *softly, lightly* and *gently* – all share a similar function, to describe tender physical contact. Verb lemmas that frequently occur after these adverbs also indicate less aggressive forms of physical contact: KISS (48), STROKE (38), TOUCH (29), RUB (24), BRUSH (23), SQUEEZE (21), PUSH (19), SUCK (19), CARESS (19), MASSAGE (16) and LICK (12). The use of these adverbs is contrasted with the rougher verb keywords that are found in the gay texts, e.g. *shove, grab, shoot*.

However, as well as differences based on physicality between the two sets of texts, there are a number of verbs which do not occur with significant differences in frequency when the two sets of texts are compared together, but do occur as key when the texts are compared against the FROWN corpus of general written American English. Both the gay and lesbian texts make significantly frequent use of 'violent' verbs such as *bit, biting, explode, exploded, grab* and *pounding* as well as more tender verbs like *caress, eased, hug, loved, nuzzled* and *stroked*. This suggests that it is not the case that all of the gay texts are violent and all of the lesbian texts are gentle, but that where there are differences based on these sorts of verbs, the gay texts are more likely to employ the violent verb constructions than the lesbian texts.

Language

As Scott (1999) notes, one of the most noticeable aspects of keyword lists is the amount of proper nouns that are found. For the comparison of the gay and lesbian texts, about 30 per cent of the keywords were proper nouns, comprising mainly of Christian names. However, names are not chosen at random in erotic narratives – they hold connotative meanings, and at different times, certain names are deemed to be more sexually attractive than others for specific cultures. It was unsurprising that names like Edna and Harold, with their (current) associations with older people, did not appear in any of the narratives. However, while both male and female names were chosen because of their positive associations in contemporary society, the average length of names in the two lists differs – it is 4.1 letters for the gay texts and 5.7 for the lesbian texts. The male names also tend to be monosyllabic, and are often shortened versions of other names, e.g. Mike, Tom, Bill. Shortened names are one possible marker of informalisation (Goodman 1996), suggesting that the gay male texts may adhere to a more informal style than the lesbian texts.

Looking at the keywords that describe people (excluding proper nouns), there are some predictable differences based on gender between the two text types, for example: *man*, *boy* and *brother* occur in the gay texts whereas *woman*, *girl* and *sister* appear in the lesbian texts. One non-gender-specific person keyword in the gay texts is *buyers*, which occurs only in one text, concerned with an underwear design company. However, there are other more interesting differences. For example, the gay texts include a number of derogatory words: *cocksucker*, *fag*, *faggot* and *fucker* (Table 6.7). These terms are almost always used when one sexual participant is talking (and often issuing an imperative) to another participant: *'You liked eating my dick, didn't you cocksucker?'* ('Army Buddies'); *'Yeah fucker, stick that finger in'* ('Jack Black and the Pizza Boy'); *'Suck it Faggot. EAT MEEE...!'* ('Doing Straight Mike'). *Fucker* and *cocksucker* are therefore used in their literal senses, the character is named because of the act he performs. In some cases, *fucker* is used to refer to a person's penis: *'That fucker is a mile wide!'* ('Fringe Benefits') or anus: *'Hold that fucker open!'* ('Wedding Bell Blueboys'). *Cocksucker* is often used, not so much as a term of endearment, but in a positive way, e.g.: *'I'm a great cocksucker, ain't I Frank'* ('Horny Guys Tails from Minnesota'); *'Hey buddy, I got me a real hot cocksucker over here'* ('The Barber's Chair'). Of the 47 cases of the word being used, about half of them have such positive connotations, with L1 collocates indicating ability at the task (*amazing, prized, born, seasoned, expert, hellacious, great, primo, steady* and *good*) or enthusiasm (*insatiable, eager*). Negative descriptions of cocksuckers occur less frequently: *crazy* occurs twice whereas *sleazy* and *sloppy* occur once each. However, in these cases, there is still an element of approbation and good humour associated with the label:

Table 6.7 Keywords suggesting discourses surrounding language use in gay and lesbian erotic narratives

Discourse	Keywords	Frequency	
		Gay texts	Lesbian texts
Gay men's language is informal, non-standard and often impolite	fucker	40	3
	cocksucker	46	2
	faggot/fag	49	1
	stuff	195	84
	yeah	638	144
	shit	335	95
	hell	292	120
	fuckin	162	3
	ain't	76	3
	wanna	135	30
	gotta	70	7
	gonna	210	91
	'em	58	11
	kinda	84	19
	real	368	115
	hey	252	151
	damn	205	88
	good	1479	1165
Lesbians' language is politer, more affectionate and more standardised	hello	26	95
	bye	7	50
	thank	77	167
	yes	383	682
	OK	224	342
	oh	718	1118
	lovely	42	122
	honey	25	148
	darling	4	52
	dear	16	171
	baby	126	329
	sweetie	3	43
	redhead	2	101
	brunette	2	81
	blonde	61	232

A devil-may-care smile spread across his face as he watched me clean up his still-hard prick. 'You crazy cocksucker, you,' he laughed. Giving him a wink, I took my mouth off his cock and replied, 'You're welcome, buddy. Anytime.'

('Prick Tease')

His mischievous blue eyes twinkled and a broad grin spread across his still-boyish face as he stretched his arms across the back of the sofa. 'I just bet you do, you sleazy cocksucker, you.'

('Prick Tease')

The big stud was holding onto Carmine's head for support, keeping him locked between his widely spread, straining thighs and allowing the crazy cocksucker to take over all the work for a little while.

('Wedding Bell Blueboys')

'Longer than you been waitin' to get back at my dick, you sloppy cock-sucker you!'

('Wedding Bell Blueboys')

The terms *fucker* and *cocksucker* are used to delineate sexual and gendered roles in the gay texts – the label *faggot/fag* is given by masculine men in the story, those who are predominantly heterosexual and take an insertor role during gay sex, but it is not a word which they call themselves. This distinction is indicative of the *stud–queen binary*, described by Waugh (1996: 54) as a common representation in pre-Stonewall gay fiction. Only 25 of the gay texts (or about 6 per cent) contain *fag/faggot*; in most of the texts, the roles between participants are not outlined in this way. *Cocksucker* occurs in 38 texts while *fucker* occurs in 26. However, taken as a whole, one of the following words – *faggot, fag, cocksucker* or *fucker* – occurs at least once in 69 (19.4 per cent) of the gay texts.

Another gay abstract noun keyword is *stuff*, qualifying for a wide set of functions, due to its non-specificness. It can refer to sexual activity: *'Where did you learn to do that stuff to a guy's dick?'* ('Lil Buddy'); clothing or other possessions: *Then we'll put your stuff in the dryer* ('Cyclist'); drugs: *'The stuff is expensive enough as it is'* ('UPS'); or act as a general noun: *As cocks went, it was quality stuff* ('Stag Night'). *Stuff* is a good indicator of informalisation within the gay texts, common to spoken discourse.

Words that express positive evaluation also show an interesting difference between the two sets of texts. For gay men, *good* is a keyword, whereas the equivalent is *lovely* in the lesbian texts. However, the way that the two words are used is quite different. *Lovely* holds the status of being one of Lakoff's 'empty adjectives', associated with the female lexicon, in studies of male and female language differences (1975). In the lesbian texts it is most often used to describe objects, e.g. faces, breasts, bodies, buttocks, whereas in the gay texts *good* is used to indicate feelings of pleasure during sex: the phrase FEEL *(adverbial modifiers) good* occurs 247 times. *Good* also frequently follows the verbs TASTE, LOOK and SMELL. In addition *good* functions in a variety of idiomatic phrases such as *good looking* (76), *good friend(s)* (53), *good time* (32), *good look* (24), *good thing* (15), *good job* (15) and *good shape* (11).

The lesbian texts tend to include affectionate keywords like *dear, honey, baby*, *darling* and *sweetie*, rather than derogatory or ambivalent words: '*Ginger, honey, your whole fist is inside my cunt*' ('Ginger'); '*Oh baby,*' Kathy *moaned* ('Confessions'). About 10 per cent of these constructions use the possessive pronoun *my* in spoken utterances made by one character to another, e.g.: '*I know my darling, just hold on!*' ('If I Give You My Heart'). The gay texts do not feature any of these possessive types of utterances. In the case of *honey*, which occurs only 25 times in the gay texts, 12 (48 per cent) of these cases refer to food, whereas for the lesbian texts only 43 (29 per cent) of the 148 cases refer to honey in the literal sense.

The word *dyke*, which is a lesbian keyword, occurring 45 times, has only three cases where it is used in a similar way to *fag* or *cocksucker*, having the form of an insult but the function of approbation, e.g. *Kathy moaned her approval*. '*You little dyke tramp*' ('Old Self').

Another feature of the lesbian texts is metonymy, where one feature of an object is used to refer to the whole (for example a member of a bureaucratic organisation may be referred to as a *suit*). In the lesbian texts metonymy occurs when a person's hair colour is used to represent their whole identity. So *redhead*, *blonde* and *brunette* appear as keywords. In about 60 per cent of cases, these words are preceded by the definite pronoun *the*: *She knew that the tall blonde was something of a sexual adventurer* ('Behind the Curtain'). Overall, in 74 per cent of uses of these terms, the word functions as a noun, rather than an adjective. Often, the character's name has been revealed earlier in the story: '*What do you think Jess?*' she asked. *The tall redhead was flustered* ('Discoveries'). While the hair colour of participants is often referred to in the gay texts, it is rarely used in this nominal way – it occurs only twice, as opposed to 200 times in the lesbian texts. So while lesbian characters are more likely to be referred to by descriptions of hair colour (e.g. *redhead*), the gay characters are more likely to be given labels that describe their sexual roles (e.g. *cocksucker*).

One word that is not key in either set of texts is the word *bitch*. However, when the texts are compared separately to the FROWN corpus of general American written English, *bitch* is key in both the gay and lesbian texts. In the gay texts, it is generally used in a similar way to *cocksucker*, e.g.: '*Yes, I am your bitch! I'm your cocksucking whore*' ('Beginner's Luck'). In the lesbian texts, *bitch* is also used in the sense of (willing) sexual subservience, but it is also used in a different sense, to simply refer to a bad person: *She would not be subject to the abuse any more. Fucking bitch! Lizbeth screamed* ('Untitled 6').

Eight keywords which appeared in the gay texts were non-standard spellings: *fuckin*, *ain't*, *wanna*, *gotta*, *gonna*, *'em*, *kinda* and *doin*. *Real* also occurred as a gay keyword, mainly because it was frequently used as a non-standard alternative to *really* in the gay texts. There were no such non-standard equivalents in the lesbian list of keywords. Most of these keywords often occur in reported speech (*kinda* is the exception, which also occurs frequently as non-reported speech). *Fuckin*, *kinda* and *real* have adverbial roles while *wanna*, *gotta* and *gonna* are semi-modals, most often preceding words like *cum, come, shoot, fuck* and *have sex*. As with the adjectival keyword *ready* (see below), these phrases show the importance of the *orgasm* within the gay narratives. Characters frequently announce that they want to, have got to, and are going to have one: *'I gotta cum, I gotta cum!' he whimpered* ('Three Times in the County Seat'); *'Oh son of a bitch. I'm gonna shoot, gonna shoot my fucking load into a dude's mouth'* ('Married Hunk'). The use of non-standard language as prestige has long-reaching associations with 'men's talk' (e.g. Trudgill 1974, Milroy and Milroy 1978). The erotic narratives therefore seek to emulate gendered ways of speaking which are viewed as traditionally being associated with 'typical' men and women.

When we look at the category of discourse markers (Stenström 1990) – words that are often used in spoken discourse, either to mark boundaries between stretches of discourse, to express social functions or to function as general exclamations – there are differences in the types of words that appear as keywords in the two sets of texts. The lesbian discourse markers function as politer expressions of social discourse: *hello, bye, thank*. Agreement also occurs: *yes, ok*. The final lesbian discourse marker keyword, *oh*, is often described as a news receipt (Atkinson 1992: 208), indicating when a character orients to a piece of new information, e.g. to mean 'Oh, I didn't know that . . .'. However, in the lesbian narratives, *oh* occurs in a variety of expressions of pleasure or emotion: *oh yes* (20), *oh god* (46), *oh my god* (68), *oh my gosh* (8). In contrast, the gay discourse markers (*yeah*,[6] *shit, hell, damn* and *hey*) are less polite: compare the non-standard *yeah* with *yes*. Three of these keywords are also taboo words: *shit, hell* and *damn* (the latter a fossilised religious taboo word). When gay characters express pleasure, they are much more likely to swear than a lesbian character. However, the swear words also occur in non-sexual situations, where they function as intensifiers: *'She's not your damn property!'* ('Straight Military Brat'); *Everything seems to bore the hell out of me* ('Apathy and Promiscuity'); *'I suppose all of you had a damn good time'* ('Seven in a Barn').

Confidence

In contrast with the sexual verbs, the lesbian texts contain many more social verbs (those which primarily refer to communication between characters) as keywords (Table 6.8). Characters in the lesbian texts often *giggle* or *smile*. They also *blush* more often, becoming embarrassed at the sexual situation that they find themselves in: *She was rewarded by seeing Roxanne blush a deep crimson* ('One Night at the Jefferson'). The keyword *replied* suggests that dialogues occur more often in the lesbian texts, especially as there are no equivalent general dialogue keywords in the list of gay keywords. Also *asks* and *asked* appear as lesbian keywords. Pragmatically, *ask* is politer than *demand*, but less subservient than *plead* or *beg*. Again, it suggests dialogue, but also a form of communication in which questions or favours are asked. When *asked* occurs during sexual encounters, it indicates that the characters are vocalising their desires: *In between the kisses she asked me if I wanted her to fuck me* ('The Boss'); *'Ready?' Colleen asked as she tightened the last strap* ('The Classified Ad'). In contrast, the gay social verb keywords *grunted* and *groaned* (see Table 6.6) are always vocal accompaniments to sex, implying a more animalistic form of communication, rather than characters asking each other questions. Both of these words have the capacity to describe how something is said, e.g.: *'Let's get on the bed,' I groaned* ('For Old Times' Sake'). However, in 92 per cent of the cases of these words, grunts and groans occur as descriptions of noises, rather than vocalisations that contain recognisable words. In the other 8 per cent of cases, where words are said, they tend to be short exclamations: *'Oooh yes'* ('Brother-in-law 1'); *'Uh huh'* ('Making Matt'); *'Mmmm, that's nice'* ('Long Lost Lovers'); *'Oh fuck, I'm pissed'* ('I Got the Taste').

Interestingly, *grinned* occurs as a gay keyword, mirroring the use of *smiled* in the lesbian texts. The strongest adverbial collocate of *grinned* is *broadly* (MI score 4.53), whereas *big grin*, *huge grin* and *broad grin* occur 13, six and five times in the gay texts respectively, suggesting a semantic prosody of grinning associated with largeness. Male facial expressions of positive emotion are therefore somewhat theatrically exaggerated. On the other hand, in the lesbian keywords list, *smile* collocates with *coy* (MI 3.56) and *smiles* collocates with *shy* (3.75). We also find the phrases *warm smile* (21 occurrences), *small smile* (16), *soft smile* (4), *smiled nervously* (4) and *smiled softly* (3). For the gay characters, *smiled* strongly collocates with *broadly* (MI 4.27)

Table 6.8 Keywords suggesting discourses of gender-related confidence in gay and lesbian erotic narratives

Discourse	*Keywords*	*Frequency*	
		Gay texts	*Lesbian texts*
Gay men are confident and assertive	grinned	153	74
	get	2196	1734
	getting	862	605
	got	1180	1156
Lesbians are coy and shy	blush	15	56
	giggle	13	51
	giggled	28	103
	giggling	11	48
Lesbians are social	smile	331	528
	smiled	430	717
	replied	248	495
	asks	17	67
	asked	1163	1419

and *widely* (3.78). I would suggest that this shows a difference in the way that the gay and lesbian characters are constructed – gay men are more certain with expressions of emotion, whereas with the lesbian characters there is more hesitation and suppression.

One set of keywords that is not easily explained is the high presence of the lemma GET in the gay texts. *Get, getting* and *got* (all key) occur a total of 4938 times in the gay texts, and 3504 in the lesbian texts. Literally, the lemma implies possession – to get something is to take it. However, in reality, GET is most often used in other, less literal constructions, which often sees it incorporated into idiomatic phrases: *get my drift, get more accustomed to, get it over with, get home*. In the gay texts, a reasonably sized proportion of the idiomatic uses of GET are sexual: *get hard/harder* (117 occurrences), *get off* (41), *get (down) on {PRONOUN} knees* (37), *get fucked* (33), *get naked* (25), *get turned on* (21), *get undressed* (16), *get into bed* (14), *get hot* (14), *get it on* (13), *get horny* (13), *get laid* (11), *get excited* (10), *get aroused* (8). The occurrences of GET in the lesbian texts tend to be used less often within sexual idioms, exceptions being *get wet* (22) and *get wetter* (10). But on the whole GET tends to occur much more often in the lesbian texts as part of non-sexual phrases such as *get up* (246), *get to know* (27) and *get home* (42).

If we look at *get* phrases that indicate arousal or sexual activity (*get off, get fucked, get turned on, get hot, get it on, get horny, get laid, get excited, get aroused*), they total 165 in the gay texts and 107 in the lesbian texts. On the other hand (as described earlier), in the lesbian keywords *passion* is often used in more detailed descriptions of arousal: *With each breath the passion grew* ('Old Self'); *With that, overcome with emotion and passion she pulled me up to her head and kissed me* ('Lisa Spreads Her Wings'). I would therefore argue that *get* is used as a narrative device in the gay texts to summarise actions or activities in a perfunctory manner, without the need for further elaboration, whereas the lesbian texts tend to focus more on details of particular events.

Kept, which is another keyword in the gay texts, is used in a similar way to *get*, in that it outlines an activity or behaviour without needing to resort to a detailed description of it. In this case, the activity is ongoing: *I kept gently sucking as he relaxed and his dick went soft* ('Party Boy David'). However, with the discussion of the words *get* and *kept* we have started to move away from looking at constructions of characters in terms of personal confidence, in order to focus on narrative structure. I wish to conclude this chapter therefore by examining in more detail issues of narrative surrounding pronoun use and focus.

Perspective

In terms of pronouns, as we would expect, male pronouns feature as keywords in the gay texts, while female pronouns are key in the lesbian texts. However, there are other differences which are more unexpected (Table 6.9). The first person pronouns *me, my, I, I'd* and *we* are keywords in the gay texts, whereas the lesbian texts have more third-person plural pronouns: *they, their* and *them*. This suggests that more gay texts are written in first person narratives, and an analysis of this reveals it to be the case (about 89 per cent of the gay texts are in the first person, while this figure is 64 per cent for the lesbian texts). Stylistically, this has the effect of making the gay narratives appear more confessional and also suggests a higher level of conversationalisation (Fairclough 1995) – these are stories where the narrator appears to be talking directly to the reader about himself. However, *you* (a keyword in the lesbian texts) also implies conversationalisation, in that it is most often used when one character within the text addresses another. This shows one of the main differences between the two types of texts. The gay texts feature a direct address to the reader, the lesbian texts feature more cases of characters addressing each other.

Perhaps the most inexplicable person-centred keyword in the lesbian texts is the word *people* itself. *People*, being non-specific, is often used to orient the characters to the wider society outside the confines of the erotic encounter, to refer to popular opinions or norms, or more specifically, to indicate that one character is widely viewed as attractive: *I always loved it when people noticed my curves* ('Alicia'); *What do you think people would say about a girl who has lipstick on her face?* ('Kailen'); *'Come on over here, let's get out of these people's way'* ('Chunky Bodybuilder'). The lesbian texts are therefore more focused on norms and opinions that occur outside the immediate setting of the narrative.

Table 6.9 Keywords suggesting discourses of perspective in gay and lesbian erotic narratives

Discourse	Keywords	Frequency	
		Gay texts	Lesbian texts
Gay men's narratives are	I	37,169	29,069
stylistically egocentric	me	10,281	8753
	my	20,695	16,482
	I'd	852	552
	we	5176	4151
Lesbian's narratives feature	you	7902	8700
more interaction and	they	1820	2460
concern about others	their	942	1478
	them	1541	2183
	people	253	388

Focus

The adjectival keywords are perhaps where some of the clearest differences between the two sets of texts can be found. For example, in terms of size, gay keywords express largeness: *thick, big, huge, broad, fat, massive, bulging,* whereas the lesbian keywords refer to smallness: *small, smaller, little* (Table 6.10). While there are significant differences in the frequencies of these sets of words, the ways that they are used in the two text types also differs. For example, in the lesbian texts, *fat* usually contains negative associations connected with being overweight: *'I'm not beautiful. I'm fat'* ('Lillian'); *Danielle tried on so many outfits and asked her opinion so many times that Dawn half heartedly considered telling her they made her look fat from then on so she could go home* ('A Mile in Her Heels'). However, in the gay texts, *fat* is generally used as a term of praise when describing a penis: *It was beautiful. Long fat, cut and just as black as he was* ('Kelly'); *'Man, you got a nice fat one on you, don't you?'* ('Sharing the Bed With Uncle Ron').

In terms of material state, the gay keywords are concerned with hardness: *throbbing, stiff, muscled, meaty, solid, rigid,* whereas the lesbian keywords mainly indicate softness (the exception being *pert*). Most of the gay identity adjectival keywords are traditionally connected to masculinity (*muscular, manly, masculine, gay, queer, male, macho*), whereas the lesbian ones are to do with femininity (*female, feminine, sexy, womanly, lesbian*). And words concerning taste are savoury or salty for the gay keywords (*sweaty, salty, mushroom, beefy*), whereas the only lesbian taste keyword is *sweet*. These categories of adjectives most often refer to men's penises, bodies, chests, testicles, muscles, buttocks, shoulders, faces, arms and fingers. The lesbian adjectives refer to breasts, nipples, bodies, lips, hands, tongues, flesh, legs and faces. Unsurprisingly, men are *handsome*, and women are *beautiful*. Another way that masculine identities are noted in the gay texts is in descriptions of bodies which imply they have been achieved by hard labour rather than at the gym: *He would of* [sic] *been close to 6 foot tall with short dark hair and from the look of his overalls a fairly decent looking body. Not one of those lame gym toned bodies either it was more to do with the hard manual work we had to do* ('Apprentice Plumber'); *'Anyway, I'm not sure what you mean about the difference between work and gyms.' 'I guess they think its {sic} more masculine and natural than a gym body'* ('UPS'); *His body was not only gym hard, but work hard* ('Rick and Me'); *He was well toned, without the obvious bulges of gym muscles, his shoulders were particularly well defined, and I wondered if he was a swimmer* ('Desk Job'). Gym-toned bodies are therefore viewed as lame, obvious and less natural or masculine than 'work' bodies, again suggesting that working-class masculine identities are preferred and seen as more authentic.

In order to understand better that the representations of male and female attributes are discursive, it should be pointed out that in Ancient Greece, a small penis was preferred (Keuls 1985: 68), so the 'bigger the better' discourse is not universal. In addition, larger women have been viewed as

Table 6.10 Keywords suggesting discourses of focus in gay and lesbian erotic narratives

Discourse	Keywords	Frequency	
		Gay texts	Lesbian texts
Gay men are orgasm-centred and sex is penetrative	up	5751	5114
	down	3890	3243
	into	3786	3319
	off	2516	1711
	got	1880	1156
	ready	452	308
The bigger the better	inch	295	157
	inches	301	129
	big	863	397
	thick	474	132
	huge	293	99
	fat	168	39
	broad	118	23
	massive	99	27
	bulging	48	7
Lesbians note certain surroundings in more detail	lace	5	85
	silk	26	101
	satin	4	49
	red	184	365
	black	295	505
	pink	79	175
	gaze	46	108
	eyes	1283	1659
How something is done is important	light	286	483
	voice	254	433
	tone	42	111
	remove	46	106
	removed	111	212
	door	644	977
	moment	412	618
Small is beautiful	small	361	721
	smaller	37	178
	little	286	423

attractive in western society in the past and in other societies (consider for example the Baroque paintings of Paul Reubens 1577–1640). Small is not always viewed as beautiful.

There are no gay male keywords that are colours or refer to materials.

While the lesbian keywords *lace*, *silk* and *satin* could be adjectives or nouns, they usually occur as modifiers to nouns (particularly clothing), e.g. *I had on one of my favourite black silk 'nothing' dresses* ('Girls Night Out'). The lesbian keywords *red*, *black* and *pink* are also often used to describe clothing, but can also refer to objects, e.g. *red wine* (nine occurrences), the colour of a person's skin (*black woman* (33)), or body parts (*black* or *red hair* (73), *red* or *pink lips* (32), *pink nipples* (34)). On the whole, women refer to colours more often than men – the total combined frequencies for *white*, *black*, *green*, *yellow*, *red*, *blue*, *brown*, *pink* and *orange* is 2051 in the lesbian texts and 1450 in the gay male texts.

Prepositional keywords generally tend to be linked closely to the mechanics of sexual activity, and the differences between the gay and lesbian keywords in this category tend to reflect this. Three prepositional lesbian keywords are *between*, *within* and *beneath*. *Between*, for example, is often used to refer to a locus of sexual interest: *between her/my legs* (308), *between my/her lips* (58), *between my/her thighs* (39), *between my/her teeth* (26), *between my/her fingers* (23). *Within* refers more explicitly to penetration: *Pressing her face within the girl's open valley as far as she could, Barbara swallowed surge upon surge of womanly joy* ('Adventures on Flight 109'). However, *within* is also sometimes used to refer to a short passage of time, e.g.: *within seconds* (11), *within moments* (9), *within (x) minutes* (11). *Beneath* occurs mainly when noting that one person is lying on top of another: *'Now come over here and crawl beneath me and wiggle it in my pussy'* ('Mrs Jackson – The Seduction'), or in descriptions of the naked body: *She slipped her hand up under Rachel's T-shirt and fondled the naked flesh beneath it* ('One for the Night').

The gay texts tend to contain more prepositions as keywords (see Table 6.11). Interestingly, in Table 6.11 the prepositions which are gay keywords occur much more frequently overall than those which are lesbian keywords.

Table 6.11 Overall frequencies of prepositional keywords in both sets of texts

	Lesbian	Gay
Lesbian keywords		
between	1222	828
within	263	157
beneath	177	90
Gay keywords		
up	5114	5751
down	3234	3890
out	4004	4659
about	2461	2879
into	3318	3786
off	1711	2516

Why is this the case? What are here being bundled together as prepositions may have non-prepositional uses; often, for example, occurring in a
variety of idiomatic phrases which are difficult to translate literally, e.g.:
what did you get up to; *he's doing my head in*; *I caught up with an old friend*; *we
ended up asleep*. As with the word *got*, this idiomatic use of prepositional
phrases is more prevalent in the gay texts than the lesbian texts. In addition,
many of these idiomatic phrases have directly sexual meanings. The most
frequent verb collocate of *down*, *out* and *off* is *pulled*, and this verb also occurs
in the top five verb collocates of *into* and *up*, generally being sexual in nature:
he gave me a long kiss while he pulled up my shirt ('The Performance'); *I pulled
out the butt plug* ('Zeke's Come Undone'); *Blake pulled off of us both* ('Skin
Diving'); *He slowly pulled down his boxers* ('Having a Fag'). Other common
sexual collocates include SPEED *up* (referring to thrusting penetrative activity
during sex), *cleaned up* (after having sex), *swell up* (to refer to an erection), *suck
off* and *reached down*. The prepositions *down*, *out*, *into* and *up* particularly refer
to the act of penetration: *I forced it into his body* ('Rained Out'); *Ben, being
experienced more in taking a cock up his ass, could still not get all ten inches of Mark*
('Coastline'); *I let his balls out of my mouth* ('Party Time'); *I slid his whole dick
down my throat* ('Carlos').

The gay prepositional keywords in their typical contexts therefore refer to
a more extreme form of penetration than the lesbian keyword *within*.
Particularly, *down* and *up* suggest that penetration is much deeper. The
phrase *up and down* occurs 429 times in the gay texts (and 236 times in the
lesbian texts), mainly being used to describe repetition of penetration.

The gay keyword *ready* reveals an interesting difference in the narrative
structure of the two sets of texts. *Ready* usually occurs when someone is
ready to orgasm, and it is used to signify that this is about to happen: *By
now I was about ready to shoot my load all over him* ('Religious Friend'). In the
lesbian texts, *ready* occurs less often and has a wider range of uses: '*Hello
sleepy, dinner is just about ready*' ('What Tommy, Anna and I did'). The frequent use of *ready* in the gay texts therefore implies the build-up to orgasm
and its importance within the gay narratives. As Dyer (1992: 293) suggests,
gay erotica is a goal-directed narrative: 'The desire that drives porn narrative
forward is the desire to come, to have an orgasm.'

While the narrative focus on the gay texts seems to be based on penetration and orgasm, the lesbian texts tend to have a wider focus, which gives a
more detailed description of a situation. For example, *voice* is also a keyword
in the lesbian texts (433 versus 254 occurrences in the gay texts). While
lemma forms like *say*, *ask* and *reply* are often used in narratives to indicate
speech, *voice* has a different function − it is often used to show *how* something is spoken, e.g.: '*This is totally new,*' *Lauren replied, her voice just above a
whisper* ('One Night at the Jefferson'); *In a very shy voice, I mentioned this to
Maya* ('Convent Education'); *A small rational voice deep within her cried out*
('Sarah and Sister Theresa'). As with eyes, the voice is used in order to
implicitly show how people are feeling. *Tone* also appears as a lesbian

keyword, used to refer to how someone is speaking: *Immediately her tone changed, from a haughty clip to a more familiar and trusting voice* ('Mrs Jackson – The Seduction').

The gaze is important in both the gay and lesbian texts (both sets of texts have comparably similar high frequencies of the lemmas LOOK and SEE). However, gaze appears to play a more important role in the lesbian texts. The word *gaze* is itself a keyword in the lesbian texts. The word *eyes* occurs as key in the lesbian texts, with phrases such as *closed/opened/averted/lowered {PRONOUN} eyes*, or *looked/stared into {PRONOUN} eyes* being popular. In addition, eyes *meet* with each other (19 occurrences), are *glued to* (19), *riveted to* (6) or *locked* on to (17) other people in the lesbian narratives. So in the lesbian texts, descriptions of *eyes* are a way that contact between characters is signified, the connection between two sets of eyes being described in terms that are akin to physical contact. These phrases in the lesbian texts also suggest that the gaze is mutual or two-way. The total frequency of phrases which imply mutual watching, e.g. *looked (back) at each other, watched one another*, etc., is 57 for the gay texts and 81 for the lesbian texts. On the other hand, phrases which imply one-way watching, e.g. *looked at him, stared at me, watched her*, etc., are higher in the gay texts (983 versus 906). While this difference is small, it does suggest that gaze in the gay male texts is more similar to Berger's (1972) concept of the objectifying, unidirectional male gaze, than for the lesbian texts. Eyes are also used in the narratives to show what people are thinking or feeling, e.g. *Diane's eyes lit with fire* ('Through Dani's Eyes'); *Roxanne's eyes widened a bit* ('One Night at the Jefferson'); *The green eyes looked intently into hers* ('The Storm'), something which occurs more often in the lesbian texts.

Interestingly *light* is a keyword in the lesbian texts, functioning in a number of different ways. In terms of a noun, it can refer to actual luminosity such as the light in a room or natural sunlight. But it can also be used in metaphorical phrases such as *to shed light on the matter* or *to have a warning light go off in your head*. It is rarely used as a verb in the erotic narratives, but often occurs as an adjective, usually to describe the lightness of someone's touch, or the shade of a person's hair, eyes or clothing or furniture. *Light* therefore often occurs in descriptions, either of the atmosphere of a room or of people or other objects: *The only light on was a pink and purple lava lamp she had on her computer desk* ('Friends Forever'); *Her naturally tan skin looked lovely against the light blue patterned fabric* ('Lisa Spreads Her Wings').

As already shown, the lemma GET is a keyword in the gay texts, often occurring either in sexual constructions, for example *get naked/undressed* occurs 41 times in the gay texts, whereas this construction appears only 15 times in lesbian texts. Instead, an equivalent construction in the lesbian texts involves the word *remove* or *removed*, which occurs 318 times, as opposed to 157 times in the gay texts.

Remove is most often used in conjunction with single items of clothing, or lists of clothing, e.g. *There she removed her blouse and what was left of her bra and threw herself naked on the bed* ('Catherine's Submission'). On the other hand, *get naked/undressed* implies that clothes are taken off indiscriminately and quickly, even urgently, not one at a time. The following example from the gay texts shows how nakedness is immediately followed by sexual activity: *Steve and I quickly got naked and when Kevin pulled his cock out of Randy's mouth asked us if we wanted some* ('Party Time'). Another example illustrates the urgency associated with *get naked*: *'And now,' John said in a stern and deliberate voice, 'you'd better get naked entirely. Hurry up!'* ('Seven in a Barn'). Undressing, however, appears to be an activity which writers of the lesbian texts seem to linger over for longer:

> *Staring into her smiling green eyes I removed my bra and dropped it on top of my discarded shirt. She lifted her eyebrow and dropped her eyes to my waist once she heard me undo my jeans. Slowly I pulled them down to my hips, stepping out, leaving me in nothing but silky, pink, string bikini panties. Kari's eyes darken and I could see that I was causing her to lose some control, given {sic} me the courage I needed to continue. In a slow teasing manner I removed my panties watching her eyes darken more as she watch {sic} my panties descend to the pile of discarded clothes.*
>
> (The Massage)

While the word *door* is frequent in both sets of data (978 lesbian texts versus 645 gay texts), it occurs significantly more in the lesbian texts and is an unexpected keyword. One noticeable aspect of the way that *door* is used in the lesbian texts is that it more often occurs with a variety of preceding adjectives, e.g. *metal door, screen door, sliding door, front door, wooden door*. However, it is difficult to point to other ways that doors are used *differently* in the lesbian texts, they are just referred to more frequently – characters tend to *open, close, lock, hear, walk out of* and *push* doors in both sets of texts. In a sense, then, doors function as ways that characters can either be introduced into or removed from a scene (the narrative equivalent of 'exit stage left'), or ways that new scenes can be introduced. *A sharp knock at the door interrupted her* ('Ebony and Ivory'); *We were met at the door by Carrie, half of the couple who owned the place* ('All Female Networking Group').

However, doors also hide secrets, unexpected events can occur behind them, and they are therefore narratively important in that they help to build suspense. A character who walks through a doorway early in an erotic narrative is often also walking through a symbolic door, making a decision to have sex. But doors can also accidentally allow unwitting characters to stumble upon sexual encounters – introducing them to a new world. For example: *I'm about to turn off the shower when the door opens and Jeff walks in, naked* ('Washington Conference'); *I flung open the door to see something of a shock* ('A Primitive Hope'); *When I pushed open the door, I couldn't believe what I saw. Nicky was naked* ('Girls Night Out With Nicky'). Characters who express uncertainty or inability to make a choice are unable to pass through doors:

She hesitates by the door, tears in her eyes ('Blackcurrent'); *At the door I hesitated. It took me a few minutes to build up my courage but finally I entered* ('Student Nurse'). Doors also place the setting of the narrative indoors, and are important for signifying privacy: *Then we closed the door and locked it* ('Mildred'); *And just to be sure, I stood from the chair, and closed the door to the office before drawing the blinds on the window* ('The Art of Seduction'). I would therefore suggest that doors in erotic narratives function as emotional, as well as physical boundaries, and are often used in ways that help to reveal the characters' emotional states or choices.

Moment(s) is an interesting lesbian keyword, occurring 799 times. A moment refers to a short, unspecific period of time, and is usually used to show that something has taken place within that period: *'Is this what you want,' I asked in a moment of intoxicated confidence* ('Muff to Mouth and Back Again'); *She hesitated for a moment, and instead slid the small card into her pocket* ('Adventures on Flight 109'). Moments are therefore used as a narrative device that focuses on small, understated details, which help to enhance the atmosphere or mood of the story. They suggest fleeting emotions or actions, which often occur within the larger structure of the narrative. Moments can add ambivalence and complexity to the stories.

Conclusion

A keyword analysis is admittedly problematic. It is limited to the lexical level of analysis so it will not reveal all of the linguistic differences between the two sets of texts (and it cannot reveal any of the similarities). Taken separately, accounts of individual keywords do not prevent a particularly convincing argument about contrasting discourses in lesbian and gay erotica. For example, the fact that *big* occurs more often in gay texts than lesbian texts, and the opposite is true of *small*, might suggest one thing, but such an analysis, when it stands alone, overlooks the possibility that numerous other adjectives of size might occur as keywords in the lesbian texts, outweighing the significance of two cases like *big* and *small*. It also doesn't mean that gay texts necessarily feature big things – the keyword may always appear in the phrase 'not big'. However, this analysis has considered all of the keywords that were found, in the hope that the sum of the keywords will be greater than its parts, while I carried out concordances of keywords to allow us to see exactly what contexts they occurred in.

So what are the main differences in terms of discourses that have emerged? First, it needs to be acknowledged again that the discourses such as 'sex is work' for gay men and 'lesbians are gentle and tender' consist of *ideal* representations of gay or lesbian sex, not representations of what such sex is actually like. So put simply, expressions of idealised gay and lesbian desire are linked strongly to gender construction: the gay texts utilise a discourse of masculinity, whereas the lesbian texts have one based on femininity. Both texts feature characters, contexts and styles of writing that are consistent with stereotypical, hegemonic, heterosexual gender roles, the only difference being that these characters also engage in gay or lesbian sex. So gay men are constructed as big, tough and confident. They watch or play sports, drink beer, use non-standard or impolite language and experience desire as an almost mechanistic urge to penetrate and ejaculate. Sex is viewed in terms of hard work, it is rough, to the point of almost being violent, sometimes a painful experience that must be endured, and lust is demonstrated via physical action rather than by references to feelings. The grunts and groans that accompany gay sex make it almost animalistic, an urge, rather than anything to do with attachment or love. Gay erotic narratives tend to focus more on the narrator, experienced via a first-person point of view.

On the other hand, lesbians are represented as smaller, softer and less sure of themselves. They are more likely to drink tea or wine and listen to music. Atmosphere and emotions are important features of the narratives, as is conversation, before and during sex. Language is more formal, polite and gentle, and there are more references to the passage of time, depth of feelings, subtleties of mood and surroundings. Lesbian erotic narratives place more distance between the reader and the characters by having the story occur from a third-person point of view. Also, characters within lesbian narratives communicate with each other more, they act coyly, blushing and giggling more often. How people say or do things is viewed as important. Love and relationships are also viewed as more important, and on the whole, physical contact is more tender.

Some of the differences reveal similar strategies. For example, beer and wine both serve as the same narrative device in the gay and lesbian texts respectively – to loosen inhibitions so that sex can occur. However, they also serve another function, to establish gendered situations and identities, designed to enhance the reader's understanding and enjoyment of the story. A class discourse also appears to run through the different narratives – masculinity is related to working-class male identities – shown through the emphasis on non-standard language, work metaphors, beer-drinking and sports-watching. On the other hand, femininity is constructed as middle-class – for example, using polite language, sipping tea or drinking wine.

The texts are therefore sites of *heterosexual* gender (and class) stereotyping – men are constructed as hyper-masculine/working class, while women are hyper-feminine/middle class. Oddly, the sorts of differences that the keywords analysis has revealed is similar to the early essays or studies on male and female difference by researchers like Lakoff. Also, the analysis mirrors findings on erotica written from heterosexual perspectives. Hoey (1997) found that heterosexual men's erotica was primarily concerned with opportunity-taking and focused on their own arousal rather than that of the woman. Heterosexual women's erotic narratives were more likely to be concerned with desire arousal and fulfilment and were more likely to attribute arousal to men. Hoey concludes that 'many men think of [women] as sex objects' (1997: 104), which may suggest that the primary factor in erotic narratives is not sexuality but gender – gay men and heterosexual men may frame desire in similar ways.

However, it should be borne in mind that the erotic narratives are imagined, idealised accounts of gender (although some are presented as 'true stories'). In a sense, the use of such hyper-gendered gay and lesbian stereotypes could be viewed as transgressive, especially when considered in relation to other discourses of homosexuality which argue that gay men are effeminate or gay women masculine. So people who engage in gay sex are constructed as the same as (or even *more* stereotypically gendered) than heterosexual people. In some cases, they actually characterise themselves as heterosexual, and their experiences are surprising to them. In a sense, the narratives therefore represent a queering of hegemonic heterosexuality – the latent potential within everyone, especially those whom we'd least expect, to enjoy gay sex. But it could also be argued that the narratives, being fictional, focus on situations that people would *like* to happen, but are perhaps unlikely to occur – the characters and situations are often unattainable – erotic fantasy in this case amplifying what is possible within the constraints of reality. Heterosexual 'gay' characters may offer a sense of the best of both worlds – for example, a nominally heterosexual man may be very sexually experienced with women (and therefore constructed as virile and masculine), but, having never had gay sex before, within the confines of the narrative they are also constructed as 'untouched'. The combination of discourses of initiation *and* virility/experience is therefore more likely to appeal to a wider set of readers.

However, alternatively it could be argued that the narratives present a narrowly defined, extreme discourse of gay and lesbian identity, which erases the possibility of more realistic or inclusive possible identities. For example, what place do effeminate or upper-class gay men have in these texts? It could be argued that gay people (as with heterosexual people) have placed a high premium on stereotypical gendered identities. As Harris (1997: 158) notes: 'literary pornography is often based on acts of disavowal, as in the case of the nongay homosexual.' The extent to which this is due to the influence of other (more explicitly homophobic) discourses, a desire to possess the unattainable, or a genuine attraction to masculine and feminine stereotypes is difficult to ascertain. With that said, the nature of a keywords analysis is that similarities between texts will not be shown. So there may be other types of gendered identities, more common to both texts, but they will not be revealed in the keywords list because they occur with roughly equal frequency in both sets of narratives. An analysis of the most frequent words in both sets of data revealed a high proportion of the keywords that were already analysed. Therefore many of the keywords examined were not only key, but they occurred often, revealing them to be instrumental in constructing the most important discourses that occur in the two sets of narratives. In addition, an analysis of words that were key in both sets of texts when compared to the FROWN corpus of general written American English revealed that the majority of them tended to be used in ways that did not index gender.

So the characters in the narratives tend to be gendered as heterosexual ideals who merely happen to engage in gay sex. The discourse of compulsory homosexuality could therefore be viewed as a way of responding to an opposing discourse that assumes that everyone is heterosexual. However, at the same time, by featuring so many characters who to all intents and purposes *are* heterosexual, the narratives make it more difficult for many gay men or lesbians to personally identify with the actors within. Gay and lesbian identities are therefore co-opted out of such narratives: sexual *behaviour* may be homosexual but gender/sexual *identity* is heterosexual.

It is impossible to make claims in relationship to the authors of the texts, or be completely certain as to the intended audiences – for example, given the well-attested interest of many heterosexual men in lesbian erotica, the lesbian texts found on the website could have been mainly created and consumed by heterosexual men. However, the texts' existence contributes to a discourse of homosexuality which will be perpetuated whenever someone looks for or discovers the website where they are archived. The texts therefore construct 'ideal' ways of being gay or lesbian, whoever the audience is.

However, an ideal sexual partner is not necessarily someone who would be an ideal romantic partner, work colleague or friend. Therefore an analysis of erotica only tells us so much about 'perfectly gendered' gay or lesbian *sexual* stereotypes. Outside of the bedroom (or sauna or hayloft, etc.), such ideals may be viewed more cynically or with contempt. For example, the stud who services an entire rugby team may not be viewed as long-term partner material. These 'perfectly-gendered' performances are therefore limited to erotic discourse and should not be viewed as fully representative of gay ideals across a wider range of discourse. Perhaps the gay narratives tell us something about the ways that ideal gay sex is characterised – as a merely physical activity – literally as *action*, rather than something involving commitment or deep emotional feelings. This may explain why non-monogamy or promiscuity tends to be viewed as less important by some gay men. However, conversely, the narratives may simply serve to *reinforce* social expectations, i.e. that women *should* find it more difficult than men to separate sex and love, because this is what the narratives tell us.

Erotic narratives therefore function as instructional discourses in the same way that advertisements instruct heterosexual women to desire taller boyfriends (Goffman 1976, Eckert 2002: 109). Erotic narratives inform people about the ways that they should ideally act and feel when having sex, and what sort of qualities or activities they ought to find desirable. The rather homogeneous sets of gay and lesbian erotic narratives therefore point to a definition of desire that is somewhat restricted. These 'vanilla' forms of gay and lesbian erotica are characterised by a uniformity of discourse types, suggesting that gender and desire are strongly linked and that heterosexual gender ideals still hold strong.

7 Making safer sex sexy

Border crossing, informalisation and gay identity in sexual health documentation

> For gay men, condoms must now become as sexy as jockstraps.
> (University of California researcher reporting on ways to prevent HIV
> infection, December 17, 1985)

On July 3, 1981 on page 20 of the *New York Times*, an article reported an outbreak of the rare cancer Kaposi's sarcoma in 41 previously healthy gay men. Nine of the men who had been tested were found to have severe defects in their immune systems. In the same month, the *Morbidity and Mortality Weekly Report* published an article about six gay men in Los Angeles who had died of a rare pneumonia, *pneumocistis carinii* (PCP). The disease which caused immune deficiencies leading to 'opportunistic infections' was labelled AIDS (Acquired Immuno-Deficiency Syndrome). On April 27, 1983 *NBC Nightly News* broadcasted a report that a virus, originally called the Human T-cell Lymphotopic Virus, Type III (HTLV-III) might be responsible for AIDS. Later the virus was known simply as HIV (Human Immuno-deficiency Virus).

Early responses to AIDS were characterised by panic, scape-goating and homophobia. For example, in the USA on May 6 1983, a doctor on ABC's *Good Morning America* told viewers that although AIDS is 'still confined to male homosexuals, Haitians, and haemophiliacs', it could soon spread to 'normal people'. In the same year, state legislators in Austin, Texas claimed that 'the diseases now being transmitted by homosexuals ... threaten to destroy the public health of the state of Texas' and attempted to recriminalise homosexual acts between consenting adults as well as banning homosexuals from taking jobs in teaching, food-handling or 'any other position of public leadership or responsibility' (Rutledge 1989: 20). In 1988 in the UK, Margaret Thatcher's Conservative Government produced legislation which banned the 'promotion of homosexuality' by local education authorities. British tabloid newspapers referred to AIDS as a 'gay plague'. However, it was soon clear that AIDS was a problem for society as a whole, rather than particular groups. As the estimated number of years to finding a cure or vaccination was constantly revised, it became apparent that people would need to be informed about reliable methods of preventing transmission.

The early British safer sex educational materials were characterised by a moral approach which foregrounded abstinence, monogamy and marriage as ideal ways to prevent HIV transmission, echoing Rich's 1980 *compulsory heterosexuality* discourse, and dismissed by Campbell (1987) as 'penetration propaganda'. However, partly due to the activism of the gay community, later materials recognised that non-heterosexual identities existed and reflected a less morally prescriptive stance.

Since the First World War, press ads, leaflets and posters have been the mainstay of health education in the West (Naidoo and Wills 1994). Wilton (1997: 81) points out that HIV/AIDS health education is unique because it is 'a self-consciously ethical discourse which is ... obliged to be fairly explicit about sexual activities'. The link between sexual health and erotica stretches back to at least the 1930s – early films such as *Forbidden Desire* (1936), *Know For Sure* (1939), *Sex Hygiene* (1942) and *VD-Damaged Goods* (1962) justified their sensationalistic content by framing it in terms of being an important message about health. Similarly, early American gay 'beefcake' magazines placed importance on physical grooming, cleanliness and regular exercise. For example, in the July 1957 issue of *Tomorrow's Man*, which features 74 photographs of bare-chested muscular men, articles included 'Sex Hygiene is Important' which warned readers against 'clinging perspiration' and 'Bodybuilding in the Summer' which gave dietary tips such as 'eat lean meats and plenty of leafy vegetables'.

Past audiences who wanted to consume erotic material could therefore be assured that there were socially sanctioned reasons for doing so. Ironically, in today's society where erotica is much more pervasive and there is less moral approbation attached to viewing it, the same technique is now employed in reverse – health documentation is disguised as erotica in order to persuade audiences to pay attention to it. The 'hyper-erotic' presentation of advice for gay men has long been argued as the exemplary discursive matrix for sexual health promotion. For example, Watney (1989: 129) writes:

> Changes in sexual behaviour cannot be forced, they can only be achieved through consent, consent which incorporates change into the very structure of sexual fantasy. Hence the urgent, the desperate need to eroticise information about safe sex, if tens of thousands or more lives are not to be cruelly sacrificed on the twin alters of prudery and homophobia.

With regards to HIV and other sexually transmitted infections, health promotional materials were initially referred to as 'safe sex advice' although the term *safe sex* has since been reformulated as *safer sex*, the gradable adjective advising that all forms of sex have risk attached to them, but some are riskier (or safer) than others.

However, the creators of safer sex documentation are faced with a number of dilemmas. The first is in targeting the appropriate audience. As seen with some of the more mainstream public sites where homosexuality is discussed (e.g. tabloid newspapers), negative or ambivalent discourses are still reasonably common, Therefore, due to the negative stereotyping of homosexuality, men who engage in sex with other men may not choose to view themselves in terms of possessing a gay identity. Attempting to target such men as 'gay' may therefore ensure that they do not read the advice. In addition, producers of such texts need to take into account the level of sexual activity their audience engages in: for example, do they assume that their audience are already participating in unsafe activities or usually have safer sex or have had little or no sexual experience? The way that such audiences will be addressed and constructed by such documentation is therefore likely to be different in each case – and where an audience is always likely to consist of *all* of the above types, plus others, writing with a specific identity in mind is likely to alienate a proportion of the target audience.

A second problem, assuming that a potential audience is targeted adequately, concerns *effectively* transmitting a safer sex message. Because sexually transmitted infections can kill or lead to unpleasant symptoms, there is a danger that the intended readership will choose to disregard sexual health messages because anything thematically related to infection (including safer sex), will be distressing to contemplate. Also, such messages may be associated with behaviour change – or having to forgo or restrict enjoyable sexual activities. While fear-based approaches *have* been found to be effective in changing health-related attitudes and behaviour (Robberson and Rogers 1988), it seems to be the cognitive appraisal of the information in the communication that mediates persuasion, rather than the fear aroused by the message (Rogers 1983).

Third, gay men may feel that they are being judged or singled out as at risk because of the existing negative discourse that labels them as predatory, raging, promiscuous, rampant, etc. As Watney (1989: 126) points out: 'Gay sex: read as "promiscuous", is being medically redefined as unsafe. Aids takes us back to the pre-modern world, with disease restored to its ancient theological status as punishment.' Anger at being targeted or shame because of the negative discourse surrounding promiscuity may also mean that some gay men could feel they don't need safer sex advice, or that it's too late for them because they may already be HIV positive, or even that they don't deserve it. Robberson and Rogers (1988) point out that persuasive messages that appeal to positive self-esteem are more effective than those that appeal to negative self-esteem. Therefore safer sex advice needs to take into account how its message is likely to affect the self-worth of a gay audience, which may already be primed to associate HIV as a form of moral punishment for homosexuality or promiscuity. Because safer sex advice needs to effectively persuade people to modify their behaviour (or continue their current safer sex behaviour), it must ensure that its audience is receptive and will engage with the promotional materials without being forced to and without feeling preached at.

Finally, even when an audience has been targeted and persuaded to read the materials, another problem concerns what advice to give. Which behaviours should be changed? Is it realistic to tell people to give up certain sexual activities altogether? Should monogamy or abstinence be recommended? And how should the advice be given? Should it be categorical, e.g. 'you must not do X', or persuasive, 'it's a good idea to do X'?

Wilton (1997: 82) examined safer sex leaflets produced for gay men by the Terrence Higgins Trust in 1992 and concluded that

> the 'gay man' constructed by HIV/AIDS health education materials is almost exclusively a sexual creature . . . Most leaflets and posters are lavishly illustrated, often in full colour, with highly sexualised and sex-positive images (usually photographs of healthy, beautiful young men) and extremely explicit.

She warns that such materials may exclude some gay men. However, in examining materials designed for other groups of people, she argues that 'lesbians are barely present in the discursive field, [heterosexual] women [are] erotophobic bearers both of sexual responsibility and the active male erotic gaze and straight men [are] invisible and proper originators/owners of erotic desire/pleasure/agency' (1997: 105).

The Terrence Higgins Trust is the leading HIV and AIDS charity in the UK and the largest in Europe. It was established in 1982 and named after one of the first people in the UK to die with AIDS. As well as delivering health promotion campaigns it also provides advice, counselling, complementary therapies, support groups, training courses and buddying/mentoring schemes. Although the Trust was originally formed by gay men, it does not target any specific group of people exclusively – recent health campaigns have focused on African people, women with HIV, gay men, young people, professionals working in the field and policy-makers. As the Terrence Higgins Trust is one of the leading exponents of safer sex materials for gay men in the UK, it was decided to carry out a corpus-based examination of more recent materials (from 2000 onwards) in order to determine the current discourses that surround the interface between sexuality, morality and health education, particularly bearing in mind the dilemmas faced by safer sex educators and the fact that a number of competing public discourses of homosexuality are already in existence. Of all of the texts examined in this book, those which feature safer sex discourses are potentially the most important of all – for some people they may mean the difference between life and death.

Border crossing

The corpus used in this chapter consists of 12 texts produced by the Terrence Higgins Trust between 2000 and 2003 to promote safer sex, consisting of a total of 51,180 words (hereby referred to as the THT Corpus).[1] These texts were available from the Trust website at www.tht.org.uk. Titles, dates of publication, word counts and brief descriptions of each are shown in Table 7.1.

It should be seen from the table that some of the materials do not appear to be about safer sex from their descriptions, although they are targeted at a gay audience. Instead, some take a number of other forms: travel guides, survey results and gay sex guides. The *Exposed!* series of documentation resembles a gay lifestyle or scene magazine, similar in design to many commercially available publications such as *Gay Times*, *Boyz* and *Attitude*. For example, the cover of *Exposed!* 1 has a picture of a muscular man wearing a pair of swimming trunks and touching himself provocatively (Figure 7.1). The man's face is cropped below the eyes, placing focus on an anonymous body. The word *exposed* is printed in pink in Impact font (size 155), apart from the characters X and ! which are in black, while the subheading 'the truth about what we get up to' appears in size 16 above it. In addition, the words 'Plus your chance to win a DVD player' appear in the bottom right corner, in a pink circle. The only indication that this is not a lifestyle magazine are the words 'CAUTION: Explicit material for gay men only' written in the bottom left-hand corner, at 90 degrees from the rest of the text in size 9 Andale Mono font.

The remainder of the leaflet is written in a highly visual style, combining images and text together in a variety of font styles, sizes, colours and orientations

Table 7.1 Safer sex documentation

Name	Date	Words	Description
The Manual	2002	13,022	Sexually transmitted infections and clinics – a guide for gay men.
The Bottom Line	2003	10,105	All you'll ever need to know about your arse and his.
Up, Up and Away!	2002	4892	Holiday hints for gay men travelling to European destinations.
Come Fly With Me!	2002	4424	Holiday hints for gay men travelling to long haul destinations.
Exposed! 1	2000	4701	Gay sex, the truth about what we get up to.
Exposed! 2	2001	1862	Gay sex, how much would you reveal?
Exposed! 3	2002	2933	Rubbered, lust 'n' latex. Let's get to grips with it!
All the f***ing facts	2000	1285	Facts for life guide.
Gay men and combination therapy	2003	1571	A guide for gay men on HAART.
man{sex}man	2002	2683	Basic information about sex between men.
Out and About	2003	2381	Advice for young gay and bisexual men.
National Gay Men's Sex Survey 2001	2002	1357	Just how many UK gay men are circumcised and other fruity statistics.

Figure 7.1 Cover of *Exposed!* 1.

(text sometimes appears upside down, within coloured boxes or laid over pictures). Later in the magazine a photo story combines text and photographs in order to present a narrative about gay men having sex. Table 7.2 shows some of the headlines from pages within *Exposed!* 1, their accompanying pictures and the topic under discussion.

Table 7.2 Topics and accompanying visuals/text in *Exposed!* 1

Headline	Picture	Topic
Top Bottom	Two men wearing black leather clothing and chains	What difference for HIV does it make whether you fuck or get fucked?
Leave it out!	Two naked men wearing soldier's hats having anal sex	Pulling out before cumming
A Game of Two Halves	Two men wearing football kits and kissing	What if one of you has HIV and the other doesn't?
Tools of the Trade	A group of six men wearing hard hats and vests	Using condoms
Suits you Sir!	A man wearing dungarees and a gold chain	Different brands of condoms
Heavy load	A shirtless weightlifter	Information about viral load
Hitching a ride	A skinhead wearing black leather	Passing on HIV from one man to another

The headlines and pictures combine to create a visual/language pun, common in advertising or in the tabloid press. The headlines also access themes to do with masculinity or gay erotica – for example 'Tools of the Trade' signifies men who work with tools (e.g. blue-collar labour), while at the same time both *tool* and *trade* have alternative sexual meanings within the gay subculture. *Tool* can be used as a slang term for the penis, whereas *trade* refers to a casual sexual partner. Other masculine-related imagery includes football, weightlifting, motorcycles and the military. Therefore, one strategy of ensuring that safer sex information will be attended to is to present it within themes which access gay masculine ideals, being similar to those found in Chapters 5 (personal adverts) and 6 (erotic narratives). The concept of *border crossing* (Goodman 1996) is also relevant here – the idea that styles and language associated with one textual genre have crossed over into another (often for persuasive purposes). Information is therefore presented as entertainment and in a format which will be already recognisable to many gay men.

One way that this border crossing is achieved is by the use of second person interrogative structures or the promise of revealing sexual information. For example, the sub-heading in *Exposed!* 2 is 'Gay sex – how much would you reveal?' Interestingly, the title of the documentation has several readings relating to the meaning of the word *exposed* – e.g. nudity, revealing sexual secrets, or getting an infection. The results of the *National Gay Men's Sex Survey 2001* asks readers how many men are circumcised, whereas *The Manual* uses a question and answer format throughout, like an Internet 'frequently asked questions' list, or similar to the 'passnotes' features used by some British newspapers.

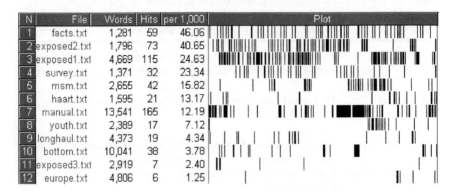

Figure 7.2 Distribution of the word *HIV* across the THT Corpus.

How and when is the subject of HIV first approached in the THT documentation? Figure 7.2 shows the distribution of the acronym *HIV* across each text, as a uniform plot (i.e. the texts are not the same size in length, but their sizes have been standardised in order to make comparisons between them easier).

Although the subject of HIV is generally mentioned once or twice at the beginning of each document, this can be explained by the fact that it usually occurs in the table of contents or in the title of one of the organisations connected to the production of the leaflet (e.g. CHAPS Community HIV and AIDS Prevention Strategy). But it can be seen that after the initial mention in the table of contents, there can be quite a gap before HIV is referred to again. For example, in the *Out and About* pamphlet (shown as 'youth' in Figure 7.2), HIV is not mentioned until three-quarters of the way through the documentation. Similarly, the document on travel to Europe (shown as 'europe' in Figure 7.2) makes five of its six references to HIV in the final fifth of the text. The MSM and HAART documents, as well as *The Manual*, also tend to focus more on HIV towards the end. The first reference to HIV in the MSM document is in the phrase 'This booklet has been written for men who don't have HIV'. The *Gay Men's Survey* has a space at the beginning of the document when it talks about the number of circumcised men before bringing up HIV in later survey results.

While border crossing can work with two or more genres (e.g. information and entertainment) it can also work within a single genre (e.g. just information) but with two or more subjects. So another form of border crossing involves embedding information about HIV within information about other subjects. This occurs in the *Out and About* pamphlet, which is about gay youth and coming out, and in the two travel guides, and the *Bottom Line* pamphlet, which includes a section describing seven positions to have anal sex, e.g.: 'The straddle aka The Cowboy, Doggiestyle...' and 'tips for better

bonking'. In addition, the *Bottom Line* includes explanations of sexual practices and the slang terms associated with them. Such glossaries access a discourse of gay subcultural knowledge, whereby the gay culture is viewed as
having a secret 'language' which is unlikely to be known by those outside it.
Words such as *fisting, scat, felching, rimming, douching, dildos* and *love eggs* are
presented as headings, with detailed explanations about what each one
means. *The Manual* also features a 'gay' glossary of sex-related terms including *active, the clap, fisting, mutual masturbation, pre-cum, rimming* and *scat.*
Therefore the documentation emulates publications such as *The Queen's
Lexicon* (Rodgers 1972), *The Book of Gay Slang* (Ellison and Fosberry 1996)
and *Fantabulosa* (Baker 2002b), that have both charted and helped to vali-
date the existence of a secret gay language. As well as learning new words,
the information in the THT Corpus is often presented in the form of short
'fun facts'. The phrase 'Did you know?' occurs 17 times in the corpus,
whereas the phrase 'Condom Fact' occurs three times. In addition, information is often presented as a list of bullet points, e.g.:

> Things to do if you're bullied –
>
> * Let somebody know it's happening.
> * Write down what happened to you.
> * Write down who you've told about the bullying and what they do
>   about it.

An examination of the two travel guides reveals another form of border
crossing – this time by embedding safer sex advice within the format of a
'scene guide'. Such guides are another recognisable facet of gay culture, providing information about what facilities are available for gay people in
various cities of the world, as well as warning people about which places to
avoid. *The Spartacus Guide* published annually by Bruno Gmuder Verlag is
one of the most famous examples of a gay scene guide.

Four of the leaflets feature competitions (see Figure 7.3) occurring
towards the end of the documents. Competitions are common features of gay
lifestyle magazines, usually offering the readers a chance to win commodities
by answering a number of questions. The competitions in the THT texts
offer prizes such as 'hot and horny films' or a gay travel guide. However, the
questions refer to safer sex and require the reader to have understood the
information in the leaflet, e.g.: '1 If a man doesn't tell you he's HIV positive

N	File	Words	Hits	per 1,000	Plot
1	exposed2.txt	1,796	3	1.67	
2	exposed3.txt	2,919	4	1.37	
3	longhaul.txt	4,373	3	0.69	
4	europe.txt	4,806	3	0.62	

Figure 7.3 Distribution of the word *competition* across the THT Corpus.

before sex it means a) he must be HIV negative b) he could be HIV negative or HIV positive. 2 Give one reason a guy with HIV might not tell you he has it.' Therefore one way that audiences are encouraged to assimilate safer sex advice is by offering the chance of winning commercial goods in exchange.

A number of the leaflets are therefore 'disguised' as other types of texts (scene guides, gay glossaries, erotica, lifestyle magazines, competitions) – genres which combine information with entertainment and will be easily recognised by many gay men. While references to HIV and other infections occur in all of the THT texts, they generally do not tend to occur in the first sections of the documents, suggesting that the reader will engage with the texts in a different way, before discovering information about safer sex within. Audiences who have started to read a text may feel they have already invested some effort into it so may be more likely to continue, while texts which 'bombard' the reader with the sensitive subject of HIV from the outset may be more likely to be put down. Such a strategy is a common feature of advertising, which often uses a joke or interesting distraction to hook an audience, before revealing what the product is about. In this case, the 'product' is not a consumer durable, but attitudes and associated behaviours involving safer sex.[2]

One way of examining the prevailing discourses within the THT Corpus is to consider which words are used most frequently and what alternatives could have been used, both in terms of lexical preference, but also in terms of the ways that such words are presented in the context of a phrase, clause or sentence. Lexical preference is different from semantic preference in that it is based on the appearance of the same word occurring much more frequently than when other, similar words could be used. For example, if a writer chooses the word *chair* rather than *chairperson* then their lexical preference contributes towards a discourse of gender equality. Lexical preference is different from the notion of collocation because such words do not necessarily have to collocate in a text with any others – they may simply be frequent (although it can be illuminating to examine their collocates).

The notion of a frequency-based analysis is therefore different to that of keyword analysis. Keywords do not have to occur particularly frequently in a text, only more often than would be expected when compared to a larger 'benchmark' corpus. However, the most frequent lexical items in a text do not have to be key (although sometimes they are).

By focusing only on the most frequent nouns, we can get an idea of the semantic focus of the text. Table 7.3 shows the frequencies of the ten highest occurring content words in the THT Corpus (plurals are given for nouns where applicable).[3] In order to analyse how these words are employed in the construction of discourses of homosexuality within the THT texts, I have focused on a variety of corpus-based techniques in this chapter. As well as examining lexical preference (asking why one word occurs more often than a related synonym), I have also looked at collocations, and common

Table 7.3 The most frequent adjectives and nouns in the THT Corpus

Rank	Word	Frequency
1	HIV	594
2	gay	384
3	man/men	378
4	condom(s)	343
5	sex	294
6	infection(s)	266
7	arse(s)	223
8	person/people	165
9	risk(s)	128
10	health	99

grammatical and dispersion patterns. In some cases I have examined lower frequency words when a discussion of them is related in an important way to the main lexical concepts in the texts. The initial question which fuelled the examination of safer sex documentation was: how do the texts construct gay identity in relation to the existing discourses of homosexuality already examined earlier in the book (e.g. the homophobic tabloid discourses, the hyper-masculine discourses in erotic texts and personal adverts and the discourses of camp and social aspiration in *Will & Grace*)? I was also interested in the construction of homosexuality as a behaviour or an identity in these texts, a particularly salient discursive focus considering that the texts are concerned with changing sexual *behaviour* yet some homophobic discourses have characterised homosexuality as just a behaviour (and, in particular, a behaviour involving anal sex).

Safer sex

The most frequent lexical word in the corpus is the acronym *HIV*, occurring 594 times. While other types of infection are also discussed, none of them are mentioned as frequently (*herpes* 51, *warts* 50, *syphilis* 47, *gonorrhoea* 36, *crabs* 29). *AIDS*, the disease which can develop as a result of HIV infection, occurs only 37 times in the corpus, and in 23 cases is mentioned as part of the name of a charity or association, e.g.: London Gay Men Fighting AIDS or CHAPS Community HIV and AIDS Prevention Strategy. The focus of the texts is therefore the virus that causes AIDS, not AIDS itself.

We have already seen that discussion of HIV is often delayed in the safer sex pamphlets, possibly as a strategy to engage with the reader by discussing less taboo subjects first. However, once the subject of HIV is addressed, the text creators need to rely on other strategies. How are people who have HIV described in the corpus? The most common way is to use a structure of noun + prepositional phrase, e.g. *men with HIV* (30), *man with HIV* (20), *people with HIV* (9), *guy with HIV* (3), *someone with HIV* (2), *person with HIV*

(1). People can also be described as *living with HIV* (2) or *living well with HIV* (4), but they can also be *infected with HIV* (7) or *diagnosed* with it (1).

Another way is to use the phrase *HIV positive* (38 occurrences). This phrase is often preceded by the verb BE (19 times), but can also include the verb *tested* (3) or *diagnosed* (1). Two related terms to *HIV positive* are *HIV negative* (27) and *HIV status* (15). People can TEST *HIV positive* (or *negative*) (6).

One issue with using corpus data that we need to be aware of is that it only tells us the choices that writers have used, not the choices that they *didn't* use. It is possible to express HIV status or HIV transmission in many ways, which were not employed by the THT, for example by using verb phrases such as *suffering from, caught, contract, spread*. So which verbs *are* used in order to signify the way that people can become HIV positive? Occurring at the 1L node in order of frequency: HAVE (93), PASS *on* (54), GET (54), PICK *up* (5), GIVE (1) or TRANSMIT (1).

Language used to talk about HIV infection therefore contains a lexical preference for non-intentional transmission. For example:

> *Later Will wants to reduce the risk of getting HIV.*
> *The only way to know for sure if you have HIV is to get an HIV test.*
> *What carries more risk of HIV being passed on?*

Verbs which presuppose that HIV infection is caused on purpose are much less frequent than those which indicate that it has happened accidentally. So the word *give* is used only once, by a fictitious HIV positive gay man to explain why he uses condoms: 'Helps me not to give HIV to other blokes.' Use of *give* is not directly associated with the main narrative 'voice' of the texts. The verb *transmit* is used in the phrase 'Fingering or fisting is unlikely to transmit HIV . . .', which places responsibility in terms of a behaviour, not a person.

On the other hand, verb phrases like PASS *on* do not directly assume intention, e.g. 'A man with HIV fucking an uninfected man is more likely to pass on HIV.' The verb GET makes the subject the person or people who are infected, rather than the person who is infecting, e.g.: 'Some men have got HIV from sucking men off.' The most frequent verb used in relation to HIV is HAVE, which also tends not to place emphasis on the process of getting infected, but places the point of infection as something which happened at some undisclosed past time: 'You can't tell who has HIV by looking.'

Responsibility regarding the transmission of HIV is therefore framed in two ways. A man who infects someone else with HIV is not characterised as 1) doing it on purpose, or 2) held accountable. For example, in a photo story in *Exposed!* 1, an HIV positive man has anal sex with another man, without using a condom. The HIV positive man withdraws before he ejaculates but then thinks: 'Well, I pulled out OK but look: blood! And I make a lot of pre-cum. Has this guy just been at risk of getting HIV?' In the latter sentence, the subject is 'this guy', the HIV positive man does not refer to himself at all, and HIV is represented as a 'risk'. The sentence is passive and because it contains no agent, is ergative – compare it to: 'Has this guy just been at risk of getting HIV by/from me?' or 'Have I put this guy at risk of getting HIV?'

One of the functions of the passive is to omit the agent (Biber *et al.* 1999: 477). However, as Stubbs (2001b: 158) points out, there are many reasons for omitting the agent – in order to be deliberately ambiguous, to obscure blame, because the information is obvious or unimportant, or in order to place the focus in a certain way. We could argue in this case that the absence of the agent is intended to not place blame on HIV+ people. But perhaps in this case it is not necessary to explicitly state the agent, as it is already implied earlier in the text: 'I made a lot of pre-cum.' What may be more useful then is to consider more general patterns of verb usage in connection to HIV infection.

As described above, HIV is referred to in connection with GET, rather than GIVE, placing the emphasis on the person being infected rather than the person with HIV. Compare, for example, a hypothetical alternative thought bubble which says, 'Have I given him HIV?' and agency is shown in a much different light. HIV infection is also framed as a question, i.e. a possibility rather than an absolute state – compare the construction to the declarative 'I've given him HIV!' It is the combination of grammar and lexis which suggests evidence that this utterance has been carefully constructed in order to avoid the presentation of blame.

Additional evidence for taking a non-blaming stance is found if we look at the word *reasons* in the corpus. In just under half of the occurrences of this word (6 out of 13), they refer to reasons why men don't tell other people that they are HIV positive: 'There are plenty of reasons why a man might choose not to tell ... you might react badly ... you might tell others ... and anyway, if you're going to have safer sex, why do you need to know? Are you still expecting to be told?'; 'Ask some men who do know and they might feel they just can't tell – often for good reasons.' Other reasons include 'When I tell you, you often clear off, I want you to know me as a person first I might talk about HIV later. If I tell you might turn nasty on me. I don't want you "counselling" me about HIV, my health and all that! I'm after a shag. Talking about HIV is a real passion killer.' So crucially, reasons for not telling another person about HIV status are seen to be plentiful and also valid.

While responsibility concerning passing on HIV (or other infections) is downplayed, responsibility for (not) getting HIV is made implicit. While imperative phrases such as 'you should use condoms' or 'don't have anal sex' do not occur in the corpus, a number of more subtle strategies offer a safer sex message, based on individual choice and responsibility.

For example, if the third most common noun lemma in the corpus MAN is examined, we find that the plural *men* occurs 313 times, while *man* only occurs 65 times. A significant proportion of uses of *men* refer to types of behaviour by non-specific numbers of men: *some men* (42 occurrences), *many men* (17), *most men* (15), *a lot of men* (3) and *lots of men* (2). These cases are often used alongside suggestions about practices that could be viewed as being a good idea – because other people do them: 'Although many men have problems to begin with, most men get used to condoms with practise. Some men say extra-strong condoms make them feel safer'; 'Some men have regular check-ups for STIs so that they can have any infection treated quickly'; 'Some men with HIV wear a condom to stop cum or pre-cum getting in their partner's mouth when being sucked off.' These descriptions of what other men do are not evaluated in the text, they are simply presented as possibilities. Yet their association with the behaviour or experiences of the majority or a significant number of people has the effect of normalising or validating them. Another aspect of these constructions is that they usually include an additional clause which explains the reasoning behind the activity: 'Some men use lubricant, fuck less hard and for less time *to reduce the chances of HIV being passed on when they fuck without condoms*'; 'Some men have a check up every few months *just to be sure they haven't got any infections without knowing*'; 'Some men use the facts in this book *to make it less likely that they will get or pass on HIV*' (italics added). In 30 out of 42 cases of *some men* and 9 out of 15 cases of *many men*, the noun phrase appears at the beginning of the sentence – therefore the structure of safer sex 'advice' follows the most common pattern of Frequency + Behaviour + Reason. A similar pattern is found with the less frequent nouns *people* (occurring 134 times) and *guys* (occurring 40 times). *Some* occurs with *people* 16 times and with *guys* seven times, *most* occurs with *people* nine times and with *guys* three times, *many* occurs with *people* ten times, while, *plenty of* and *lots of* occur once each with *guys*.

It should be also noted that advice is given implicitly – it is not presented in the form of there being a single 'correct' way to have safer sex. So, in the examples above, there is advice on activities which will help reduce the risk of HIV when *not* using a condom. However, on the whole, stressing condom use plays an important role in the presentation of safer sex behaviour for gay men. The words *condoms* and *condom* occur 343 times collectively, which makes forms of the lemma CONDOM the fourth most frequent noun in the corpus. The phrase USE *a condom* occurs 22 times while USE *condoms* occurs 45 times. However, these phrases never occur as imperatives. Instead, other grammatical constructions appear. The most common is to use an *-ing* clause, rather than a human actor as the subject: 'Using a condom should help stop herpes being passed on through sucking or fucking'; 'Using condoms will greatly reduce the risk of getting NSU from fucking and sucking.' These examples have no human actors at all – for example, the word *you* or *someone* could have been inserted before the word *getting* in the latter case. The *-ing* clause as subject occurs in 21 cases of the 59 cases of USE as a verb occurring before *condom*. Another technique is to word the sentence as a first-person declarative: 'I don't know if I've got HIV or not, so I use a condom every time'; 'In a casual encounter, if I ask if they want to use a condom but they're happy not to, then that's their choice.' As with the *some men* structure, using a vox pop narrative via real or imaginary speakers allows advice to be given in terms of an opinion or 'voiced behaviour' – again validating the behaviour as one worth considering. In ten cases of USE occurring before *condom*, the strategy of citing majority behaviours is used, with phrases like *some men, most men, lots of couples* and *most of us* appearing. Pairing USE *condom(s)* with a second person pronoun (e.g. *you* or *your*) is a strategy that is used much more infrequently, occurring eight times and shown below:

> If you don't have HIV and decide not to use condoms for cocksucking, you can reduce the risk of picking up HIV by . . .
> If you have HIV and decide not to use condoms for cocksucking, you can reduce the risk of passing on HIV by . . .
> If you decide not to use condoms for cocksucking you can reduce the risks by . . .
> Your chances of getting an STI can depend on whether you use condoms or not.
> You can reduce the risk by avoiding contact with shit, proper hand washing and using condoms.
> You can reduce the chances of getting one by using condoms.
> Practising if you're a beginner or had problems using condoms.
> Whether or not to use condoms with your regular partner.

Again, none of these examples instruct the reader implicitly to use condoms. Six of them use the modal verb *can* linked to the risk or chance of HIV infection. *Can* is used to refer to permission, possibility or ability (Biber *et al.* 1999: 485). While the distinction can sometimes be ambiguous, in the above cases, *can* seems to indicate possibility. In addition, four of the above sentences make use of a conditional *if* clause while one uses *whether*. All of these cases therefore reference possibility rather than certainty. Condom use is not presented as a failsafe way of preventing infection, and the reader is never explicitly directed to use them. Instead, by the use of other strategies, a condom is shown to be a good idea but not the only option for gay men.

Another important word, *risk(s)*, occurs 128 times in the corpus (the ninth most frequent lexical word) and also refers to the modality of infection. *Risk* is used in preference to *chance/chances* which only occur 37 times, of which 28 refer to sexually transmitted infections, or the words *possibility* or *danger* which never occur in the corpus. In the THT Corpus *risk* collocates with the following words (mutual information log base 2 scores are shown): *infecting* 4.64, *reduce* 4.45, *cuts* 4.15, *passing* 4.11, *low* 3.92, *almost* 3.79, *picking* 3.57, *past* 3.38, *high* 3.26 and *there's* 3.22. A look at the strongest collocates of *risk* in the BNC (calculated via log–log) show that most of them relate to danger in some way: usually personal (*cancer* (41.2), *injury* (29.8), *disease* (26.4), *suicide* (25.2)) or financial (*non-market* (33.6), *management* (23.7), *premium* (39.2)). *Risk* is therefore what Crystal (2001: 170) calls a loaded word, one which contains negative associations embedded within it (hence collocates such as *infecting, disease, injury* and *suicide*). However, some collocations of *risk* in the THT Corpus frame the concept as an amount that can vary: *low, reduce, high, almost* – suggesting that risk is something which, while a matter of probability, is also subject to some human control, unlike concepts such as *danger* or *chance*. *Risk* and its collocates therefore emphasise human agency. Note that *reduce* is a strong collocate of *risk* whereas its antonym *increase* is not. One example of *risk* which demonstrates how it relates to personal choice is the sentence: 'Whether it's a risk you're happy taking is for you and him to decide.'

The THT Corpus mentions *infection(s)* 266 times (the sixth most common lexical word), in preference of *disease(s)* which only occurs 11 times. This is contrasted with the frequency of these words in the BNC – where *infection* occurs 2700 times as opposed to *disease*'s 8858 occurrences. Sixty-seven cases of *infection(s)* in the THT corpus appear in the phrase *sexually transmitted infection(s)*. The popularity of this phrase is shown by the fact that it also appears as the acronym *STI* 32 times. *Sexually transmitted disease(s)* occurs four times, whereas *STD* occurs five times in the corpus. *Venereal disease* only occurs once, while *VD* occurs twice. All three phrases are used as rough synonyms of each other within the THT Corpus, although a clear preference is shown for *sexually transmitted infection*. Why is this the case? Again, the BNC provides a clue. Strong collocates of *infection* (using log–log) are the words *spread* (34.3), *risk* (35.5), *prevalence* (30.0), *preventing* (28.6), *susceptible* (27.8), *diagnosed* (25.6), *resistance* (24.6), *immunity* (23.8) and *eradicated* (23.2). On the other hand, collocates of *disease* are *severity* (44.8), *patients* (43.4), *malignant* (42.6), *symptomatic* (37.7), *chronic* (53.6), *incurable* (34.2), *sufferers* (32.5) and *severe* (31.1). In general British English, *infection* is therefore associated with transmission (how is something transmitted and how can it be stopped?), whereas *disease* is connected to symptoms (how bad are the symptoms and will they go away?). So while both words are 'loaded', the negative connotations of *disease* are stronger than those of *infection*. By using the word *infection* in the THT texts, emphasis is again placed on the point of transmission and its prevention, rather than dwelling on symptoms. This finding is in keeping with the high frequency of the word *HIV* in the corpus and the low frequency of *AIDS*. Further evidence for the leaflet's de-emphasis of AIDS or other diseases is found by the tenth most frequent noun in the corpus – *health*, which occurs 99 times. *Health* collocates most strongly in the THT Corpus with *advisor* (5.37), *sexual* (4.95), *centres* (4.57) and *project* (4.40), occurring in phrases such as *health advisor* (17 times), *sexual health* (31, of which 17 are *sexual health clinic*) and *gay men's health project* (7).

One strategy that the advertisers therefore have used is to not focus on the potential long-term consequences of becoming HIV positive, ensuring that readers will not become too traumatised by the safer sex advice and not pay attention to it. However, another form of emotional arousal – one based on a pleasurable response – is used in order to ensure that the message will be read. Instead of fear, the leaflets promote sexual desire via explicit sexual images and text. A closer look at how sexual language is used in the Corpus would therefore be useful.

Informalisation

Another top-ten word, *arse*, demonstrates an aspect of the informal language which the texts employ. *Arse* occurs 217 times (the seventh most frequent lexical word), whereas the plural form appears on seven occasions. *Arse* is shown as being a synonym for anus in one case: 'Then the shit moves into your rectum and out of your anus (arse) through your two anal sphincters' (*The Bottom Line*). Alternatives for *arse* are rare: *anus* occurs only twice, *bottom* occurs ten times but refers to the sexual role of being passive rather than meaning anus. *Butt* occurs six times, while *bum* appears seven times. There is a definite lexical preference for *arse* over other terms.

A look at the most frequent collocates of *arse* in the THT Corpus reveals a possible reason for this choice. A number of the collocates which occur one place to the left of *arse* are possessive constructions: *someone's* (13), *their* (10), *his* (7), *man's* (4). However, the two most frequent collocates at L1 are *the* and *your*, both occurring 69 times each. Therefore, when *arse* is used, it is often one of the cases where the text talks directly to the reader (e.g. the high frequency of the phrase *your arse*). By using an informal rather than scientific term, the text attempts to engage with the reader on a 'common sense' level. The word also accesses the language variety of gay erotica – *arse* occurs in the gay erotic narratives corpus (see Chapter 6) 164 times, although *ass* appears 2153 times. I would argue that *ass* and *arse* are variants of the same word. The difference in orthographic form is most likely due to pronunciation variation between American English and British English – British uses the long vowel /ɑː/ whereas American employs the short vowel /æ/. *Ass* does not appear at all in the THT texts, although it is popular in the erotic narrative corpus because most of the stories within it are by American writers.

In order to see if this type of informalisation was restricted just to *arse* or whether it occurred across other concepts, the frequencies of other informal lexis and their alternatives in the THT Corpus are shown in Table 7.4 below.

In all cases but one (*gonorrhoea*) the informal word is used in preference to the formal one. Taken as a whole, *your* collocates one place immediately to the left of the informal words in the left-hand column 112 times, while *you* collocates in the same position 23 times (accounting for 14.0 per cent of the 963 cases). With the formal words in the right-hand column, *your* and *you* occur five times and once respectively (accounting for 3.3 per cent of the 149

Table 7.4 Informal lexis used in the THT Corpus

Informal lexis		Formal lexis	
ARSE	223	ANUS/ANAL	35
DICK	24	PENIS	1
COCK	104		
FUCK	252	anal sex	25
cum (noun)	12	semen	5
		sperm	1
cum (verb)	77	ORGASM	6
lube	65	lubricant	18
shit	63	faeces/fecal	0
SUCK	69	oral sex	10
crabs	29	lice	9
piss	27	urine	3
spit	12	saliva	0
clap	6	gonorrhoea	36
total	963	total	149

cases). Therefore, second person pronouns occur in the THT texts almost three times as often next to informal words as they do with formal ones. However, it may be the case that *all* pronouns, not just second person ones, appear in connection with informal words in the corpus. The only other L1 pronoun collocates with the words in the table are *his* (19 occurrences) and *their* (28 occurrences), which do not occur at all with the formal lexis. So when sexual terminology is addressed directly to the reader, the most common strategy is to use informal language. Additionally, informal language is restricted to a number of areas in the corpus – sexual body parts and experiences and waste products. All three areas could be viewed as tabooed in society. However, other tabooed topics such as names of infections tend not to be informalised in the texts. Genital warts, syphilis, herpes, HIV and chlamydia are not generally referred to by non-standard terms. This could be because there are fewer commonly known slang words for these infections. A total of 21 out of 29 cases of *crabs* are in scare quotes, and the proportion rises to five out of six for *(the) clap*. The strategy of using informal language about sexually transmitted infections is made more explicit, with the informality being marked. The other non-standard words never receive scare quotes.

Vernacular language is therefore most strongly connected to the positive aspects of sex (orgasm, body parts, sexual acts) rather than possible negative outcomes (e.g. infections).

Arguably, the use of informal language for sexual terms when directly addressing the audience is in keeping with the 'border crossing' strategy of the health documents – presenting information in an accessible, involved way. Over-reliance on scientific 'medical' terminology might make the narrative sound too detached or possibly judgemental about sexual practices. In addition, the familiar terms access an erotic discourse which is accentuated by the 'photo story' format in some of the texts. For example, in *Exposed!* 2 the characters in a photo story have speech bubbles that say 'Tasty! I'll give him one alright', 'He's well fit' and 'Horny body! I want him to fuck me.' In *Exposed!* 1 characters say 'Phwoargh! Tasty! Looks like I'll be getting a good screw tonight', 'Don't cum inside me will ya!', 'Urghhh!! I've cum' and 'Fuck! He said he'd not cum in me but he did.' Informal lexis (*tasty, well fit, screw, horny*), vocalisation of emotion (*phwoargh, urrghhh, fuck*), non-standard spellings and grammatical forms (*cum, ya, said he'd not cum*) and fragments of speech (*Looks like . . ., Horny body!*) are linked to expressions of desire and sexual activity, emulating the language of gay male erotic narratives (see Chapter 6).

However, there is another aspect of this type of non-standard language – it emphasises a form of masculinity associated with working-class heterosexual men (Trudgill 1974: 94). For example, *tasty* occurs in the BNC four times near the word *she* (when a man is speaking) but doesn't collocate with *he*. Casting gay men as stereotypically masculine in the THT texts fulfils a number of purposes. It encourages the reader to focus on the characters and their actions because such traits are viewed as highly desirable to gay men – note for example the high frequency of terms such as *straight-acting* and *masculine* in the corpus of personal adverts (Chapter 5), or the hyper-masculine identity constructions in the gay men's erotic narratives corpus (Chapter 6). Additionally, presenting gay men as being masculine runs counter to discourses of gay effeminacy. Not all such discourses are wholly negative; for example, Jack – the effeminate stereotype in *Will & Grace* (Chapter 4) – is shown to be entertaining and politically aware. However, discourses of gay effeminacy tend to show such men in a camp, humorous, asexual role – a source of laughter rather than sexual desire. The fictional characters in the THT texts contest the discourse of gay effeminacy by presenting an alternative discourse which shows gay men as 'real men' who desire and are desirable. For example, in the leaflet *The Bottom Line*, passive sexual acts are reconceptualised as not being feminine: 'Some straight people still ask about gay couples "who's the man, who's the woman"? Reality is, these days most of us do it both ways. We might prefer one role more but that says nothing about how "manly" we are.' And in the youth advice leaflet, a character says 'Everyone thinks you're into glitter and girly things. But I'm just a regular lad into the same things as everyone else.'

A higher proportion of the informal language in the THT Corpus is therefore found in the vox pops language of the fictional characters as opposed to the main narrative 'voice' of the texts. For example, in *Gay men and combination therapy*, the narrative voice says, 'Things that some men have found helpful' and then lists advice in the form of first-person quotes: 'If I get a bit hammered when I'm out I just try to drink loads of water to stop me drying out'; 'If I've copped off I just take a bathroom break after sex, men usually don't think anything's odd with that.'

Sexuality

If the language used in the texts tends to presuppose a masculine audience (or one who finds masculinity desirable), then in what other ways are sexual identities constructed? *Gay* is the second highest lexical word in the THT Corpus, occurring 384 times. The texts show a strong lexical preference for this term – *homosexual* never occurs, nor do pejorative words like *sissy*, *puff*, *fag* or *faggot*. *Queer* occurs six times in the Europe travel guide leaflet, but it is always used as part of the title 'Queer Year' which gives calendar dates for gay events in different cities. *Bisexual* occurs 26 times, of which 24 occurrences are as part of the phrase 'gay and bisexual' or 'gay or bisexual'. Bisexuality is therefore rarely viewed as a salient identity but something to be connected to (and overshadowed) by gay identities. As *gay* occurs proportionally most often in the Europe leaflet and least often in the MSM leaflet it is worth investigating how sexual identity is constructed in these two leaflets in more detail.

The *man{sex}man* leaflet has the lowest occurrence of the word *gay* in the texts (see Figure 7.4) at 1.88 per thousand words. A set of terms that seem to be used in this leaflet as an alternative to *gay* focus on sexual activity or desire rather than identity and include phrases such as 'guys who have sex with other men' (one occurrence), 'men who have sex with other men' (one), 'Men who love Men' (one), 'Men who'd had sex with another man' (two), 'sex with men' (five occurrences) and 'sex with other men' (five occurrences). Just over half (eight) of all these phrases in the whole corpus occurred in the *man{sex}man* leaflet. Other aspects of the leaflet reinforce the idea that sexuality isn't a fixed identity. On pages 2–3, six drawings of men of different ages (teens to late 40s/early 50s), ethnic origins (black, Asian, white) and clothing styles (suits, casual, sports gear) are shown, each with a phrase describing their sexual identity, e.g.: 'I'm gay', 'I don't know', 'I'm bisexual', 'I'm just me'. This leaflet emphasises the diversity of men who have sex with men, e.g.: 'Sex can be what you want it to be... Not everyone enjoys

N	File	Words	Hits	per 1,000	Plot
1	europe.txt	4,806	117	24.34	
2	youth.txt	2,389	42	17.58	
3	longhaul.txt	4,373	74	16.92	
4	survey.txt	1,371	15	10.94	
5	exposed2.txt	1,796	12	6.68	
6	exposed3.txt	2,919	19	6.51	
7	exposed1.txt	4,669	20	4.28	
8	manual.txt	13,541	51	3.77	
9	haart.txt	1,595	5	3.13	
10	facts.txt	1,281	4	3.12	
11	bottom.txt	10,041	20	1.99	
12	msm.txt	2,655	5	1.88	

Figure 7.4 Distribution of the word *gay* across the THT Corpus.

the same things...' The leaflet also celebrates sex as a matter of personal choice: 'Sex is great! Sex with other men is what you make it.'

Davies *et al.* (1990) describe the origins of the term *MSM*. Project Sigma researchers, among others, had found that large numbers of men who had sex with other men did not identify as gay – many of them were married and maintained a heterosexual identity. Wilton (1997: 78) critiques the creation of the term as part of a process called identifaction/identificating:

> This label, useful though it was to health educators and researchers, was neither chosen by the men themselves nor adopted by them once coined. It was, in other words, an entirely assigned identity, not subject to the usual processes of resistance, incorporation, performance and negotiation which constitute gender identities.

While Wilton's argument is valid, it is difficult to think of a way of addressing a group who are not willing to acknowledge their own existence. The THT's strategy of using different phrases such as 'sex with men' at least places categorisation beyond having to acknowledge identity and locates it within behaviour/desire instead.

Other leaflets in the THT Corpus are more explicitly written for a gay male audience, particularly the travel guides, the young person's guide and the *Exposed!* 'magazine' series. How about cases where *gay* is used instead? Words which occur one place to the right of *gay* do tend to relate to identity (*men* (85), *people* (four), *youth* (four), *couples* (three), *man* (two), *adults* (one)). Sexual activity tends not to co-occur with *gay*, with *sex* only appearing as an R1 collocate seven times. So the term *gay sex* is very infrequent. Instead, when sex is referred to, it is as an act that is not based on sexuality, e.g. *fucking* (105 occurrences), *sucking* (53) and *rimming* (28) or simply as *sex* (294 occurrences in total). Sexual activity then is not explicitly defined as gay (nor is homosexuality directly linked to sexual activity), a finding in keeping with the use of phrases like 'men who have sex with men'. Instead, *gay* collocates with words that connect it to lifestyle: either places (*venues* (14), *bars* (14), *nudist beach* (three), *beach* (three), *hot spots* (two), *hotels* (two), *stores* (two), *club* (two), *bookshop* (two), *shops* (one), *restaurants* (one), *resorts* (one), *pubs* (one), *accommodation* (one)), media (*press* (eight), *maps* (six), *magazines* (three), *travel guides* (two)) or the notion of a community (*scene* (23), *Pride* (five), *community* (two)).

Gay is therefore often associated with places – this is partly due to the fact that two of the pamphlets are travel guides and offer lists of places that are assumed to be of interest to gay men. In this sense, another discourse of gay identity is accessed here – one that is not primarily based on sexual activity or desire for other men, but of the gay man as a tourist, a consumer and a reveller. For example, in *Gay men and combination therapy*, a vox pops quote talks about the side-effects of taking drugs for HIV: 'Diarrhoea and sickness – sometimes the worst bit about needing the toilet in a hurry is that a lot of pubs and clubs have poor toilets and no loo paper.' Here there is the assumption that gay men *do* go to pubs and clubs and, therefore, this advice is relevant to them.

In the Europe guide, the reader is instructed on how to navigate his way through the Yumbo Centre in Playa del Ingles which is described as a shopping mall by day and a 'gay playground' by night: 'Don't bother arriving before 11 pm unless eating first in the restaurants. Start on the bottom level, move up to level 2 with its more sex-oriented bars, peaking on the top level sometime after midnight, then back down a level to the cruisy bars and clubs.' The use of imperative verb phrases in this guide, e.g.: 'don't bother arriving ... start on the bottom level...' assumes that the reader will *want* to visit the sex-oriented and 'cruisy' bars and clubs.

Later in the Europe guide, the reader is given information about some sand dunes in Gran Caneria: 'The (in)famous sand dunes at Maspalomas – 20 mins walk from Playa del Ingles – offer daytime cruising. Head for kiosk 7 with the rainbow flag.' Again, the verb *head* not only instructs the reader how to reach the sand dunes but could be read as an *invitational imperative* (Omoniyi 1998: 6), or a way of normalising cruising activity while on holiday. These instructions do not make use of modal verbs or a correlative subordinator such as 'if you want to go cruising then...' or 'although it may not be your thing, the sand dunes can be found at...' in order to imply that cruising is not something that all gay men do or want to do. Later in a section entitled 'Survival tips', readers are warned: 'Don't leave valuables unattended when you go off to explore the dunes.' The use of *when* here again assumes that the reader *will* engage in that activity. And in the section on Mykonos, the reader is instructed to 'Bare all on the gay nudist beach.' One sentence which does use an *if* clause is 'If you have sex with quite a few men while you're away ... it's a good idea to get a check-up at a clinic once you're home.' This advice is presented in less categorical terms as the instructions about how to reach the sand dunes; hedging the imperative 'get a check-up' with the phrase 'it's a good idea to'. In addition, the phrase 'sex with quite a few men' is vague but can be interpreted as implying that there's a possibility that gay men will have multiple sexual partners while on holiday. The Europe travel guide gives a checklist of important items for readers to remember to take on holiday with them, including condoms and lube. And in the sex survey pamphlet, readers are asked: 'So boys, of all the dicks you've seen how many of them came with or without a foreskin.' Again, there is the normative presupposition that the reader will have had a fair amount of sexual experience; the phrase 'all the dicks you've seen' implies the reader will have seen a lot of them.

The travel guides make other assumptions about what constitutes a likely gay identity. For example, during advice about protection from sunburn on holiday the sentence 'Cropped/shaved heads burn extra fast – cover up with cap or sun block (at least Factor 15)' appears. The advice does not appear to cover people who are naturally bald but instead assumes that readers who don't have hair have consciously chosen this style by cropping or shaving their head – thus following current fashions. The fact that the only travel destinations that are written about in the guides are large cities (Paris, New York, Berlin, etc.) that have sizeable gay scenes also constructs gay men as being likely to want to go to such places. This effectively accesses the discourse of gay men as sophisticated consumers, suggesting that they are going to be confident, discerning travellers who like to holiday in urban capitals that are associated with culture and capitalism. Such places reflect the aspirational discourse found in the *Will & Grace* scripts (Chapter 4). Non-urban locations that do not have large gay scenes are therefore not viewed to be particularly relevant to the audience. The gay reader is therefore constructed as the sort of person who will want to go to gay bars, clubs, shops or cruising grounds while on holiday.

As well as writing about sexual health, some of the pamphlets refer to drug use. A distinction is made between legal (e.g. to counter infections) and illegal drugs. For example, in *The Bottom Line*, there is a section on taking illegal drugs anally:

> Some people take drugs by putting them up their arse, sometimes called a 'Booty Bump'. This can be done with many powdered drugs or crushed tablets dissolved in water. Drugs taken anally include Speed (including methamphetamine aka 'Crystal Meth'), Ecstasy or Cocaine and Heroin.

The 'some people' noun phrase here echoes the indirect safer sex advice about condom use described above, therefore providing instructions to people on how drugs can be taken. The section also describes different ways of taking drugs anally: '"Dabbing" is another way of taking drugs anally. It involves putting a finger into the arse with powdered drug on it. "Stuffing" involves putting into the arse a powdered drug wrapped in a cigarette paper or inserting a tablet into the rectum.'

The THT texts sometimes assume that the reader will take drugs or has taken them. For example, the recommended treatment for Hepatitis A is 'rest and no booze or party drugs for months'. Injuries from fisting are described as due to 'going too fast, drugs clouding your judgement or not being prepared or relaxed'.

Advice about drugs does not recommend abstinence but instead focuses on the legal consequences of taking them:

> the scene in San Francisco is a lot less drug-orientated than much of the clubbing scene in the UK. However, party drugs like cocaine and ecstasy are available if you know where to look but are illegal. It's worth remembering that if you are caught with drugs in the United States and convicted, it may affect or even exclude you from returning to the country in the future.

The texts also warn about the strength of drugs: 'The drugs in this part of the country are particularly strong (cocaine especially) so don't get piggy.' So rather than warning readers not to take drugs, the texts warn them not to take too many ('don't get piggy'). Such advice contradicts earlier British drug campaigns which have categorically advised abstinence from all drugs, using messages such as 'Just Say No'.

Therefore gay identity is associated with hedonism (drug taking, cruising for sex), although the authors of the leaflets do not make a negative moral judgement about this. In fact, being able to accept pleasure is viewed as a positive consequence of gay sexuality: 'Being gay is about having the sex we want and like – not about denying what gives us pleasure.' At the same time, heterosexuality is presented in a more negative light: 'Unlike most straight people, we aren't chained to the idea sex has to mean someone getting fucked.' Heterosexuality is therefore seen as resulting in restrictive and prescriptive sex roles. In contrast, gay men are characterised as having a wide repertoire of sexual behaviours to choose from, and also the *right* to decide which ones they want to engage in:

> Just 'cos you're a gay man doesn't mean you must have anal sex! It's your right to say yes or no to it. No-one has the right to make you feel pressured to do it. Lots of guys have great sex that doesn't involve fucking. Often we're too busy sucking, snogging, rimming, fingering and all that other stuff!

The texts therefore regularly construct the audience as one which is sexually experienced and versatile. This 'sex-positive' discourse is moral in that it accesses ideas related to humanism – that people have the right to their own happiness and should be given free will to decide their own fate. However, this is a different sort of moral discourse to one which views homosexuality as wrong, unnatural or against God's will.

Discussion

A number of discourses relating to male homosexuality appear in the THT Corpus, reflecting the fact that different strategies are used in individual texts to 'reach' a specific type of audience. For example, the *man{sex}man* pamphlet emphasises sexual behaviour between men as something that doesn't necessarily have anything to do with being gay, and that people don't have to be given 'labels'. In this pamphlet men who have sex with men are seen as being *individuals* – each with a completely different identity, preferences for sexual activity and way of conceptualising himself. However, in the travel guides, men who have sex with men are constructed as being *gay*, sophisticated travellers who are interested in going to holiday destinations that are urban centres with a large commercial gay scene, likely to go to bars and clubs, take drugs and engage in anonymous sex with multiple partners. Indeed, the texts go beyond such assumptions that readers of the texts may engage in these activities by implicitly inviting them to do so through the use of invitational imperatives. The reader of the texts not only has his gay identity discursively constructed for him, but is also discursively *instructed* in how to be a gay man. The notion of the gay man as consumer is exploited in the leaflets by using competitions in order to ensure that the safer sex message is attended to. Prizes such as gay travel guides or 'hot and horny' videos again construct gay men in a certain way, implying that these are the sorts of commodities they should be interested in possessing.

However, in addition to these two contrasting discourses (men who have sex with other men versus gay men as part of the commercial gay scene) is a third one which is based on masculine iconography and language – the gay man as the masculine ideal. Images of sports (footballers, bodybuilders) or occupations (soldiers, builders) appear alongside vernacular words and phrases associated with stereotypical 'men's language', helping to construct another type of aspirational gay identity – one which audiences are expected to be both attracted to and want to resemble. Such representations are a staple of gay erotica (see Chapter 6) and it could be argued are useful in that they will counter homophobic 'effeminate' representations of gay men as well as being more likely to hold the reader's attention by tapping in to what Leap (1996: 150) calls the 'gay erotic imaginary'. However, in showing such ideals, readers may feel inadequate – that their bodies and lifestyles don't match that of the men depicted in the leaflets. The use of language associated with working-class masculinity may not be viewed as relevant to middle-class or professional men, while some readers may feel that the sex that they have is not as exciting, varied, celebratory or in sufficient quantity as the sex experienced by the men in the leaflets.

Therefore, the goals of the Terrence Higgins Trust health promotional materials are inadvertently conflicted – on the one hand they must be careful not to reproduce homophobic discourses (which means downplaying notions of 'blame' and shame in favour of personal responsibility and agency) and by showing gay men to be masculine rather than effeminate. Second, they must bear in mind that some men do not identify as gay (again, possibly due to homophobia, although there may be other reasons), while others consciously identify as gay, to the point where the identity will impinge on non-sexual aspects of lifestyle such as fashion or choice of holiday. Third, they need to focus on changing sexual *behaviours*, although also acknowledging that, for some people, sexuality is more a question of desire or identity rather than acts. Fourth, they must balance techniques of holding attention by showing images of attractive men while ensuring that the reader sufficiently identifies with those images. Finally, the sexual health message must not be too invasive – although by embedding it within other types of texts (competitions, lifestyle magazines, sex manuals and travel guides) the producers must make assumptions about what gay identity constitutes, while also emphasising that all gay people are different and that sexual health is a matter of personal choice.

Such conflicts therefore account for the unique use of language in the texts as well as the border crossing and informalisation of the safer sex genre. Referring back to the issues that safer sex promoters need to take into account, outlined at the beginning of this chapter, it appears that most of the leaflets aimed at gay men tend to assume that the reader is already relatively sexually experienced, not prudish and has some contact with the gay scene (perhaps because such men are assumed to be in the majority and/or most at risk). However, one way that the Terrence Higgins Trust has addressed the issue of different understandings of homosexuality is by producing a range of leaflets which discursively construct different types of subjects, e.g. the HIV positive gay man, the young gay man, the scene-aware gay man or the man who has sex with men. However, the presence of three, somewhat conflicting, main discourses of gay identity found in the safer sex texts (homosexuality as individual behaviour/desire, as lifestyle/collective identity, and as gender performance/aspirational masculinity) is therefore indicative of the current feeling of ambiguity around gay identity. It is with this thought that I turn to the final chapter.

8 Conclusion

Corpora and identity

Having come this far, I hope I have demonstrated that it is possible to employ a variety of corpus-based methodologies on a range of text types in order to uncover evidence for discourses and identity constructions.

I would argue that the use of corpora has helped a great deal in countering hypotheses and expectations that I held before I began this research. Before writing some of the preceding chapters, I already held expectations concerning what I was going to find. For example, even before reading any of the erotic narratives analysed in Chapter 6, I hypothesised that there would be a focus on traditional constructions of masculinity in the gay male texts as opposed to femininity in the lesbian texts. However, in other cases, my familiarity with texts provided no help in determining prevailing discourses. For example, I had hypothesised that overt references to masculinity in the personal adverts in *Gay Times* would simply increase at a steady rate from the 1970s to the present day (which I guessed would be due to the increased commercialisation of the male body in the media). However, I was surprised to find that the increase only lasted up to the early 1990s, and had fallen back to previous levels by the year 2000. With the analysis of the tabloid newspapers in Chapter 3, I was already aware that such newspapers tended to portray gay men in negative ways. However, I was unaware of the variety of (often conflicting) discourse types that existed. I also did not find much evidence of the discourses I had expected to be present. For example, I had expected to see gay men constructed as silly, inconsequential or feminine. Instead, I found that they were much more frequently represented as a danger, particularly in the *Daily Mail*, in terms of being politically strident and violent.

A qualitative, smaller-scale analysis of these texts would therefore not have been as helpful for this study – on reading the texts during the process of collecting data, it became clear that certain aspects had stood out to me as being interesting and/or appearing typical. Such aspects could have therefore fuelled a qualitative analysis where I might have subconsciously (or not) looked for further examples which supported my initial hypotheses and overlooked patterns that were present but more difficult to notice. One asset of a corpus-based approach then is that it helped to remove some of my own biases. The picture of discourse that has emerged from this analysis is *not* what I had expected to find.

However, that is not to say that researcher bias played no role in influencing the analysis. For example, my focus on 'vanilla' erotic texts featuring adult gay men and women in Chapter 6 meant that I overlooked a much wider range of gay sexuality that was featured in the erotic texts archive, including categories such as 'watersports', 'young friends', 'incest' and 'S/M'. My unwillingness to examine such texts was partly due to concerns about the legality of storing these texts on my computer, partly due to personal disinterest/distaste in such subjects and partly due to a somewhat subjective belief that such texts would not reflect majority or traditionally public discourses of homosexuality.

So while the vanilla 'adult friends' section of the erotic archive was much larger than other sections, there was a range of types of gay sexual desire that I ignored. The presence of such narratives should not be taken as evidence that behaviours such as incest or S/M occur with great frequency among gay people, rather that they are topics that some people find compelling to write about, just as the large number of vanilla stories involving masculine muscular men does not imply that all gay sex occurs between such people. By downplaying different types of gay male desire, I am aware that I am influenced by current discourses which cast certain forms of sexuality (particularly incest and paedophilia) as immoral, in a way that may have been less likely to be the case in the past or in other cultures.

My own biases aside though, the analyses in the preceding chapters have been informative in unearthing old and newer discourses of mainstream homosexuality and the links or inconsistencies between them. Before I go on to look at these discourses in more detail, I wish to examine some of the other issues concerning taking a corpus-based approach to texts on gender/sexuality.

One problem that I noted in Chapter 1 is that corpus analysis is primarily based on orthographic texts, so aspects of visual or performative communication are going to be more difficult to elicit. This was particularly relevant in Chapters 2, 3, 4 and 7, where written language worked in conjunction with images or speech. For example, when examining data from *Will & Grace*, at times it was difficult to judge from a concordance line whether characters were being ironic or joking. Again, tone of voice, posture or context going back over a long period of time would be required to interpret the text correctly. In some cases I supplemented the corpus-based approach by referring to these other forms of communication (for example, Karen's high-pitched voice in the *Will & Grace* episodes, or the pictures of masculine men in the sexual health documentation). Therefore, while a corpus-based approach may be useful in many cases, it cannot be relied on exclusively in every text, particularly with texts that involve pictures or spoken language, unless a more detailed annotation system is employed in order to take into account speech prosody or visual analysis.

A further aspect of the corpus-based approach to discourse analysis is that some texts were more self-selecting than others. In particular, texts that were relatively short and contained a reasonably restricted use of language (e.g. personal adverts, erotic stories) were easy to collect and resulted in recognisably quantifiable patterns. In addition, uncovering such patterns only required the analysis of thousands rather than millions of words. Other texts, which are subject to more internal variation, such as a gay novel or magazine, may require the researcher to undertake more ambitious corpus-building projects in order to elicit similar linguistic patterns. Additionally, texts that already existed in an accessible, searchable electronic form (such as the House of Lords debates or web-based newspaper archives) were more likely to be used than those which had to be scanned or typed in by hand. I had particular difficulty in collecting corpus data that consisted of naturally occurring spoken language. Although two of my chapters are concerned with spoken data (the House of Lords debates and the *Will & Grace* scripts), both are to a greater or lesser extent forms of 'prepared' speech.

As I had noted in Chapter 1, it is sometimes difficult to account for absence in corpus data, unless the researcher knows what to look for, or the text is compared with a larger reference corpus. Negative keywords may also highlight lexical items which occur much less frequently than expected. In addition, the range of processes and tools that are available to the corpus linguist does not lend itself to a single optimum way to analyse data. I have tried to illustrate a variety of possible types of corpus-based analysis of discourse, employing keywords, part of speech and grammatical annotation, collocation, semantic preference, discourse prosody, dispersal patterns and frequency lists. Again, researcher intuition is required in order to choose an appropriate methodology and to interpret the results. For example, in Chapter 5 the corpus analysis showed that gay men were more concerned with using terms relating to masculinity in 1991 than in other years. However, the corpus did not explain *why* this was the case. I have therefore needed to explain the results by placing them in the larger context of societal change – the quantitative analysis requiring interpretative explanations in order to make sense. Fitting the corpus results into a wider range of studies – Sanderson's (1995) analysis of the homophobic content of British newspapers in the light of HIV, attitude surveys from 1983–2000 from British Social Attitudes surveys on homosexuality (Jowell 1996, Jowell *et al.* 1992, 1999, 2000), and critiques of the changing representations of heterosexual masculinity (Bronksi 1998, Simpson 1994) – helped to piece together evidence which offers one explanation as to why gay men became more concerned with representing themselves as 'straight-acting' during the early 1990s.

However, as with all forms of analysis, explanations are interpretative and the reader may disagree with my conclusions. I welcome the fact that a range of alternative accounts exists for the corpus data. At least in devising alternative explanations for my data they will be starting from a place where they are being asked to account for quantifiable patterns, or carry out their own research based on the theories and hypotheses I have used in order to explain my results.

While corpus techniques should not be rejected, the boundaries between qualitative and quantitative forms of analysis, structuralist and post-structuralist accounts, difference and discourse need to be shown as being more inter-related than they are currently accounted for. These forms are better viewed as linked components in a single system rather than separate, conflicting and incompatible approaches to knowledge. I hope that this book has presented a complementary method of discourse analysis to researchers of language and gender/sexuality. I do not offer it as a superior or replacement approach to the methodologies which are more commonly used in these fields, but one which may be considered worthwhile and not dismissed as a shallow form of 'number-crunching' as has unfortunately been the case in the past.

Discourse and gay men

The analysis of a range of publicly available texts which construct male homosexuality has been useful in showing the wealth of discourse types surrounding the subject. Any one of the analytical chapters in this book could have functioned as a stand-alone article but it is only by considering the discourses found in them within the larger context of the discourses in the other chapters, and considering how they contradict or support each other, that we can build a larger picture of the way that homosexuality is currently constructed in public discourse in western society.

So what discoveries have been made about discourses of homosexuality from the preceding chapters? One of my initial research questions was to uncover dominant and competing discourses. It is clear that, unlike previous decades, there is no single 'dominant' discourse of homosexuality at present; rather there are a number of related yet conflicting discourses, which point to a dramatic reformulation of the way that western society conceptualises sexuality and gay men view themselves.

In writing this book I have elicited three interlinked sites of contestation that I have found useful in understanding the ways that gay men are currently discursively constructed. These are *definitions*, *homophobia* and *aspiration*.

Definitions

The first site of contestation involves how homosexuality itself is defined by both mainstream and gay culture. From examining the House of Lords debates it is clear that one of the clashes between discourses comes from a long-established notion of homosexuality as consisting of a form (or forms) of behaviour (hence the use of terms like *practising homosexual, commit an act of buggery* and *homosexual activities*) versus a relatively newer reconceptualisation of homosexuality as an identity-based community (shown by terms such as *sexual orientation, gay scene, pride* and *liberation*). Both discourses do not have to be mutually exclusive, although they are often presented as such. However, neither is completely satisfactory when examined alone, leading to inconsistencies and the possibility of exclusion or miscategorisation in both cases. For example, the idea of homosexuality as a set of behaviours (most often sexual acts) omits the possibility that people may not have sex but still identify as gay. Other sorts of behaviours that become associated with gay men have the effect of stereotyping, often in a negative way, e.g. the way that newspaper tabloids characterise gay men as promiscuous, outrageously flamboyant and attempting to convert children. The 'homosexuality as behaviour' discourse is therefore one which is frequently implicitly homophobic, relying on nineteenth- and twentieth-century medical, religious and legal discourses which cast gay men as criminal deviants. This discourse is not, however, limited to homophobic texts: it appears in a slightly different form in gay personal adverts, where terms such as *active, passive* and *versatile* frame homosexuality around the act of penetration. In this case, it is not simply the act of gay sex which denotes homosexuality, but a range of acts or preferences for certain types of act which denote different *types* of gay men. In addition, the 'homosexuality as behaviour' discourse has been adopted and reclaimed by safer sex workers in order to target men who do not consider themselves to be gay but have sex with men. Ironically though, in some cases, the reluctance of such men to identify as gay may be a result of homophobic discourses such as 'homosexuality as behaviour' in the first place.

On the other hand, the 'gay identity' discourse offers an alternative, more positive conceptualisation of homosexuality, suggesting that gay men are defined by more than what they do or don't do in bed, and that they are a social group who deserve the same political rights and freedom of expression as everyone else. The concept of gay identity has allowed notions such as 'gay pride' and the idea of 'coming out' to come into being. The identity discourse has therefore sprung in resistance from the less positive 'behaviour' discourse.

The presence of both types of discourse within the same texts shows the difficulty that people have in defining what they mean by the term *gay* and the fact that different conceptualisations may be useful at different times. For example, in the tabloid newspapers gay people are alternatively constructed as people who 'indulge' in sexual behaviours (rather than being able to maintain relationships) while at other times they are a group or community with a political 'agenda' or shared interests beyond sex.

It could be argued that the 'gay identity' discourse sometimes oversimplifies the notion of community, where everyone has (or should have) similar goals, values and preferences. This homogeneous identity is therefore found in discourses which presuppose that gay men are likely to want to attend nightclubs, gay holiday resorts and cruise for anonymous sex (such as those found in the safer sex documentation in Chapter 7). While the newer notion of a gay identity as community is an important advancement in terms of uniting numbers of people, promoting awareness from a sense of shared oppression and allowing an identity to be named and claimed rather than a behaviour that is named and shamed, the sense of community can be exclusionary or restrict choices. Some people may not want to claim a gay identity if they feel that they will be faced with a set of expectations from a community they do not particularly identify with. For political reasons, the idea of a 'gay identity' is therefore useful, yet also problematic.

Therefore, in order to make sense of the ways that society currently understands homosexuality, we need to be aware that it exists as a set of inter-related, yet fluctuating, components including sexual and non-sexual behaviour and identity (both at the individual and community-based level). A third theory which has more recently been put forward as a potential framework for research into language and sexuality is based around the concept of *desire* and is influenced by the psychoanalytical work of Lacan (1998) among others. Psychoanalytical theory has been influential in fields as diverse as literary theory, anthropology and film criticism (e.g. Mulvey 1989). Framing sexuality as desire helps to address the conflicting positions of identity and behaviour, but this theory also poses questions. For example, how does one objectively and confidently study the unconscious or the existence of repression – both important facets of desire?[1] Also, psychoanalytical theories are often based on arguments that can be difficult to falsify, involving interpretations of experiences that infants have before they are able to speak and will later not be able to recall. And what political consequences would there be for gay people or other minority groups in focusing sexuality around desire rather than identity?

However, accepting the importance of desire in discourses of sexuality is useful, particularly in enabling us to answer questions concerning fantasy and idealised identities. Desire influences both how someone wishes to be perceived and the kinds of identities that they find attractive or unattractive. Why certain sexual identities are seen as more desirable than others and the ways in which such identities are constructed in discourse are questions which can be usefully addressed by researchers, and such issues are examined in more detail in relation to the corpus data in the section on aspirational identities below.

There may be other reasons why gay people do not initially 'come out' or identify as gay (while still having gay sex). The issue of sexual regulation in the form of homophobia has already been mentioned above, and I now want to discuss how discourses surrounding this subject have permeated through all forms of public texts addressing homosexuality.

Homophobia

Homophobia is still present in a range of public texts, particularly within those written from conservative perspectives, although the form that homophobia takes is now very different to the moral panics that characterised mid-twentieth-century discourses of homosexuality. Public homophobia is now shaped by an awareness of competing discourses, particularly those of gay community and the notion of equal rights. Where homophobia is present, it is therefore often more subtle – shown by under-representations or non-representations, associations with individuals who are already demonised (Hitler, Osama Bin Laden) or seemingly casual collocations between homosexuality and other lexis which imply relationship transience, political and sexual extremism, secrecy or outrageousness. Another way that homophobia is implied is via irony or jokes, as in the *Mirror* article which complained about gay policemen holding hands.

Such discourses are therefore less easy to contest – the ambiguous intent of humour means that the interlocutor has a ready-made means of saving face by replying with 'I was only joking', which also serves to ensure that whoever confronts him or her will be seen as humourless or overly sensitive. Less obvious examples of homophobia involving an unfortunate co-occurrence in a single news article are more likely to be overlooked or seen as too insignificant to be worth complaining about. It is only when a public text is openly or crudely homophobic (as in the case of the *Sun*'s 'We hope this doesn't put you off your cornflakes' article regarding a same-sex kiss) that there is likely to be reaction from readers. In addition, elements of the same discourse can have different effects depending on the context that it appears in. Both tabloid newspapers and gay erotic texts utilise a discourse of gay men as having the sexual appetites of animals, although in the former this is characterised as a disturbingly negative trait associated with being predatory whereas in the latter it is seen as a positive sign of virility.

Homophobia can also be disguised, excused or negated, as in the House of Lords debates whereby speakers justified an existing inequality (the age of consent) by reframing the debate in terms of another issue which was viewed as more important, such as the need to protect boys *and* girls from the apparent dangers of anal sex (not homosexuality per se).

It should not be thought that homophobic discourses are always noticed or contested, even by gay people. For example, a poll carried out on the British gay community website www.outintheuk.com in 2002 asked the question: 'Which newspaper do you read regularly, if at all?' Of the 2012 voters who replied, 5.5 per cent said that they read the *Daily Mail* (about 111 people). As shown in Chapter 3, in the past the *Daily Mail* has taken a disapproving stance towards homosexuality. So while the *Daily Mail* is not the favourite choice for gay men who use this website,[2] the presence of homophobic discourses in a newspaper does not ensure that *all* gay men will opt not to buy it; the reasons for this apparent paradox are worthy of further research. Perhaps negative tabloid discourses are now so subtle that they pass unnoticed, or they are accepted by some gay men because they are not as bad as they could be.

It is therefore perhaps not surprising that homophobia also pervades texts which are not written from a mainstream point of view. For example, in the *Will & Grace* scripts, characters make puns such as 'Knock Knock. Anyone homo?' and stereotyping phrases such as 'The gays really love their rules'. While such examples are used in a joking manner which is not intended to be offensive to gay viewers, at the same time, the characters and situations in *Will & Grace* are carefully scripted so that they will not appear to be too overtly sexual. The two central gay characters are constructed by accessing a range of different stereotypically masculine and feminine gender traits – Jack is camp, promiscuous and bitchy, whereas Will is more masculine, sensitive and domesticated yet almost asexual. A third character, Karen, displays linguistic traits associated with drag queens, but is played by a woman, perhaps as a way of ensuring that the sitcom does not have too many 'officially' gay characters in it. *Will & Grace* addresses homophobia and makes use of camp humour while suggesting that heterosexual women can form intense friendships with gay men, but gay sex occurs rarely and off-screen. In addition, the audience primarily identifies from a heterosexual point of view. The sitcom's central premise is framed as Grace's 'problem' of being in love with a gay man she can't have. We are led to wish 'If only Will was heterosexual' rather than 'If only Grace was a gay man'.

Homophobic terms such as *cocksucker*, *fag* and *faggot* also appear in gay erotic narratives, although they are often used to show the paradoxically 'heterosexual' status of some of the characters or as reclaimed words – *cocksucker* is almost always a term of praise. Homophobia is therefore increasingly characterised by a sense of ambiguity, both from mainstream and gay culture, suggesting another way that discourses of homosexuality are currently engaged in a struggle between vilification and acceptance.

Linked to the notion of homophobia are discourses surrounding AIDS, which continue to have an effect on the way that gay men view themselves and are constructed by others. The longitudinal analysis of personal adverts in *Gay Times* showed that there was a definite move towards a reconceptualisation of gay identity in terms of discreet, 'non-scene' masculinity during the period directly following the moral panic over AIDS in the 1980s and the subsequent adoption of legislation designed to prevent the 'promotion' of homosexuality by local education authorities in the UK. While many gay men have traditionally found masculinity to be a desirable trait, references to identities that emulated stereotypical male heterosexuality reached a peak during 1991, falling to previous levels as attitudes towards homosexuality became less reactionary over the 1990s.

However, the AIDS crisis continues to affect how gay men are characterised, making the task of designing safer sex documentation an extremely delicate issue. The use of agency in leaflets, e.g. 'Has this guy just been at risk of getting HIV?', and lexical choices which favour words like *risk* and *infection* over terms like *transmit* and *disease*, demonstrate the importance attached to not framing gay men as irresponsible. However, at the same time a balance must be found between giving advice and not appearing moralistic or issuing diktats. Tactics such as informal language use and delaying references to HIV until later in the pamphlets demonstrate attempts to engage with the reader in a down-to-earth, non-threatening way. Sexual health documentation therefore plays down references to gay men being infected with HIV in favour of representing them as enjoying as much sex as they want in a responsible way.

Therefore, homophobia has impacted upon a wide range of newer texts that reference homosexuality. Traces of homophobic discourses, although now contested, run through all of the texts examined. Homophobia may be acknowledged in different ways, but it is still a driving force in the construction of newer discourses. It is perhaps not so surprising that the word *gay* continues to evolve, taking on negative meanings which seem to undo the activism that was first used to reclaim the word as a positive descriptor (remember the gay exam timetable from Chapter 1). This polysemy reflects the ambivalence that parts of society feel towards homosexuality.

The newer discourses of homosexuality based around the notion of gay identity have also helped to create a consumer type which is viewed as having a large disposable income and fewer financial responsibilities than the average heterosexual man. The concept of the 'pink pound', although disputed (Badgett 2001), has therefore emerged in tandem with increased acceptance of homosexuality in western society. At the same time, the construction of gay men as a category of consumers has led to the third site of contestation – that of aspirational identities.

Aspiration

Advances in gender equality and increasing openness about sexuality since the 1970s have resulted in businesses realising that male identities were an untapped source of financial opportunity. Male bodies could be used to sell goods in much the same way that female bodies had been used previously. Such representations in the media resulted in the exposure of the male body, something which had ordinarily been backgrounded to the minority hobby of body-building (or to discreetly wrapped gay magazines). Muscular bodies in mainstream advertising strengthened the link between masculinity, physicality and heterosexuality.

The commercialisation of gay culture (seen from the popularity of lifestyle magazines filled with advertising such as *Attitude* and *Gay Times*) has helped to raise the profile of homosexuality, yet at the same time has resulted in a newer set of aspirational concerns faced by gay men. The idea of 'gay pride' has resulted in a sense of celebratory sexuality whereby gay men are urged to 'be themselves' or 'have the sex they want'. However, in reality, discourses within gay male culture have outlined an increasingly narrow set of characteristics which appear to promote conformity rather than diversity. For example, the erotic narratives in Chapter 6 feature muscular, masculine men, and the personal adverts from *Gay Times* in Chapter 5 also show that many people are attempting to construct themselves in terms of such a masculine ideal. Such images are also found in *Will & Grace*, where Will is constructed as the perfect (unattainable) partner to both Grace and Jack – wealthy, professional, masculine (yet sensitive) and physically attractive. Will therefore has a lot in common with the 'new man' (Jackson *et al.* 2001), an identity which is normally linked to heterosexual males. While there are many reasons why Will does not return Jack's feelings, I would argue that an important one concerns the fact that Will's more masculine gender performance is rated as possessing a higher market value than Jack's effeminate one. Such aspirational ideals again undermine the notion of a gay community where everyone is equally welcome, instead creating a hegemonic hierarchy where certain forms of identity are more highly rated than others. With the adoption of aspirational and hegemonic gay identities (see also Rowe 2000), an 'arms' race of a different kind has emerged – one based, among other things, around the circumference of one's biceps. Such representations are deemed to be so attractive and alluring that they are used in an increasingly wide range of contexts, including sexual health documentation, where masculine, muscular men not only show readers how to engage in safer sex, but also offer them a template for the way that their own sexual identities should be constructed.

It could be argued that masculine identities based on muscularity are based on appropriations of traditional male working-class identities, whereby muscular, tanned bodies were achieved through daily labour. However, as Talbot (1998: 193) points out: 'Real social power does not reside in big muscles . . . Power resides elsewhere: in being at the head of a corporation, a general leading an army, a senator or an MP.' The power from muscular bodies is therefore often symbolic or restricted to a particular community of practice. Large or toned muscles offer one form of power then, which for gay men is likely to make them more successful in the sexual marketplace and instil a sense of confidence. Because such muscles are rarely needed to carry out manual labour, instead they become presentational, a form of cultural rather than physical capital, the result of gym membership, protein supplements or steroids, personal trainers and the free time required to carry out a regular exercise routine. Muscularity is therefore increasingly a signifier of middle-class, rather than working-class, identity – a desire to obtain authentic masculinity – although the fact that the body is achieved in an air-conditioned gym rather than a building site means that such authenticity is out of reach. The gym-toned body is also different from the muscular body acquired by hard labour. It is more sculpted, emphasising certain sets of muscles (particularly pectorals and abdominals), and often combined with a narrower waist or shaved chest. However, the gay erotic narratives in

Chapter 6 are often concerned with unreconstructed 'authentic' masculinity, based on sports, the armed forces, manual labour and big men engaging in rough sex. The refutation of gym-trained bodies as 'obvious' or 'lame' suggests that, for some, such bodies are viewed as inadequate approximations.

The corpus data also indicate that sexuality cannot be examined as an isolated phenomenon, but is strongly linked to other aspects of identity which must be considered in concert in order to make sense of discourses surrounding homosexuality. For example, the preoccupation with masculinity among gay men, coupled with the use (or rejection) of camp humour, suggests two sites where gender and sexuality intersect. However, gender and sexuality are also linked to social class, as shown by the gay erotic narratives and, to a lesser extent, the safer sex documentation and the *Will & Grace* scripts. In the erotic narratives, masculinity is conceptualised as physical capital, being a working-class trait, hence the framing of gay sex as 'work', men's bodies as machines and the use of informal, explicit 'male' language. However, in *Will & Grace*, another form of ideal gay identity is constructed, one which is based upon cultural capital – gay men as wealthy, well-connected, socially superior, urban arbiters of good taste. These two possible ideals of gay identity (working class/masculine/authentic, middle- or upper-class/cultured/witty) are constructed as incompatible. There can only ever be an approximation of working-class masculinity, based on the adoption of codes such as clothing and muscularity, but it will always be at odds with a tastefully decorated home in a fashionable postcode.

Aspirational discourses of homosexuality therefore simultaneously pull gay men in different ways – achieving both sets of 'ideals' is likely to be extremely difficult. However, it should be noted that it is not just gay men who have become subject to discourses that encourage them to 'buy into' conflicting identities. Such a dilemma is similar to that faced by women since the late twentieth century, where they are expected to be perfect mothers and physically attractive wives yet also hold down a job and maintain their own independence, social life and interests. It also mirrors the identity crisis faced by heterosexual men, who are presented with a carefree, ironic, irresponsible, hedonistic 'lad' identity yet are also expected to earn great amounts of money which can be converted into a wealthy lifestyle, while becoming a breadwinner and perfect father.

As well as class and gender, age is also an important aspect of the way that sexual identity is conceptualised. For example, the debate in the House of Lords over the age of consent for anal sex and the tabloid panics over gay men adopting children indicate one of the ways that homophobic discourses draw on other types of identity in order to make their point. Sexuality is constructed as being unstable and unfixed in young people (particularly so for boys), hence the need to protect young people from the influences of homosexuality lest they be 'ruined for life' in the words of Lord Longford. At the same time, youth is another highly valued trait to gay culture (although it could be argued that it is a highly valued trait in mainstream culture too), shown by the fact that the words *young* and *younger* consistently appeared as popular adjectives in the *Gay Times* personal adverts. Youthfulness is therefore another factor in the construction of a hegemonic gay identity, suggesting that one ideal would be a combination of a muscular 'adult' body, with a youthful boyish face (another difficult-to-achieve set of criteria).

It should not be thought that the creation of hegemonic homosexualities began with the commercialisation of gay culture during the late twentieth century. Images from the pre-Stonewall era have shown that muscular, youthful, masculine bodies have formed part of the gay imaginary for many decades (Waugh 2002). However, the situation has been more fully articulated with the event of subcultural commercialisation, which has coincided with the rise of the discourse of 'gay identity' (as opposed to homosexuality as a 'deviant behaviour'). Therefore discourses surrounding homosexuality have changed from the notion of homosexual behaviour as 'always wrong', to the reconceptualisation that some types of gay identity are better than others. And while these newer forms are far removed from the conceptions of such identity in terms of sickness, disease, criminality, abnormality, unnaturalness and shame, they are instead based around visibility, pride and conflicting ideals of cultural capital. While analogies to *Animal Farm* could be made (all gay men are equal but some are more equal than others), the situation must certainly be said to be preferable to preceding constructions of gay identity. It should also be noted that the discourses surrounding gay identity are continually evolving and also related to a wider trend towards the commercialisation of identity which is present in mainstream western society. Possibly if older homophobic discourses are laid to rest, this will result in a stronger sense of security, and a growing acknowledgement of the potentially bisexual nature of humanity (see Kinsey *et al.* 1948). The hard distinction between gay and heterosexual identities may therefore be eroded. On the other hand, discourses based around aspirational and hegemonic homosexuality may multiply, particularly if they continue to be exploited for commercial interests.

Foucault (1972, 1976, 1979) argues that the purpose of discourse is to ensure that a certain view of the world is accepted as 'common-sense' without question. Discourses are therefore in the best interests of groups who want to maintain power. To paraphrase Rich (1980), the discourse of compulsory heterosexuality is one way that men have maintained power over women – by ensuring that women marry and have children, they can be more easily excluded from the workforce or promotion. Another way that homophobia has ensured power over gay men *and* women is by associating gay men in general with female sexual behaviour (e.g. being penetrated) and feminine gender identities and then stigmatising such men. Such a message holds that gay men are like women – and female identities are not as good as male ones.[3] However, power is not absolute – different people can have access to different types of power at different times.

Foucault contrasts *sovereign power* with *disciplinary power*, or what Fairclough (1989: 33) similarly formulates as *coercion* or *consent*. The former is exercised by the state or sovereign, who had the power to punish, coerce or kill people. Disciplinary power, on the other hand, is a way of ensuring that people exercise self-control, or submit to the will of 'experts'. For Foucault, disciplinary power is a much more efficient method of control than sovereign power. The earlier discourses of homosexuality, grounded in homophobia, were examples of sovereign power at work, when homosexuality was punishable by imprisonment. However, the newer discourses, with their focus on gender and class aspiration, still attempt to impose a form of control on gay men, although through disciplinary power. Disciplinary power also fits the needs of a capitalist society. Aspirant discourses of homosexuality create a need for self-improvement, which can be attained through purchasing commodities and also by representing oneself as a sexual commodity. However, the conflicting aspirant discourses ensure that there will *always* be room for improvement – nobody is likely to be able to satisfy all of the aspirational criteria.

It is therefore possible to relate all of the sites of discourse found in this book back to capitalism. The more obviously homophobic discourses found in the House of Lords and tabloid news echo a period where long-term, permanent, heterosexual relationships along with marriage, procreation and women being expected to stay at home to look after children were deemed necessary or at least optimal for the functioning of capitalist society and for the prosperity and survival of individuals within that society. Children were important because they could be sent to work, and because they could look after their parents when they were too infirm to work. Because rates of child mortality were higher, the ability to procreate was highly valued. Any social practice which compromised these optimum conditions was tabooed: divorce, promiscuity, women having careers, homosexuality. However, in contemporary western society, procreation is no longer a necessity for survival into old age: people are expected to provide for their long-term health and comfort with pension schemes and medical insurance. With post-liberation discourses of homosexuality, we find an increasing commodification of certain types of gay identity, based on cultural capital, lifestyle, the fashion cycle and the body. Same-sex desire, once repressed as anathema to capitalism, is now harnessed and exploited, as a way of ensuring that people continue to earn and spend.

This is a somewhat ambivalent conclusion to make about the current direction that discourses of homosexuality are taking, although it is in keeping with the ambivalence towards homosexuality that was found in many of the text types that were examined in the book. For many gay men, it is likely that the newer discourses are more welcome than the older criminalising ones. However, this does not necessarily mean that they will go uncontested or remain frozen indefinitely. And it is with the view that discourses are prone to change that I turn to the final section of the book.

Further directions

On a happier note, I hope that this book has shown the worth of carrying out corpus-based studies of discourse and identities. While my analysis covered a wide range of publicly available texts, there were others which I did not include for reasons of space or access. Such texts are likely to shed further light on discourse and homosexuality, including academic writing, graffiti in public restrooms, gay blogs (web-based diaries or journals written by gay people), documentation from gay rights groups such as Stonewall and Outrage, nightclub flyers, gay cartoons, religious and political texts that reference homosexuality, lifestyle questionnaires issued by banks and insurance companies, policy documentation on discrimination in the workplace and references to homosexuality in mainstream television or advertising. Because the texts that I examined had mainly focused on British and American producers, they could therefore be said to be representative of westernised, English-speaking discourses surrounding homosexuality – the story of globalisation is particularly linked to American culture. However, discourses produced in the UK and America do not represent the fuller picture of how homosexuality is conceived throughout the world. In many cultures, homosexuality is constructed differently – the idea of 'gay pride' or the gay community is therefore moot. Study of such cultures, particularly in reference to how they resolve discourses of homosexuality based around identity/behaviour/desire, homophobia and aspiration, will be enlightening.

It may also be useful to examine sites of discourse that focus on less mainstream or hegemonic constructions of gay identity – for example, by looking at literature written by and for groups such as *bears* (hairy, chubby gay men who do not fit the youthful stereotype), S/M lovers, older gay men and religious gay groups. An investigation into how such 'minority' gay discourses are constructed in relationship to the dominant ones (both from within and without mainstream gay culture) would complement this study. In addition, a comparison with discourses that occur in *private* settings (as opposed to the publicly available text types examined in this book) is also needed. Researchers may find that discourses that occur in such contexts are less straightforward to collect, particularly in terms of addressing ethics and the observer paradox, and also, finding examples of such discourses that are representative of mainstream thinking may be more difficult as the nature of private discourse means that fewer people will be engaged in the creation or reception of a single 'text'. Sites of private discourse could include letters, personal diary entries, spoken conversations, chat room 'conversations' or other 'communities of practice', phone sex or utterances made in other sexual settings such as gay saunas or cruising areas. Counselling or medical settings may also provide examples of discourse – for example, interactions which occur in sexual health clinics or calls to gay telephone advice lines.

With the exception of the personal advertisements in Chapter 5, the data I examined were all sampled from within a relatively short time period. It is clear that, at least at present, discourses of homosexuality are not static, and therefore comparative studies which revisit the same sorts of texts in the future should reveal the extent to which they have changed. For example, at the completion of this book, I have noticed that discourses surrounding homosexuality have already developed since writing commenced. Consider this description of the American television programme *Queer Eye for the Straight Guy*, taken from Bravo TV's website at http://www.bravotv.com/ Queer_Eye_for_the_Straight_Guy/:

> They are the Fab Five: an elite team of gay men dedicated to extolling the simple virtues of style, taste and class. Each week their mission is to transform a style-deficient and culture-deprived straight man from drab to fab in each of their respective categories: fashion, food & wine, interior design, grooming and culture.

This programme furthers the public discourse of gay men as sophisticated consumers by presenting them as *experts* with something of value to offer heterosexual men. A number of television programmes have utilised similar 'makeover' formats, including *Brian's Boyfriends* (UK), *Fairy Godfathers* (UK) and *Straight Dates by Gay Mates* (USA). Such a discourse suggests that the features associated with one kind of aspirational homosexuality should also be applied to heterosexual masculinity – helping to blur some of the traditional ways that *gay* and *heterosexual* are viewed. This discourse is also embodied in terms such as *stray* (a blend of *straight* and *gay*) or *just gay enough*, which suggest that heterosexual men could benefit, particularly in terms of their success with women, from possessing a few (stereotypically) 'gay' traits.

However, at the same time, it could be argued that the discourse of gay men as sophisticated lifestyle experts continues to offer a narrowly defined view of homosexuality – why are gay men viewed as good advisers in the categories of fashion and interior design rather than say, car maintenance, map-reading or martial arts? Why are heterosexual men seen to be in need of advice on grooming and culture? Therefore, while this 'expert' discourse is positive in that it shows gay men as relatively powerful and knowledge-able in some areas, at the same time the view that gay men are only experts in areas traditionally associated with femininity is reinforced. Future research focusing on discourses in programmes like *Queer Eye for the Straight Guy* will be able to plot the extent that gay identities are accepted or cele-brated while being represented in restricted ways. In addition, we could examine how discourses of homosexuality cross over into constructions of heterosexuality. Will aspirant male heterosexuality increasingly resemble aspirant male homosexuality, with a focus on both working-class masculin-ity and refinement?

Longitudinal studies of discourses of homosexuality could also be back-dated – for example, by carrying out a corpus-based analysis of how the tabloid newspapers constructed homosexuality in the 1980s or the 1950s, or by comparing current sexual health documentation with leaflets that appeared a decade previously. And one problem with studies of language and sexual identity is that, all too often, it is gay male identity which is researched (something which I am guilty of); therefore, corpus-informed analyses of discourses of lesbian, bisexual, transsexual and heterosexual identities would provide further understanding of the way that sexuality is constructed in society and how it is also related to other aspects of identity. It is short-sighted to examine gay sexuality without considering other forms of sexuality, which is one reason why I tried to draw my data from different sources where possible (e.g. by looking at discourses of hetero- as well as homosexuality in the tabloid press, by looking at how erotic narratives differed when the subjects were lesbian or gay).

To summarise, earlier mainstream homophobic public discourses that have categorised the 'homosexual' as a criminal, medical oddity or 'woman in a man's body' have found themselves in competition with a range of newer discourses, not imposed from an outsider perspective but from within. Such discourses, while containing more positive representations, reveal contradictions as well as overlaps, resulting in a sense of ambiguity about what exactly constitutes a gay man. One discourse foregrounds a sense of community, pride and openness, yet also suggests that gay men are a homogeneous group that have shared interests and tastes. Another repackages the negative 'homosexual as someone who has anal sex' discourse by continuing to focus on sex but as something which is celebratory and pleasurable. In this sense, sex between men can occur outside of the gay community, and the term *gay* is backgrounded, in favour of a discourse of individual identity based on desire and/or sexual behaviour. There are also two aspirational discourses of homosexuality – which, in effect, act as extensions of the new discourses just mentioned. The first depicts gay men as sophisticated, urbanite, witty consumers who possess good taste and are socially well-connected. The second suggests that gay men possess muscular, healthy bodies, enjoy perfect sex and appear hyper-masculine and/or working-class. While both aspirational discourses appear to be contradictory, they both tend to cluster around representations of gay men that are young and beautiful, and both increasingly rely on the purchase of commodities to be achieved.

While such ideals appear narrow, the discourses surrounding homosexuality are more widespread, publicised, accessible and varied than any period in the history of western civilisation. In terms of gaining legal and social equality gay people have come a long way in a short period of time – however, the existence of numerous conflicting discourses, both from inside and outside gay culture, indicates that their journey is far from over.

Appendix

Grammatical tags used in Chapter 4

CLAWS C7 Tag set

APPGE	possessive pronoun, pre-nominal (e.g. my, your, our)
AT	article (e.g. the, no)
AT1	singular article (e.g. a, an, every)
BCL	before-clause marker (e.g. in order (that), in order (to))
CC	coordinating conjunction (e.g. and, or)
CCB	adversative coordinating conjunction (but)
CS	subordinating conjunction (e.g. if, because, unless, so, for)
CSA	as (as conjunction)
CSN	than (as conjunction)
CST	that (as conjunction)
CSW	whether (as conjunction)
DA	after-determiner or post-determiner capable of pronominal function (e.g. such, former, same)
DA1	singular after-determiner (e.g. little, much)
DA2	plural after-determiner (e.g. few, several, many)
DAR	comparative after-determiner (e.g. more, less, fewer)
DAT	superlative after-determiner (e.g. most, least, fewest)
DB	before determiner or pre-determiner capable of pronominal function (all, half)
DB2	plural before-determiner (both)
DD	determiner (capable of pronominal function) (e.g. any, some)
DD1	singular determiner (e.g. this, that, another)
DD2	plural determiner (these, those)
DDQ	wh-determiner (which, what)
DDQGE	wh-determiner, genitive (whose)
DDQV	wh-ever determiner (whichever, whatever)
EX	existential there
FO	formula
FU	unclassified word

FW	foreign word
GE	germanic genitive marker (or 's)
IF	for (as preposition)
II	general preposition
IO	of (as preposition)
IW	with, without (as prepositions)
JJ	general adjective
JJR	general comparative adjective (e.g. older, better, stronger)
JJT	general superlative adjective (e.g. oldest, best, strongest)
JK	catenative adjective (*able in* be able to, *willing in* be willing to)
MC	cardinal number, neutral for number (two, three...)
MC1	singular cardinal number (one)
MC2	plural cardinal number (e.g. sixes, sevens)
MCGE	genitive cardinal number, neutral for number (twos, 100s)
MCMC	hyphenated number (40–50, 1770–1827)
MD	ordinal number (e.g. first, second, next, last)
MF	fraction, neutral for number (e.g. quarters, two-thirds)
ND1	singular noun of direction (e.g. north, southeast)
NN	common noun, neutral for number (e.g. sheep, cod, headquarters)
NN1	singular common noun (e.g. book, girl)
NN2	plural common noun (e.g. books, girls)
NNA	following noun of title (e.g. M.A.)
NNB	preceding noun of title (e.g. Mr., Prof.)
NNL1	singular locative noun (e.g. Island, Street)
NNL2	plural locative noun (e.g. Islands, Streets)
NNO	numeral noun, neutral for number (e.g. dozen, hundred)
NNO2	numeral noun, plural (e.g. hundreds, thousands)
NNT1	temporal noun, singular (e.g. day, week, year)
NNT2	temporal noun, plural (e.g. days, weeks, years)
NNU	unit of measurement, neutral for number (e.g. in, cc)
NNU1	singular unit of measurement (e.g. inch, centimetre)
NNU2	plural unit of measurement (e.g. ins., feet)
NP	proper noun, neutral for number (e.g. IBM, Andes)
NP1	singular proper noun (e.g. London, Jane, Frederick)
NP2	plural proper noun (e.g. Browns, Reagans, Koreas)
NPD1	singular weekday noun (e.g. Sunday)
NPD2	plural weekday noun (e.g. Sundays)
NPM1	singular month noun (e.g. October)
NPM2	plural month noun (e.g. Octobers)
PN	indefinite pronoun, neutral for number (none)
PN1	indefinite pronoun, singular (e.g. anyone, everything, nobody, one)
PNQO	objective wh-pronoun (whom)
PNQS	subjective wh-pronoun (who)
PNQV	wh-ever pronoun (whoever)

PNX1	reflexive indefinite pronoun (oneself)
PPGE	nominal possessive personal pronoun (e.g. mine, yours)
PPH1	3rd person singular neuter personal pronoun (it)
PPHO1	3rd person singular objective personal pronoun (him, her)
PPHO2	3rd person plural objective personal pronoun (them)
PPHS1	3rd person singular subjective personal pronoun (he, she)
PPHS2	3rd person plural subjective personal pronoun (they)
PPIO1	1st person singular objective personal pronoun (me)
PPIO2	1st person plural objective personal pronoun (us)
PPIS1	1st person singular subjective personal pronoun (I)
PPIS2	1st person plural subjective personal pronoun (we)
PPX1	singular reflexive personal pronoun (e.g. yourself, itself)
PPX2	plural reflexive personal pronoun (e.g. yourselves, themselves)
PPY	2nd person personal pronoun (you)
RA	adverb, after nominal head (e.g. else, galore)
REX	adverb introducing appositional constructions (namely, e.g.)
RG	degree adverb (very, so, too)
RGQ	wh-degree adverb (how)
RGQV	wh-ever degree adverb (however)
RGR	comparative degree adverb (more, less)
RGT	superlative degree adverb (most, least)
RL	locative adverb (e.g. alongside, forward)
RP	prep. adverb, particle (e.g. about, in)
RPK	prep. adverb, catenative (*about* in be about to)
RR	general adverb
RRQ	wh-general adverb (where, when, why, how)
RRQV	wh-ever general adverb (wherever, whenever)
RRR	comparative general adverb (e.g. better, longer)
RRT	superlative general adverb (e.g. best, longest)
RT	quasi-nominal adverb of time (e.g. now, tomorrow)
TO	infinitive marker (to)
UH	interjection (e.g. oh, yes, um)
VB0	be, base form (finite, i.e. imperative, subjunctive)
VBDR	were
VBDZ	was
VBG	being
VBI	be, infinitive (To be or not . . . It will be . . .)
VBM	am
VBN	been
VBR	are
VBZ	is
VD0	do, base form (finite)
VDD	did
VDG	doing
VDI	do, infinitive (I may do . . . To do . . .)

VDN	done
VDZ	does
VH0	have, base form (finite)
VHD	had (past tense)
VHG	having
VHI	have, infinitive
VHN	had (past participle)
VHZ	has
VM	modal auxiliary (can, will, would, etc.)
VMK	modal catenative (ought, used)
VV0	base form of lexical verb (e.g. give, work)
VVD	past tense of lexical verb (e.g. gave, worked)
VVG	-ing participle of lexical verb (e.g. giving, working)
VVGK	-ing participle catenative (going in, be going to)
VVI	infinitive (e.g. to give... It will work...)
VVN	past participle of lexical verb (e.g. given, worked)
VVNK	past participle catenative (e.g. *bound* in be bound to)
VVZ	-s form of lexical verb (e.g. gives, works)
XX	not, n't
ZZ1	singular letter of the alphabet (e.g. A, b)
ZZ2	plural letter of the alphabet (e.g. As, bs)

Semantic tags used in Chapter 4

USAS Tag set

A1	GENERAL AND ABSTRACT TERMS
A1.1.1	General actions, making, etc.
A1.1.2	Damaging and destroying
A1.2	Suitability
A1.3	Caution
A1.4	Chance, luck
A1.5	Use
A1.5.1	Using
A1.5.2	Usefulness
A1.6	Physical/mental
A1.7	Constraint
A1.8	Inclusion/Exclusion
A1.9	Avoiding
A2	Affect
A2.1	Affect: modify, change
A2.2	Affect: cause/connected
A3	Being
A4	Classification
A4.1	Generally kinds, groups, examples

A4.2	Particular/general; detail
A5	Evaluation
A5.1	Evaluation: good/bad
A5.2	Evaluation: true/false
A5.3	Evaluation: accuracy
A5.4	Evaluation: authenticity
A6	Comparing
A6.1	Comparing: similar/different
A6.2	Comparing: usual/unusual
A6.3	Comparing: variety
A7	Definite (+modals)
A8	Seem
A9	Getting and giving; possession
A10	Open/closed; hiding/hidden; finding; showing
A11	Importance
A11.1	Importance: important
A11.2	Importance: noticeability
A12	Easy/difficult
A13	Degree
A13.1	Degree: non-specific
A13.2	Degree: maximisers
A13.3	Degree: boosters
A13.4	Degree: approximators
A13.5	Degree: compromisers
A13.6	Degree: diminishers
A13.7	Degree: minimisers
A14	Exclusivisers/particularisers
A15	Safety/danger
B1	Anatomy and physiology
B2	Health and disease
B3	Medicines and medical treatment
B4	Cleaning and personal care
B5	Clothes and personal belongings
C1	Arts and crafts
E1	EMOTIONAL ACTIONS, STATES AND PROCESSES General
E2	Liking
E3	Calm/violent/angry
E4	Happy/sad
E4.1	Happy/sad: happy
E4.2	Happy/sad: contentment
E5	Fear/bravery/shock
E6	Worry, concern, confident
F1	Food
F2	Drinks
F3	Cigarettes and drugs

F4	Farming and horticulture
G1	Government, politics and elections
G1.1	Government, etc.
G1.2	Politics
G2	Crime, law and order
G2.1	Crime, law and order: law and order
G2.2	General ethics
G3	Warfare, defence and the army; weapons
H1	Architecture and kinds of houses and buildings
H2	Parts of buildings
H3	Areas around or near houses
H4	Residence
H5	Furniture and household fittings
I1	Money generally
I1.1	Money: affluence
I1.2	Money: debts
I1.3	Money: price
I2	Business
I2.1	Business: generally
I2.2	Business: selling
I3	Work and employment
I3.1	Work and employment: generally
I3.2	Work and employment: professionalism
I4	Industry
K1	Entertainment generally
K2	Music and related activities
K3	Recorded sound, etc.
K4	Drama, the theatre and showbusiness
K5	Sports and games generally
K5.1	Sports
K5.2	Games
K6	Children's games and toys
L1	Life and living things
L2	Living creatures generally
L3	Plants
M1	Moving, coming and going
M2	Putting, taking, pulling, pushing, transporting, etc.
M3	Vehicles and transport on land
M4	Shipping, swimming, etc.
M5	Aircraft and flying
M6	Location and direction
M7	Places
M8	Remaining/stationary
N1	Numbers
N2	Mathematics

N3	Measurement
N3.1	Measurement: general
N3.2	Measurement: size
N3.3	Measurement: distance
N3.4	Measurement: volume
N3.5	Measurement: weight
N3.6	Measurement: area
N3.7	Measurement: length and height
N3.8	Measurement: speed
N4	Linear order
N5	Quantities
N5.1	Entirety; maximum
N5.2	Exceeding; waste
N6	Frequency, etc.
O1	Substances and materials generally
O1.1	Substances and materials generally: solid
O1.2	Substances and materials generally: liquid
O1.3	Substances and materials generally: gas
O2	Objects generally
O3	Electricity and electrical equipment
O4	Physical attributes
O4.1	General appearance and physical properties
O4.2	Judgement of appearance (pretty, etc.)
O4.3	Colour and colour patterns
O4.4	Shape
O4.5	Texture
O4.6	Temperature
P1	Education in general
Q1	LINGUISTIC ACTIONS, STATES AND PROCESSES; COMMUNICATION
Q1.1	LINGUISTIC ACTIONS, STATES AND PROCESSES; COMMUNICATION
Q1.2	Paper documents and writing
Q1.3	Telecommunications
Q2	Speech acts
Q2.1	Speech, etc.: communicative
Q2.2	Speech acts
Q3	Language, speech and grammar
Q4	The media
Q4.1	The media: books
Q4.2	The media: newspapers, etc.
Q4.3	The media: TV, radio and cinema
S1	SOCIAL ACTIONS, STATES AND PROCESSES
S1.1.2	Reciprocity
S1.1.3	Participation

S1.1.4	Deserve, etc.
S1.2	Personality traits
S1.2.1	Approachability and friendliness
S1.2.2	Avarice
S1.2.3	Egoism
S1.2.4	Politeness
S1.2.5	Toughness; strong/weak
S1.2.6	Sensible
S2	People
S2.1	People: female
S2.2	People: male
S3	Relationship
S3.1	Relationship: general
S3.2	Relationship: intimate/sexual
S4	Kin
S5	Groups and affiliation
S6	Obligation and necessity
S7	Power relationship
S7.1	Power, organising
S7.2	Respect
S7.3	Competition
S7.4	Permission
S8	Helping/hindering
S9	Religion and the supernatural
T1	Time
T1.1	Time: general
T1.1.1	Time: general: past
T1.1.2	Time: general: present; simultaneous
T1.1.3	Time: general: future
T1.2	Time: momentary
T1.3	Time: period
T2	Time: beginning and ending
T3	Time: old, new and young; age
T4	Time: early/late
W1	The universe
W2	Light
W3	Geographical terms
W4	Weather
W5	Green issues
X1	PSYCHOLOGICAL ACTIONS, STATES AND PROCESSES
X2	Mental actions and processes
X2.1	Thought, belief
X2.2	Knowledge
X2.3	Learn
X2.4	Investigate, examine, test, search

X2.5	Understand
X2.6	Expect
X3	Sensory
X3.1	Sensory: taste
X3.2	Sensory: sound
X3.3	Sensory: touch
X3.4	Sensory: sight
X3.5	Sensory: smell
X4	Mental object
X4.1	Mental object: conceptual object
X4.2	Mental object: means, method
X5	Attention
X5.1	Attention
X5.2	Interest/boredom/excited/energetic
X6	Deciding
X7	Wanting; planning; choosing
X8	Trying
X9	Ability
X9.1	Ability: ability, intelligence
X9.2	Ability: success and failure
Y1	Science and technology in general
Y2	Information technology and computing
Z0	Unmatched proper noun
Z1	Personal names
Z2	Geographical names
Z3	Other proper names
Z4	Discourse bin
Z5	Grammatical bin
Z6	Negative
Z7	If
Z8	Pronouns, etc.
Z9	Trash can
Z99	Unmatched

Notes

1 What can I do with a naked corpus?

1 The term *homosexual* was originally coined by Karl Maria Kertbeny in the 1860s as a more positive alternative to an existing term *pederast*. Kertbeny claimed that many homosexuals were more masculine than other men, being superior to heterosexuals. However, the word was quickly adopted by doctors, including Richard von Krafft-Ebing, who concluded that homosexuality was a form of inherited medical illness, resulting in effeminacy.

2 To give an example, during one week of writing this book, newspapers reported that the Anglican Church was locked in debate over the appropriacy of appointing an openly gay Bishop. At the same time, the British government published plans to give gay and lesbian couples the same rights as their married heterosexual counterparts by allowing them to call themselves 'registered civil partners'. Meanwhile, the largest employer in the USA, Wal-Mart, expanded its equal opportunities policy to cover sexual orientation, only a week after the Supreme Court abolished a law in Texas against sodomy. Finally, there was media controversy over the fact that Rebekah Wade, current editor of the UK's largest selling newspaper, the *Sun*, appeared in the top ten of the *Guardian* newspaper's annual list of the most influential people in the British media. Since replacing David Yelland at the beginning of 2003, Wade oversaw a rise in the number of homophobic stories and comments in the newspaper. For example, a still from a music video which featured two men kissing was captioned with 'We hope this doesn't put you off your cornflakes' (February 11, 2003).

3 I use the term *queer* based on essays by Seidman (1993) and Warner (1993) to refer to a collective of identities that are defined in opposition to society's standards of what is 'normal' or hegemonic. Queer Theory assumes that identities are fluid, multiple and overlapping and is concerned with highlighting the ways in which hegemonies are maintained, for example by examining language practices.

4 While the focus of work on language and identities has often been gender and/or sexuality, I would argue that other attributes such as age, class, health and ethnicity are also important. Our identities consist of a range of interacting attributes – however, what is interesting about identity is that some identities are viewed as more salient or problematic than others.

5 Thanks to Susan Russell for this argument. At the same time, for words like *feminist* and *sexist* to have been invented in the first place, conditions must have existed whereby it was possible to recognise and give labels to such concepts. Discourse and language use are therefore related, reinforcing processes.

6 In the 100-million word British National Corpus, *gay man* appears 17 times, *homosexual man* occurs six times and *heterosexual man* appears once. *Straight man*

appears 20 times, of which only two occurrences refer to sexuality (the others mainly refer to the 'straight man' of a comedy duo). *Man* (without these sexuality markers) occurs 58,834 times.

7 See Leap 1996.

8 We need to bear in mind that a small number of occurrences of *gay* in the British National Corpus will involve the older 'carefree' meaning or be used as a personal name, so will not refer to homosexuality.

9 These were *The Three Little Pigs, Sleeping Beauty, Snow White, The Ugly Duckling, Cinderella, Rumpelstiltzkin, Hansel and Gretel* and *Rapunzel*.

10 Negative keywords are only given in cases where a word occurs once or more in the text under study. Words that never occur in the smaller text, although they occur often in the reference corpus, will not be shown as keywords in Word-Smith Tools.

11 In the BNC, *bystander* and *innocent* have a log–log score of 36.7 (which suggests high collocation). The word *bystander* (when not collocating with *innocent*) often occurs in legal texts, usually to label a victim of crime. Weaker collocates of bystander include *powerless, neutral, frightened* and *unfortunate*. It could be suggested then that in legal texts *bystander* is set up in opposition to something else (the accused) whose guilt is to be ascertained.

12 See Oakes (1998), Chapter 4, for more detailed information about different ways to calculate collocations.

13 The top ten collocates of *gay* in the BNC (using log–log) are *lesbian, lesbians, men, switchboard, liberation, bisexual, rights, activists, gordons* and *communities*. The top ten collocates of *homosexual* are *men, heterosexual, seroconverted, bisexual, non-homosexual, acts, sensibility, hiv-1, male* and *behaviour. Gay* therefore strongly collocates with words connected to political reform and community, whereas *homosexual* collocates with concepts of behaviour and disease.

14 In two of the corpora that I examine in this book – the *Will & Grace* scripts and the Terrence Higgins Trust safer sex documentation – visuals play a role in the construction of discourses.

2 Unnatural Acts: the House of Lords debates on gay male law reform

1 The last time the Monarch seriously considered refusing Royal Assent was in the period 1912–14, during the crisis concerning the partition of Ireland. The opponents of Prime Minister Asquith urged King George V to refuse Royal Assent to the Government of Ireland Bill, or to force a general election. In the end, the King said that he might be prepared to intervene in this way to avoid a national catastrophe, but otherwise it was not the job of the Monarch to get involved in politics.

2 The 1967 Sexual Offences Act decriminalised homosexual acts in private between two consenting adult males over the age of 21. It did not apply to members of the armed forces, merchant seamen or residents of the Channel Isles or the Isle of Man, where homosexuality remained illegal.

3 An internal debate among the anti-reformers about whether the Baroness' amendment was a compromise, and the extent to which this was a good or bad thing, resulted in the word *compromise* appearing as a keyword in the anti-reform texts.

4 This data was collected from the UK Government's web service at http://www.publications.parliament.uk/.

5 Peter Tatchell is a British campaigner for gay and human rights and one of the founders of the queer rights direct action group OutRage in 1990.

6 Initially, I compared both sets of House of Lords texts against the one-million word FLOB corpus of written English. However, the resulting keywords in both lists turned out to be similar to each other (for example, the words *noble, I, Lord, Bill, Young, that, homosexual* and *amendment* all appeared within the top ten keywords for both lists). This reflected the fact that both texts came from the same language variety, rather than illuminating differences in position. It was decided, then, that comparing the two House of Lords sets of data against each other would help to reveal differences.

7 A *p* value of 0.0005 means that there is a 1 in 2000 danger of being wrong in claiming a relationship. In the social sciences, a 1 in 20 (or $p < 0.5$) risk is usually considered to be acceptable. However, as Scott (1999) notes, in a keywords analysis, the notion of risk is less important than the notion of selectivity. Using $p = 0.5$ on the House of Lords data would give 492 keywords. Making the *p* value smaller is a way of reducing the number of keywords found to only those which reveal the most significant differences between the two sets of texts.

8 The wording, or similar wording, to the 1885 Criminal Law Amendment Act has been reproduced in the creation of laws in other countries. For example, section 377a of Singapore's penal code states: 'Any male person who, in public or private, commits or abets the commission of or procures the commission by any male person of, any act of gross indecency with another male person, shall be punished with imprisonment for a term which may extend to 2 years.' In Tasmania, it remains an offence for males to engage in 'unnatural sexual intercourse' or 'acts of gross indecency' whether the conduct occurs in public or private.

9 Lord Longford's position about homosexuality is somewhat unusual, even among the anti-reformers – his belief that homosexuality can be 'taught', for example, and his use of the phrase 'homosexual object' which doesn't fit well into the discourses of identity or behaviour that the other debaters tend to access.

10 In a survey of literature on the subject, Cass (1983: 108) notes that homosexual identity can be used to mean '(1) defining oneself as gay, (2) a sense of self as gay, (3) image of self as homosexual, (4) the way a homosexual person is, and (5) consistent behavior in relation to homosexual-related activity.'

11 For example: *The Problem of Ego Identity* (1956); *Identity and The Life Cycle* (1959).

12 See http://news.bbc.co.uk/1/hi/talking_point/138062.stm.

13 A similar attempt to boost the credibility of those against reform had been used the year before by Brian Souter, the owner of the company Stagecoach, who had campaigned against the repeal of Section 2A, the Scottish version of Clause 28 which banned the 'promotion of homosexuality' by local education authorities. Mr Souter funded a private referendum, sending out 3.9 million ballots slips to Scottish citizens. Of those who voted, 86.6 per cent were in favour of keeping the section, whereas 13.2 per cent voted for repeal. Although Souter's 'keep the clause' campaign was criticised by gay rights groups, who pointed out that the *overall* response rate was only 34 per cent, and that 3,000,000 ballot slips were undeliverable because the poll had been based on the 1999 electoral register, Souter said it was a clear vindication of his efforts (the *Guardian*, May 31, 2000: 6).

3 Flamboyant, predatory, self-confessed homosexual: discourse prosodies in the British tabloid press

1 More recently, some broadsheet newspapers (e.g. the *Independent* and *The Times*) have published 'tabloid-sized' versions alongside their usual broadsheet format.

2 See http://www.telegraph.co.uk/pressoffice/graphics/research/nrs12mar02.pdf.

3 It is important to note the difference between readership figures and circulation

figures. The former refers to the number of newspapers that are sold, while the latter refers to the number of people who read them. As most newspapers are read by more than one person, the actual number of newspapers that are sold will be lower than its circulation.

4 *Lady doctor* occurs 13 times in the BNC, *woman doctor* occurs 20 times and *female doctor* occurs three times. *Male doctor* also occurs three times, whereas *man doctor* only occurs once. *Doctor* without these gender markers occurs 10,104 times.

5 It could be argued that all 'three-in-a-bed romps' contain some degree of homosexual behaviour as there will always be at least two people of the same sex taking part.

6 Josh Rafter ran a housing business in the gay district of Soho and revealed his sexuality within hours of entering the *Big Brother* house, so his status as a 'closet homosexual' is somewhat debatable.

7 Note that, as this article fell short of the period under study by five days, it was not included in the corpus-based analysis.

4 True Man' and 'McFairyland': gay identities in an American sitcom

1 Audience ratings for individual episodes of *Will & Grace* can be found at: http://www.durfee.net/will/ratings.htm.

2 Nielson ratings are usually given as two numbers: rating/share, e.g. 6.2/16. There are an estimated 99.4 million television households in the USA. A single 'ratings' point represents 1 per cent, or 994,000 households. The 'share' is the percentage of television sets in use tuned to a specific programme. For example, a rating of 6.2 means that approximately 616,280 households watched the programme, representing a 16 per cent share of the total viewing population at that time.

3 The central premise of *Will & Grace* (the relationship between a heterosexual woman and a gay man) is also found in the films *My Best Friend's Wedding* (1997), *The Object of My Affection* (1998) and *The Next Best Thing* (2000).

4 A small number of articles in the newspaper corpus examined in Chapter 3 used a somewhat stronger version of the 'what a shame . . .' discourse, rephrasing it as a 'waste'. For example: 'When I told her he was happily and openly gay, she sighed and said: "What a waste"' (the *Daily Mail*, January 20, 2002), 'You're gorgeous, you are. What a waste' (the *Daily Mail*, July 7, 2000).

5 Karen appears to have a power which at times borders on the supernatural. For example, in episode 1.15 she guesses that Grace has had sex (twice) with Will's brother. Karen is constructed as a bored and powerful middle-aged woman, which is in many ways similar to the character of the witch Endora in the 1960s sitcom *Bewitched* (about witches with magical powers). In one episode the link between *Bewitched* and *Will & Grace* is made explicit when Karen calls a rival wealthy friend (played by Joan Collins) 'Endora'.

6 The off-screen spouse or relative is a staple of many other sitcoms, including the character of Maris in *Frasier*, Vera in *Cheers* and Sheridan in *Keeping Up Appearances*. The humour in such characters arises from the fact that they are often constructed as 'larger than life' and by the irony that such non-presences can play such important roles in the lives of other on-screen characters.

7 In later seasons of *Will & Grace*, Will is sometimes shown as being more stereotypically 'gay' – for example, in one episode he queues all night for Barry Manilow tickets.

8 Another reading of Karen's scripting as a 'gay man' may be partly due to the gender/sexuality of the scriptwriters, who may be more skilful at representing camp speech as opposed to women's speech.

9 One genre of language use which I would argue contains uses of 'heterosexual

camp' is in action/adventure fiction. For example, heterosexual action heroes like James Bond often make litotic, bemused quips or non-sequiturs when faced with danger (often to show that they are unruffled by their predicament) which is similar to the inversion of established rhetorical routines, while the theatrical threats issued by villains in this genre could be said to consist of a different type of camp.

5 'No effeminates please': discourses of gay men's personal adverts

1 For example, the UK magazine *Films and Filming*, while not being an explicitly gay magazine, regularly featured 'coded' advertisements from 'bachelors' seeking friendships with other men in the 1950s and 1960s.
2 Gay Liberation paralleled and was connected to the Civil Rights, students' and Women's Liberation movements of the 1960s/1970s. It was linked to the 'struggle against sexism' (Young 1972: 7) and was one of the first movements to instil a sense of pride for gay men and lesbians.
3 Russo (1987) gives numerous examples of effeminate representations of homosexuality in the cinema, while Sanderson (1995) focuses on such constructions in the popular British press.
4 Bears are gay men who generally possess one or more of the following traits: a hairy body, beard and/or moustache, large or tubby build, muscular development and masculine behaviour.
5 I chose four nine-year periods, not because I felt that these periods had any historical significance, but because I felt that a nine-year gap between each data type would be long enough to show up significant shifts in discourses of homosexuality. For the sake of roundness, I had initially wanted to sample ten-year periods, but as the earliest data I had access to was 1973 and the latest was 2000, this would not have allowed me to incorporate both of these years in the analysis.
6 Not all advertisers were concerned with presenting themselves as stereotypically attractive – a very small number stressed attributes such as *old* or *fat*, which were often used to present an 'honest' or 'humorous' identity: e.g. 'No timewasters – I'm too old for it.'
7 It is beyond the scope of this chapter to carry out a full analysis of the relationship between gay personal adverts and the images found in gay magazines, but Dotson (1999: 125–37) gives an analysis of representations of the male body within the gay magazine genre.
8 The mean sentence length in the corpus was eight words. For this reason, unless stated, collocates were calculated on the basis of occurring four words to the left and four words to the right of a target word.
9 Differences across time based on frequency data presented in Tables 6.6–6.9 were also significant at the 0.001 per cent level.
10 In terms of hair colour, *blondes* are cited most often (27 times as opposed to 15 times for *dark* hair, the next highest category).
11 It would have been useful to extend the range of this survey to look at attitudes in the 1970s. However, 1983 was the first year that this question was added to the British Social Attitudes survey.

6 As big as a beercan: a comparative keyword analysis of lesbian and gay male erotic narratives

1 Such narratives can also have a second function: to give descriptions of tabooed, extreme or unusual sexual activities, acting as a way of expressing behaviours or

desires that may be seen as socially unacceptable or illegal. For example, some of the sub-categories within the Nifty Archive included *adult youth* (about 'cross-generational relationships'), *authoritarian* (about 'bondage, control, S&M and authority figures'), *urination* and *incest*. In this chapter I only look at stories within the *adult friends* sub-category (consensual adult relationships) because these stories tended to focus on the former, more idealised, non-tabooed types of gay sexual relationships that I was interested in studying. Also, there were ethical, legal and moral implications of studying narratives involving, say, 'intergenerational sex' which makes such research problematic. See also Chapter 8.

2 Comparing gay erotica with heterosexual erotica was difficult because hetero-sexual texts use language about and by men *and* women. Questions such as 'Are gay men constructed differently from heterosexual men?' in erotica become more difficult to answer because the male utterances or characterisations in the hetero-sexual text have to be teased apart from those that are about women.

3 With that said, the archive I took the narratives from did specify a few guidelines. These included rejecting stories that contained 'rape or coercion of minors or abusive situations involving minors, graphic violence, unwilling participants, dangerous sexual acts, or published works'. Writers were also advised about the text format to submit their story in and to include disclaimers if their story con-tained references to famous people.

4 Lesbian texts: standardised type token ratio: 40.08, average word length, 4.18, average sentence length: 17.72. Gay texts: standardised type token ratio: 40.01, average word length, 4.02, average sentence length: 17.73.

5 The presence of beer in the gay texts has a third function, whereby men's genitals are admiringly compared to beercans (hence the title of the chapter).

6 *Yeah* can be classed as both a discourse marker and a non-standard spelling.

7 Making safer sex sexy: border crossing, informalisation and gay identity in sexual health documentation

1 In addition, the 100-million word British National Corpus is used in this chapter at times in order to compare the language in the THT with general British English.

2 It could be argued, however, that safer sex advertising would have some economic benefit to governments who would have to spend less money on providing medical services for people with HIV and AIDS if larger numbers of people 'bought' into the product of safer sex.

3 *Gay* is included in this table; although it is generally used as an adjective, it can have noun status.

8 Conclusion

1 One question about sexuality which relates to desire and repression is the issue of bisexuality. If bisexuality is as common as Kinsey (1948) suggests (e.g. 37 per cent of the total male population has at least some overt homosexual experience to the point of orgasm between adolescence and old age) then why are references to bisexuality not more common in our society? The BNC has fewer references to bisexuality than it does to homosexuality and heterosexuality, e.g. *bisexual* occurs 81 times, *homosexual* occurs 253 times and *heterosexual* occurs 377 times. The word transsexual, although far more rare, occurs 75 times in the BNC, almost as many times as *bisexual*. This would suggest a discourse of *bisexual invisibility*, possibly based around the repression or negation of bisexual desire.

2 The *Guardian* was the most popular newspaper at 20 per cent, although 29 per cent of respondents said they did not regularly read a newspaper.
3 On the other hand, hegemonic discourses of lesbian identity have either erased the possibility altogether or sanctioned lesbian sexual behaviour as both erotic and exotic (for heterosexual men), while at the same time erasing the notion of a stable lesbian identity (with the view that 'all a lesbian needs is a good man'). Such discourses therefore still maintain male heterosexual hegemony.

References

Anderson, B. (1983) *Imagined Communities: Reflections on the Origins and Spread of Nationalism*. London: Verso.

Armistead, N. (1974) *Reconstructing Social Psychology*. Harmondsworth: Penguin.

Atkinson, D. (1999) *Scientific Discourse in Sociohistorical Context*. Mahwah: Erlbaum.

Atkinson, J. M. (1992) 'Displaying neutrality: formal aspects of informal court proceedings.' In P. Drew and J. Heritage (eds) *Talk at Work*. Cambridge: Cambridge University Press, pp. 199–211.

Badgett, M. L. V. (2001) *Money, Myths and Change – The Economic Lives of Lesbians and Gay Men*. Chicago: University of Chicago Press.

Baker, P. (2002a) *Polari: The Lost Language of Gay Men*. London: Routledge.

Baker, P. (2002b) *Fantabulosa: A Dictionary of Polari and Gay Slang*. London: Continuum.

Baker, P. and Stanley, J. (2003) *Hello Sailor: The Hidden History of Gay Men at Sea*. London: Pearson.

Bakhtin, M. (1984) *Problems in Dostoevsky's Poetics*. Minneapolis: University of Minnesota Press.

Barrett, R. (1997) 'The "Homo-genius" Speech Community.' In A. Livia and K. Hall (eds) *Queerly Phrased*. Oxford: Oxford Studies in Sociolinguistics, pp. 181–201.

BBC News (2001) *Reform 1999: The Eleventh Hour of the Eleventh Day*. Online, available at: http://news.bbc.co.uk/hi/english/static/in_depth/uk_politics/2001/open_politics/lords/reform_1999.stm.

Becker, H. (1972) 'Whose side are we on?' In J. D. Douglas (ed.) *The Relevance of Sociology*. New York: Appleton-Century-Crofts, pp. 99–111.

Beetham, M. (1996) *A Magazine of Her Own? Domesticity and Desire in the Woman's Magazine 1800–1914*. London: Routledge.

Bell, A. (1991) *The Language of News Media*. Oxford: Blackwell.

Bell, S. (1981) *How to Abolish the Lords*. Fabian Tract 476, Fabian Society, London.

Berger, J. (1972) *Ways of Seeing*. London: Pelican.

Bergvall, V. L. (1999) 'Toward a comprehensive theory of language and gender.' *Language in Society* 28: 273–93.

Berry-Rogghe, G. L. E. (1973) 'The computation of collocations and their relevance in lexical studies.' In A. J. Aitken, R. Bailey and N. Hamilton-Smith (eds) *The Computer and Literary Studies*. Edinburgh: Edinburgh University Press, pp. 103–12.

Biber, D. (1988) *Variation Across Speech and Writing*. Cambridge: Cambridge University Press.

Biber, D. (1998) *Corpus Linguistics: Investigating Language Structure and Use*. Cambridge: Cambridge University Press.

Biber, D. and Burges, J. (2001) 'Historical shifts in the language of women and men: gender differences in dramatic dialogue.' In D. Biber and S. Conrad (eds) *Variation in English: Multi-Dimensional Studies*. London: Longman, pp. 157–70.

Biber, D., Johansson, S., Leech, G., Conrad, S. and Finegan, E. (1999) *Longman Grammar of Spoken and Written English*. London: Longman.

Blachford, G. (1981) 'Male dominance and the gay world.' In K. Plummer (ed.) *The Making of the Modern Homosexual*. London: Hutchinson, pp. 184–210.

Bolton, R. (1995) 'Sex talk: bodies and behaviours in gay erotica.' In W. Leap (ed.) *Beyond the Lavender Lexicon*. Amsterdam: Gordon and Breach, pp. 173–206.

Borsley, R. D. and Ingham, R. (2002) 'Grow your own linguistics? On some applied linguistics' views of the subject.' *Lingua Franca* 112: 1–6.

Bourdieu, P. (1978) 'Sport and social class.' *Social Science Information* 17: 6, 819–40.

Bourdieu, P. (1986) 'The forms of capital.' In J. Richardson (ed.) *Theory and Society* 14: 6, 723–44.

Bright, S. (2001) *How to Write a Dirty Story: Reading and Publishing Erotica*. New York: Fireside.

Brockett, G. (1991) *History of the Theatre*, 6th edn. New York: Allyn and Bacon.

Bronski, M. (1998) *The Pleasure Principle. Sex, Backlash and the Struggle for Gay Freedom*. New York: St Martin's Press.

Brown, P. (1973) *Radical Psychology*. London: Tavistock.

Brown, P. and Levinson, S. C. (1987) *Politeness: Some Universals in Language Usage*. Cambridge: Cambridge University Press.

Brownmiller, S. (1975) *Against Our Will: Men, Women and Rape*. London: Secker and Warburg.

Bruthiaux, P. (1994) 'Functional variation in the language of classified ads', *Perspectives: Working Papers of the Department of English*, City Polytechnic of Hong Kong, 6: 2, 21–40.

Bryman, A. (1988) *Quantity and Quality in Social Research*. London: Unwin Hyman.

Bucholtz, M., Liang, A. C. and Sutton, L. A. (1999) *Reinventing Identities: The Gendered Self in Discourse*. Oxford: Oxford University Press.

Burchill, J. (2002) 'For the hell of it.' The *Guardian*, Saturday July 20, 2002.

Burr, V. (1995) *An Introduction to Social Constructionism*. London: Routledge.

Butler, J. (1990) *Gender Trouble: Feminism and the Subversion of Identity*. New York: Routledge.

Caldas-Coulthard, C. R. and Moon, R. (1999) 'Curvy, hunky, kinky: using corpora as tools in critical analysis.' Paper read at the Critical Discourse Analysis Meeting, University of Birmingham.

Caldas-Coulthard, C. R. and van Leeuwen, T. (2002) 'Stunning, shimmering, iridescent: toys as the representation of gendered social actors.' In L. Litosseliti and J. Sunderland (eds) *Gender Identity and Discourse Analysis*. Amsterdam: John Benjamin, pp. 91–108.

Caldwell, J. T. (1995) *Televisuality: Style, Crisis and Authority in American Television*. New Jersey: Rutgers University Press.

Cameron, K. (1993) 'The numbers game: what percentage of the population is gay?' Talk presented at a seminar entitled *The Gay Nineties*, Crystal City, Virginia. Online, available at: http://www.familyresearchinst.org/FRI_AIM_Talk.html.

Campbell, B. (1987) 'Bealine.' *Marxism Today* (December): 9.

Campbell-Kibler, K., Podesva, R. J., Roberts, S. J. and Wong, A. (eds) (2002) *Language and Sexuality: Contesting Meaning in Theory and Practice*. California: CSLI Publications.

Cass, V. C. (1983) 'Homosexual identity: a concept in need of a definition.' *Journal of Homosexuality* 9 (winter 1983/spring 1984): 107–8.

Chirrey, D. (2003) '"I hereby come out": what sort of speech act is coming out?' *Journal of Sociolinguistics* 7: 1, 24–37.

Chouliaraki, L. and Fairclough, N. (1999) *Discourse in Late Modernity*. Edinburgh: Edinburgh University Press.

Cicourel, A. V. (1964) *Method and Measurement in Sociology*. New York: Free Press.

Clear, J., Fox, G., Francis, G., Krishnamurthy, R. and Moon, R. (1996) 'COBUILD: the state of the art.' *International Journal of Corpus Linguistics* 1: 303–14.

Connell, R. W. (1995) *Masculinities*. Polity: Cambridge.

Coulthard, M. (1993) 'On beginning the study of forensic texts: corpus concordance collocation.' In M. Hoey (ed.) *Data Description Discourse: Papers on the English Language in Honour of John McH Sinclair*. London: HarperCollins, pp. 86–97.

Cracknell, R. (2000) Lords reform: the interim house: background statistics. *Research Paper 00/61*. House of Commons.

Crystal, D. (2001) *The Cambridge Encyclopaedia of the English Language*. Cambridge: Cambridge University Press.

Crystal, D. and Davy, D. (1975) *Advanced Conversational English*. London: Longman.

Culpeper, J. (2001) 'Computers, language and characterisation: an analysis of six characters in Romeo and Juliet.' *Conversation in Life and in Literature. Papers from the ASLA symposium*, Uppsala, 11–30.

Danet, B. (1980) '"Baby" or "fetus": language and the construction of reality in a manslaughter trial.' *Semiotica* 32: 1/2, 187–219.

Darsey, J. (1981). '"Gayspeak": A Response.' In J. Chesebro (ed.) *Gayspeak: Gay Male and Lesbian Communication*. New York: Pilgrim Press, pp. 58–67.

David, H. (1997) *On Queer Street: A Social History of British Homosexuality 1895–1995*. London: HarperCollins.

Davies, P. M., Coxon, A. P. M. and McManus, T. J. (1990) *Longitudinal Study of the Sexual Behaviour of Homosexual Males under the Impact of AIDS: A Final Report to the Department of Health* (Project SIGMA Working Papers). London: Department of Health.

Denzin, N. K. (1988) 'Qualitative analysis for social scientists.' *Contemporary Sociology* 17: 3, 430–2.

Derrida, J. (1974) *Of Grammatology*. Baltimore: Johns Hopkins Press.

Derrida, J. (1978) *Writing and Difference*. Chicago: University of Chicago Press.

Derrida, J. (1981) *Dissemination*. Chicago: University of Chicago Press.

Dotson, E. W. (1999) *Behold the Man: The Hype and Selling of Male Beauty in Media and Culture*. New York: Harrington Park Press.

Dunning, T. (1993) 'Accurate methods for the statistics of surprise and coincidence.' *Computational Linguistics* 19: 1, 61–74.

Dworkin, A. (1981) *Pornography: Men Possessing Women*. New York: G. P. Putman's Sons.

Dyer, R. (1992) 'Coming to terms: gay pornography.' In R. Dyer, *Only Entertainment*. London: Routledge, pp. 121–34.

Eckert, P. (2002) 'Demystifying sexuality and desire.' In K. Campbell-Kibler *et al.* (eds) *Language and Sexuality*. California: CSLI Publications, pp. 99 110.

Eckert, P. and McConnell-Ginet, S. (1992) 'Think practically and look locally: language and gender as community-based practice.' *Annual Review of Anthropology* 21: 461–90.

Eckert, P. and McConnell-Ginet, S. (1999) 'New generalisations and explanations in language and gender research.' *Language in Society* 28: 185–201.

Eckert, P. and McConnell-Ginet, S. (2003) *Language and Gender*. Cambridge: Cambridge University Press.

Edwards, T. (1994) *Erotics and Politics: Gay Male Sexuality, Masculinity and Feminism*. London: Routledge.

Ellison, M. J. and Fosberry, C. T. (1996) *A Queer Companion*. London: Abson Books.

Epstein, S. (1998) 'Gay politics, ethnic identity: the limits of social constructionism.' In P. M. Nardi and B. E. Schneider (eds) *Social Perspectives in Lesbian and Gay Studies*. London: Routledge, pp. 134–59. Reprinted from *Socialist Review 93/94* (May–August 1987): 9–54.

Erfurt, J. (1985) 'Partnerwunsch und Textproduktion: Zur Strujtur der Intentionalitat in Heiratsanzeigen.' *Zeit für Phonetik, Sprachwiss und Kommunikforsch* 38: 3, 309–20.

Erikson, E. (1956) 'The problem of ego identity.' *Journal of the American Psychoanalytic Association* 4: 56–121.

Eysenk, H. J. (1953) *The Structure of Human Personality*. New York: Wiley.

Fairclough, N. (1989) *Language and Power*. London: Longman.

Fairclough, N. (1995) *Critical Discourse Analysis: The Critical Study of Language*. London: Longman.

Fairclough, N. (2000) *New Labour, New Language?* London: Routledge.

Farrell, R. A. (1972) 'The argot of the homosexual subculture.' *Anthropological Linguistics*, 14: 3, 97–109.

Ferguson, M. (1983) *Forever Feminine: Women's Magazines and the Cult of Femininity*. London: Heinemann.

Fields, J. and Casper, L. M. (2001) *America's Families and Living Arrangements*. Washington, DC: US Census Bureau.

Firth, J. R. (1935) 'The techniques of semantics.' *Transactions of the Philological Society* 36–72.

Firth, J. R. (1957) *Papers in Linguistics 1934–1951*. London: Oxford University Press.

Fishman, P. (1983) 'Interaction: the work women do.' In B. Thorne, C. Kramarae and N. Henley (eds) *Language, Gender and Society*. Rowley: Newbury House, pp. 89–101.

Flowerdew, J. (1997) 'The discourse of colonial withdrawal: a case study in the creation of mythic discourse.' *Discourse and Society* 8: 453–77.

Forestier, G. (1981) *Le théâtre dans le théâtre sur la scènce française du XVIIe siècle*. Genève: Droz.

Foucault, M. (1972) *The Archaeology of Knowledge*. London: Tavistock.

Foucault, M. (1976) *The History of Sexuality: An Introduction*. Harmondsworth: Penguin.

Foucault, M. (1979) *Discipline and Punish*. Harmondsworth: Penguin.

Fowler, R. G. and Kress, G. R. (1979) 'Critical linguistics.' In R. G. Fowler, G. R. Kress, A. A. Trew and R. I. V. Hodge (eds) *Language and Control*. London: Routledge, pp. 185–213.

Garside, R. and Smith, N. (1997) 'A hybrid grammatical tagger: CLAWS4.' In

R. Garside, G. Leech and A. McEnery (eds) *Corpus Annotation: Linguistic Information from Computer Text Corpora*. London: Longman, pp. 102–21.

Gergen, K. J. (1973) 'Social psychology as history.' *Journal of Personality and Social Psychology* 26: 309–20.

Gibson, O. (2003) 'Sales dip may push Mirror under 2m: Morgan accepts war stance could reduce circulation to 70-year low.' The *Guardian*, April 2, 2003.

Gill, R. (1993) 'Justifying justice: broadcasters' accounts of inequality in radio.' In E. Burnman and I. Parker (eds) *Discourse Analytic Research*. London: Routledge, pp. 75–93.

Gleason, P. (1983) 'Identifying identity: a semantic history.' *Journal of American History* 69: 4, 910–31.

Goffman, E. (1963) *Stigma: Notes on the Management of Spoiled Identity*. Englewood Cliffs: Prentice-Hall.

Goffman, E. (1976) 'Gender advertisements.' *Studies in the Anthropology of Visual Communication* 3: 69–154.

Goodman, S. (1996) 'Market forces speak English.' In S. Goodman and D. Graddol (eds) *Redesigning English: New Tests, New Identities*. London: Routledge, pp. 141–80.

Gough, V. and Talbot, M. (1996) ' "Guilt over games boys play": coherence as a focus for examining the constitution of heterosexual subjectivity.' In C. R. Caldas-Coulthard and M. Coulthard (eds) *Texts and Practices: Readings in Critical Discourse Analysis*. London: Routledge, pp. 214–30.

Graddol, D. (1996) 'Global English, global culture?' In S. Goodman and D. Graddol (eds) *Redesigning English: New Tests, New Identities*. London: Routledge, pp. 181–238.

Gramsci, A. (1985) *Selections from the Cultural Writings 1921–1926*. D. Forgacs and G. Nowell Smith (eds), trans. W. Boelhower. London: Lawrence and Wishart.

Granger, S. (2002) 'A bird's-eye view of learner corpus research.' In S. Granger, J. Hung and S. Petch-Tyson (eds) *Computer Learner Corpora, Second Language Acquisition and Foreign Language Teaching*. Amsterdam: John Benjamins, pp. 3–33.

Hacking, I. (1990) *The Taming of Chance*. Cambridge: Cambridge University Press.

Hall, S., Critcher, C., Jefferson, T., Clarke, J. and Roberts, B. (1978) *Policing the Crisis: Mugging, the State, and Law and Order*. London: Macmillan.

Halliday, M. A. K. (1978) *Language as a Social Semiotic: the Social Interpretation of Language and Meaning*. London: Edward Arnold Ltd.

Hamamoto, D. (1990) *Nervous Laughter: Television Situation Comedy and Liberal Democratic Ideology*. New York: Praeger.

Hantzis, D. M. and Lehr, V. (1994) 'Whose desire? Lesbian (non) sexuality and television's perpetuation of hetero/sexism.' In R. J. Ringer (ed.) *Queer Words, Queer Images: Communication and the Construction of Homosexuality*. New York: New York University Press, pp. 107–21.

Harré, R. and Secord, P. F. (1972) *The Explanation of Social Behaviour*. Oxford: Blackwell.

Harris, D. (1997) *The Rise and Fall of Gay Culture*. New York: Ballantine Books.

Harvey, K. (2000) 'Describing camp talk: language/pragmatics/politics.' *Language and Literature* 9: 3, 240–60.

Harvey, K. and Shalom, C. (eds) (1997) *Language and Desire*. London: Routledge.

Hayes, J. (1976) 'Gayspeak.' *The Quarterly Journal of Speech* 62: 256–66. Reprinted in J. W. Chesebro (ed.) (1981) *Gayspeak: Gay Male and Lesbian Communication*. New York: Pilgrim Press, pp. 43–57.

Henley, N., Miller, M. D., Beazley, A., Nguyen, D. K., Kaminsky, D. and Sanders, R. (2002) 'Frequency and specificity of referents to violence in news reports of anti-gay attacks.' *Discourse and Society* 13: 1, 75–104.

Hermes, J. (1995) *Reading Women's Magazines: An Analysis of Everyday Media Use.* Oxford: Polity Press.

Heywood, J. (1997) 'The object of desire is the object of contempt: representations of masculinity in *Straight to Hell* magazine.' In S. Johnson and U. Meinhof (eds) *Language and Masculinity.* London: Blackwell, pp. 188–207.

Hoey, M. (1986) 'The discourse colony: a preliminary study of a neglected discourse type.' In M. Coulthard (ed.) *Talking about Text: Studies Presented to David Brazil on his Retirement*, Discourse Analysis Monograph no. 13, English Language Research, University of Birmingham, 1–26.

Hoey, M. (1997) 'The organization of narratives of desire: a study of first-person erotic fantasies.' In K. Harvey and C. Shalom (eds) *Language and Desire.* London: Routledge, pp. 85–105.

Holleran, A. (2000) 'The Alpha Queen.' *The Gay and Lesbian Review* 7: 3, 65–6.

Holloway, W. (1981) ' "I just wanted to kill a woman", Why? The Ripper and male sexuality.' *Feminist Review* 9: 33–40.

Holloway, W. (1984) 'Gender difference and the production of subjectivity.' In J. Henriques, W. Holloway, C. Urwin, C. Venn and V. Walkerdine (eds) *Changing the Subject: Psychology, Social Regulation and Subjectivity.* London: Methuen, pp. 227–339.

Holmes, J. (2001) 'A corpus based view of gender in New Zealand English.' In M. Hellinger and H. Bussman (eds) *Gender Across Languages. The Linguistic Representation of Women and Men.* Vol. 1. Amsterdam: John Benjamins, pp. 115–36.

House of Lords (2002a) 'The House of Lords.' In *An Introduction to Parliament.* Parliamentary Copyright House of Lords.

House of Lords (2002b) 'The work of the House of Lords – its role, functions and powers.' *House of Lords Briefing.* Parliamentary Copyright House of Lords.

Hov, L. (1990) *Thalias første døtre. Skuespillerinderne i 1500- og 1600-tallets europæiske teater.* Oslo: Solum/København: Nansengade Antikvariat og Forlag.

Hubert, S. J. (1999) 'What's wrong with this picture? The politics of Ellen's coming out party.' *The Journal of Popular Culture* 33: 2, 31–6.

Hunston, S. (2002) *Corpora in Applied Linguistics.* Cambridge: Cambridge University Press.

Jackson, P., Stevenson, N. and Brooks, K. (2001) *Making Sense of Men's Magazines.* Cambridge: Polity Press.

Jaworski, A. and Coupland, N. (eds) (1999) *The Discourse Reader.* London: Routledge.

Jenkins, P. (1992) *Intimate Enemies: Moral Panics in Contemporary Great Britain.* New York: de Gruyter.

Jespersen, O. (1922) *Language: its Nature, Development and Origin.* London: Allen and Unwin.

Jivani, A. (1997) *It's Not Unusual: A History of Lesbian and Gay Britain in the Twentieth Century.* London: Michael O'Mara.

Johansson, S. (1991) 'Times change and so do corpora.' In K. Aijmer and B. Altenburg (eds) *English Corpus Linguistics: Studies in Honour of Jan Svartvik.* London, Longman, pp. 305–14.

Johns, T. (1997) 'Contexts: the background, development and trialling of a concordance-based CALL program.' In A. Wichmann, S. Fligelstone, T. McEnery and G. Knowles (eds) *Teaching and Language Corpora*. London: Longman, pp. 100–15.

Johnson, S. and Meinhof, U. L. (eds) (1997) *Language and Masculinity.* London: Blackwell.

Johnson, S., Culpeper, J. and Suhr, S. (2003) 'From "politically correct councillors" to "Blairite nonsense": discourses of political correctness in three British newspapers.' *Discourse and Society* 14: 1, 28–47.

Jowell, R. (1996) *British Social Attitudes, the 13th Report.* Aldershot: Ashgate.

Jowell, R., Brook, L., Prior, G. and Taylor, B. (1992) *British Social Attitudes, the 9th Report.* Aldershot: Ashgate Publishing.

Jowell, R., Curtice, J., Park, A. and Thomson, S. (1999) *British Social Attitudes, the 16th Report: Who Shares New Labour Values?* Aldershot: Ashgate.

Jowell, R., Park, A., Thomson, K., Jarvis, L., Bromley, C. and Stratford, N. (2000) *British Social Attitudes, the 17th Report: Focusing on Diversity.* London: Sage.

Käding, J. (1897) *Häufigkeitswörterbuch der deutschen Sprache.* Steglitz: privately published.

Kanner, M. (2003) 'Can *Will and Grace* Be "Queered"?' *The Gay and Lesbian Review* 10: 4, 34–5.

Katz, J. (1983) *Gay/Lesbian Almanac: A New Documentary.* New York: Harper and Row.

Keuls, E. (1985) *The Reign of the Phallus: Sexual Politics in Ancient Athens.* New York: Harper and Row.

Kilgarriff, A. (1996a) *Using Word Frequency Lists to Measure Corpus Homogeneity and Similarity between Corpora.* Information Technology Research Institute, University of Brighton, April 18.

Kilgarriff, A. (1996b) 'Corpus similarly and homogeneity via word frequency.' *EURALEX Proceedings*, Gothenburg, Sweden, August.

Kilgarriff, A. and Tugwell, D. (2001) 'WASP-bench: an MT lexicographers' workstation supporting state-of-the-art lexical disambiguation.' *Proceedings of MT Summit VII*, Santiago de Compostela, 187–90.

Kinsey, A. C., Pomeroy, B. and Martin, C. E. (1948) *Sexual Behavior in the Human Male.* Philadelphia: W.B. Saunders; Bloomington: Indiana University Press.

Lacan, J. (1998) *The Four Fundamental Concepts of Psychoanalysis.* New York: Norton.

Lakoff, R. (1975) *Language and Woman's Place.* New York: HarperCollins.

Lave, J. and Wenger, E. (1991) *Situated Learning: Legitimate Peripheral Participation.* Cambridge: Cambridge University Press.

Leap, W. (1996) *Word's Out: Gay Men's English.* Minneapolis: University of Minnesota Press.

Litosseliti, L. and Sunderland, J. (eds) (2002) *Gender Identity and Discourse Analysis.* Amsterdam: John Benjamins.

Livia, A. and Hall, K. (eds) (1997). *Queerly Phrased.* Oxford: Oxford Studies in Sociolinguistics.

Longino, Helen E. (1980) 'What is pornography?' In L. Lederer (ed.) *Take Back the Night: Women On Pornography.* New York: William Morrow and Co. Inc., pp. 40–54.

Louw, B. (1993) 'Irony in the text or insincerity in the writer? The diagnostic potential of semantic prosodies.' In M. Baker, G. Francis and E. Tognini-Bonelli (eds) *Text and Technology.* Amsterdam: John Benjamins, pp. 157–76.

Louw, B. (1997) 'The role of corpora in critical literary appreciation.' In A. Wichmann, S. Fligelstone, T. McEnery and G. Knowles (eds) *Teaching and Language Corpora*. London: Longman, pp. 140–251.

McArthur, T. (1981) *Longman Lexicon of Contemporary English*. London: Longman.

McEnery, T. (2005) *Swearing in English*. London: Routledge.

McEnery, T. and Wilson, A. (1996) *Corpus Linguistics*. Edinburgh: Edinburgh University Press.

McEnery, T., Baker, P. and Hardie, A. (2000) 'Swearing and abuse in modern British English.' In B. Lewandowska-Tomaszczyk and J. Melia (eds) *PALC 99 Practical Applications in Language Corpora*. Hamburg: Peter Lang, pp. 37–48.

McIlvenny, P. (1996) 'Heckling and Hyde Park: verbal audience participation in popular public discourse.' *Language in Society* 25: 1, 27–60.

Marc, D. (1989) *Comic Visions: Television Comedy and American Culture*. Boston: Unwin Hyman.

Marley, C. (2002) 'Popping the question: questions and modality in written dating advertisements.' *Discourse Studies* 4: 1, 75–98.

Marsh, A. (1976) 'Who hates the blacks?' *New Society* (September 23): 649–52.

Milroy, J. and Milroy, L. (1978) 'Belfast: change and variation in an urban vernacular.' In P. Trudgill (ed.) *Sociolinguistic Patterns in British English*. London: Edward Arnold, pp. 19–36.

Montagu, A. (1967) *The Anatomy of Swearing*. London: Collier-Macmillan.

Morrish, L. (2002) ' "That's so typical of Peter – as soon as there's a cock-up he tries to sit on it": British Broadsheet Press versus Peter Mandleson 1996–2001.' Paper given at the *9th Annual American University Conference on Lavender Languages and Linguistics*.

Mulvey, L. (1989) *Visual and Other Pleasures*. Bloomington and Indianapolis: Indiana University Press.

Naidoo, J. and Wills, J. (1994) *Health Promotion: Foundations for Practice*. London: Ballière, Tindall.

Nair, B. R. (1992) 'Gender, genre and generative grammar: deconstructing the matrimonial column.' In M. Toolan (ed.) *Language, Text and Context: Essays in Stylistics*. London and New York: Routledge, pp. 227–54.

Norton, R. (1992) *Mother Clap's Molly House. The Gay Subculture in England 1700-1830*. London: Gay Men's Press.

Oakes, M. (1998) *Statistics for Corpus Linguistics*. Edinburgh: Edinburgh University Press.

O'Kelly, L. (1994) 'Kiss a few frogs, land a prince.' *Observer*, July 10, 1994, 23.

Omoniyi, T. (1998) 'The discourse of tourism advertisements: packaging nation and ideology in Singapore.' *Working Papers in Applied Linguistics*, 4: 22, 2–14. London: Thames Valley University.

Parker, I. (1992) *Discourse Dynamics: Critical Analysis for Social and Individual Psychology*. London: Routledge.

Parker, I. (1994) 'Qualitative research.' In P. Banister, E. Burnman, I. Parker, M. Taylor and C. Tindall (eds) *Qualitative Methods in Psychology*. Buckingham: Open University Press, pp. 1–16.

Parker, I. and Burnman, E. (1993) 'Against discursive imperialism, empiricism and constructionism: thirty-two problems with discourse analysis.' In E. Burnman and I. Parker (eds) *Discourse Analytic Research*. London: Routledge, pp. 155–72.

Piper, A. (2000) 'Some people have credit cards and others have giro cheques: "individuals" and "people" as lifelong learners in late modernity.' *Discourse and Society* 11: 515–42.

Plotz, D. (2000) 'Luke Skywalker is gay?' *Slate* April 14. Online, available at: http://slate.msn.com/id/80225/.

Potter, J. and Wetherell, M. (1987) *Discourse and Social Psychology*. London: Sage.

Power, Lisa (1995) *No Bath but Plenty of Bubbles: An Oral History of the Gay Liberation Front 1970–73*. London, Cassell.

Pratt, M. L. (1987) 'Linguistic utopias.' In N. Fabb, D. Attridge, A. Durant and C. MacCabe (eds) *The Linguistics of Writing: Arguments Between Language and Literature*. Manchester: Manchester University Press, pp. 48–66.

Precht, K. (2002) 'Gender differences in affect, evidentiality, and hedging in American conversation.' Paper presented at the annual meeting of the Linguistic Society of America, San Francisco.

Preyer, W. (1889) *The Mind of the Child*. New York: Appleton. Translation of original German edition of 1882.

Provencher, D. M. (2004) 'Sealed with a kiss: heteronormative narrative strategies in NBC's *Will and Grace*.' In M. Dalton and L. Linder (eds) *America Viewed and Skewed: Television Situation Comedies*. New York: SUNY Press.

Quirk, R. (1960) 'Towards a description of English usage.' *Transactions of the Philological Society* 40–61.

Rayson, P. (2001) *Wmatrix: a Web-based Corpus Processing Environment*. Software demonstration presented at ICAME 2001 conference, Université catholique de Louvain, Belgium, May 16–20.

Rayson, P., Leech, G. and Hodges, M. (1997) 'Social differentiation in the use of English vocabulary: some analyses of the conversational component of the British National Corpus.' *International Journal of Corpus Linguistics* 2: 133–50.

Rey, J. M. (2001) 'Changing gender roles in popular culture: dialogue in *Star Trek* episodes from 1966 to 1993.' In D. Biber and S. Conrad (eds) *Variation in English: Multi-Dimensional Studies*. London: Longman, pp. 138–56.

Rich, A. (1980) 'Compulsory heterosexuality and lesbian existence.' *Signs: Journal of Women in Culture and Society* 5: 4, 631–60.

Robberson, M. R. and Rogers, W. P. (1988) 'Beyond fear appeals: negative and positive persuasive appeals to health and self esteem.' *Journal of Applied Social Psychology* 18: 3, 277–87.

Rodgers, B. (1972) *The Queen's Vernacular*. San Francisco: Straight Arrow Books.

Rogers, R. W. (1983) 'Cognitive and physiological processes in fear appeals and attitude change. A revised theory of protection motivation.' In J. Caciioppo and R. Petty (eds) *Social Psychophysiology*. New York: Guildford Press, pp. 153–76.

Rowe, C. (2000) *True Gay – Hegemonic Homosexuality?: Representations of Gayness in Conversations Between Gay Men*. Unpublished M.A. Dissertation, Lancaster.

Russo, V. (1987) *The Celluloid Closet*. New York: Harper and Row.

Rutledge, L. (1989) *The Gay Fireside Companion*. Boston: Alyson.

Sanderson, T. (1995) *Mediawatch*, London: Gay Men's Press.

Sarup, T. R. (1988) *An Introductory Guide to Post-structuralism and Postmodernism*. Hemel Hempstead: Harvester Wheatsheaf.

Saussure, F. de (1974) *Course in General Linguistics* (trans. W. Baskin). London: Fontana.

Schiller, H. I. (1976) *Communication and Cultural Domination*. New York: International Arts and Sciences Press.

Schmid, H.-J. and Fauth, J. (2003) 'Women's and men's style: fact or fiction? New grammatical evidence.' Paper presented at the Corpus Linguistics Conference, Lancaster, March.

Scott, M. (1999) *WordSmith Tools Help Manual*. Version 3.0. Mike Scott and Oxford University Press.

Scott, M. (2000) 'Focussing on the text and its key words.' In L. Burnard and T. McEnery (eds) *Rethinking Language Pedagogy from a Corpus Perspective*. Frankfurt: Peter Lang, pp. 103–22.

Scott, M. (2001) 'Comparing corpora and identifying key words, collocations, and frequency distributions through the WordSmith Tools suite of computer programs.' In M. Ghadessy, A. Henry and R. L. Roseberry (eds) *Small Corpus Studies and ELT: Theory and Practice*. Amsterdam: John Benjamins, pp. 47–67.

Sedgwick, E. K. (1991) *Epistemology of the Closet*. Hemel Hempstead: Harvester Wheatsheaf.

Seidman, S. (1993) 'Identity and politics in a "postmodern" gay culture: some historical and conceptual notes.' In M. Warner (ed.) *Fear of a Queer Planet: Queer Politics and Social Theory*. Minneapolis: University of Minnesota Press, pp. 105–42.

Shalom, C. (1997) 'That great supermarket of desire: attributes of the desired other in personal advertisements.' In K. Harvey and C. Shalom (eds) *Language and Desire*. London: Routledge, pp. 186–203.

Sherrard, C. (1991) 'Developing discourse analysis.' *Journal of General Psychology* 118: 2, 171–9.

Silverman, D. (1993) *Interpreting Qualitative Data: Methods for Analysing Talk, Text and Interaction*. London: Sage.

Simpson, M. (1994) *Male Impersonators*. London: Cassell.

Sinclair, J. (1991) *Corpus, Concordance, Collocation*. Oxford: Oxford University Press.

Sinclair, J. M. (1999) 'A way with common words.' In H. Hasselgård and S. Oksefjell (eds) *Out of Corpora: Studies in Honour of Stig Johansson*. Amsterdam: Rodopi, pp. 157–79.

Smith, N., McEnery, A. M. and Ivanic, R. (1998) 'Issues in transcribing a corpus of children's hand-written projects.' *Literary and Linguistic Computing* 13: 4, 217–25.

Smithard, T. (2001) 'Young Guns York', *York Vision*, Online Issue 128. Online, available at: http://vision.york.ac.uk/articles/128/news/40223.shtml.

Snyder, M. and Gangestad, S. W. (1986) 'On the nature of self-monitoring: matters of assessment, matters of validity.' *Journal of Personality and Social Psychology* 54: 972–9.

Spencer, C. (1995) *Homosexuality: A History*. London: Fourth Estate.

Stanley, J. P. (1970) 'Homosexual slang.' *American Speech* 45: 45–59.

Steinem, G. (1978) 'Erotica and pornography: a clear and present difference.' *Ms.* November.

Stenström, A.-B. (1990) 'Lexical items peculiar to spoken discourse.' In J. Svartvik (ed.) *The London–Lund Corpus of Spoken English: Description and Research*. Lund Studies in English 82. Lund: Lund University Press, pp. 137–75.

Stubbs, M. (1996) *Text and Corpus Analysis*. London: Blackwell.

Stubbs, M. (2001a) 'Texts, corpora and problems of interpretation: a response to Widdowson.' *Applied Linguistics* 22: 2, 149–72.

Stubbs, M. (2001b) *Words and Phrases: Corpus Studies of Lexical Semantics*. London: Blackwell.

Stubbs, M. (2002) 'On text and corpus analysis: a reply to Borsley and Ingham.' *Lingua Franca* 112: 7–11.

Stubbs, M. and Gerbig, A. (1993) 'Human and inhuman geography: on the computer-assisted analysis of long texts.' In M. Hoey (ed.) *Data, Description, Discourse.* London: HarperCollins, pp. 64–85.

Sunderland, J. (2004) *Gendered Discourses.* London: Palgrave.

Swann, J. (2002) 'Yes, but is it gender?' In L. Litosseliti and J. Sunderland (eds) *Gender Identity and Discourse Analysis.* Amsterdam: John Benjamins, pp. 43–67.

Taine, H. (1877) 'On the acquisition of language by children.' *Mind* 2: 252–9.

Talbot, M. (1998) *Language and Gender: An Introduction.* Oxford: Polity.

Taylor, E. (1989) *Primetime Families.* Berkeley: University of California Press.

Thompson, K. (1998) *Moral Panics.* London: Routledge.

Thorne, J. and Coupland, J. (1998) 'Articulations of same sex desire: lesbian and gay male dating advertisements.' *Journal of Sociolinguistics* 2/3: 223–57.

Trudgill, P. (1974) *The Social Differentiation of English in Norwich.* Cambridge: Cambridge University Press.

Trumbach, R. (1991) 'The birth of the queen: sodomy and the emergence of gender equality in modern culture, 1660–1750.' In M. B. Duberman, M. Vicinus and G. Chauncey (eds) *Hidden From History.* London: Penguin, pp. 129–40.

van Dijk, T. (1991) *Racism and the Press.* London: Routledge.

Warner, M. (1993). 'Introduction.' In M. Warner (ed.) *Fear of a Queer Planet: Queer Politics and Social Theory.* Minneapolis: University of Minnesota Press, pp. vii–xxxi.

Waterhouse, K. (1993) *On Newspaper Style.* London: Penguin.

Watney, S. (1989) *Policing Desire: Pornography, AIDS and the Media.* Minneapolis: University of Minnesota Press.

Waugh, T. (1996) 'Cockteaser.' In J. Doyle, J. Flatley and J. Muñoz (eds) *Pop Out: Queer Warhol.* Durham: Duke University Press, pp. 51–77.

Waugh, T. (2002) *Out/Lines: Underground Gay Graphics From Before Stonewall.* Vancouver: Arsenal Pulp Press.

West, C. and Zimmerman, D. (1983) 'Small insults: a study of interruptions in cross-sex conversations between unacquainted persons.' In B. Thorne, C. Kramarae and N. Henley (eds) *Language, Gender and Society.* Rowley: Newbury House, pp. 102–17.

Wickens, P. (1998) 'Comparative analysis of the use of projecting clauses in pedagogical legal genres.' Paper read at the 25th International Systemic-Functional Congress, University of Wales, Cardiff, July.

Widdowson, H. G. (2000) 'On the limitations of linguistics applied.' *Applied Linguistics* 21: 1, 3–25.

Williams, R. (1976) *Keywords.* London: Fontana.

Wilson, A. and Thomas, J. (1997) 'Semantic annotation.' In R. Garside, G. Leech and A. McEnery (eds) *Corpus Annotation: Linguistic Information from Computer Texts.* London: Longman, pp. 55–65.

Wilton, T. (1997) *Sexualities in Health and Social Care.* Buckingham: Open University Press.

Wolfenden, Lord J. F. (1957) *Wolfenden Report.* Issued by Her Majesty's Stationers, 5 September.

Woolls, D. and Coulthard, M. (1998) 'Tools for the trade.' *Forensic Linguistics* 5: 33–57.

Young, A. (1972) 'Out of the closets, into the streets.' In K. Jay and A. Young (eds) *Out of the Closets*. New York: Douglas.

Zeeland, S. (1996) *The Masculine Marine*. New York: Harrington Park Press.

Zwicky, A. (1997) 'Two lavender issues for linguists.' In A. Livia and K. Hall (eds) *Queerly Phrased*. Oxford: *Oxford Studies in Sociolinguistics*, pp. 21–34.

Index